JAMES JOYCE AND
SAMARITAN HOSPITALITY

In memory of Weldon Thornton, my mentor and beloved teacher at
Chapel Hill and James Joyce scholar extraordinaire (1934–2021):
Thank you for your sacrificial care of and love for your students,
including me, all these years.

Love is patient, love is kind. It does not envy, it does not boast,
it is not proud. . . .
Love never dies.
1 Corinthians 13:4, 8a

JAMES JOYCE AND SAMARITAN HOSPITALITY

Postcritical and Postsecular Reading in
Dubliners and *Ulysses*

Richard Rankin Russell

EDINBURGH
University Press

Edinburgh University Press is one of the leading university presses in the UK. We publish academic books and journals in our selected subject areas across the humanities and social sciences, combining cutting-edge scholarship with high editorial and production values to produce academic works of lasting importance. For more information visit our website: edinburghuniversitypress.com

© Richard Rankin Russell 2023, 2024

Edinburgh University Press Ltd
The Tun – Holyrood Road
12(2f) Jackson's Entry
Edinburgh EH8 8PJ

First published in hardback by Edinburgh University Press 2023

Typeset in 10/12.5 Adobe Sabon by
IDSUK (DataConnection) Ltd

A CIP record for this book is available from the British Library

ISBN 978 1 4744 9900 2 (hardback)
ISBN 978 1 4744 9901 9 (paperback)
ISBN 978 1 4744 9902 6 (webready PDF)
ISBN 978 1 4744 9903 3 (epub)

The right of Richard Rankin Russell to be identified as the author of this work has been asserted in accordance with the Copyright, Designs and Patents Act 1988, and the Copyright and Related Rights Regulations 2003 (SI No. 2498).

CONTENTS

Preface and Acknowledgments	vi
List of Abbreviations	x
Introduction	1
1 Haunted by Hospitality in "The Dead"	19
2 Joyce, Scripture, and Autobiographical Rescue Narratives	42
3 Rewriting the Good Samaritan Parable: The Fictional Rescue Narratives of "Grace" and "Circe"	63
4 Bloom as Stranger and Samaritan in "Cyclops," "Oxen of the Sun," and "Circe"	87
5 "In orthodox Samaritan fashion": The Parabolic Encounter between Stephen and Bloom in "Eumaeus"	122
6 Home to "Ithaca" and "Penelope": Bloom's Hospitality and Stephen and Molly's Reactions	160
7 Enfleshed Ethics and the Responsibility of the Reader in the Good Samaritan Parable and the "Nostos" of *Ulysses*	180
Coda: "Go thou and do likewise": Postcritical and Postsecular Reading through a Joycean Hermeneutics of Hospitality	198
Works Cited	212
Index	228

PREFACE AND ACKNOWLEDGMENTS

The inspiration for this book emerged from a graduate seminar on Yeats and Joyce that I taught at Baylor University in the fall semester of 2016. After spending half the semester on Yeats's poetry, drama, and prose, we spent the second half on Joyce, reading *A Portrait of the Artist as a Young Man* and *Ulysses*. Turning back to *Ulysses* is always a daunting task, and as always, I felt compelled to rehearse others' arguments about the novel while admitting I had few original readings of my own. Valid as some of those established readings are, I found myself wishing for a new theory that would illuminate the novel for my students and myself. Late that semester, when we started the "Nostos," or last three episodes, I discovered my entrée. It comes in the first sentence of "Eumaeus," the sixteenth episode: "Preparatory to anything else Mr Bloom brushed off the greater bulk of the shavings and handed Stephen the hat and ashplant and bucked him up generally in orthodox Samaritan fashion which he very badly needed" (*U* 15.1–3). I had always tended to distrust this circumlocutious narrator, who is not only long-winded but also vague and who fumbles to accurately convey conversation in this episode. What I realized for the first time after recognizing the reference this narrator makes to the Good Samaritan narrative as recounted in Luke 10:25–37 was that the narrator nonetheless *can* describe the actions in this episode clearly (and often does). Actions, then as now, still matter more than words for some of us, and Joyce chose to admiringly portray Leopold Bloom's charitable actions at crucial moments earlier in the novel and especially beginning in the second half of "Circe," the fifteenth episode, continuing through "Eumaeus" and "Ithaca." A significant portion of that excessively long episode rendered as a sort of phantasmagoric expressionistic drama, I later realized, begins "staging" the Good Samaritan narrative that will be referenced in the opening sentence of "Eumaeus." Later still, I would realize that Joyce dramatizes this parable in this crucial section of "Circe" in verbatim phrases and sentences he "recycled" from "Grace," the penultimate story in his collection *Dubliners*.

But first, I had to investigate the criticism I was sure had long ago exhausted the reference to the well-known Lukan story, as I told my seminar students other Joyceans must have done. The fifth chapter of this book explains how little work until now has been conducted on this reference—and how confusing and even contradictory that criticism is. I decided to write a short note about the reference, then I began wondering why Joyce would start the last section of his novel with such a clear reference to this narrative.

I gradually came to understand, as I worked through the implications of the Lukan narrative for not only the last four episodes of the novel but also its entirety, that Joyce was still dwelling both upon his assault in June 1904 in Dublin and a mugging in March 1907 in Rome—events that led him to imagine himself as part of this parable in the role of the wounded traveler. Joyce seems to have reimagined the likely apocryphal origins of the novel—his supposed rescue by a putatively Jewish gentleman, Alfred H. Hunter, after Joyce spoke to a young woman one evening that fateful June in Dublin and was beaten up by her escort. As I will discuss later, however, it is much less clear that Joyce himself was rescued after this beating, and, significantly, he mentions nothing of a rescuer in his letter about the incident to his dear friend Constantine Curran. And he apparently made no mention of his Roman mugging to his brother Stanislaus afterwards in 1907. I have come to believe that Joyce wanted so much to be rescued on those two long-ago evenings that he made up the story of Mr. Hunter's rescue of him in 1904 and then reveled in the crowd's helping him in Rome after his assault. Out of that "true"—because much-desired— Dublin fiction, he then wrote a novel that explored a protagonist who had developed a habitus of rescuing others and who unhesitatingly swung into action to help Stephen Dedalus that evening in Nighttown when he is attacked by a constable at a brothel. Having actually been attacked himself and not rescued in the Dublin incident gave Joyce acute insight into Stephen's mindset in "Circe" and helped him develop this narrative arc as a compelling version of the parable concerning the traveler who was waylaid on the road from Jerusalem to Jericho in the Lukan narrative. In a episodes-long burst of narrative optimism, Joyce gives Stephen, a fictitious version of his earlier self, a genial rescuer in the person of Leopold Bloom, who helps him get out of an entanglement with the police and feeds him at a cabman's shelter, and who then takes him home. As I argue, Joyce's depiction of Bloom's rescue of Stephen signifies in heretofore unexplored ways their profound connection and stands as a fictional example of how we should be hospitable to others.

As I read more of the commentaries on what might be Christ's best-known parable, and as I thought through Joyce's portrayal of it, I finally realized that Joyce was inviting us to be readers who would model Bloom's generosity and who would develop a habitus of generous and generative reading. The coda of this study explores what would happen if literary criticism moved away from the suspicious critique of literature long deplored by Paul Ricoeur and others and into an empathetic, open literary criticism espoused recently by Rita Felski and others.

I am deeply grateful to Anne Fogarty, Professor of James Joyce Studies at University College, Dublin, for an invitation to deliver a lecture to the 2017 James Joyce Summer School in Dublin, which spurred me to begin developing my argument, particularly in relation to the "Eumaeus" episode. While in Dublin, Anne herself and her colleague Luca Crispi (also of UCD) were most encouraging about this embryonic project, as were local Joyce scholars Christine O'Neill and Terence Killeen, along with Leah Flack of Marquette University. They collectively told me there was something to this project and convinced me I should carry through with it. Luca was very helpful as I developed my summer school lecture into an article that was eventually published in *Dublin James Joyce Journal* 10 (2017) as "'Who Is My Neighbour?': Leopold Bloom and the Parable of the Good Samaritan." I am thankful to Luca and to Anne Fogarty for permission to reprint a portion of this material in this book. Vicki Mahaffey encouraged me in my reading of the novel at the 2017 meeting of the Association for Literary Scholars, Critics, and Writers (ALSCW) in Dallas. A conversation at the 2018 meeting of the ALSCW at Vanderbilt University with my graduate school colleague Farrell O'Gorman, now Chair of the English department at Belmont Abbey College, and with Brian Richardson of Ohio State University, helped me realize that I needed to write a separate book on Protestantism and Joyce and focus this project on reading *Ulysses* through the Good Samaritan narrative. At that point, I began splitting what had become an unwieldy and excessively long book manuscript into two.

I'm very grateful to all the above-mentioned friends and scholars, along with Joseph Heininger of Dominican University, Marilynn Richtarik of Georgia State University, and another graduate school friend from Chapel Hill days, Bryan Giemza of Texas Tech University, for their continued encouragement on this project. Bryan's support of me and friendship over many years is one of the great boons of my life.

Two Joyce scholars in particular have influenced my approach here: the late Weldon Thornton, William R. and Jeanne H. Jordan Professor of English Emeritus, University of North Carolina-Chapel Hill, and Declan

Kiberd, Donald and Marilyn Keough Professor of Irish Studies and Professor of English Emeritus, Notre Dame University. Weldon's work is foundational for anyone hoping to read or write on Joyce. He directed my dissertation (not on Joyce) over twenty years ago and he has always insisted on reading Joyce closely and with attention to his penchant for *caritas*, as, for example, when Bloom helps both the blind stripling and Stephen Dedalus. Weldon graciously and thoroughly read my M.Phil. thesis on Joyce from the University of Glasgow in the fall of 1995 after I entered the University of North Carolina at Chapel Hill; my thesis on hunger in *Ulysses* was shockingly ignorant and misguided, but he took the time to edit and critique it for me, a perfect stranger, exemplifying hospitality. I have never met a more vibrant and spirited teacher and close reader. He believed in my potential as a literary critic at a particularly dark time in my life. He was there for me for over a quarter-century, and he was greatly encouraging as I thought through and wrote this book and the other manuscript on Joyce and Protestantism that has emerged from this endeavor. This book is lovingly and gratefully dedicated to him.

Declan taught a wonderful Joyce seminar that I was privileged to take and which was sponsored by West Virginia University during a memorable week in June 2000. The seminar previewed arguments Declan would later develop into his thoughtful study, *Ulysses and Us*. That book's insistence on reading *Ulysses* as wisdom literature complemented Weldon's approach to the novel and I realize now that both scholars—different as their approach to *Ulysses* can be—saw that the core of it was humanistic empathy for others.

As always, I must express grateful thanks to my wife Hannah ("gracious gift of God") and my sons Connor and Aidan Russell. They ground me and give me joy. I would know little of empathy and hospitality without their loving presence in my life.

Finally, I am grateful to the literature acquisitions editor at Edinburgh University Press, Jackie Jones, and her professional staff. Jackie was an early supporter of this book, and I will never forget opening her encouraging email to me in early August of 2020 during the fearful and anxious time of the global coronavirus crisis. She told me she thought my proposal was "deft" and "probing," and even claimed that reading it was "uplifting." And so I hope it is.

Once again, *Soli Deo Gloria*. Christ alone is the author and perfecter of my faith and I am inexpressibly grateful to Him for His death on a cross for my sins and that of other believers and for His resurrection that gives us eternal life.

ABBREVIATIONS

D	James Joyce	*Dubliners: Text, Criticism, and Notes.* Ed. Robert Scholes and A. Walton Litz. New York: Penguin, 1969.
FW	James Joyce	*Finnegans Wake.* Ed. Robbert-Jan Henkes, Erik Bindervoet, and Finn Fordham. Oxford: Oxford World's Classics, 2012.
JJ2	Richard Ellmann	*James Joyce.* New and revised ed. New York: Oxford University Press, 1982.
P	James Joyce	*A Portrait of the Artist as a Young Man: Text, Criticism, and Notes.* Ed. Chester G. Anderson. New York: Viking, 1968.
SL	James Joyce	*Selected Letters of James Joyce.* Ed. Richard Ellmann. New York: Viking, 1975.
U	James Joyce	*Ulysses.* Ed. Hans Walter Gabler. New York: Vintage, 1986.

INTRODUCTION

CREATIVE AND CARING READING IN JOYCE

On July 24, 2010, the *Irish Independent* ran a story that might have been startling for those familiar with the alleged origins of James Joyce's *Ulysses*. The paper's security editor, Tom Brady, reported that "A man was in *garda* custody last night after a father-to-be was stabbed to death when he attempted to break up a row. Good Samaritan James Joyce (20) was struck several times in the upper body with a domestic knife."[1] The writer James Joyce was also putatively involved in a fight 106 years before this incident and was rescued by a Good Samaritan—or so the legend goes. The truth, however, is much more complicated. And understanding this likely apocryphal incident and its effect on Joyce and *Ulysses* reveals a writer and a novel indebted to this specific parable and to Scripture more generally.

    Ulysses gradually reveals the faultiness of Stephen Dedalus's notion of hyper-elitist artistic predestination and his embrace of extreme atomistic individualism derived from a caricature of the Reformation in *A Portrait of the Artist as a Young Man* by showing him slowly moving into a type of heterogeneous community epitomized by Christ's pluralist parable of the Good Samaritan. The question of what it means to be a neighbor—a good neighbor, even—dominates much of Joyce's *Ulysses* and became increasingly important to the peripatetic Joyce while in exile from Ireland. While living in Rome in 1906, he regretted not reproducing in *Dubliners* the "hospitality" of Dublin, which he claimed to his brother Stanislaus, "does not exist elsewhere in Europe" (*SL* 110). The two central characters of *Ulysses*, Stephen and Leopold Bloom, are often rebuffed by their neighbors—Stephen by Buck Mulligan and Haines, Bloom by a whole series of Dubliners—and gradually drift toward each other. The central, long-planned-for event of the novel occurs with their meeting in the second half of the "Oxen of the Sun" episode and continues through the apocalyptic, overly long "Circe" episode, and the parabolic episodes of "Eumaeus" and "Ithaca," even "Penelope." Bloom tries to be neighborly to Stephen, fatherly even, and his actions here and earlier in encounters with others in the novel are depicted as re-enactments of the Good Samaritan parable, perhaps Jesus' most famous story of this kind in Scripture.

Using the well-known but invigorating language of parable gave Joyce the opportunity to convincingly show how great art might proceed from solitude but always enacts a reciprocal process of reception with a community—within the pages of *Ulysses*, within the heart, mind, and soul of its readers. As George Steiner argues, if an artistic act is intended to be "intelligible, 'private language' becomes lexical and shared." For instance, if Stephen is to succeed as an artist, his gnomic pronouncements must themselves be transmuted into something shared, palatable, understandable. Steiner posits that "[w]hat the poet aims for," and what I believe Joyce sought himself, "is that novelty of combinations which will suggest to the listener, to the reader, a corona, a new-lit sphere of perceptible meanings, of radiant energy, at once understandable and adding to (transcending) what is already to hand."[2] *Ulysses* gives us that "new-lit sphere of perceptible meanings, of radiant energy," and in so doing, creates the kind of community that the Stephen of *A Portrait of the Artist* disdains yet secretly desires. And it does so by drawing deeply upon the Lukan narratives that Joyce valued in the Bible, particularly that of the Good Samaritan, that stranger who un-homes our settled notions of who our neighbor truly is, and who asks us to make new neighbors, new homes, new communities across time and place and race.

The novel's parabolic arc drawn from that specific parable has generally been occluded, in part because of Joyce's own reluctance to directly reveal the novel's parabolic nature; but Hugh Kenner reminded us long ago that there is much that "the book does not offer to say to us," and suggests that "we may learn how largely *Ulysses* is a book of silences despite its din of specifying."[3] I also find Derek Attridge's claim in *The Singularity of Literature* particularly appropriate to my argument here: "some sense of strangeness, mystery, or unfathomability is involved in every encounter with the literary. Even a work one knows well, if it retains its inventiveness, possesses an enigmatic quality; one cannot put one's finger on the sources of its power, one does not know where its meanings end."[4] In this study, I enter some of these enigmatic, silent spaces in *Dubliners* and *Ulysses*, seeking to make them sing their secrets—their parabolic resonances. My argument is inspired in part by Attridge's description of creative reading—"not one that overrides the work's conventionally determined meanings in the name of imaginative freedom but rather one that, in its striving to do full justice to the work, is obliged to go beyond existing conventions." Reading in this way involves "attending to that which can barely be heard, registering what is unique about the shaping of language, thought, and feeling in this particular work. It involves a suspension of habits, a willingness to rethink old positions in order to apprehend the work's inaugural power."[5] And make no mistake: literary works need us to read them creatively. They "need our devotion," as Rita Felski argues. Moreover, "[t]heir existence depends on being taken up by readers or viewers or listeners, as figures through whom they must pass." Thus, "[a]rtworks must be *activated* to exist."[6]

Reading *Ulysses* anew, I also finally argue, enables not only fresh apprehension of the parabolic arc over its last five episodes, but also a recognition of what Felski has termed elsewhere the "sociability" of works of art, an "indispensable element" of which is "a work's dexterity in soliciting and sustaining attachments."[7] How does a novel like *Ulysses* draw us to it, generate affection for it and its characters, perhaps even lead us into caring for the Other? In part, it achieves this care by teaching us to read affectively through its reinscription of such stories as the Good Samaritan parable. Felski, summarizing Marielle Macé's work on incorporating affective experience into the act of interpretation, characterizes this "affective engagement" as "the very means by which literary works are able to reach, reorient, and even reconfigure their readers."[8] Joyce wanted *Ulysses* to do just that and to create more caring readers.

Karen Lawrence argues that the "thematic of hospitality runs throughout Joyce's oeuvre, from *Dubliners* to *Finnegans Wake*,"[9] and apprehending afresh the hospitality ethic of particular stories from *Dubliners* and *Ulysses* as a hospitality narrative structured in part by the Good Samaritan parable may return us to something of what Attridge terms the "work's inaugural power." We might then perceive how Joyce begins exploring hospitality narratives generally in *Ulysses* as a warm and welcoming fiction that invites us into its world of 1904 Dublin, allowing us to linger on the relationship between Leopold Bloom and Stephen Dedalus and to understand how they re-enact this greatest of all parables, with important implications for us as readers who should become hospitable in turn to these characters and others with whom we come in contact outside the pages of the novel.[10]

Joyce and the Turn toward Religion in Literary Studies

Apart from scattered important early books on Joyce and Catholicism,[11] along with several seminal studies of Joyce and Judaism in the late 1980s and 1990s,[12] Joyce criticism did not turn back in any serious way to considerations of belief in his work until the early twenty-first century, in part because of its long historicist turn; as Jean Kane notes, "historicist Joyce criticism of the last decades [apart from the Judaism and Joyce studies] largely ignored 'religion' as a category of deep analysis."[13] Although this book takes for granted the importance of embedding literature in its particular histories—textual, cultural, material, political—I focus more on the aesthetic, affective and theological dimensions of Joyce's fiction and, in doing so, find, as Mark Knight and Emma Mason have argued, that "the distinctiveness of literature tends to be brought out by the disciplines of theology and philosophy instead of being suppressed by them."[14] Like them, I believe that "[w]ith religion, literature makes space for feeling, emotion, and the communities of readers who experience life and thought in particular ways; with philosophy, literature shares a determination to question received wisdom and pursue new modes of thought."[15] The sort of religiously and philosophically oriented literary criticism I seek to practice here restores our attention to the primacy of the literary work itself in all its strangeness and variousness, hopefully leading to a new understanding of Joyce's great interest in hospitality—and to the growing body of postcritical reading theory wherein readers practice hospitality to the literary text and ideally to others.

The "modernity as secularization" thesis has been contested by a series of studies in recent years, which are part of the general religious turn in literary studies and of the increasing recognition of the modernist novel's particular debt to religion and Joyce's ongoing interaction with questions of religion despite his leaving the Catholic Church.[16] As Kane has pointed out in her study of how religion is employed to represent minority characters in the fiction of Joyce and Rushdie, "[d]iscarded as a preoccupation of New Critical aesthetics and structuralist master codes, belief appears as a topic of interest in relation to institutional-political histories, magic realist myth, or economic analogue when it bears upon literary production at all."[17] In 2005, however, the well-known literary theorist Stanley Fish announced in a provocative column in *The Chronicle of Higher Education*, entitled "One University under God?", that the religious turn in literary studies would replace high theory and the triumvirate of race, class, and gender as "the center of intellectual energy in the academy" in the wake of Derrida's death.[18] Fish's prediction may have been overstated, but certainly the religious turn in literary studies has become a major area of interest for many scholars. Michael W. Kaufmann's article, "The Religious, the Secular, and Literary Studies: Rethinking the Secularization Narrative in Histories of the Profession," remains essential reading on the subject. Kaufmann's opening statement challenges a formerly essential underpinning of literary studies: "Histories of the profession of literary studies have long been underwritten by a narrative of secularization. It seems generally accepted that while the discipline and its practitioners were once more religious, literary studies is now a decidedly secular enterprise."[19] His patient survey of the religious turn in literary studies shows that by 2007, and even before, some major literary critics were questioning the jettisoning of religion in literary criticism and theorizing religion's persistence in literature through, for example, the emergence of postsecularism.

A number of critical studies have appeared in the last fifteen years that have signaled literary studies' religious turn, including several important studies of Joyce. These include John McClure's *Partial Faiths: Postsecular Fiction in the Age of Pynchon and Morrison* (2007), Emer Nolan's *Catholic Emancipations: Irish Fiction from Thomas Moore to James Joyce* (2007), Roy Gottfried's *Joyce's Misbelief* (2008), Mary Lowe-Evans's *Catholic Nostalgia in Joyce and Company* (2008), Pericles Lewis's *Religious Experience and the Modernist Novel* (2010), and Amy Hungerford's *Postmodern Belief: American Literature and Religion since 1960* (2010). More recently, there are Justin Neuman's *Fiction beyond Secularism* (2014), Lynne Hinojosa's *Puritanism and Modernist Novels* (2015), William Franke's *Secular Scriptures: Modern Theological Poetics in the Wake of Dante* (2015), Colum Power's *James Joyce's Catholic Categories* (2016), Susan Felch's edited *The Cambridge Companion to Literature and Religion* (2016), Steve Pinkerton's *Blasphemous Modernism: The 20th-Century Word Made Flesh* (2017), Matthew Mutter's *Restless Secularism: Modernism and the Religious Inheritance* (2017), Farrell O'Gorman's *Catholicism and American Borders in the Gothic Literary Imagination* (2017), Chrissie van Mierlo's *James Joyce and Catholicism: The Apostate's Wake* (2017), Michael Hurley's *Faith in Poetry: Verse Style as a Mode of Religious Belief* (2017), Christopher Herbert's *Evangelical Gothic: The English Novel and the Religious War on Virtue from Wesley to* Dracula (2019), and Kieran Quinlan's *Seamus Heaney and the End of Catholic Ireland* (2020), to name just a few of the most influential such studies.[20] There are book series on literature and religion at major presses as well, such as those published by Baylor University Press and Bloomsbury (along with a recently concluded series on Literature, Religion, and Postsecular Studies at Ohio State University Press), and a series of journals continue to focus on the subject, including *Christianity and Literature, Religion and Literature, Religion and the Arts, Theology and Literature,* and *Renascence: Essays on Values in Literature*, among others. More and more, including in Irish literary studies, literary scholars have begun taking seriously how literature is informed by particular religious practices and cultures.[21]

Joyce's heretical stances in religion and politics and other areas were predicated upon his ferocious individualism and independence, which were themselves, seemingly paradoxically, coupled with a profound privileging of a community of individuals who could not only recognize and tend to the needs of the Other, but finally enfold the Other into a radical community of difference grounded in love. In order to imagine this community, Joyce felt it necessary to rebel against the restrictive Irish Catholicism in which he had been raised. Roy Gottfried, for instance, points out that having been reared a Catholic, Joyce "is particularly interested in assaulting the unitary power of the Vatican, both in religious terms and in terms of hegemony; being Irish, he is particularly resistant to the subsuming of his local identity as a Dubliner into the larger one of a universal Catholic," and thus, "heretics as particular persons and agents appear as almost obsessive components in Stephen [Dedalus]'s thinking and are widely present in Joyce's work."[22] Joyce had left the Catholic Church well before he wrote *Ulysses* and moved to the continent, and he sought to radically challenge religious authority, especially that of the Catholic Church in his day, along with British colonialism. Yet while acknowledging these challenges, this book also takes seriously Joyce's vast array of allusions to a wide variety of texts across different fields, focusing upon his engagement with scriptural narratives—particularly that of the Lukan parable of the Good Samaritan—to demonstrate his rebellion against established orthodoxies and privileging of a secularized figure who became a major model for Leopold Bloom, Joyce's Everyman who epitomized his embrace of pacifism, love, and community, particularly his concept of the neighbor.

Literary Studies and Hospitality

In his magisterial study, *Hospitality and Treachery in Western Literature*, James A. W. Heffernan observes that "[i]n spite of its ubiquity and its pervasiveness in literature, hospitality has long been slighted by literary theorists and critics."[23] The relative neglect of hospitality in literary studies is a lacuna that desperately needs to be addressed, although there have been welcome advances such as Heffernan's important work and others.[24] At a time when all of us are supposedly closer to each other than ever before thanks to advances in the speed and scale of communication, we are nonetheless farther apart—strangers passing through the spaces of Facebook, Twitter, and other social media. A thick, rich concept of hospitality drawn from the nexus of religion and literature might enable us to apprehend anew a concept of neighborliness and care for others in the midst of a hardening of various divides, especially since, as Heffernan so convincingly argues, being hospitable involves developing an ethic of vulnerability and potentially being betrayed, even wounded or killed.

But hospitality as a subject can be difficult to comprehend, and its etymologies convey something of its ambiguity. As Christopher Yates has argued, "It is a subject matter that, once broached, resists the categories of abstraction and the determinative instruments of analysis" because it "has a history and a depth, just as it carries marks of urgency, weight, and discovery in our present moment."[25] Moreover, hospitality can be uncomfortable to study since it displays a "trajectory of reflection well aware that its subject matter consists in an event that interrogates those who study it."[26] After surveying the etymological origins of the word, including *hospes* and *hospitis*, denoting "host, guest, or stranger," and *hostis*, denoting "stranger as friend or foe," Yates concludes that it is "a word pregnant with the potential to signify passage and mercy, or exclusion and punishment, thereby placing supplicants, states, and scholars alike on the brink of a rather decisive threshold."[27] And J. Hillis Miller points out that "host" and "guest" contain the same root: "*ghos-ti*, stranger, guest, host, properly 'someone with whom one has reciprocal duties of hospitality.'"[28]

To these etymological complications, which he also traces, Heffernan additionally reflects upon the Greek word *xenos*, with its multiplicity of meanings:

> It can mean either "guest" or "host"; it can designate a friend with whom you have a hereditary treaty of hospitality, such as the child of someone whom you once entertained or who once entertained you; it can mean anyone who is entitled to the rights of hospitality simply because he or she is a stranger; or it can denote a complete stranger, a *barbaros*, or foreigner.[29]

Sadly, in English, "the word *xenos* seems to leave but a single trace: xenophobia, fear of strangers, which can all too easily turn into virulent hatred of them."[30] Heffernan draws on late theories about hospitality developed by Jacques Derrida, particularly his notion of absolute or unconditional hospitality, which would banish the hatred sometimes visited on guests or visitors that is expressed in "xenophobia."

One of Joyce's exemplars, Homer, gave antiquity its most extended treatment of *xenia* in the *Odyssey*. In fact, it might best be thought of as an extended study in hospitality. In his study of hospitality scenes in the *Odyssey*, Steve Reece argues that the pervasiveness of such scenes in that epic arise because "the tales of a young traveler on a quest for information and of a warrior wandering homeward from abroad are naturally conducive to this theme." He further posits that "[i]n a practical sense . . . the *Odyssey* may be regarded as a sequence of hospitality scenes."[31] Homer's elaborate incorporation of hospitality scenes—Reece considers 38 elements that recur repeatedly in eighteen different such scenes—into his narrative, along with the way in which he puts those scenes into conversation with each other, a practice that Reece likens to a composer arranging "variations on a common musical theme," seems downright, well, Joycean, we might say in looking back to that epic.[32] Because of his long admiration for Homer and decision to base *Ulysses*' structure loosely upon the *Odyssey*, Joyce certainly would have known the concept of *xenia*. Moreover, he undoubtedly also would have realized how much Homer's epic becomes a study of hospitality and admired how Homer "staged" so many different scenes of hospitality and related them to each other so intricately. Homeric hospitality thus helps inspire and undergird Joyce's interest in and development of hospitality theory in his fiction, particularly in *Ulysses*.

And yet Joyce's reading of Christian, not pagan, hospitality finally became even more influential for his development of this theme in *Ulysses*. Drawing on

Jesus' admonition to take care of strangers in Matthew 25:34–46, Heffernan argues that "Christ makes the eternal fate of everyone wholly dependent on our hospitality to strangers," claiming "it is scarcely possible to overstate the moral importance of hospitality in the New Testament." While he actually overstates the case in arguing that "our response to needy strangers on earth" is "the *sole determinant* of our eternal life" (emphasis his), neglecting our need for a Savior because of the abiding presence of original sin, it is difficult to disagree with him that "Christ places hospitality at the very center of his teachings."[33] As we will see in the course of this study, Joyce knew and took seriously the concept of Christian hospitality, finding it particularly appealing in the Lukan narrative and in then-contemporary biographies of Jesus that stressed his humanist qualities.

In a series of works written in the late 1990s and early 2000s, including his study *Of Hospitality*, but also a significant chapter on the subject in *Acts of Religion*, Derrida formulated a thick concept of hospitality that seems perhaps unachievable by humans, but is nonetheless an ideal for him. As Heffernan puts it in characterizing Derrida's theory of absolute hospitality, "While conventional hospitality is conditional, based on laws of reciprocity and mutual obligation between individuals or groups, absolute hospitality is unconditional," and thus, as Derrida claims, it requires

> that I open up my home . . . to the absolute, anonymous other, and that I give place to them, that I let them come, let them arrive, and take place in the place I offer them, without asking of them either reciprocity (entering into a pact) or even their names.[34]

As I will argue later, my main issue with Derrida's theory of hospitality, which in general I commend for its emphasis on prodigality, concerns its anti-incarnational stance whereby the Other becomes an abstraction, over against the Christian concept of hospitality, epitomized by Christ's literal offering of Himself on the cross. Unfortunately, the extensive research that has been conducted on Joyce and Derrida does not seek to understand Joycean hospitality through the important Derridean contributions to the subject.[35]

This book often looks to Christian-inspired hospitality theories such as those promulgated by Paul Ricoeur and Richard Kearney that arise from my specific textual readings of Joyce's fiction—particularly the theory of hospitality he develops in *Ulysses* from dwelling upon and incorporating the Lukan parable of the Good Samaritan. In *Strangers, Gods, and Monsters: Interpreting Otherness*, Kearney has argued convincingly that "we often project onto others those unconscious fears from which we recoil in ourselves. Rather than acknowledge that we are deep down answerable to an alterity which unsettles us, we devise all sorts of evasion strategies." Such strategies include our scapegoating of strangers or our turning them into monsters, in the process refusing "to recognize the stranger in front of us as a singular other who responds, in turn, to the singular otherness in each of us. We refuse to acknowledge ourselves-as-others."[36] I share Kearney's commitment to what he calls a "diacritical hermeneutics" of the Other, which is distinct from both a romantic and a radical hermeneutics. Practitioners of romantic hermeneutics such as Schleiermacher, Dilthey, and Gadamer tended to argue that philosophical interpretation should "unite the consciousness of one subject with that of another," in the process recovering "some lost original consciousness by way of rendering what is past contemporaneous with our present modes of comprehension." In such a model, the Other loses its alterity and so do I; each is rendered nonsingular, and the productive tension of otherness is effaced. On the other hand, as Kearney succinctly puts it, those who have posited a radical hermeneutics such as Derrida, Blanchot, and Lyotard tend to reject "the model of appropriation, insisting on the unmediatable and ultimately sublime nature of alterity." Further, "in defiance of a community of minds, this uncompromising stance holds out for irreducible difference and separation."[37] In this model, the Other can never become part of us, nor we part of her. Friendship, community remain unattainable, just over an infinitely unreachable horizon, although desirable.

Instead of these two hermeneutical extremes, Kearney articulates his diacritical hermeneutics as exploring "possibilities of intercommunion between distinct but not incomparable selves." Thus, "friendship begins by welcoming difference (*dia-legein*). It champions the practice of dialogue between self and other, while refusing to submit to the reductionist dialectics of egology governed by the logos of the Same."[38] Kearney's diacritical notion of hermeneutics not only seems most appropriate to our apprehension of our interactions with the stranger on a daily basis but also to understanding Joyce's deep concern with hospitality and the stranger.

Because of the contradictory etymology of "hospitality," we are given a choice, a threshold opportunity, as it were—to embrace the stranger or to fear and repudiate him. Hospitality is thus never an inert concept but always an *action incumbent on us* when encountering the Other—drawing the stranger to us or repelling her, welcoming him or repudiating him. As readers we practice hospitality unconsciously with the characters we meet whom we either love or loathe. In both *Dubliners* and *Ulysses*, Joyce invites us into a particularly rich series of hospitable situations in which we explore meetings that strangers have with those in the inner circles of power and culture. In his fiction, we are asked to begin practicing a diacritical hermeneutics, in the process getting to know strangers and ourselves more deeply.

Ireland, Hospitality, and Joyce

Although Ireland has long been marketed as a hospitable culture, especially by its tourist board, John Brannigan has pointed out that the modern Irish state was founded in part in a hostility to ethnic others, and further, that the "representation of foreigners, and the political rhetoric surrounding aliens, suggests that Irish hospitality was usually conditional, and often problematic in terms of how the foreigner was marked out as the symbolic embodiment of exoticism, immorality, or rootless modernity."[39] As we will see in my discussion of the treatment of Leopold Bloom in *Ulysses*, his darker skin and supposed Jewishness mark him out as Other—and he is verbally maligned by a series of characters throughout much of the novel and almost physically attacked late in the "Cyclops" episode. Joyce rebelled against many institutions and attitudes in his lifetime—the Irish Catholic Church, the British imperial state, excessive nationalism—but in his repeated portrayals of hospitable acts by his fictional characters, he rejected the insular characteristics of Irish hospitality he recognized, even as he celebrated more inviting aspects of it. As an Irish exile living abroad for much of his adult life, he knew keenly the importance of truly welcoming others—of being hospitable—and he gradually developed an ethic of hospitality in major works such as *Dubliners* and *Ulysses* wherein strange and startling acts of kindness and *caritas* erupt between unlikely characters and in improbable locations such as bars and brothels.

Likening Joyce to a monk in 1968, Darcy O'Brien claimed that "his ideals were supernal, mythical, exalted, impossible" and further termed them part of Joyce's "spiritual idealism."[40] This notion of Joyce as a spiritual idealist has not received enough attention among even those critics sympathetic to his spiritual aims. More recently, Jack Dudley has reclaimed what he terms the "spiritual Joyce," a concept amply supported by Joyce's recourse to the language of spirit, spirituality, and spiritualism, which pervades his prose. As Dudley puts it,

> Joyce consistently appropriated the religious resources of his Catholic background not for secular ends, at least not how we use the term today, nor [for] merely aesthetic purposes. Instead, Joyce intended what he himself called "spiritual" purposes, a mystical transcendence that drew its meaning from concepts like divinity and soul.

Further, Dudley argues that "[t]his term, 'spiritual,' not only emerges as central to his view of art and life, but generates new ways of reading stories like 'Grace' when it helps us see those stories advance a specifically transcendent vision." Dudley defines the transcendent for Joyce as how his writings "maintained a sense of sacredness, religious valence, and mystical meaning that transcends mere matter," and yet which is "distinct from that preached by the Roman Catholicism of his time, which taught that transcendence was above and beyond the physical world and bestowed by God alone, through the Roman Catholic Church alone."[41] What Dudley posits as Joyce's location of transcendence in the material world is compelling. I argue further that Joycean transcendence may reach its apotheosis in its grounding in our material flesh through concepts of reaching out to the Other in hospitable practice, epitomized by the Good Samaritan parable.

Toward a Hospitality Ethic in *Dubliners* and *Ulysses*

My exploration in the next chapter of the various aspects of hospitality that are often thwarted and occasionally accepted in *Dubliners* suggests the differing manifestations of hospitality and how Joyce inflects the concept in many of those stories. In Chapter 1, I offer a reconsideration of hospitality in *Dubliners* that counters the still-dominant reading of that volume of short stories as bifurcated between the concerns of the first fourteen stories and those of "The Dead," which Joyce wrote after having moved to the continent. Rather than suddenly appreciating hospitality while in his long European exile and writing about it only in "The Dead," Joyce actually meditates upon hospitality in many of the preceding stories, including the Good Samaritan-inspired "Grace." This chapter offers a substantial reading of "The Dead" through theories of hospitality, showing how Gabriel becomes a true host at the end of the story by welcoming both the intimate stranger of his wife Gretta and the truly strange ghost of Michael Furey into his heart. Through this process of opening himself to another, inspired as well by meditating on Christological symbols in the graveyard where Furey is buried, Gabriel now has a chance to become the hospitable, attentive husband that Gretta needs and desires. By attending so closely to Gabriel's transformation into a figure of hospitality (however embryonically), Joyce signals his own determination to further explore this subject in his later fiction—and to suggest how readers might become more hospitable by steeping themselves in the lives of others.

In Chapter 2, I detail Joyce's turn toward Scripture, showing how his burgeoning theories of literature were informed by his forays into Scripture, beginning with his transcription of the Book of Revelation when he was 16 years old as an act of rebellion against the Catholic Church. While there are a vast number of allusions in the novel, the two major sources for it are, as Robert Alter has argued, Homer's *Odyssey* and the Bible: "unlike all the other non-Homeric allusions in *Ulysses*, the Bible serves, in a manner nearly symmetrical with the *Odyssey*, as a fundamental allusive matrix for Joyce's novel."[42] Declan Kiberd has posited *Ulysses* as akin to the Bible in its function as wisdom literature, not only observing that the New Testament was a major part of the creation of the novel, but also noting that Joyce sought to "reconfigure earlier classics, making *Ulysses* both their fulfilment and itself an open, prophetic book," much as the Old Testament was.[43] Joyce's interest in Scripture manifests itself throughout the novel, but particularly, for my purposes, in his appropriation of the Good Samaritan parable from the New Testament, signaled at the beginning of the "Nostos" section of *Ulysses*, the last three episodes of the novel that start with "Eumaeus," the most understudied episode.

This chapter concludes by examining how Joyce took the actual incident of his physical assault in 1904, after which he was allegedly helped to his feet by a local (supposedly Jewish) gentleman, as one of the major inspirations for his novel—what I call a "true fiction"—and began understanding it as a manifestation of the Good Samaritan parable, just as he did with the later incident of his mugging in Rome. As a heretic, a rebel, Joyce was drawn to this parable precisely because its hero transgressed the orthodoxies of his day and helped a wounded traveler from another "tribe" beaten to near death. Certainly there were other inspirations for the novel: Joyce's walking out for the first time with his eventual wife Nora Barnacle on June 16, 1904, the day on which he chose to set the novel; his desire to write an epic of the body; a marked motivation to supersede English literature and create a truly Irish novel that attended to ordinary people; and certainly not least, a need to declare religious and political independence from both the Irish Catholic Church and the British imperial state. Yet Joyce's long-held desire to write a story about this partially apocryphal incident remained a guiding inspiration for the novel.

Chapter 3 begins by exploring Joyce's affinity for scriptural narrative, in particular his interest in the narratives of Luke and Acts and the parables therein. Mr. Kernan and Bloom's interaction in the cemetery in "Hades" connects these two characters, further linking "Grace" to "Circe," both narratives featuring rescues that re-enact the Good Samaritan parable. It then shows how Bloom's rescue of Stephen in "Circe," the fifteenth episode of *Ulysses*, turns out to be a rewriting (at times verbatim) of the opening scene of his 1905 short story "Grace," in which Kernan falls down the steps of a pub and is rescued by a cyclist. This chapter finally ponders how particular contours of that parable structure some of the significant action and dialogue late in "Circe" when Bloom rescues Stephen—homeless since leaving the Martello Tower that morning—and saves him both from further attack by a soldier and from a police inquiry.

Chapter 4 charts Bloom's transformation from Stranger in the "anti-hospitality" episode of "Cyclops," where he assumes a Jewish identity, into Samaritan, briefly, in "Oxen of the Sun," and in particular "Circe," where he assumes a secular Christ-like identity. This chapter also shows how Bloom has pursued Stephen to the Westland Row railway station after "Oxen of the Sun" and before "Circe," where he finds Stephen with an injured hand, likely from striking Buck Mulligan. Also temporarily homeless, himself earlier attacked, particularly in "Cyclops," Bloom empathizes with Stephen's rootless state and wounded condition. In "Circe," Bloom finally rejects the closing vision of his dead son Rudy in favor of "adopting" Stephen Dedalus as a living heir, over whom he mutters a Masonic oath. I introduce a reading of Bloom not just as a Mason here, but also as a likely holder of the Masonic side order of the Good Samaritan degree. Finally, I assess how Bloom's instinctive and profoundly creative actions in his rescue of Stephen align him with the hated Samaritan from the Lukan narrative and suggest his *agape* love for this beaten Stranger.

The fifth chapter gives an extended reading of the sixteenth episode of the novel, "Eumaeus," which, even though it is rife with misunderstandings and seemingly hampered by a circumlocutious narrator, nonetheless is revealed to be a deeply and warmly humanistic episode that I situate in the context of the Good Samaritan parable. After evaluating the vexed issue of that episode's confusing style and recovering it, to some degree, as capable of conveying truth and beauty, this chapter also surveys the critical misapprehensions that have obtained from readings of the reference to this parable at the beginning of "Eumaeus," and critiques most of those readings by showing Joyce's clear interest in introducing the parable as a primary intertext for the "Nostos" section, not as a throwaway, to pun on an advertisement that is discarded early in the novel but continues to reappear periodically. Even though the two will separate later that evening, I show how Bloom's rescue, while not affirmed verbally in any substantial way by Stephen, nonetheless becomes profound by nature of its enfleshment when Stephen leans on Bloom's arm and lets him guide them toward his home.

Bloom's *caritas* toward Stephen also models charity for the young man, who in turn starts becoming charitable by loaning Corley some money. This parable-driven episode reveals that even though Stephen, "playing" the role of the downtrodden beaten man from Christ's parable, often rejects Bloom's ministrations, Bloom's care for him triumphantly finishes inscribing a narrative of care and concern that runs throughout the novel. Bloom can care so well for Stephen because he knows what it is like to be usurped by an invader in his own home and because he has been verbally assaulted repeatedly that day and throughout his life. This parabolic plot gives us "the curve of an emotion" put into enacted practice that Joyce had sought long ago in his essay, "A Portrait of an Artist," and that emotion, raised to the height of the virtue of charity, repeatedly enacted by Bloom, becomes a major arc of the novel—at least for these two major characters.[44]

The sixth chapter focuses on "Ithaca" and "Penelope," building upon Margot Norris's theory in *Virgin and Veteran Readings of Ulysses* that Stephen's seeming rejection of Bloom in his recitation of the anti-Semitic ballad in "Ithaca" actually may be followed by his spreading the story of Bloom's generosity throughout Dublin, combating the rumors circulating about Bloom as a stereotypically stingy Jew. This chapter also examines, through theories of beauty articulated by Jean-Louis Chrétien and Elaine Scarry, how Stephen and Bloom jointly experience the beauty of the nighttime sky in "Ithaca," a moment that makes them newly receptive and hospitable to each other. It concludes by assessing how Molly's embodiedness in "Penelope" casts her as the figurative innkeeper from the Good Samaritan parable, receptive to taking in both Bloom, formerly cast as the Stranger, now Samaritan, and Stephen, the newly wounded Stranger, although her desire to help Stephen is undercut by her wanting to bed him as well. Strikingly, Molly reaffirms her relationship with Bloom after offering hospitality in the form of her bed and body to Blazes Boylan the previous afternoon, a usurper who abuses her hospitality and treats her roughly during sex over against Bloom's much more tender and deferential sexual practices.

The seventh chapter shows how reading the novel parabolically not only helps us to apprehend the deep relationship Bloom establishes with Stephen over the course of a few hours but also suggests how Joyce recruits us as readers to have pity on Bloom and Stephen and to act charitably toward them in our minds and ideally toward those around us. The Good Samaritan parable throws the question of rescue and charity back on the reader, asking us to become neighbors of such fictional characters as Stephen and Bloom and, thus, to start inculcating charitable attitudes in ourselves. Hence, Joyce finally reaches out beyond sectarian boundaries—Catholic, Protestant, Jewish, other—and toward a deeply ethical, enfleshed ethics, inspired by Christ's attitude toward the stranger, grounded in charity toward the Other that warmly suggests our common deep humanity and our inextricably reciprocal natures. This enfleshed Joycean ethics, informed by Paul Ricoeur's extensive philosophical and theological investigations of the Good Samaritan parable, beginning with his seminal essay, "The Socius and the Neighbor," also takes its bearings from Richard Kearney's concept of "carnal hermeneutics" in understanding how touch enables us to begin knowing others as neighbors.

The parable of the Good Samaritan perhaps captures the essence of hospitality most profitably and profoundly for Joyce. Certainly, the Samaritan parable became for him, in the years he was writing *Ulysses*, the *ne plus ultra* of how to treat others generously and lovingly, including the reader, whom he also wanted to gather into his extra-literary community. Apprehending that novel's parabolic instantiation of community reveals Joyce's ongoing attempt to reach out in love to his readers in what became his secular scripture.

What would it mean for *Ulysses* studies to understand the parabolic arc of the Good Samaritan that is enacted across the last several episodes of the novel, but anticipated at significant moments earlier? First of all, it would, it should lead inevitably to some qualified revision of Weldon Thornton's assertion that "Joyce simply does not value narrative enough to protect it over against his other interests and agendas in *Ulysses*."[45] In fact, Joyce valued narrative so much that he realized that using parables to partially structure his novel would help achieve his narrative goals, which were inherently ethical.[46] Thus, he grasped that "[a]s a narrative unit, parable is distinctly unsatisfactory. It leaves the reader with a crux—a narrative dilemma without a solution to be found directly within the parable itself."[47] Moreover, my renewed emphasis on a sorely neglected strand of Joyce's interest in narrative leads to an enhanced appreciation of the role of narrative in the novel and could thus profitably enable us to grapple all over again with Joyce's excursions in various styles. Such a treatment is beyond the scope of this study, but it is worth further exploration. More important, such an emphasis on *Ulysses* as parabolic enables us to think through a variety of intertwined issues, such as the inspiration for the novel, its structure, its importance for Stephen and Bloom's relationship, its emphasis on Joyce's thinking about Jesus' teachings, and finally, what a consideration of the importance of this parable portends for our sense of the novel's ending, or, rather, its tentative conclusions.

My coda offers an overview of other avenues for reading hospitality in Joyce that future critics might explore, then it extends my reading of Joyce's Samaritan hospitality into a hermeneutics of generosity in terms informed in part by those articulated in Rita Felski's *The Limits of Critique*—her exemplary investigation of postcritical literary studies—but which is also influenced by what has become known as "postsecular criticism." Felski returns to Ricoeur's rejection of the so-called "hermeneutics of suspicion" and explores how we might approach literary works through a spirit of generosity and even hospitality, drawing others into this generative way of reading. This coda also draws on Felski's recent study *Hooked: Art and Attachment*, wherein she articulates a compelling theory of how literary works appeal to us through our "co-production" of them, part of what she terms literature's particular and peculiar work of "attachment." And postsecular criticism, as shown by critics such as Lori Branch, Mark Knight, and Tracy Fassenden, among others, maintains that the metaphysical questions and concerns raised by faith—at the heart of our practices as readers and critics and human beings—become fully part of our meaning-making that binds us together in our common enterprise. *Ulysses* uncannily anticipates both the rise of the postcritical and the postsecular, asking us to consider how attending to the lingering authority of both biblical texts and secular works that draw deeply upon them such as *Ulysses* might unsettle the authoritative notions of self that we have erected, in the process leading us out of ourselves and into a potential communion with fictional and actual Others, who are finally and inextricably part of ourselves.

Notes

1. Brady, "Suspect Quizzed after 'Good Samaritan' Stabbed to Death," n.p.
2. Steiner, *Grammars of Creation*, 147.
3. Kenner, *Ulysses*, 48.
4. Attridge, *The Singularity of Literature*, 77.
5. Ibid., 80.
6. Felski, *Hooked: Art and Attachment*, 7.
7. Felski, *The Limits of Critique*, 166.
8. Ibid., 177, drawing on Macé, *Façons de lire, manières d'être*.

9. Lawrence, *Who's Afraid of James Joyce?*, 151.
10. The previous extended exploration of hospitality in Joyce, Jean-Michel Rabatè's *James Joyce and the Politics of Egoism*, places it in a dialogue with Joyce's egoism as a member of the avant-garde of his day. As will become clear, my notion of Joyce's hospitality is quite different from Rabatè's since I stress its origins in Joyce's deep knowledge of the Good Samaritan parable and the theological criticism that has accrued around that parable, particularly its grounding in an embodied, incarnational ethics that views love as an action toward others, even those who do not wish to be loved.
11. See, for instance, Kevin Sullivan's *Joyce among the Jesuits* (1958), J. Mitchell Morse's *The Sympathetic Alien: James Joyce and Catholicism* (1959), William T. Noon's *Joyce and Aquinas* (1963), and later ones such as Robert Boyle's *James Joyce's Pauline Vision: A Catholic Exposition* (1978) and Beryl Schlossman's theoretically informed *Joyce's Catholic Comedy of Language* (1985).
12. See especially Ira Nadel's *Joyce and the Jews: Culture and Texts* (1989), Neil Davison's *James Joyce, Ulysses, and the Construction of Jewish Identity* (1998), and Marilyn Reizbaum's *James Joyce's Judaic Other* (1999).
13. Kane, *Conspicuous Bodies: Provincial Belief and the Making of Joyce and Rushdie*, 69.
14. Knight and Mason, "Saving Literary Criticism," 153.
15. Ibid., 153–4. I should immediately note that the rise of "affect" studies, including those dealing with empathy, have also been important for me in thinking through hospitality in Joyce's fiction, though I rarely cite them in this study. In this regard, see Meghan Marie Hammond's helpful study, *Empathy and the Psychology of Literary Modernism*, which helpfully charts the turn from sympathy in Victorian and Edwardian fiction to modernist fiction's new focus on empathy in her introduction, 1–31.
16. Geert Lernout's study *Help My Unbelief: James Joyce and Religion* represents a major exception to this trend: it rejects any real, lingering influence of Joyce's earlier Catholicism on his major works. While Lernout at least engages deeply with the question of Joyce and religion, however, in Brandon Kershner's essay for the *Cambridge Companion to Ulysses*, simply entitled "Intertextuality," he seems to believe that such questions were dealt with only in a period dominated by New Criticism, when such critics "paid special attention to Christian references in literary works that were not on the surface Christian." These critics "were eager to discover and interpret them even in the work of an admitted apostate like Joyce, since his writing was still permeated with Biblical tags and echoes of the Church Fathers" (175). Apart from his positive appreciation of J. Mitchell Morse's *The Sympathetic Alien* and more negative appraisal of Virginia Moseley's *Joyce and the Bible*, Kershner's condescension toward such readings emerges clearly here.
17. Kane, *Conspicuous Bodies*, 8.
18. Fish, "One University under God?". He also argued that universities needed to "take religion seriously . . . not as a phenomenon to be analyzed at arm's length, but as a candidate for the truth."
19. Kaufmann, "The Religious, the Secular, and Literary Studies," 607.

20. I was pleased to find that Kane includes a similar such list to my own; she also includes Lernout's study, Gian Balsamo's *Joyce's Messianism: Dante, Negative Existence, and the Messianic Self* (2004), and Stephen Sicari's *Joyce's Modernist Allegory* (2001). See Kane, *Conspicuous Bodies*, 172 n7.
21. For instance, Cóilín Owens's editorial, "Religion and Irish Studies," published in the fall 2007 issue of *Irish Literary Supplement*, marked a somewhat strident call for more work on religion within the field. Owens cited a number of instances where he felt religion was ignored, misrepresented, or attacked, including at the 2005 Notre Dame meeting of the American Conference for Irish Studies (ACIS) and at the 2006 St. Louis meeting of ACIS. His statement that "The failure to recognize the value of religion—except as some sort of social marker or emotional handicap—diminishes the claim of Irish Studies to [be] a serious academic enterprise" is undeniable and welcome. While he calls for elements of the mysticism of the Protestant-raised Yeats, the metempsychosis of the Protestant-raised Synge, the Catholic influences on Joyce, and the religious aspects of the Protestant-raised Beckett, Denis Devlin, Patrick Kavanagh, and Seán O Ríordán (these last three all raised Catholic), to be appreciated, however, he is mostly concerned about how "anti-Catholic sentiments" have led to what he perceives as an "indifference or hostility to the religious dimensions of Irish history, literature, and social custom [that] appears to be on the rise." Tongue-in-cheek, he goes on to declare, "When that indifference escalates into unembarrassed bigotry and is provided a privileged space under the umbrella of academic freedom and is apparently accepted without demur, it is time to declare oneself a protestant [sic]." Yet Owens himself spends most of his editorial defending the Catholic Church from, for example, what he sees as an overstated reputation for pedophile priests, and argues that "The Catholic Church, for all its much publicized problems, remains the principal beacon of Christian love in a world where the guiding principle in every sphere of life—including much academic endeavor—appears to be individual self advancement" (Owens, "Religion and Irish Studies," 2). A year later, Owens attacked Gottfried's groundbreaking study, *Joyce's Misbelief*, a major influence for my understanding of Joyce's interest in Scripture, including the Lukan Good Samaritan parable, for its audacity in advancing the incontrovertible thesis that Joyce reacted against the magisterium of the Irish Catholic Church by transcribing Revelation and otherwise engaging in practices that are traditionally Protestant.
22. Gottfried, *Joyce's Misbelief*, 107.
23. Heffernan, *Hospitality and Treachery in Western Literature*, 2.
24. See, for instance, Mike Marais's 2009 study, *Secretary of the Invisible: The Idea of Hospitality in the Fiction of J. M. Coetzee*, which draws on theories of hospitality articulated by both Levinas and Derrida.
25. Yates, "Introduction, Hospitality: Imagining the Stranger," 515.
26. Ibid., 515–16.
27. Ibid., 516.
28. Miller, "The Critic as Host," 220–1.
29. Heffernan, *Hospitality and Treachery in Western Literature*, 3.
30. Ibid.

31. Reece, *The Stranger's Welcome: Oral Theory and the Aesthetics of the Homeric Hospitality Scene*, 191.
32. See ibid., 6–7, for the recurring elements across those scenes, and 192 for a comparison of their arrangement to a symphony.
33. Heffernan, *Hospitality and Treachery in Western Literature*, 9. There would be considerable warrant, however, for developing an argument that sees Christ's body as torn for believers on the cross as the supremely hospitable act.
34. Ibid., 3, citing Derrida, *Of Hospitality*, 25.
35. See, for instance, the many essays collected in *Derrida and Joyce: Texts and Contexts*, edited by Andrew J. Mitchell and Sam Slote, and the monographs by Peter Mahon, *Imagining Joyce and Derrida: Between Finnegans Wake and Glas*, and Alan Roughley, *Reading Derrida Reading Joyce*.
36. Kearney, *Strangers, Gods, and Monsters*, 5.
37. Ibid., 17.
38. Ibid., 18.
39. Brannigan, *Race in Modern Irish Literature and Culture*, 155.
40. O'Brien, *The Conscience of James Joyce*, 245, 246.
41. Dudley, "From 'Spiritual Paralysis' to 'Spiritual Liberation': Joyce's Samaritan 'Grace,'" 180.
42. Alter, *Canon and Creativity*, 152.
43. Kiberd, *Ulysses and Us*, 297.
44. Joyce, "A Portrait of the Artist," 258.
45. Thornton, "The Greatness of *Ulysses*," 34.
46. Although she attends relatively little to how Joyce's ethics were influenced by his being steeped in Christianity, including his knowledge of the Bible, Marian Eide's *Ethical Joyce* remains the fullest examination of Joyce's ethics—particularly across his writing.
47. Mahaffey and Shashaty, "Introduction," 17.

I

HAUNTED BY HOSPITALITY IN "THE DEAD"

Joyce's cast of characters in *Dubliners*, often from the margins of society, gives credence to Frank O'Connor's claim in *The Lonely Voice* that rather than heroes, who often feature in novels, the short story has instead highlighted "submerged population groups," and thus, that "[a]lways in the short story there is this sense of outlawed figures wandering about on the fringes of society," resulting in "an intense awareness of human loneliness."[1] Vicki Mahaffey has cogently argued that "[e]ach of Joyce's works reflects an increasingly sharper awareness that an appreciation of otherness . . . is only enhanced through encounters with the unfamiliar," and we see this process of appreciating otherness beginning in *Dubliners*, most richly and deeply in "The Dead."[2] Immersing himself in so many lives, real and imagined, different from his own gave Joyce immense insights into appreciating the importance of hospitality toward others.

The two final stories in *Dubliners*, "Grace" and "The Dead," celebrate Irish hospitality, the former through recourse to the Good Samaritan parable, the latter by affirming Irish hospitality more generally, through a New Year's feast of food, conversation, music, and drink, and more specifically, through Gabriel Conroy finally allowing himself to imaginatively, empathetically enter into the life of a dead teenager whom his wife had cared for many years before. As we will see in Chapter 3, "Grace" actually reproduces the main lineaments of the Good Samaritan parable in its opening pages when the drunken Mr. Kernan falls down the steps of a pub into the men's toilets and is rescued by a kindly cyclist and a helpful crowd. More startlingly, Joyce then reproduces verbatim parts of that parabolic opening in the "Circe" chapter of *Ulysses* to narrate the Good Samaritan Leopold Bloom's rescue of the wounded traveler, Stephen Dedalus. Joyce criticism has tended to argue that the paralysis that runs throughout the volume is suddenly replaced with the theme of hospitality in "The Dead," which was written after Joyce had come to appreciate Irish hospitality while living in Italy—as if the question of hospitality appeared suddenly, Athena-like, out of his head. Instead, he had been meditating upon aspects of hospitality in his life and his work for years.

Many of the stories in *Dubliners* that precede "Grace" and "The Dead" also meditate on hospitality—real or imagined—usually perversions of it. The first story, "The Sisters," features a wake at the titular sisters' home where they offer food and drink to their guests, who have come to mourn their brother the priest, a positive manifestation of hospitality that is undermined by the ambiguous relationship that the young boy had with the priest. Karen Lawrence offers the best analysis of hospitality in this story, arguing that "Joyce mines the reversals and paradoxes implicit in the act of hospitality that are present etymologically in the Latin word from which 'host' derives, *hostia*, meaning sacrifice and victim."[3] The young boy thus "hosts" the priest in trying to hear his confession in retrospect: "[T]he grey face still followed me. It murmured, and I understood that it desired to confess something. . . . I felt that I too was smiling feebly as if to absolve the simoniac of his sin" (*D* 11). Lawrence posits that Joyce's use of "simony" (*D* 9) and "simoniac" in the context of the boy's relationship with the priest suggests that he is introducing "the perversion of responsibility to the Infinite," because "sacred hospitality is a gift and not a sale. In the pact between them, the boy senses an unsavory bribe of some sort, an erotic exchange that accompanies tutelage in the mysteries of priestly ritual."[4] Whatever "erotic exchange" might have been offered by the priest to the boy (which the boy hopefully rejected), this constitutes a clear abuse of hospitality by a figure representing the most trusted vocation in Irish society at the time.

The mean and stinting hospitality in the homes of the main characters in the subsequent stories "Araby" and "Eveline" forms the impetus for their major decisions. The young boy of "Araby," who lives with his aunt and uncle, enjoys little emotional warmth, and thus he is drawn to the titular bazaar to obtain a gift for his boyhood crush. And Eveline's home is filled with the rage and violence of her father, who drinks her wages and verbally abuses her. Yet the hospitality offered her by a figure outside her world might be even worse. She too is drawn outside the home and nearly leaves for Argentina with the ironically named Frank, who might be trying to sell her into prostitution in Buenos Aires. Frank, as her potential host, likely will abuse his hospitality to her.

Then there is the horrible mother Mrs. Mooney, who has forced an arranged marriage between her daughter and one of her lodgers in "The Boarding House," abuses the hospitality she offers her lodgers, and yet acts as if her hospitality has been violated. As she rehearses the conversation she will have with Bob Doran, who has slept with her daughter (and possibly gotten her pregnant), she pictures herself haranguing him, drawing on notions of hospitality: "She had allowed him to live beneath her roof, assuming that he was a man of honour, and he had simply abused her *hospitality*" (D 64; my emphasis). The truth, however, is that during the affair, Polly, her daughter, knows that "her mother's persistent silence could not be misunderstood. There had been no open complicity between mother and daughter, no open understanding but, though people in the house began to talk of the affair, still Mrs. Mooney did not intervene" (D 63). While this rich story has been profitably read by Donald Torchiana as both a perverse parody of the Immaculate Conception and an illustration of the forced Irish marriage,[5] Joyce clearly takes pains to critique the false hospitality narrative modeled by Mrs. Mooney to her male lodgers, before whom she parades her daughter, finally entrapping Bob Doran. And who can forget the abusive home of Farrington—abjectly lacking in hospitality—in a later story, "Counterparts," which concludes with him viciously beating his son with a stick, physically reproducing the abuse his boss Alleyne has given him earlier in the day?

Hospitality—or its lack—is generative, as "Counterparts" demonstrates. Kindness to strangers can become infectious, with the recipient of the unexpected act reproducing it later for another. Conversely, those who are expecting hospitality and are instead abused or offered malformed versions of hospitality can become stunted personally and in their expectations of others. Such potential guests may be correspondingly less likely to offer hospitality to others in need when they encounter them—or may even abuse them.

By the time he came to write "The Dead" in 1907, the concluding story of *Dubliners* that celebrates positive aspects of that city's hospitality, Joyce, who was already pondering and writing about hospitality in negative ways in many of the earlier stories, saw Irish hospitality and warmth in a new light, despite his continuing revulsion against the excesses of the Irish Catholic Church and the British imperial state. As Richard Ellmann has pointed out, "That he began ["The Dead"] with a party was due, at least in part, to Joyce's feeling that the rest of the stories in *Dubliners* had not completed his picture of the city." Thus, "[i]n a letter of September 25, 1906, he had written his brother from Rome to say that some elements of Dublin had been left out of his stories: 'I have not reproduced its ingenuous insularity and its hospitality, the latter *virtue* so far as I can see does not exist elsewhere in Europe.'" Ellmann calls attention to Gabriel Conroy's after-dinner speech praising "Ireland for this very virtue of hospitality," and further notes that Joyce based Gabriel's great-aunts, the Misses Morkan, on his own "hospitable great-aunts Mrs. Callanan and Mrs. Lyons," and associated them and Mrs. Callanan's daughter Mary Ellen with earlier festive occasions at their home at 15 Usher's Island (*JJ2* 245).

Joyce strikingly contrasts the warm and inviting Morkan home with the other homes portrayed in the collection: the cloistered, claustrophobic, and distinctly unfriendly-to-children homes of "The Sisters" and "Araby"; the abusive and poverty-stricken homes of "Eveline" and "Counterparts"; the brothel-like home of "The Boarding House"; the austere and lonely home of Mr. James Duffy in "A Painful Case." Although it is described early in "The Dead" as a "dark gaunt house" (*D* 176), the Misses Morkans' home overflows with light and warmth and hospitality on the occasion of their annual dance and dinner.

Moreover, "The Dead," written after he had left Ireland and was in Rome, overflows with Joyce's appreciation of Irish hospitality, characterized by profligacy and generosity, which he contrasts throughout the story with Gabriel Conroy's pettiness and selfishness. Colm Tóibín has pointed out that "[i]n the time between writing 'Grace' and writing 'The Dead,' scrupulous meanness in Joyce gave way to a hesitant, hushed generosity."[6] And Mary Power has shown that the perceived waning of Irish hospitality was "much analyzed and lamented in the [Irish] popular press in 1904" in publications ranging from *The United Irishman* to *Irish Society and Review* to *The Bystander*, and that Joyce with his capacious knowledge of his home city, including its periodicals, likely knew of such discussions.[7] Gabriel's final journey out of that selfishness in the conclusion presages the type of hospitality grounded in selfless generosity that Joyce would champion throughout the rest of his life and particularly in *Ulysses* by drawing upon the intertext of the Good Samaritan parable.

It is important, however, to distinguish Gabriel's false praise of hospitality during his after-dinner speech—remarks that are made to contrast what he thinks is the nationalist Miss Ivors's begrudging behavior during the earlier dance—from Joyce's general approval of Irish hospitality, evident in the tone of the story, others' generally charitable behavior, and the abundance of food and drink. These earlier instances of hospitality culminate with Gabriel's own emergent generous hospitality as he muses upon Michael Furey's "sacrifice" for Gretta. Critics writing on the story have not always made this distinction between Gabriel's fake rhetorical embrace of hospitality in his speech and the real examples of hospitality offered by other characters. Vincent P. Pecora argues, for instance, that the story "does seem to be about the institution—the great tradition—of 'genuine warm-hearted Irish hospitality' ('Dead,' 203), but not in any uncritical or laudatory way." Instead, he believes "the socially embedded attitude toward hospitality and generosity that Gabriel invokes in his speech becomes in the end nothing more than the codified expression of the myth of self-sacrifice, or grateful oppression, lying at the heart of Joyce's Dublin."[8] Pecora assumes that the story examines Ireland's self-sacrifice as an act of cultural resistance to British colonization, and while I have argued elsewhere that "The Dead" reveals a major, lingering anxiety about Protestant, imperial domination that intensified during the run-up to the Home Rule crisis of 1912–14,[9] nevertheless, Pecora misses the genuinely hospitable thrust of the story that persists despite this political subtext.[10]

If we attend to the story closely, several early facets of Joycean hospitality reveal themselves that anticipate several contours of my understanding of *Ulysses* as a hospitality text; one of these strands concerns hospitality as a *habitus*, or repeated act. Each year, we are told, Gabriel's great-aunts and their niece host this dance and dinner: "It was always a great affair, the Misses Morkan's annual dance. Everybody who knew them came to it, members of the family, old friends of the family, the members of Julia's choir, any of Kate's pupils that were grown up enough and even some of Mary Jane's pupils too" (*D* 175). Partly because of their habitus of hospitality, the continuity of the party ensures its success: "Never once had it fallen flat. For years and years it had gone off in splendid style, as long as anyone could remember. . ." (*D* 175–6). Hospitality, repeated, becomes engrained in the mind of a community such that it gathers them in over time, leading them repeatedly into situations of being generously hosted, creating reciprocal feelings of good will and amiability. As we will see later in my analysis of *Ulysses*, Leopold Bloom also often practices hospitality, but his community's uneasiness around him (predicated in part on their revulsion against his supposed Jewishness) leads them to jettison him from their membership, and even his hospitable acts are subject to question. Here, however, in the pages of the greatest short story in English, hospitality is so well-established and organic that it becomes a beacon of warmth, even hope, to all who attend this annual dance and dinner party.

Risks come with hospitality, and practicing it can even be dangerous. In his brilliant, far-ranging study of hospitality and treachery in Western literature, James Heffernan muses that "if hospitality can occasionally furnish something like the pleasures of love, it also resembles love in exposing all of its parties to the perils of intimacy." Since "[t]o fall in love is to give someone the power to break your heart," likewise, "[t]o ask one or more people into your home, whether to dine at your table, sleep under your roof, or simply converse, is to give them the power to complicate your life right up to the act of taking it."[11] As an example, Heffernan cites the murder of two Dartmouth professors in January of 2001 by two teenage boys who gained admittance to their home by pretending to be conducting a survey, and who then stabbed them to death to obtain their ATM cards. This instance of hospitality "ambushed by treachery" encapsulates Heffernan's argument.[12]

In "The Dead," as Gabriel Conroy participates in the various ritualized acts of hospitality at his great-aunts' Epiphany party on January 6, he is the character whom Karen Lawrence terms "the would-be host, the male spokesperson for the female acts of hospitality," the "sovereign presence in the story, the host who presides."[13] But he then feels "ambushed" by what he sees as his wife's treachery when she movingly recalls a teenaged boyfriend who died long ago.

Crucially, however, the death that must occur for true Joycean hospitality to flourish is a metaphorical one for Gabriel—he dies to his old selfish self in the conclusion. This true self-sacrifice is grounded in an ethic of Christian sacrifice, suggesting how, for Joyce, Christianity could continue to provide a foundation for an ethic of hospitality even though he no longer believed in its doctrines. This general ethic of Christian-inspired hospitality would take parabolic shape in *Ulysses* as Joyce reinscribed the Good Samaritan parable in the novel, crucially beginning in and continuing through three of its last four episodes.

In "The Dead," another facet of this warm Irish hospitality Joyce celebrates concerns the abundance of food at the party. The scene must be one of the most famous eating episodes in English, and select passages from it illustrate Joyce's approval of this gustatory profligacy: "A fat brown goose lay at one end of the table and at the other end, on a bed of creased paper strewn with sprigs of parsley, lay a great ham, stripped of its outer skin and peppered over with crust crumbs, a neat paper frill round its shin and beside this was a round of spiced beef" (*D* 196). And this is just the meat! There are also "hot floury potatoes" (*D* 197), jellies, blancmange and jam, raisins and almonds, figs, custard, "chocolates and sweets wrapped in silver papers and a glass vase in which stood some tall celery stalks" (*D* 196). Oranges, apples, and a pudding finish the food, and these are surrounded by port, sherry and "three squads of bottles of stout and ale and minerals..." (*D* 197). For a country only fifty years or so removed from the greatest calamity in its history—the Great Hunger or Irish Famine—this meal suggests not just bodily necessities but something like sheer luxury in a still penurious time. The overflowing abundance of food and drink is matched only by Mary Jane, Aunt Kate, and Aunt Julia's desire to generously serve others at the meal, suggested in a long passage that follows this parade of gustatory delights. The general atmosphere is almost carnivalistic, jovial, fun: "There was a great deal of confusion and laughter and noise, the noise of orders and counter-orders, of knives and forks, of corks and glass-stoppers" (*D* 197).

Note that while Gabriel does carve the goose and distribute the meat, he is not sufficiently caught up in the spirit of hospitality as Mary Jane and his aunts are. Instead, he finds respite in the carving after his awkward encounters earlier in the story with the maid Lily and the Irish nationalist Miss Ivors. Thus, we are told that "[h]e felt quite at ease now for he was an expert carver and liked nothing better than to find himself at the head of a well-laden table" (*D* 197). And yet this refuge cannot sufficiently render Gabriel truly hospitable, nor can his attempts to tend to Freddy Malins in the story, who is getting steadily more drunk, nor does his toast to his aunts' hospitality. Paul K. Saint-Amour even believes that the story "exhibits a suspicion of hospitality in its populous spaces and in Gabriel Conroy's toast."[14] But again, we must distinguish between Gabriel's feigned public hospitality and a real and robust hospitality evinced by others as they eat, drink, converse, and dance—and between Gabriel's stinting spirit for most of the story and his final receptivity to the persistent ghost of Michael Furey, who hovers over the Conroys' marriage in the conclusion and whose narrative helps precipitate Gabriel's growing warm hospitality.

Gabriel's mental rehearsal of his toast and his actual delivery of it especially deserve further consideration, since he seemingly predicates it upon a robust sense of prodigal hospitality epitomized by his great-aunts and niece. In rehearsing mentally what he will shortly say and in twitting the current generation, which he sees epitomized by Miss Ivors, he invokes the hospitality of the Morkans' generation:

> *Ladies and Gentlemen, the generation which is now on the wane among us may have had its faults but for my part I think it had certain qualities of hospitality, of humour, of humanity, which the new and very serious and hypereducated generation that is growing up around us seems to me to lack.* (D 192)

But immediately, he thinks, "Very good: that was one for Miss Ivors. What did he care that his aunts were only two ignorant old women?" (*D* 192). This last belief strikingly demonstrates Gabriel's pettiness and lack of care for these elderly, kind hosts. It will take Gretta's revelation of Michael Furey's seemingly sacrificial death and her emotional collapse afterward to actually teach Gabriel to care for his great-aunts, for Furey, and Gretta, becoming truly imaginatively generous, empathetic, and thus finally hospitable, an ethic deepened by his final reflection on the snow-covered Christological landscape of the graveyard where Furey is buried.

For someone who has little to no real sense of hospitality himself—whose encounters with Lily and Miss Ivors and even with Gretta earlier in the story are indeed marked by a distinct lack of hospitality—Gabriel certainly evokes the term repeatedly in his actual speech. But does it lose its meaning and force with each repetition? Consider his remarks in his toast: "It is not the first time that we have gathered together under this *hospitable* roof, around this *hospitable* board. It is not the first time that we have been the recipients—or perhaps, I had better say, the victims—of the *hospitality* of certain good ladies" (*D* 202). The repetitions, of course, signal the *repeated hospitality* of his aunts and Mary Jane—their hospitable habitus—over the years to the assembled partygoers; but concurrently, they contrastingly show Gabriel himself to be a creature of surfaces, one given to repetitive rhetorical flourishes that invoke abstractions. And privately, as we have already seen and will see again, he chooses to highlight the hospitality of his three kinswomen to contrast what he sees as the nationalist Miss Ivors' grasping nature.

It is nonetheless striking that the continentally oriented Gabriel, fond of his galoshes and cycling trips to Belgium, privileges Ireland as a site of hospitality out of all the countries he has known, almost despite himself. So he continues, moving on from praising the Morkans' hospitality to that of Ireland as a whole: "—I feel more strongly with every recurring year that our country has no tradition which does it so much honour and which it should guard so jealously as that of its hospitality" (*D* 202). Furthermore, he argues, "It is a tradition that is unique as far as my experience goes (and I have visited not a few places abroad) among the modern nations" (*D* 203), a comment that uncannily echoes Joyce's remark about Irish hospitality in his 1906 letter to Stanislaus cited above. Notice even here, before Gabriel singles out what he sees as the lack of hospitality by Miss Ivors and her cohort, that he is implicitly reminding her (even though she has already left the party) and the others that he does indeed know his own country—better than she does—and that its qualities do not inhere in a misguided romantic nationalism, but in a prodigal openness and warmth to others. Thus does Gabriel turn his continental excursions—the very thing for which Ivors criticizes him—into a way of expressing his expertise on national expressions of hospitality, despite his own relative lack of it.

Even though he admits that others have noted "that with us it is rather a failing than anything to be boasted of," he persists in his praise of Irish hospitality, claiming "it is, to my mind, a princely failing, and one that I trust will long be cultivated among us" (*D* 203). Even failed attempts at hospitality, he suggests, are superior to no attempts at all—perhaps thinking of his giving a coin to the maid Lily earlier to cover up his embarrassment at their encounter—and implicitly admitting that even this very speech, invoking as it does repeated rhetorical expressions of hospitality, constitutes a failure. In this tacit admission, he fulfills the prophecy he spoke to himself earlier after his conversation with Lily: "He would *fail* with them just as he had *failed* with the girl in the pantry. He had taken up a wrong tone. His whole speech was a mistake from first to last, an utter *failure*" (*D* 179; my emphases). So *Gabriel's speech becomes a self-fulfilling prophecy, at least as much about its predicted performative failure*, even while he ostensibly praises his hostesses' hospitality. One could scarcely find a more selfish oratorical performance, one brought into relief by the genuine hospitality being practiced all around him. Even though he goes on to praise "the tradition of genuine warm-hearted courteous Irish hospitality" (*D* 203), which he sees as a bequest from innumerable Irish forebears and as a legacy the Irish must leave to their descendants, the attentive reader knows that Gabriel remains cold, icy—dedicated to protecting himself from the literal snow he has previously brought into this house of hospitality on his galoshes—and by extension, to defending himself from showing any unselfish emotions.

Gabriel's speechifying grows in power as it proceeds and as the audience affirms it, but at crucial junctures, Joyce leads us to realize that much of it is a pointed riposte to the departed Miss Ivors. Thus, after a "hearty murmur of assent" runs "around the table" following his extended praise of the three women's hospitality and that of Ireland, he quickly realizes that "Miss Ivors was not there and that she had gone away discourteously. . ." (D 203). Condemned in his own mind for her profound lack of hospitality, Miss Ivors becomes the verbal target of what follows. Unknown to his audience, she stands for the "new generation growing up in our midst," which he fears "will lack those qualities of humanity, of hospitality, of kindly humour which belonged to an older day" (D 203). Miss Ivors is the blank screen upon which Gabriel projects these antitheses of hospitality, but which he himself, ironically, manifests.

While many commentators have articulated part of the motivation of Gabriel's speech as inhering in his displeasure at Miss Ivors' treatment of him, what is often not noticed about the speech is his refusal of the claims of the dead on the living—another indication of his inherent selfishness and lack of hospitality. Significantly, in the conclusion of the story, Gabriel admits the dead—the projected dead Aunt Julia and the long-dead Michael Furey—into his life and heart and enters into their emotional and spiritual lives, finally and truly becoming the hospitable host that he has falsely played throughout. During the speech, however, while he notes that they will "still cherish in our hearts the memory of those dead and gone great ones whose fame the world will not willingly let die" (D 203), he quickly rejects the call of the dead upon him and the others, musing that despite "thoughts of the past, of youth, of changes, of absent faces that we miss here tonight," were "we to brood upon them always we could not find the heart to go on bravely with our work among the living" (D 204). Because "[w]e have all of us living duties and living affections which claim, and rightly claim, our strenuous endeavours," he vows not to linger on the past, remarking, "I will not let any gloomy moralizing intrude upon us here to-night" (D 204). He then praises his great-aunts and niece for their various gifts and the dinner guests toast them and sing "They Are Jolly Gay Fellows" (D 204–5). Gabriel has successfully avoided dwelling upon the entreaties of the dead here, reducing such pleas and thoughts to "gloomy moralizing," but he cannot escape the beckoning, hospitable ghost of Michael Furey for much longer.

It takes Gretta's dramatic revelation of Michael Furey's having died for her when she was a teenager to jolt Gabriel out of his smug complacency and become truly hospitable. He undergoes this conversion to hospitality as he opens himself to the sufferings of others—first Furey's, followed by a succession of others, including his aunts and Gretta—for the first time. In beginning to die to himself and his selfish needs, Gabriel starts becoming hospitable, likely for the first time in his life. The story is rarely taught or thought about in this way. Instead, we are told (or think ourselves) that Gabriel is either fading out and will remain emotionally cold because he cannot compete with Michael Furey's sacrificial love, or that he is spurred on to generous new heights of love for Gretta by Furey's example—a sort of emotional superfluity. And a third option remains—that he is merely withdrawing into a sort of position of supreme artistic neutrality. But the second option, which I favor and have generally taught to my students over many years, actually sells the ethic of Joycean hospitality short in the story. Yes, Gabriel is generous at the end of the story: "Generous tears filled his eyes" (*D* 223). But that substantial and real generosity (not an inchoate wallowing in emotion) emerges from, is predicated upon, his finally opening himself to the entrance of Michael Furey, the Stranger, into his and Gretta's marriage.

Furey is first an unwelcome guest to Gabriel, by whose memory he feels assailed. After Gretta tells him melodramatically, "—I think he died for me," Gabriel is haunted by Furey's specter: "A vague terror seized Gabriel at this answer as if, at that hour when he had hoped to triumph, some impalpable and vindictive being was coming against him, gathering forces against him in its vague world" (*D* 220). But then, after "he shook himself free of it with an effort of reason," he "continued to caress her hand" (*D* 220), maintaining an embodied connection to his wife as he slowly draws out from her the story of Furey's death, likely from pneumonia, as he stood outside her window the night she left for the convent in Dublin. This enfleshed attempt at understanding her enables his own slow emergence into becoming a more empathetic human being. Slowly, as Gretta dissolves into tears, Gabriel "held her hand for a moment longer, irresolutely, and then, shy of intruding on her grief, let it fall gently and walked quietly to the window" (*D* 221–2). This deference to Gretta signals his own new unwillingness to impose his desires upon her—and a new, enfleshed openness to others' desires and feelings.

He then starts imagining other lives than his own, entering into them—all through Furey's spectral example that swims before his eyes. By allowing Furey into his heart, mind, and, yes, soul (the closing language is inherently Christological), Gabriel figuratively allows Furey late entrance to the feast that everyone enjoyed earlier, not giving him actual food and drink, but lavishing him with abundant attention and headspace—a real communion with the living and the dead. Revivifying the dead Furey in this way, Gabriel thus imagines himself into his short life and suffering in the rain that fateful night under Gretta's window. In so doing, Gabriel takes the Stranger into his marriage, *briefly even becoming both Furey and Gretta*, as we shall see; comforts them (or at least their memory); and is himself permanently changed, made more hospitable, generous, empathetic.

Joyce, a gifted tenor himself, leads us and Gabriel into the lives of the dead and thus into the heart of hospitality through two songs that hover over the story and betoken betrayal and jealousy, respectively. One of these is the oft-remarked "The Lass of Aughrim" which the tenor Bartell D'Arcy sings, and which moves Gretta to remember Michael Furey; the other, unsung in the text of the story but present in Joyce's mind while he drafted it, is Thomas Moore's "O, Ye Dead!" Gabriel must grapple with both betrayal and jealousy, represented respectively by these songs, in order to receive Michael Furey and his wife hospitably into his marriage and transform it.

"The Lass of Aughrim" has, as Luke Thurston points out, "a fragile luminescence or phantasmal emanation,"[15] and thus, not only does the song speak of a haunting relationship, but it also seems to color the air in a ghostly manner. The narrator of "The Dead" tells us that "[t]he voice, made plaintive by distance and by the singer's hoarseness, faintly illuminated the cadence of the air with words expressing grief. . ." (D 210). Notice Joyce's assonantal diction here—"plaintive," "faintly"—which contributes to the melodic performance of the song itself. "Faintly" will recur in the last sentence of the story, set in chiasmus with the snow—"falling faintly" and "faintly falling" on the graveyard where Michael Furey is buried (D 224)—and its appearance here anticipates, even proleptically "haunts" that concluding sentence with an echo of the performance of that song, sung originally to Gretta by Furey (D 219), and sung this fateful night by D'Arcy.

There are multiple versions of the song, but most of them "reproduce a dialogue between Lord Gregory and the young woman whom he has seduced and abandoned with a child," as Margot Norris points out.[16] The song speaks of the exchanges between Lord Gregory and the lass, which always favor him: He gives her a "black tin" ring and she a "beaten gold" one to him.[17] He then gives her a smock of "Scotch cloth," while she gives him one "of the holland fine." And the last "gift" he gives her was the baby who resulted from his rape of her. She shows up at his home drenched in rain (which must recall Joyce's depiction of the shivering Furey standing in the rain calling up to Gretta long ago) and plaintively says in the refrain, "My babe lies cold within my arms; / Lord Gregory let me in."[18] In the story itself, Gabriel hears part of three lines from this last stanza: "O, the rain falls on my heavy locks / And the dew wets my skin, / My babe lies cold. . ." (D 210). In each instance, Gregory could have been hospitable or at least kind to the Lass of Aughrim, but he betrayed her with each "gift" he gave her. He seems to have promised marriage to her and she likely gives herself (hospitably) to him with that expectation, but then he deserts her and refuses her entrance to his lordly home.

While this song that laments Lord Gregory's lack of hospitality functions positively to enable Furey, the shivering, rain-soaked ghost from her past, to visit Gretta this fateful night, the ballad and her recounted memory of Furey's love for her nonetheless make Gabriel feel (wrongly) that he has been betrayed. Even though he did not even know Gretta at the time, he misunderstands how she has perceived this story from her past, musing toward the end of the story, "He thought of how she who lay beside him had locked in her heart for so many years that image of her lover's eyes when he had told her that he did not wish to live" (D 223). That "locked" is the crucial verb here, and it could be read as "locked away, never to be explored"; but instead, Gabriel seems to think Gretta has "locked" this memory in her heart as a precious jewel to be treasured and viewed repeatedly. In this reading, Gabriel feels he has been betrayed *over and over* by Gretta in the course of their marriage. This process can be understood as the reverse of a habitus of hospitality; instead of repeated generous offerings as the characters have experienced at the party in the story, Gabriel believes Gretta has repeatedly betrayed him, choosing to continue to love Michael Furey.[19]

James Alexander Fraser, whose book *Joyce and Betrayal* elucidates the persistence and ubiquity of this theme in Joyce's later writing, questions Gabriel's feeling himself betrayed in "The Dead," asking (understandably), "Is the complex sense of loss and self-awareness that Gabriel experiences in 'The Dead' really a sense of having been betrayed? Has Gretta betrayed him with the memory of the dead Michael Furey?" Fraser muses that, given Joyce's notes for *Exiles*, "where he discusses the virginity of the soul . . . perhaps she has," and he sees betrayal as one of his "defining themes in *Dubliners*," but he argues that "he does not make it the centerpiece or keystone of the book in the way that he does with those texts I am dealing with here."[20] Fair enough: I do not believe that Gretta has thought of Michael Furey in many years myself. But understanding Gabriel's sense of betrayal nonetheless becomes crucial to our apprehending Joyce's development of hospitality—the reverse of betrayal, perceived or actual.

The treachery inherent in the story not only shows Gabriel's temporary feeling of betrayal, but it helpfully contrasts his later receptivity and hospitality toward Furey's ghost. Heffernan has shown how treachery often uncomfortably colors or enters into situations between hosts and guests, perhaps supremely so in the example of Judas's betrayal of Christ at the Last Supper, which Heffernan terms "the first Communion," and which "primordially marks the intersection of hospitality and treachery."[21] Gabriel is no Christ figure, as Joyce intermittently and ambiguously suggests Leopold Bloom is in *Ulysses*, but through dwelling upon the feelings of betrayal produced in Gabriel by Gretta's mournful recollection of Michael Furey, prompted by the recitation of "The Lass of Aughrim," Gabriel slowly emerges as a sort of sacrificial host—grudgingly, at first—welcoming those whom he believes have betrayed him such as Gretta and Furey. Happily, Gabriel, through this "hosting" of his wife and her long-ago boyfriend, will sacrificially die to his old self in the closing passages of the story, born into a new and generous, hospitable self.

Gabriel is also beset by jealousy, an emotion Joyce knew very well. We know from Ellmann's biography that a man named Michael "Sonny" Bodkin courted Nora Barnacle and that he became ill with tuberculosis and then was bedridden. Not long after he took ill, Nora resolved to leave Galway and go to Dublin, whereupon Bodkin "stole out of his sickroom, in spite of the rainy weather, to sing to her under an apple tree and bid her goodbye" (*JJ2* 243). After arriving in Dublin, Nora learned that Bodkin had died and when she "met Joyce she was first attracted to him, as she told a sister, because he resembled Sonny Bodkin" (*JJ2* 243). Any man would have been jealous, and so Joyce was: "The notion of being in some sense in rivalry with a dead man buried in the little cemetery at Rahoon was one that came easily, and gallingly, to a man of Joyce's jealous disposition" (*JJ2* 243).

Brenda Maddox, on the other hand, argues in her biography of Nora Joyce that the likelier model for Michael Furey was a young man named Michael Feeney, a teenaged schoolteacher on whom Nora had a crush when she was nearly 13. Feeney died in February of 1897 following typhoid fever, then pneumonia, and he was buried in Rahoon Cemetery, only two miles from Galway City.[22] As Maddox argues, "The proximity of Michael Feeney's death in February to that of Nora's grandmother on New Year's Day and the occasion of her leaving her grandmother's home make Feeney a closer model for the fictional Michael Furey than Nora's later admirer, Michael Bodkin, who has been widely cast in the part." Feeney, moreover, was five months short of 17 when he died, whereas Bodkin died at 20. Finally, the "shift from *Feeney* to *Furey* is the kind of association of sounds that Joyce liked—what psychologists call a Klanglink."[23] Certainly, Gabriel Conroy is a fictional creation, and Maddox admits that Nora was smitten with Michael Bodkin as well, who was also buried in Rahoon Cemetery; and she suggests finally that "[i]n all likelihood, Joyce fused Nora's memories of her two lost friends."[24] Whatever the truth behind the model for Michael Furey, Joyce knew well the jealousy he intended his fictional character to suffer, and depicted that jealousy deftly as a result here and elsewhere in his oeuvre.[25]

Furthermore, when Stanislaus told his brother about hearing Plunket Greene, an Irish baritone, sing one of Thomas Moore's Irish Melodies, "O, Ye Dead!," Joyce became obsessed with the song and learned to sing it himself because he recognized the jealousy of the dead for the world of the living. Thus, Ellmann posits, "His feelings about his wife's dead lover found a dramatic counterpart in the jealousy of the dead for the living in Moore's song: it would seem that the living and the dead are jealous of each other" (*JJ2* 244). The song's words, however, such as those in the second verse, have larger implications than Ellmann notices. For instance, Joyce may have transformed the line, "we are shadows cold and wan" (qtd. in *JJ2* 244), into some of the phrases that echo so resonantly in the story's conclusion. When Gabriel thinks of Aunt Julia dying, for example, he muses, "She, too, would soon be a *shade* with the *shade* of Patrick Morkan and his horse" (*D* 222; my emphases). Soon after this passage, Joyce suggests that Gabriel himself is becoming a sort of "cold and wan" shadow: "The air of the room chilled his shoulders. He stretched himself cautiously along under the sheets and lay down besides his wife. One by one they were all becoming *shades*" (*D* 223; my emphasis). Thus, "shadows" in Moore's song representing the dead likely became transmuted into "shade" and "shades" and are characterized by the frigid temperature experienced now by the living Gabriel himself.

Crucially, Gabriel must first become jealous of Michael Furey's love for Gretta and his seeming self-sacrifice in order then to become the sacrificial host of both his wife and this guest haunting his marriage. Jealousy of Furey, a shade from the past, makes Gabriel realize his debt to the dead—that he cannot ignore them any longer as he urged his listeners to do at the Christmas dinner table. Feeling remarkably similar to the "cold and wan" dead in the words of Moore's song, Gabriel finally senses what it must be to warmly live as another person, experiencing perhaps something of the dying Furey's furious wish to remain alive, in the concluding words of Moore's stanza about the dead: "Of the field and the flow'rs in our youth wandered o'er, / That ere, condemn'd, we go / To freeze, 'mid Hecla's snow, / We would taste it awhile, and think we live once more!" (qtd. in *JJ2* 244).

Joyce thus allows Gabriel-as-shade an opportunity to give the ghostly lover of his wife a chance to live once more—in him—thereby reanimating his marriage, in contrast to Joyce himself, who remained jealous of Bodkin and was angry that his ghost haunted his courtship and perhaps even the early days of his marriage to Nora. When Gabriel muses late in the story that "[h]is own identity was fading out into a grey impalpable world: the solid world itself which these dead had one time reared and lived in was dissolving and dwindling" (*D* 223), he has briefly become Michael Furey and thus experiences deep communion with the dead.

At the same time, Gabriel also momentarily imagines Gretta in that long-ago past when the "few light taps upon the pane made him turn to the window" (*D* 223). His eyes have been so filled with "[g]enerous" tears that they "gathered more thickly in his eyes and in the partial darkness he imagined he saw the form of a young man standing under a dripping tree" (*D* 223). Now, he seemingly, briefly believes that Furey is standing outside his and Gretta's window throwing small stones up at it ("A few light taps upon the pane") to get their attention just as he did long ago when Gretta "heard gravel thrown up against the window" (*D* 221). Gabriel at the beginning of the story or even in the middle could in no way have demonstrated such profound narrative empathy. Even though he quickly realizes that it "had begun to snow again" (*D* 223), he is sufficiently overwhelmed by tears and gazing upon frozen water that his emotional thaw runs in full spate, as does his spiritual awakening to his wife, Furey, and others, the living and the dead.[26]

But Gabriel has so thoroughly empathized with Gretta as well as Furey that rather than believing he sees Furey outside their Gresham Hotel window, as I have always assumed until recently, we should understand that he instead temporarily assumes his wife's identity long ago in Galway, when "he imagined he saw the form of a young man standing under a dripping tree." Thus, he is not only Furey in the previous passage where he becomes "chilled" and lies down, shade-like, next to Gretta, but subsequently assumes the identity of the young Gretta in the new passage that begins with "Generous tears filled Gabriel's eyes" (*D* 223). Karen Lawrence's reading of the "strange friendly pity" (*D* 222) with which Gabriel views Gretta now that she sleeps, exhausted from her retelling of the ghost story of Michael Furey, reveals the extent to which Gabriel expands his conception of host, formerly relegated to his social duties at the party. Now, Gabriel values the friendship he has with his wife, which is "strange," having replaced his lust to make love to her that evening at the Gresham. Lawrence shows that this passage indicates that "the *xenia*, the pact between the host and the stranger, comes in the unusual guise of friendship, a friendship between husband and wife," an aspect of their marriage "that had never entered the conjugal relationship before."[27] In this sense, Gabriel as host welcomes two "strangers" into their relationship—marital friendship and Michael Furey—and in the process, becomes more generous and receptive to his wife, seeing her as more of an individual than he likely has for a long time.[28]

And yet Lawrence neglects the spiritual context of the "strange friendly pity" phrase, simply asserting that it implies how Gabriel views his wife anew. Surely it does do that, but it also carries a spiritual register: the full quotation runs, "a strange friendly pity for her *entered his soul*" (*D* 222; my emphasis). Audaciously, Joyce suggests here that Gabriel's new hospitality toward his wife is a gift from beyond himself that enters "his soul." Gabriel does not somehow work himself up into a state whereby he is now more receptive to both Gretta and Furey; indeed, the story until now makes very clear he is simply incapable of reconceiving his role as host beyond that of the social duties he has already carried out that night. Instead, *a spiritual manifestation of friendly pity from beyond his ken* enters his soul and it allows him to apprehend (and briefly become) what Allen Tate argued "he has never acknowledged": "her spirit, her identity as a person" since "he knows only her body."[29] This process implies Joyce's deep conviction—as we will see throughout this book's analysis of the hospitality narrative of the Good Samaritan parable—that hospitality goes beyond mere human relationships and is predicated upon a spiritual foundation.

With his soul thus visited by this spiritual, "strange friendly pity" for his wife, Gabriel now actively imagines himself into a narrative frame that Gretta has sketched out for him and then inhabits it, inviting two more strange guests—this Stranger Michael Furey, along with the well-known Stranger of young Gretta—fully into his life, and then learning openness, generosity, and yes, hospitality from them. The considerable evidence that he does just this in these closing passages suggests the misapprehension of how hospitality works here by even so sensitive a critic as Lawrence, who believes "Gabriel, the host, is himself taken hostage by the same visitor [death, which carried away Michael Furey]," and suggests that "[t]he story ends outside the geometry of responsibility Gabriel has so carefully tried to draw" as "Michael Furey haunts the place from which he has been excluded by Gretta's silence and Gabriel's complacency."[30] On the contrary, Gabriel becomes so affected by Furey's death, which *productively* haunts both him and Gretta, that he takes on, as we have seen, in his new role of host, the identity of consecutively, Furey, then Gretta, thus finally welcoming, along with friendly pity, this long-ago couple as "guests" into his marriage as a spur for active change in it.

Paul K. Saint-Amour offers the fullest discussion until now of how to read Gabriel's growing hospitality to Gretta. Although I disagree with his opening sentence in the passage that follows, his insistence on including Gretta in this hospitality narrative as not stranger but intimate fructifies Joyce's rich, unfolding theory of hospitality in the closing pages of the story. For Saint-Amour, the scene where Gretta reveals Furey's supposed sacrifice to Gabriel,

> rather than the one that follows it, is the heart of the story's meditation on the ethical dimensions of hospitality. Such a suggestion may seem perverse, given that Gabriel extends welcome here not to a stranger but to his own wife, and only by extension to the memory she bears of a long-dead stranger. If staying with this scene seems strange, it is because hospitality narratives across a range of cultures emphasize welcoming the absolute, nameless stranger—the god, angel, ghost, mendicant, or refugee—rather than the familiar-become-strange. Against this grain, "The Dead" suggests that extreme alterity can take the form of an intimate whose disclosures vandalize the portrait of our intimacy; it suggests, by extension, that radical hospitality can be asked of us not only by the absolute stranger but also by the intimate who comes bearing absolutely strange news.[31]

Gretta becomes that intimate stranger "bearing absolutely strange news for Gabriel." But we do not have to choose between this scene and the better-known one that follows in order to understand how Gabriel is visited by a profound hospitality that allows him to briefly channel both the living Gretta and the dead Furey.

Clearly—and this fact has not been brought out sufficiently in the rich body of criticism on the story—as Gabriel listens to Gretta tell him the story, even the narration adopts a tone that we could term "hospitable." Bruce Avery indirectly makes this point when he claims that the narrator is "relinquishing his satiric voice" at this moment in the story.[32] He notes that rather "than double-voicing the narrative to paraphrase her or to parody her idioms, he relays Gretta's story about Furey in direct quotation," suggesting further that "[h]e now worries that beside Gretta's simple, emotional expression, the ironic tonality of his voice sounds small and petty, just as Gabriel's voice, as we have heard, has sounded small and petty."[33] Caught up in how he appears to us, the narrator checks his snarkiness, as we might say in today's parlance, and fascinatingly, so does Gabriel as the story proceeds. Just as the narrator, then, learns to respect and appreciate Gretta, to invite her to literally have a voice, so does Gabriel, thus revealing a double awakening to hospitality, one at the level of narration and another in Gabriel's character development.

Heffernan's reading of "The Dead" through hospitality theory helpfully illuminates the process Gabriel undergoes by welcoming both his wife and Furey in a hospitable fashion. Building on Saint-Amour's argument that the story suggests that "radical hospitality can be asked of us not only by the absolute stranger but also by the intimate who comes bearing absolutely strange news," Heffernan posits that "Gretta's revelation [about Furey] is surely uncanny," *unheimlich* in Freud's term, and it "profoundly challenges" Gabriel's "capacity to take it in, as a host might take in a guest." Moreover, Heffernan reads this crucial part of "The Dead" in juxtaposition with other narratives whereby a "guest usurps, seduces, or is offered the wife of his host,"[34] including Pierre Klossowski's later novel *Roberte Ce Soir* (1954), which itself reconstructs the host's offer of his wife to Gawain for three straight days in *Sir Gawain and the Green Knight*. Arguing that because of his jealousy of Furey earlier in the story, Gabriel's "hospitality to the ghost of his wife's long-dead suitor is not quite absolute in Derrida's sense," Heffernan convincingly holds that nevertheless, "he is far more open than either of two other [literary] hosts" whose narratives Joyce knew well: Homer's Odysseus, who slaughters his wife Penelope's suitors for their courtship of her and for "abusing his hospitality" when he finally returns home, and Angel Clare, "whose wedding night is poisoned by his wife's story of her former lover" in Hardy's 1892 novel, *Tess of the d'Urbervilles*.[35] Gabriel's welcoming not only of the intimate stranger Gretta but also of the true stranger Michael Furey—along with the strange and unsettling news Furey voices from beyond the grave—into his heart represents his transformation in front of our eyes from his previously interiorized self to a new self, open to others. Charles Taylor's conception of the self's identity as dependent upon others has special warrant here: "One is a self only among other selves. A self can never be described without reference to those who surround it."[36] Gabriel's selfhood can only become rich and full by the growth of his community not only with his familiar wife but also with this stranger and this strange news brought to him by both Gretta and Furey—an awakening out of his old, selfish self into new, generous life predicated on hospitality.

Florence Walzl's reading of "The Dead," while not employing the language of hospitality, nonetheless anticipates and captures some of the spirit and thrust of my argument. She sees Gabriel as having finally moved from "a selfish preoccupation with self to sympathy with Gretta, pity for his relatives, and love for all men. His illumination takes place when he realizes he is part of common humanity and shares its mutable state of being."[37] And yet Walzl's argument does not go far enough in articulating Joyce's radical theory of hospitality. Gabriel undoubtedly sympathizes with Gretta, but it's a sympathy that moves closer to empathy. And he certainly pities his great-aunts, but his final feeling for them is much deeper and lasting than mere pity. Finally, love for all men may overstate the case: snow may be "general" over Ireland, but I am not sure Gabriel loves everyone! Undoubtedly, Gabriel feels genuine warmth and affection for this one man, Michael Furey, who has helped him see his wife as much more than an object of mere desire, a fully fledged human who fully deserves his love and attention. All those years of being treated to his great-aunts' hospitality at this annual dinner and dance might have instilled the seed of hospitality in Gabriel that now begins to flower in the snow that falls over the last passages; yet merely being a passive recipient of hospitality cannot lead to the true, active welcome at the heart of hospitality and its major narratives such as the Good Samaritan parable, which Joyce meditated upon extensively in writing "Grace" and *Ulysses*.

Although I have issues with aspects of Derrida's theory of unconditional hospitality, such as its anti-incarnational tendency,[38] one facet of it is apposite here and illustrates Gabriel's conversion to hospitality from selfishness, especially given that he has proven unwilling throughout the story to change. Derrida remarks that "to be hospitable is to let oneself be overtaken . . . precisely where one is not ready to receive—and not only *not yet ready* but *not ready, unprepared* in a mode that is not even of the 'not yet.'"[39] Whereas, as we shall see, Leopold Bloom in *Ulysses* has actively cultivated his receptivity and hospitality to the Other, Gabriel Conroy in "The Dead" has never prepared himself to reach out to the Other through habitual acts of generosity and care. Instead, Gabriel's "reception" of his wife and Michael Furey fits Derrida's analysis of the unwilling host well:

> If, in hospitality, one must say *yes,* welcome the coming . . . say the "welcome"; one must say *yes,* there where one does not wait, *yes,* there where one does not expect, nor await oneself to, the other . . . to let oneself be swept by the coming of the wholly other, the absolutely unforeseeable . . . stranger, the uninvited visitor, the unexpected visitation beyond welcoming apparatuses. If I welcome only what I welcome, what I am ready to welcome, and that I recognize in advance because I expect the coming of the *hôte* [the one who both gives and receives hospitality] as invited, there is no hospitality.[40]

Reluctant, selfish Gabriel in no way anticipates the coming of the ghost Michael Furey from Gretta's past into his plans for sex with her that evening. He is only concerned with pursuing her sexually at this time, not finding out what has been bothering her since Bartell D'Arcy sang "The Lass of Aughrim" shortly before they left the party when she was catapulted into the past—into a memory that has not emerged for many years. Because of his unpreparedness for this "guest" at the party—a guest who in some sense travels with them to the Gresham Hotel that night—he is caught completely off guard by Furey's entrance into their married life. But also, as Derrida's argument implies, the unprepared Gabriel now has a chance to truly welcome both Gretta and Furey and learn sacrifice and empathy from him, which he certainly seems to have done in the passages where, temporarily channeling the young Gretta, he imagines Furey standing outside in the rain and throwing stones at the window.

Now, the "[g]enerous" tears that flood Gabriel's face in the story's conclusion, signifying his new, welcoming self, his hospitable self, lead to his meditation on the Christian sacrificial imagery reflected in the graveyard where Michael Furey lies. As Gabriel mentally wanders out to that "lonely churchyard" (*D* 223), where his immersion in the falling snow guides him, he perceives how "it lay thickly drifted on the crooked crosses and headstones, on the spears of the little gate, on the barren thorns" (*D* 224). The cross, symbolizing the instrument of death and torture for Christ, along with the spears, representing how he was stuck in the side by a Roman centurion holding a spear, and the thorns, signifying the crown of thorns placed on his head, together imply a Christian ethic of hospitality based on Christ's bodily suffering—dying to self in order to receive others and make them welcome out of a profound discomfort, even torture. Although Gabriel certainly cannot live up to such a model, Christ's hermeneutic of hospitality, given unconditionally despite His sure knowledge of Judas's betrayal, seems to reinforce that of Michael Furey, and likely inspires Gabriel to be more welcoming from now on toward the Other. And the chiastic prose in the story's finale—"as he heard the snow *falling faintly* through the universe and *faintly falling*"—inscribes Christ again into this last sentence through this rhetorical device signifying the Cross, and further suggests Gabriel's emotional thawing and desire to reach out in unselfish love to his wife Gretta (*D* 224; my emphasis). Thus Joyce conveys his profound interest in a Christian-derived theory of generosity and hospitality with this story, one that he fully explores and celebrates in *Ulysses* and develops into a fleshly ethic of hospitality embodied (literally) by Leopold Bloom, his heretic who performs rescues and cares for others better than any Christian in the novel.

Ellmann perhaps comes closest to recognizing this rich ethic of hospitality that Gabriel experiences and models at the end of "The Dead," although he tends to read this ethic as a more generalized unity of feeling among humankind. Ellmann argues that the falling snow seen by Gabriel from the window of the hotel in the story's conclusion

> belongs to all men, it is general, mutual. Under its canopy, all human beings, whatever their degrees of intensity, fall into union. The mutuality is that all men feel and lose feeling, all interact, all warrant *the sympathy that Gabriel now extends to Furey, to Gretta, to himself, even to old Aunt Julia.* (*JJ2* 252; my emphasis)

Gabriel certainly actively extends sympathy to these dead and living characters, but his transformation into a generous human being goes much further than Ellmann recognizes, shading into empathy and even hospitality, as I have argued. When Ellmann terms the story "a linchpin in Joyce's work," singling out its theme of cuckoldry, rhythmic detail, and "the mutual dependency of living and dead," he is surely right; but "The Dead" also shows Joyce in the process of becoming a major fictional practitioner of hospitality, one inspired in part by the "news" of Gretta's past life, Furey's sacrifice, and now Christ's sacrifice—as Gabriel's transformation is here— and one which he would develop more extensively in the character of Leopold Bloom in *Ulysses*.[41]

Joyce's specific interest in rescue narratives such as the Good Samaritan parable arose out of his general interest in hospitality and was heightened by the beating he was given in Dublin in 1904 and his mugging in Rome in 1907, as we shall see in the next chapter, and "The Dead" may even manifest his early interest in rescue narratives in the way Colm Tóibín has suggested. In *Mad, Bad, Dangerous to Know: The Fathers of Wilde, Yeats, and Joyce*, Tóibín argues for a fascinating autobiographical reading of "The Dead" that he considers part of Joyce's rescue narrative for his scurrilous father, John Stanislaus Joyce. Although he does not draw upon the Good Samaritan parable, in his extrapolating from Gabriel's generous tears, Tóibín posits that,

> In the mixing of his [Joyce's] own sensuality with his imagination of his father's sensuality, in allowing his own ghost to mingle with that of John Stanislaus Joyce, he banished his scrupulous meanness and performed an act of generosity. He rescued himself for the work that he would now make.[42]

Elsewhere, in his reading of Joyce's portrait of Stephen Dedalus's father Simon in *A Portrait of an Artist as a Young Man* as part of Joyce's recasting of his own stingy and bullying father, Tóibín argues,

> Joyce rescues his father from the sort of certainty that Stanislaus uses in his diary and his memoir and from the tone that he himself adopts in *Stephen Hero* by moving his father from the private realm, where he clearly is a bully and a monster, into the public sphere. He allows him to be the man he is with his friends rather than with his family.[43]

Tóibín's fascinating biographical retrieval project suggests strongly Joyce's privileging of rescue narratives in his life and in his fiction as part of his interest in hospitality, and suggests by implication the importance of my argument in the rest of this book for some of Joyce's major fictions to be understood as rescue narratives specifically founded on the Good Samaritan parable.

Notes

1. O'Connor, *The Lonely Voice: A Study of the Short Story*, 18, 19.
2. Mahaffey, *States of Desire: Wilde, Yeats, Joyce, and the Irish Experiment*, 143.
3. Lawrence, "Close Encounters," 135.
4. Ibid., 136.
5. See Torchiana, *Backgrounds for Joyce's* Dubliners, 109–24.
6. Tóibín, *Mad, Bad, Dangerous to Know*, 207.
7. Power, "A Note on Hospitality and 'The Dead,'" 109. The quotation from the February 13, 1904 issue of *The United Irishman* that Power singles out is particularly resonant for the story: "This grand old race of hostesses is passing away with its traditions and ideals of the past." Marie Corelli's article, "The Decay of Hospitality" in *The Bystander* (June 29, 1904, pp. 203–5), anticipates both the sumptuous dinner and Gabriel's speech, particularly when Corelli terms hospitality "'a great-souled splendid Grace,'" and in her contrast of "the simplicity and sincerity of the old to the hypocrisy and sophistication of the new" (109).
8. Pecora, *Self and Form in Modern Narrative*, 243.
9. See my essay, "Irish Unionism, North of Ireland Protestantism, and the Home Rule Question in Joyce's *Dubliners*."
10. See also Pecora, "The Inkbottle and the Paraclete," 344–59. Pecora here considers "the question of the sentimental in Joyce [apparently his term for Joycean generosity, which he identifies earlier in this essay on 346], an element of his work that I had more or less denied in my earlier reading," and tries to square that element with "Joyce's radically unsentimental technique" (352). Pecora paradoxically argues that in Gabriel, Joyce created a "character who finally gives in to the more generous impulses that Joyce himself obviously felt, all the while mischievously undermining that character, subtly parodying the larger spirit of reconciliation . . . with ambiguous details and rhetorical overkill" (358). Pecora even admits the "beautiful, redemptive language of its finale," but then argues that "the end of the story with its swoon into the comforts of oblivion is the surest sign of Joyce's own deep and irresolvable ambivalence" about "the impossible morass of personal and political claims Ireland made on him" (358, 359).
11. Heffernan, *Hospitality and Treachery in Western Literature*, 1.
12. Ibid., 2.
13. Lawrence, "Close Encounters," 137. As she further holds, "Gabriel believes in the laws of hospitality that govern the Greeks, laws that insure certain rights and privileges for the guests as they sit at table." Because he believes in "the sovereignty of the host that allows him to exclude an improper guest," he is discomfited by both Lily and Miss Ivors and what he perceives as their attacks on his role as host.
14. Saint-Amour, "'Christmas Yet to Come': Hospitality, Futurity, the *Carol*, and 'The Dead,'" 102.
15. Thurston, *Literary Ghosts from the Victorians to Modernism*, 140. Thurston also perceives Aunt Julia's song "Arrayed for the Bridal" as ghostly, linking it to "The Lass of Aughrim" through their common phantasmal performances (139–40).
16. Norris, "Words to 'The Lass of Aughrim,'" 247.
17. Qtd. in ibid., 247.

18. Ibid., 248.
19. I thus disagree with the first part of Heffernan's claim in *Hospitality and Treachery in Western Literature*: "Part of the reason for which Gretta has been so long secretly mourning the death of Michael Furey . . . is that she may feel doubly responsible for it." She becomes so upset at this moment precisely because she has not mourned Furey in ages. But as Heffernan continues, he makes a valuable point about how Gretta may have condemned herself because of her lack of hospitality long ago to Furey: "He 'died for' her, as she tells Gabriel . . . not only because he loved her but also because she was not quite generous, hospitable, and daring enough to let him into her house, let alone her bed, on the rainy night he came to see her at her grandmother's house" (291). Leaving aside the question of whether Furey literally—or purposely—died for Gretta, both of which seem doubtful to me and instead are projections by the romantic Gretta, Heffernan nonetheless offers an important insight about Gretta's desire to be more hospitable in the future. Gabriel, at least, achieves her desire as he later channels her and briefly imagines he sees Furey outside her window years ago, throwing gravel up at it.
20. Fraser, *Joyce and Betrayal*, 27, 28.
21. Heffernan, *Hospitality and Treachery in Western Literature*, 72.
22. Maddox, *Nora*, 15.
23. Ibid., 17.
24. Ibid., 17.
25. John McCourt points out in *The Years of Bloom: James Joyce in Trieste, 1904–1920*, that Joyce became jealous of Roberto Prezioso's "overzealous interest in Nora" early in 1913 (192), even if Joyce was initially "pleased Nora had such an illustrious admirer" (193). Joyce's recognition of Prezioso's fascination with Nora enabled him to "write on the themes of attraction and betrayal, marriage and infidelity and the often ambiguous nature of sexual attraction, which would dominate *Exiles* and play a significant role in *Ulysses*" (193). Even more telling evidence for understanding the theme of jealousy in "The Dead" and the persistence of Sonny Bodkin's "sacrifice" for Nora emerges in McCourt's examination of Joyce's preliminary notes for *Exiles*, which lists Prezioso's name, immediately followed by that of Bodkin (194). Also in 1913, more evidence for Joyce's continuing fascination with Bodkin and/or Feeney occurs in his poem, "She Weeps over Rahoon," collected in *Pomes Penyeach*. McCourt argues that the poem's speaker is Nora, who is remembering Michael Bodkin, or perhaps Gretta Conroy remembering her lost love Michael Furey. There are also echoes from the closing lines of "The Dead," as McCourt points out, "in the rain which 'falls softly, softly falling' in the opening lines of the poem" (240). See line 1 of "She Weeps over Rahoon" (54), and also the closing lines, which indicate that the love of the speaker and her lover (likely Nora and Joyce) will lie "cold / As his sad heart has lain / Under the moongrey nettles, the black mould / And muttering rain" (lines 9–12).
26. Pecora, who previously read this line about Gabriel's "generous tears" as ringing false in his earlier essay, "'The Dead' and the Generosity of the Word," now admits the emotional power of the story. He perceives that "There is, I now recognize, something deeply human and moving about Gretta and her sorrow," and, furthermore, muses that "I am more willing now to accept that the word *generous* as applied to

Gabriel's tears could be taken at face value, or perhaps simply as meaning 'copious,'" although he immediately states, "But it still for me reverberates with irony in the context of the story as a whole" ("The Inkbottle and the Paraclete," 357). Pecora's honest reflections on how the story has changed in his mind over the years typifies that of most readers, who continue to find depths in it beyond their original readings, as have I in thinking back through the story in terms of hospitality.

27. Lawrence, "Close Encounters," 138.
28. Ibid., 139: "[I]n this case, Gretta is transformed from Gabriel's view of the symbolic woman hearing 'Distant Music' to a haggard and very particular sleeping face."
29. Tate, "The Dead," 407.
30. Lawrence, "Close Encounters," 138.
31. Saint-Amour, "'Christmas Yet to Come,'" 103.
32. Avery, "Distant Music: Sound and the Dialogics of Satire in 'The Dead,'" 416.
33. Ibid., 417.
34. Heffernan, *Hospitality and Treachery in Western Literature*, 287.
35. Ibid., 289.
36. Taylor, *Sources of the Self: The Making of the Modern Identity*, 35.
37. Walzl, "Gabriel and Michael: The Conclusion of 'The Dead,'" 441.
38. Andrew Shepherd, *The Gift of the Other: Levinas, Derrida, and a Theology of Hospitality*, appreciates Derrida's (and Levinas's) contributions to hospitality theory, but adroitly shows their shortcomings. The most telling drawback is, as Shepherd points out, that "Derrida's two-dimensional understanding of hospitality has strongly Platonist tendencies, with an aversion to any kind of incarnation" (78–9). See his entire chapter, "Unconditional Hospitality, the Gift of Deconstruction," 46–80, for a thoroughgoing diagnosis of Derrida's persistent agnosticism, and how it is characterized by a hopeful but finally fruitless wait for a Messiah figure who never arrives.
39. Derrida, "Hostipitality," 361.
40. Ibid., 361–2.
41. Ellmann intriguingly points out that both Joyce's "Ivy Day in the Committee Room" and "The Dead" were inspired by Anatole France's short story "The Procurator of Judaea," in which Pontius Pilate never mentions presiding over Christ's trial until asked specifically; he then feigns ignorance. As Ellmann notes, "The story is overshadowed by the person whom Pilate does not recall; without him, the story would not exist. Joyce uses a similar method in 'Ivy Day' with Parnell and in 'The Dead' with Michael Furey" (*JJ2* 253). Strangely given his reading of "Ivy Day," Ellmann does not mention how not just Furey, but Christ as well, hovers over the end of "The Dead." And meditating upon His sacrifice on the cross, as we have seen, likely helps reinforce Gabriel Conroy's desire to be more hospitable in the future, a process he has begun in imagining Furey's death, his Aunt Julia's death, and caring for the grieving Gretta.
42. Tóibín, *Mad, Bad, Dangerous to Know*, 211.
43. Ibid., 216.

2

JOYCE, SCRIPTURE, AND AUTOBIOGRAPHICAL RESCUE NARRATIVES

"You should approach Joyce," said William Faulkner, "as a preacher approaches the Old Testament—with faith."
Qtd. in Declan Kiberd, *Ulysses and Us*, 312

[T]he Bible plays a distinctive role in the world of *Ulysses* that sets it apart from the brawling, untidy democracy of quotations in which it often appears to participate as no more than an equal partner with a welter of uncanonical texts, high and low.
Robert Alter, *Canon and Creativity*, 158

In this chapter, I first argue that Joyce's early turn to Scripture and scriptural narratives, and his deep familiarity with them, particularly the Gospel of Luke and his parables of the humanized Jesus, is grounded in a hospitality ethic that indelibly marked his great epic. I conclude with a brief assessment of two primary inspirations for the novel—Joyce's putative "rescue" by Alfred H. Hunter from his beating in Dublin in 1904, and Joyce's mugging and possible rescue in Rome in 1907—suggesting that these incidents enabled Joyce to read himself into the Good Samaritan parable and see in it profound fictional possibilities.

"Preparatory to anything else": Joyce's Interest in Scripture

As D. H. Lawrence slightingly acknowledged about *Ulysses* in his letter of August 15, 1928 to Aldous and Maria Huxley, Joyce thoroughly incorporated passages from Scripture in the novel to the extent, Lawrence believed, that it was merely an assemblage of quotations from other sources: "Nothing but old fags and cabbage-stumps of quotations from the Bible and all the rest..."[1] Lawrence's remark reveals the extent to which Joyce's contemporaries recognized the novel's immersion in Scripture, although later critics have by and large tended to downplay the role of scriptural narratives as intertexts in *Ulysses*. Critics who have closely examined the scriptural underpinnings of the novel, however, have apprehended their variety and pervasiveness, and furthermore, how biblical narratives enable Joyce to achieve his moral vision. For instance, Robert Alter, a leading expert on the use of Scripture in literary narratives, has argued that "[i]n the extraordinarily supple and varied uses to which the Bible is put in *Ulysses*, it is converted into a secular literary text, but perhaps not entirely secular, after all, because it is reasserted as a source of value and vision."[2] Joyce fascinatingly appealed to the authority of Scripture in articulating his vision of kindness, community, and love in *Ulysses*, even as he continued to draw on biblical narratives to protest the authority of the dominant Irish Catholic Church.

Joyce was immersed in Scripture from early on, partly as a reaction to the magisterium of the Catholic Church; as he stated in a letter to Nora of August 29, 1904, "I made secret war upon it when I was a student and declined to accept the position it offered me.... Now I make open war upon it by what I write and say and do" (*SL* 25, 26). Roy Gottfried has argued in *Joyce's Misbelief* that Joyce's transcription of the Book of Revelation when he was 16 years old as a college student at University College, Dublin, "was a highly unusual and intimate rebellious act, given the Catholic practice of not encountering scripture directly."[3] As Gottfried holds further,

> To appeal to the Bible at all is a striking move for a Catholic, indoctrinated in obedience to the clergy in its intercessory power to inform and lead. To seek and to derive authority by reading and citing directly from scripture rather than receiving it from ecclesiastical authorities (ranked from the priest up to the Pope) is a striking move of independent agency and individual choice.[4]

Finally, as Gottfried points out, "Joyce's use of the Bible has not gone unremarked in earlier criticism, although questions as to his purpose in using it have been overlooked."[5] Yet Gottfried emphasizes Joyce as such a schismatic through his turn to Scripture that he leaves out any account of Joyce's parabolic turn of mind and how he employs parables, especially the parables of Christ, to bring people together, not separate them, as would a typical schismatic.

Another influential examination of Joyce and religion, Geert Lernout's *Help My Unbelief*, intimates that it is the last word on the subject, but actually reveals his own bias against religion. As Jack Dudley has shown in the best concise refutation of Lernout's thesis, Lernout's "stridently secular understanding of Joyce" wrongly constructs an "Ellmannian consensus about Joyce's religion." Dudley argues that Lernout misrepresents Richard Ellmann's judgment on Joyce as completely uninterested in religion, whereas Ellmann instead noted multiple instances of Joyce's general interest in religion but specific rejection of the Roman Catholic Church. For instance, Dudley notes that Ellmann's statement, "He [Joyce] was no longer a Christian himself; but he converted the temple to new uses instead of trying to knock it down, regarding it as a superior kind of human folly and one which, interpreted by a secular artist, contained obscured bits of truth" (*JJ2* 66), certainly does not represent "Ellmann's ultimate judgment on Joyce's religion."[6] Not only does Lernout wrongly extrapolate from Ellmann's contention about Joyce's leaving Irish Catholicism to his alleged rejection of all religion, but he also omits mention of Ellmann's statement in 1982, the year the revised edition of his acclaimed biography appeared, that "[t]o be opposed to the Church as an institution is one thing; to be opposed to all religious feeling is another," and does not highlight Ellmann's anecdote from Stanislaus that Joyce likely believed in a deity.[7]

Moreover, Lernout often misunderstands, misrepresents, or elides Joyce's ongoing interest in Christianity and particularly in Scripture, though more recently he has discovered Joyce's deep interest in Scripture, despite relegating that fascination to Joyce's interaction with Byron's drama *Cain*.[8] Lernout facilely posits that

> Useful as a corrective to some critics' faith in Joyce's native knowledge of the Bible are Stanislaus's comments [in *My Brother's Keeper*]: "In Catholic homes and in Catholic schools the Bible is never read. . . . The Catholic Church has its own shrewd reasons for preferring to keep the Bible a sealed book in a dead language."[9]

But besides Lernout's misleadingly attributing Stanislaus's feelings about Catholicism and the Bible to Joyce, Joyce certainly would "have absorbed biblical content through . . . the Catholic liturgy," as Leland Ryken points out. *Ulysses* contains almost six dozen biblical names and 500 allusions to the Bible.[10] Moreover, we know that in thinking through the character of Stephen Dedalus for *A Portrait of the Artist as a Young Man*, Joyce copied into his notebooks the long narrative from Acts 6:8–7:4 and from 7:51–8:4 in the King James Bible[11] about one of the first deacons in the early Christian church, Stephen, who was martyred by several different Jewish groups. We also know from the catalogue of Joyce's Trieste library that he had not only a well-read copy of an 1825 edition of the Authorized (King James) Version, but also a 1912 Italian edition of the Bible and a 1902 copy of the Vulgate edition.[12]

Given Lernout's mischaracterization of Joyce's biblical knowledge, it is worth restating here some points about that knowledge made long ago by Virginia Moseley in her still valuable book, *Joyce and the Bible*. Drawing on Joyce's confession to his Italian tutor Francini-Bruni, "I love Dante almost as much as the Bible," noting that Italian was Joyce's favorite language of the eighteen he eventually acquired, and citing his comment to Stanislaus that he "placed Dante even above Shakespeare," Moseley sensibly concludes, "If Joyce's love of the Bible exceeded even his love for Dante, the Bible must have been for him a veritable cornerstone."[13] Lernout smugly claims from Moseley's subsequent contention—because "the Jesuits focused on the Christian religion, the Bible was probably the one literary work that Joyce knew best by the time he received his university degree"—that she shows "a rather limited understanding of the role of the Bible in Catholicism: later in life Joyce told his father that Catholics should not read the Bible at all."[14] And yet as Moseley points out, Joyce would have known the Douay Version and the Latin Vulgate from "a continual hearing and reading of the *Daily Missal* of the Roman Catholic Church," even though those readings "would be restricted and proscribed by authority," as Gottfried argues.[15] Fascinatingly, while Joyce likely did not study biblical texts once he matriculated at University College in Dublin, Roger McHugh has suggested that his interest in Cardinal Newman, the university's founder, "might have helped to interest him in the Bible."[16] Finally, Lernout's citation of Joyce's unattributed statement to his father that Catholics should not read the Bible may well have been delivered in a flippant tone or ironically or by way of sarcastically protesting that the Bible was not read personally by many Irish Catholics outside of church. This last possibility resonates with Joyce's suggestion to Stanislaus that "there was no thinking proletariat" in Ireland, which "he blamed on the stifling power of the priests."[17]

Joyce's anti-clericalism was pronounced but should not prevent us from realizing how saturated his mind was with Scripture, particularly such parables as that of the Good Samaritan, which was, among other things, an attack on the ecclesiastical elite of Jesus' day and thus would have resonated with his own critique of the Irish Catholic clergy. Certainly, Joyce obsessively read the Bible, especially the King James Version, as he moved away from his Catholicism, and so he would not have felt any sense that his childhood Catholicism inhibited him from doing so; indeed, as Gottfried shows, he read the King James Version as a defiant act against the Catholic Church, an attitude that steadily grew upon his departure from heavily Catholic Ireland to Italy, perhaps the only country in the world at that time that was even more Catholic.

Joyce thus sought out the otherness or strangeness of Scripture as an exile within his own country and then as an exile from Ireland abroad. On the textual question of Scripture's strangeness—and one with special import for Joyce's focus on the Stranger in his iterations and reimaginings of the Good

Samaritan parable in *Ulysses*—it is worth considering Jean-Louis Chrétien's contention about Scripture as inherently strange or other to us. In his study *Under the Gaze of the Bible*, Chrétien posits,

> If there is a Word of God, how could its manifestation ever—no matter what mode it takes—be other than a manifestation of self by self? He possesses that "strange" or "foreign" (*xenon*) character that Origen recognized: "The word of God has something of a nature alien beyond every word of anyone else—and what is God and what is a living being while being a word, what subsists in itself and what is subject to the father, has an alien nature."[18]

Joyce's incorporation of Scripture into his work, such as the Good Samaritan references in *Ulysses*, not only testifies to the importance of the Word to his literary project as one of several ur-narratives he returns to repeatedly, but also suggests how the "alien" nature of Scripture because of its manifestation of God appealed to him as an exile himself dedicated to writing about strangers such as Leopold Bloom. Welcoming the "strangeness" of Scripture into his life and work meant accommodating himself to the presence of a transcendent Other who spoke the world into being, and while Joyce left the Catholic Church, he retained a keen interest in the mysteries of the Mass and other aspects of Catholicism—and in this alien quality of Scripture.

His habitual tendency to welcome Scripture into his work, where he gave it new life, suggests how he saw himself in dialogue with it, interpreting it for himself and his fictional purposes. Chrétien's point about the "infinite movement of translation" involved in reading Scripture is apposite to Joyce's interpretation of it as he incorporates it into his fiction:

> The original of the heart of the Christian revelation is for us already a translation, at the same time that the New Testament translates, in all the senses of the word, the Old . . . . [Thus,] [t]o translate is already to interpret, to interpret again is to translate, and it is thus that the unique and divine melody . . . reaches me . . . with the harmonics and accompaniment of an immense symphonic orchestra of redactors, translators, commentators.[19]

Joyce joins that "symphonic orchestra," already in full swing, through his "translation" of scriptural narratives throughout *Ulysses*.

In keeping with his interest in Christ's teaching, including in such parables as the Good Samaritan, Joyce marked with ribbons mostly sections of the New Testament, not the Old Testament, although as Abby Bender has shown in her fine study, *Israelites in Erin: Exodus, Revolution, and the Irish Revival*, which features a convincing recuperation of the importance of the Book of Exodus for *Ulysses*—what she believes is "the central trope of the novel"—Joyce certainly knew the Old Testament very well too.[20]

Lamentably for someone who believes that Joyce was relatively ignorant of Scripture, Lernout insists on categorizing him repeatedly as a freethinker, a rationalist, even though he blandly admits that Joyce's Trieste library "shows his continued interest in religious matters."[21] Lernout's unsubstantiated claims and rush to untether Joyce from his immersion in Scripture—and even from religion more broadly—suggest his own biases and signify that he is an adherent of the narrative of modernity as secularization, a narrative that, as I demonstrated in the introduction, has been significantly challenged and now refuted by a series of critics writing on American and British and Irish literature, among other national literatures.

Although Alter convincingly posits that the *Odyssey* and the Bible are the two main allusive sources for the novel and holds that Joyce "imagines an intricate coordination and complementarity" between these two works, he points out that the language of the Bible lives on the lips of the characters in a way that Homer's epic does not: "the Anglophone Irish, with the exception of an occasional flamboyant pedant like Buck Mulligan, did not go around quoting Homer, whereas the Bible was still a common point of reference for this Judeo-Christian society . . . its more famous verses, stories, and figures textually recalled by middlebrow and highbrow alike."[22] It has been well-established that Joyce used Thom's 1904 edition of the *Official Directory of the United Kingdom of Great Britain and Ireland* as the source of his elaborate knowledge of Dublin, supplemented by his own memory and that of others, such as his brother Stanislaus. The Bible functions as a different sort of intertext for the novel: It provides source material, talking points, character analogues, history, narratives. It is the common linguistic meeting ground where Joyce's characters mix and mingle, live and have their being. His two main characters know it well, as do a host of other, minor characters.

Even more so than his characters in the novel, Joyce knew Scripture exceedingly well. Luke Gibbons has shown that Joyce was so interested in scriptural matters that he even followed the Evangelical Protestant Bible wars in Dublin and referenced them in *Ulysses*.[23] We know too that in addition to his 1825 edition of the King James Version, Joyce had in his Paris library French and English copies of the Anglican Book of Common Prayer, a work that is replete with passages from the King James translation.[24] William Franke, author of the definitive essay on Joyce and the Bible, clearly shows that "James Joyce's employment of the Bible in his literary production is vast and multifaceted."[25] Joyce's refusal to stay in the Catholic Church or join any other established church certainly does not preclude his ongoing fascination with Scripture, particularly its narrative possibilities for his own fiction, as we will see.

Like Steve Pinkerton, who draws on Gottfried's notion of misbelief to characterize Joyce as "a creative, I would add blasphemous, *mis*believer," I believe we should appreciate anew Joyce's work as simultaneously mingling the sacred and the profane:

> Drawing as they do so ubiquitously on biblical and ecclesiastical tradition and tropes, his fictions can hardly be called secular in any common sense of that term. Yet ... we must also realize the extent to which these literary sacraments are inherently ironic, revisionist, and very often profanatory.[26]

I likewise focus on how Joyce reappropriates and reconfigures a central New Testament tenet—the Good Samaritan parable—in ways that reward an ever closer reading of his "sacred" text to determine how he redolently conveys a secularized message of loving others, even those who abuse us, through a revivified concept of the neighbor. Both connected to the authority of Christ in legitimizing such a radical posture and unfettered from that authority by virtue of the novel's secularizing turn to us as those who might effect that profound neighborliness, *Ulysses* profanely but powerfully points toward a sacrificial, giving spirit to others outside narrow, bounded conceptions of ourselves.

My intent here is not to reclaim Joyce as some sort of believer—Protestant or Catholic. Lernout, and later Father Colum Power in his *James Joyce's Catholic Categories*, correctly point out that many critics have wrongly done so in attempting posthumously to co-opt Joyce back into the Christian faith. Rather, I contend that if we fail to apprehend the ongoing influence of a particular aspect of Christian theology for Joyce—Christ's parables and the dialogic relationship he perceived they set up with the listener or reader—we miss a great deal of his emphasis on hospitality in *Ulysses* and cannot truly appreciate the meeting and partial union of Bloom and Stephen, their profoundly enfleshed encounter epitomized by the Good Samaritan parable and prophesied throughout the novel. Likely reflecting his debt to the Reformation's insistence on the reader's direct experience with Scripture, Joyce's use of the Good Samaritan parable in *Ulysses* not only shows his great respect for the reader and, by extension, the burden he placed on the reader to respond to his fiction, but also displays his continued interest in forming community through bringing strangers together—Stephen and Bloom, author and reader—in parabolic storytelling.

Along with his interest in scriptural parables, Joyce evinced an interest in the last book of the Bible, Revelation, from an early age, in part as a rebellion against the Catholic Church. Gottfried's insistence on Joyce's transcription of Revelation at age 16 as crucial for the development of his art remains an important reclamation of biblical influence on Joyce. As Gottfried insightfully argues, "the copying and the reading [of this book of the Bible] must have been particularly ink-stained and wholly literal acts of apostasy and rebellion. Close scrutiny and citation of the Word for the sake of gaining authority are rebellious acts." And "[t]he transcribing of the particular section of the New Testament . . . must have been itself a gesture of *non serviam* direct[ed] at the highest authorities in Joyce's life."[27]

But there are additional literary reasons for Joyce's having been drawn to Revelation that Gottfried does not raise. David Lawton, for instance, argues that the Book of Revelation models desirable aesthetic positions, including the "*persona* of the dream vision," from which stems "the most easily accessible model of the imaginative artist who, by means of art, speaks the truth." Moreover, this model "reaches its apotheosis in the revolt of the Romantic poet against organized religion: the book makes war on itself."[28] Joyce's interest in the Romantic poets, particularly Byron and Blake, was profound and ongoing, and certainly his rebellion against organized religion was reinforced both by their rebellions and by Revelation's seeming rebellion. Furthermore, the Apocalypse's inspiring of art across various media is various and ongoing. Lawton even argues that "[i]ts vision of global destruction is a constant incentive to artistic construction," holding finally that because "[w]e celebrate that which we most fear to lose: the ephemeral," thus "Western art, Western civilization, grows out of, and has never escaped from, the shadow of the Apocalypse."[29] Joyce seems to have been similarly inspired to make art out of destruction repeatedly in his own art: Think, for instance, of how *A Portrait of the Artist* responds to the fall of Parnell and the destruction of the hopes for Irish independence, along with the apocalyptic episode "Circe" from *Ulysses*.

Joyce's ego and desire for authority may also have led him to the Book of Revelation. Lawton believes that it is "by far the most pretentious book in the Bible, and the most authoritarian—by which I mean simply that it makes more claims for its own truths than any other book," because "it is pure and deliberate fiction."[30] For a writer struggling to emerge from the iron grip of the Catholic Church, a Church that insisted only its authority could interpret Scripture, immersing himself in and transcribing Revelation and mulling over how to interpret it must have given Joyce confidence in starting to construct his own fictions and lent him considerable authority in the process.

Sangam MacDuff, who has recently analyzed the manuscript of Joyce's transcription of Revelation, has posited that "the formal structure of Revelation, organized around sequentially unfolding symbolic patterns like the seven churches, seals, trumpets, figures, and vials of Chapters 1–16, may have attracted Joyce as a model of narrative order." He further believes that the "Apocalyptic proliferation of images and symbolic associations, whose ultimate significance remains intractably obscure, can be compared to the gnomonic principles of absence and reiteration which govern Joyce's art, from the epiphanies to *Finnegans Wake*."[31] That sense of secrecy and obscurity inherent in Revelation surely appealed to a writer who claimed that in *Ulysses*, he had "put in so many enigmas and puzzles that it will keep the professors busy for centuries arguing over what I meant, and that's the only way of insuring one's immortality" (qtd. in *JJ2* 521). Bernard McGinn nods to this aspect of Revelation, noting that it is "[i]n itself arcane and full of secret allegories at whose original reference we can only guess."[32] In this prophetic fiction, replete with secrets and hidden mysteries, Joyce seems to have found a model for his future fiction. As MacDuff puts it,

> Each of Joyce's works can be considered as a revelation: the thwarted hope and dreams of *Dubliners*, the growth of the artist in *Portrait*, the extraordinariness of the ordinary in *Ulysses*, the revelation of language in the *Wake*; and each of Joyce's books alludes frequently to the Book of Revelation.[33]

Immersing himself in Revelation likely helped Joyce in his belief that he was a member of the artistic elect, since millenarian readings of Revelation "often included a sense of England as an apocalyptically elect nation,"[34] and Calvinists in the North of Ireland often used it as well to justify their sense of political election. From an early age, Joyce felt he was ordained to play a major role as a national artist, and certainly Stephen Dedalus's sense of destiny in *Portrait* and his desire to "forge in the smithy of my soul the uncreated conscience of my race" (*P* 253) derives from Joyce's similar sense that he would be the writer of his nation, even in exile, a conviction amply evidenced in his letters and essays.[35]

The "Circe" episode in *Ulysses* functions as a mini-Apocalypse and its placement in the novel prepares the reader for Joyce's epiphany of loving the Other, introduced by the reiterations Stephen and Bloom make of the Lukan parable of the Good Samaritan. Virginia Moseley claims that "Joyce's technique of hallucination in the Nighttown scene points directly to the last book of the New Testament."[36] MacDuff believes she "overstates the case," but quotes a series of references to Revelation and admits that "these examples support Moseley's reading of the Book of Revelation as the nightmare of history." Yet he immediately claims that these examples also "attest to Joyce's continuing fascination with the beasts of Apocalypse, whether evangelical or Antichristian."[37] It is not clear how MacDuff's claim contradicts Moseley's; rather, it seems to reinforce her reading of "Circe" as indebted to Revelation. Significant portions of the episode reference the Second Coming beyond the ones MacDuff cites, as, for instance, when Florry Talbot, one of the prostitutes, tells Stephen she has read in the newspapers that the Antichrist is coming (*U* 15.2135), after which newspaper boys run by with an edition of the paper proclaiming the Antichrist's safe arrival (*U* 15.2140–1). Certainly when Stephen smashes the chandelier in Bella Cohen's brothel, bringing on what the narrator calls the *"ruin of all space, shattered glass and toppling masonry*" (*U* 15.4244–5), we realize that we are, as Harry Blamires memorably put it, now in a "cosmic cataclysm in which the heroic individuality of the artist is asserted even against the light."[38] Amid the wreckage of this Apocalypse, compounded by the arrival of the police, Bloom and Stephen begin enacting the Lukan narrative of the Good Samaritan.

Although critics have thoroughly explored Joyce's interest in and artistic development of the Christian notion of epiphany in his earlier work, this concept seems to color very few major readings of *Ulysses*.[39] Many discrete epiphanies are manifested in the novel, but now, on this greater canvas, these micro-epiphanies are set in the plenum of the macro-narrative of *Ulysses* as an artistic Book of Revelation revealing its message of loving the Other.

The Good Samaritan parable embodies the major message of the novel—to love others, even those who persecute us, or those whom we do not know, or those who reject our ministrations—through a narrative subgenre that Paul Ricoeur argues forms a subset of prophetic narratives. Citing Matthew 25:31–42, a passage about how Christ will separate those who fed and clothed the sick and poor from those who ignored them, Ricoeur argues that "[t]he [Good Samaritan] parable related an encounter in the present, the prophecy relates an event at the end of history which, in retrospect, unfolds the meaning of all the encounters in history." Thus, "prophecy bears upon and unveils the meanings of encounters, encounters similar to those of the Samaritan and the stranger overpowered by thieves: to give to eat and drink, to take in the stranger, to clothe the naked, care for the sick, and visit those in prison."[40]

Declan Kiberd argues that Joyce was fascinated with how the authors of the Gospel "cannibalized and rewrote the Old Testament much as he would reconfigure earlier classics, making *Ulysses* both their fulfillment and itself an open, prophetic book." Since Joyce realized that the "words of the prophets were shot through with a utopian potential that was not completely realized until it was incarnated in the figure of the New Testament Jesus,"[41] he likewise saw himself as a new prophetic figure incarnating his wisdom about hospitality and loving our neighbor in the character of Bloom. This chapter and subsequent ones do not emphasize Bloom *only* as a secular savior figure as much as Kiberd has,[42] in part because I see Bloom functioning as not just a Good Samaritan figure (traditionally a representation of Christ in one major strand of theologians' reading of the parable), but also as the beaten Stranger, a bivalent symbol both of hospitality and woundedness.[43] Kiberd's contention that Joyce saw himself as writing a prophetic book with *Ulysses* that was based on incorporating remnants of earlier holy texts such as the Pentateuch and the New Testament seems incontrovertible and coheres with Joyce's view of himself as a prophet, steeped in knowledge of the Book of Revelation, who espoused theories of artistic election—one of a handful of such figures able to communicate their inspired messages to the masses.

Besides Kiberd—and prior to him—the only critic who has previously approached a reading of Joyce's work in this way is William Franke, who cogently argues that "Joyce is aligned with a continuous prophetic-apocalyptic movement comprising the efforts of secular writers to extend apocalyptic revelation from the Bible into the sphere of literary artistic endeavor." For Franke, because "the core of the Bible as it is refracted in Joyce consists in the Eucharistic celebration of the death of Christ, his offer of his flesh as nourishment for all," this "rite in the Bible and in Joyce alike culminates in the symbolic resurrection of the body of Christ and in the salvation and even the sanctification of the world."[44] Drawing on Thomas J. J. Altizer's *History as Apocalypse* (1985), *Genesis and Apocalypse* (1990), and *The Genesis of God: A Theological Genealogy* (1993), Franke, who is closely attuned to Joyce's blasphemies, convincingly posits that Joyce stands in a long line of not just theologians such as Augustine and Luther but also poets such as Dante, Milton, and Blake. These poets all recognized that the death of God opened up new possibilities of divinity, since "Christianity inaugurates the vision of divinity revealed in a unique, irreversible historical event, an incarnation in flesh that is a final and irrevocable submission to death (as recounted particularly in Phillipians 2: 5–11)."[45] In this moment, for "the first time in the history of religions the real and actual beginning of finite historical experience that never returns but passes toward a future that is genuinely new and apocalyptic" occurs. In this "resurrected life" that transpires after "the past has been nailed to the cross and is thus crossed out forever," it is "[o]nly now" that the "full and absolute presence of the embodied individual and the incarnate historical act [is] possible," finally "realized by Joyce in the apocalypse of *Finnegans Wake*."[46]

And yet in *Ulysses*, Joyce employed a simpler apocalyptic vision of the world in which we feed on his text and gradually see another vision growing before our eyes—the novel's epiphanic injunction that we love our neighbors. Read in this way, as part of a consistent development from his early essay "Ecce Homo," explored in the fourth chapter of this book as part of discerning his exploration of a secularized Christ, *Ulysses* manifests a central message much as John's vision on the island of Patmos does. John takes great pains to characterize his Revelation—the transfigured Son of God, with the "hairs of his head" depicted as "white, like white wool, like snow" (Rev. 1:14 ESV)—a vision meant simultaneously to terrorize non-believers and comfort believers with predictions of the Apocalypse and subsequently, heaven, which John slowly unfolds. Joyce's revelation in *Ulysses*, on the other hand, gives us Bloom, thought to be Jewish by other Dubliners, most recently baptized Catholic, who nonetheless carries a version of Christ's command to love our neighbors as ourselves in the Good Samaritan parable and reveals it to us throughout the day as he re-enacts that narrative and encounters a host of characters—Protestant and Catholic alike—who would deny that message.

Only by so feasting on that revealed, prophetic literary word can we apprehend the depth of Joyce's conviction that we should love our neighbors as ourselves.

Joyce's Assaults in 1904 and 1907 and the Good Samaritan Parable as Inspiration for *Ulysses*

We know from a letter of June 23, 1904 from Joyce to his friend Constantine P. Curran that he was assaulted, likely the previous night or on the night of June 20. He suffered a "black eye, sprained wrist, sprained ankle, cut chin, cut hand," and wryly noted, "For one role at least I seem unfit—that of man of honour. However I will not groan through the post" (*SL* 21). Strangely, though, he does not mention what caused these injuries or that he was helped by anyone afterward, though Ellmann points out that his friend Vincent Cosgrave "stood by hands in pockets" and did not help (*JJ2* 161). Joyce mentions to Curran that he is enclosing his autobiographical novel *Stephen Hero* and concludes "Yours heroically, Stephen Daedalus" (*SL* 21–2). Here, we already see Joyce adopting a Daedalian perspective—as potential hero—and conflating an actual incident in which he was beaten up with Stephen's penchant for imagining himself as hero, a motif developed more extensively in *Portrait*.

Sometime in the succeeding two years, Joyce seems to have told his brother Stanislaus that a Jewish gentleman named Alfred Henry Hunter had rescued him that evening, possibly saving him from further assault. Writing Stanislaus from Rome on September 30, 1906, Joyce attached a second postscript, intriguingly remarking, "I have a new story for Dubliners in my head. It deals with Mr. Hunter" (*SL* 112). Ellmann's footnote for this passage in his edition of the *Selected Letters* states, "The story was to be entitled 'Ulysses.' Joyce never wrote it, but as he frequently said in later life, his book *Ulysses* had its beginnings in Rome. Alfred H. Hunter was a Dubliner, rumoured to be Jewish and to have an unfaithful wife" (*SL* 112 n.1). Writing his brother again on November 13, 1906, Joyce mused, "I thought of beginning my story *Ulysses*: but I have too many cares at present," later asking in this same letter, "How do you like the name for the story about Hunter?" (*SL* 128, 131). By December 3 of that same year, he was asking Stanislaus, "Write to me also about Hunter" (*SL* 136).

Joyce's "rescue" from this fracas by Alfred Henry Hunter on the evening of June 20 or June 22, 1904 has never been verified, though it continues to be repeated by a series of critics, including those who should know better.[47] Even Peter Costello, in his 1992 treatment of Joyce's life, and Joyce's most recent biographer, Gordon Bowker, whose book appeared in 2011, argue that Hunter rescued Joyce from a fight, with Bowker's account largely reproducing the details of this incident first mooted by Ellmann in his biography. Costello strangely locates the attack on the night of September 15, 1904, after Joyce left the Martello Tower, during which he claims that Joyce got into a *second* fight after being assaulted by a girl's escort on Stephen's Green on June 22 of that year.[48] Bowker, on the other hand, argues that the incident occurred on the night of June 20 after Joyce's bout of drinking and throwing up in the lobby of the Irish Literary Theatre.[49] Ellmann explores that drunken evening at some length, then notes that a "second unsavoury episode took place later that night or soon after," after which he notes that Joyce was attacked by the escort of a young woman in St. Stephen's Green after he spoke to her (*JJ2* 161). By stating, however, that "[n]ext day Joyce lamented to Curran" the details of the fight in the June 23 letter, Ellmann implies it occurred on June 22. Costello claims the fight was in the Monto brothel quarter located behind Talbot Street (the site of Joyce's fictional Nighttown in the "Circe" episode of *Ulysses*), while Bowker admits the possibility of that location, but locates the incident at St. Stephen's Green, as does Ellmann, as we have seen.[50] Both Costello and Bowker state that Vincent Cosgrave was with Joyce and refused to help, with Costello claiming that his "friend Vincent Cosgrave refused to help him and stood idly by watching the fracas" and Bowker noting that "Cosgrave stood by and watched, hands in pockets," both confirming Ellmann's account (*JJ2* 161).[51] Finally, both argue that Alfred Hunter then rescued Joyce: Costello claims that "he picked Joyce up and took him home—either to his own house, at 28 Ballybough Road, or to his Uncle William's house nearby in North Strand, where he was staying and which was only a step away"; Bowker states, "[a]bandoned by Cosgrave, Joyce was rescued by Alfred (Hugh) Hunter," who "was a friend of his father's from Clontarf," "tall and dark (reputedly a Jew and a cuckold)," and who, "hearing of his distress took him reportedly to a flat in Eccles Street where he had lived with his separated wife Margaret."[52] Clearly, we know this: Joyce was in one fight for sure during 1904, likely in June, and his friend Cosgrave was with him and did not help him. Hunter's presence and help are much less likely.

As Terence Killeen has shown in the best short treatment of this "incident," Ellmann subtly questions whether or not Joyce was rescued from a fight by Hunter in the second edition of his biography, a revision of his definitive claim of Hunter's rescue of Joyce in the afterword he wrote for the first (Penguin) paperback edition of *Ulysses* in 1968. Ellmann does not mention the story at all in his original 1959 biography, and while "[i]t does appear in the second edition of the biography [1982] . . . [it appears] in a far more qualified fashion than in the Penguin afterword."[53] Thus, in 1968 Ellmann gave an account of a fight in 1904, then declared that Joyce "was dusted off and taken home by a man named Alfred Hunter,"[54] but in 1982, he qualified this statement heavily, noting, "[i]f Dublin report *can be trusted* . . . Joyce was *said* to have been dusted off and taken home by a man named Alfred H. Hunter," an account that is footnoted thus: "W.P. D'Arcy, a friend of Joyce's father, heard the story from John Joyce; letter to me from D'Arcy. Other confirmation is lacking."[55] Killeen shows that Hugh Kenner "produced enough evidence to show that the story of Joyce's 'rescue' from a fracas by Alfred H. Hunter rests on very shaky foundations," and that the "only other means to uphold it, apart from the tainted testimony of W.P. D'Arcy, is to decide that Stephen's rescue by Bloom at the end of 'Circe' must have biographical parallels and then to fit the evidence around this thesis." Even though Peter Costello, the first to identify the real-life Hunter as Presbyterian in upbringing, not Jewish, took this approach in his 1992 biography, *James Joyce: The Years of Growth*, I concur with Killeen that "it is too daring a leap to decide that any event narrated in a fictional work must have a parallel in 'real life' without supporting evidence."[56]

Certainly Joyce attended the funeral of Matthew Kane on July 13, 1904, as did Hunter, so he had a chance to meet him, or at least see him, in that seminal year for his career. Costello remarks that Hunter was "a tall, dark-complexioned man in his late thirties," and he "caught Joyce's interest. From his father he learnt that this person was supposed to be Jewish and to have an unfaithful wife."[57] Moreover, as Killeen points out, Joyce was fascinated by Hunter as late as 1921, when, in a letter of October 14, he asked his Aunt Josephine if she knew what had happened to him. Joyce asked her, "Also I forgot to ask what do you know about Hunter who lived in Clonliffe road..." (*SL* 286). Killeen further plausibly posits that because "Hunter was in some sense at the origin of *Ulysses*" and because of this 1921 letter to his aunt, "it seems very likely that he [Joyce] inquired about him on his two trips back to Dublin in 1909 and 1912, thereby supplementing the knowledge he already possessed at the time of his initial conception of the abortive story 'Ulysses.'"[58] I would add that we know that Joyce toured Belfast in 1909 in the hopes of placing a cinema there. It is tempting to wonder if he tried to discover anything about the Hunter family of Ballymacarret, near Belfast, at that time, even though Hunter himself had long since moved to Dublin and was married on February 15, 1898 to a Catholic woman named Margaret Cummins, who was named "Marion (or Marian) 'Brúini Hunter" in the 1911 census entry. The Hunters both became Church of Ireland members, a suggestion that they were willing to cross denominational lines as Leopold Bloom's father and Bloom himself did. Given that Hunter was born on August 30, 1866, the same year as Leopold Bloom, and that his wife's name was shared by Molly Bloom, along with the connotation that Marian Hunter had a stage persona, signaled by that "mysterious second surname," linking her to Molly the professional singer—all this suggests some salutary antecedents for Joyce's fictional Blooms.[59] As Killeen argues, drawing on Ellmann's discussion of Joyce's possible encounter with Mr. Hunter (*JJ2* 162), "Joyce did not have to know Hunter personally to be keenly interested in him."[60] Killeen convincingly concludes, "Alfred H. Hunter may or may not have rescued James Joyce from an assailant; but even if he did not, his centrality and that of his wife, to Joyce's creation has been amply confirmed."[61]

Thus, whether or not Joyce was rescued by Hunter that June night in 1904 is beside the question: Hunter helped inspire *Ulysses* and by so doing, the story of that "rescue," invented or real, gave Joyce a contemporary purchase on the Good Samaritan parable, as did Joyce's reaction to his 1907 mugging in Rome. While Ellmann shrewdly questions in the second edition of his biography whether this 1904 event actually occurred, he also makes an insightful observation that is helpful in apprehending its parabolic resonance for Joyce, noting that his "very lack of acquaintance [with Hunter] was memorable, since Joyce regarded himself as hemmed in by indifference or hostility and was the more surprised that someone unfamiliar, of temperament and background opposite to his own, should have causelessly befriended him" (*JJ2* 162). For someone who had often seen himself as a victim of sorts (compounded and enhanced by his identification from childhood with Parnell), hounded by those who would make him conform to Catholicism, propriety, or convention, Joyce found in the Good Samaritan parable a story that resonated with his own difficulties, but which also had more far-ranging applications and implications than mere autobiography.

For Ellmann, the story called "Ulysses" that Joyce abandoned might have "shown Hunter circumnavigating Dublin and, in the end, offering a lifebuoy to a castaway resembling Joyce." The crucial aspects of that planned story for Ellmann seem to be this plot and the complementary strand of Jews' ambiguous place in Europe (which Joyce found himself to occupy as an Irish exile on the continent), along with the "figure of the cuckolded Jew" (*JJ2* 230). But while these aspects remain essential to the eventual novel named *Ulysses*, Hunter's "rescue" of Joyce and the Lukan parable of the Good Samaritan were foundational to the novel and especially to the significant events in its closing episodes.

If this incident, in which Joyce was clearly beaten up in late June of 1904 but most likely *not* rescued, has proved an enduring, if misunderstood narrative in Joyce studies, his later mugging at the hands of some drinking companions in Rome during early March of 1907 remains a curiously underreported event in his life—and even more so does this second episode's function as another inspiration for *Ulysses*.[62] Let us return to Ellmann's statement explaining a neglected part of Joyce's reference to Hunter in the letters: "as he frequently said in later life, his book *Ulysses* had its beginnings in Rome" (*SL* 112 n.1). Joyce is clearly musing on Hunter in the November 13, 1906 letter to Stanislaus and considering writing a story about the incident. He felt no warmth from the Romans generally during his eight-month stay there, much preferring the Triestines he had already befriended in his time in that city, and he may have been casting his mind back to Dublin and that fight and its aftermath as a way of comforting himself—reminding himself of home with the fictitious rescue to bolster his attachment to Dublin.

Specific accounts of actual rescues back in Dublin were on his mind at this time as well. In his August 12, 1906 letter to Stanislaus, Joyce wistfully recalled the rescues performed over the years by Oliver St. John Gogarty (the model for Buck Mulligan in *Ulysses*) but also chastised him for his enabling of the continuing power of the Church and for the stratified class system of that period. Joyce mused, "Gogarty would jump into the Liffey to save a man's life but he seems to have little hesitation in condemning generations to servitude" (*SL* 94). Ellmann notes that "Gogarty rescued drowning men from the Liffey on three occasions, in 1898, 1899, and 1901" (*SL* 94 n.2). And Joyce grudgingly affirms those rescues in the opening episode of *Ulysses* when Stephen tells Mulligan, "You saved men from drowning" (*U* 1.62) and confesses his own fear of Haines's nightmare about a black panther, which had led Haines to fire a shot the previous night and narrowly miss Stephen. We know this incident was based on Samuel Chenevix Trench's nightmare that he was being attacked by a panther while staying in the Martello Tower with Joyce and Gogarty; in the event, Gogarty shot the pots that were hanging over Joyce's bed, frightening the life out of Joyce, and he left the tower that day, September 15, 1904.

Stephen's close call with the pistol might echo Joyce's own fears of the danger associated with pistols, particularly while in Rome. Along with his sense that Romans lacked warmth was his apprehension of danger there, which finally manifested itself in his mugging, after which he left to return to Trieste the next day. At first, the opening statement of his letter to Stanislaus on August 31, 1906 seems tongue-in-cheek, until we realize that Joyce's dire financial straits were compounded by his fear of robbery. Thus, he states immediately to his brother, "I have had no letter from you for nearly a fortnight so I suppose you are in great difficulties or else that you sent me money which was robbed in the post" (*SL* 98). If Stanislaus was chuckling at that point, he likely stopped after he read the very next sentence: "In the latter case I hope you have the registration receipt" (*SL* 98). Seemingly in passing, later in this same letter Joyce muses upon the hospitality given to him and Nora and Georgie, their son, by the proprietor of the wine shop who lived across from them. In the middle of a huge supper he gives them, the old man shares with Joyce his fears for his safety: "He said he was an old man and thought sometimes of buying a revolver to protect himself from assault at night in the streets and asked me did I approve of that" (*SL* 100). The famously pacifist Joyce likely did not approve, but the old man's fear lingered with him, and shortly before Joyce was mugged late in the evening of March 5/early morning of March 6, 1907, he wrote Stanislaus a long letter, likely on March 1, in which he discussed standing waiting for the deceased Giordano Bruno's funeral cortege to pass. While waiting, he was disturbed by the sight of a young Italian woman who "constantly raised slowly to her lips" a trinket that she then "rested" there, "slowing parting them [her lips], all the time gazing tranquilly about her." A horrified Joyce finally realized "that the trinket was a miniature revolver!" (*SL* 152). The incident was clearly sexual, with the woman nearly sucking the phallic revolver each time she raised it to her lips, and the Italians to whom Joyce related the story confirmed that many Italian women then wore a miniature penis as a trinket (*SL* 153). Joyce seems more disturbed, however, by the danger inherent to the woman of her accidently shooting herself.

Only four days later, having given his notice to the Nast-Kolb Schumacher Bank where he worked, and having drunk some of his considerable severance pay, Joyce was robbed of the remainder of his money by his drinking companions, and by some accounts, assaulted. Biographers differ on the exact details of the robbery, but they do agree that Joyce's money was taken late on the night of March 5/early morning hours of March 6. Costello notes only that "Joyce slipped away from Nora to celebrate [his plans to leave Rome after turning in his notice to the bank] by drinking in the Pincian Gardens" and was "reckless enough to expose his wallet to his companions," who "duly relieved him of it, adding insult to injury by pretending to be patrol officers and taking him off to the police station to report the crime."[63] Bowker also states that Joyce "had given in his notice at the bank," noting further that on the evening in question, "he drew a month's salary (250 lire) at the bank and went on a farewell spree."[64] Then, when he was "suitably drunk, two congenial bar-flies took him to a backstreet and relieved him of his bulging wallet. He returned home penniless and completely soaked from an evening downpour," after which the family left for Trieste.[65] John McCourt states simply that "[h]aving just received his monthly salary from the bank" that morning, as "he made his way home, late in the night, he was attacked by two men who robbed him of everything he had."[66]

Ellmann's account is most convincing, most sinister, and, finally, most uplifting because Joyce *is* rescued this time. After he "received his month's pay from the bank" that day, "he drank heavily in a café and indiscreetly allowed two hangers-on with whom he was talking to see the contents of his wallet. They followed him out, knocked him down, and made off with his 200 crowns" (*JJ2* 242). Fascinatingly, Ellmann then clearly links this incident to Bloom's rescue of Stephen in the novel that would spring out of both the 1904 and 1907 incidents: "In the resulting hubbub he would have been arrested, as when he first arrived in Trieste in 1904, if some people in the crowd had not recognized him and taken him home, a good deed (like Hunter's earlier) which he recalled at the end of the *Circe* episode in *Ulysses*" (*JJ2* 242). Recognized and rescued, a shaken Joyce nonetheless quickly gathered Nora and Georgie and fled Rome, the eternal city that by that time had become an eternal site of threatened and actual violence to him. Heartened by his rescue, however, and surely reminded of his 1904 assault in Dublin when he was likely *not* rescued, he began revolving both incidents in his mind, purposing to finally write about them and the comforts of hospitality—imagined and real—in a time of violence.

Clearly, Joyce's inspiration for the novel—Bloom's rescue of Stephen Dedalus—was based on a partly apocryphal Dublin story in which Joyce was undoubtedly assaulted by a stranger but likely not rescued by Hunter or anyone else, and on a truer Roman story in which Joyce was robbed and possibly assaulted by drinking companions, then perhaps rescued by a crowd. Even though he gets the chronology wrong and mistakenly believes that Joyce mentioned the Roman assault in the now-famous November 13, 1906 letter to Stanislaus as the inspiration for what he projected as a new short story for *Dubliners*, Richard Kearney's recovery of this assault in Rome captures its importance for Joyce in formulating the beginnings of what would become *Ulysses*. Although he cannot prove his claim, Kearney argues that as Joyce was "left lying in the gutter, destitute, despondent, and bleeding," he "suddenly remembered something: being assaulted several years previously (June 22, 1904) in Dublin and rescued from the gutter by a man called Hunter, 'a cuckolded Jew' who dusted him down and took him home for a cup of cocoa—in 'true Samaritan fashion,' as Joyce put it." Crucially, although Kearney also wrongly believes that Hunter rescued Joyce, his supposition that the 1907 Roman assault surfaced his memory of the 1904 Dublin assault convinces, as does his formulation of both incidents: "This repetition of woundings triggered a lost memory where an immigrant Jew came to the rescue of a wounded Dubliner and planted a seed of *caritas* in his imagination."[67]

The example of the Good Samaritan in the form of an imaginary "immigrant Jew" thus inspired *Ulysses* in larger part. And the "seed of *caritas*" planted "in his imagination" became for Joyce the heart of the novel, as we will see in later chapters. It was also both a riposte to what he saw as the hypocrisy rampant in the contemporary Irish Catholic Church and a model for neighborliness founded in hospitality to the Other. First, however, as we saw in the previous chapter, he would begin exploring hospitality more generally in the great stories of *Dubliners*, particularly in "The Dead." Along with the particular reinscription of the Good Samaritan parable in "Grace" that he would re-employ in *Ulysses*, Gabriel Conroy's eventual, gradual hospitable reception of Michael Furey became a touchstone for Joyce's developing theory of receptiveness to the Other.

Notes

1. Lawrence, *Selected Literary Criticism*, 148.
2. Alter, *Canon and Creativity*, 182–3.
3. Gottfried, *Joyce's Misbelief*, 66.
4. Ibid., 61.
5. Ibid., 67.
6. Dudley, "From 'Spiritual Paralysis' to 'Spiritual Liberation,'" 179, quoting Lernout, *Help My Unbelief*, 5.
7. Ibid., 179, quoting Ellmann, "Prologue: Two Perspectives on Joyce," 4.

8. See Lernout, *Cain—But Are You Able? The Bible, Byron, and Joyce*, especially his statement there about Joyce's knowledge of James Frazer's 1918 study *Folk-Lore in the Old Testament* and Lamy's *Commentarium in Librum Geneseos*: "It is clear that through Lamy's book Joyce was aware of the textual and logical problems associated with the text of Genesis 4. . . . And now we can also contextualize his strange plan to write a libretto based on Byron's *Cain*. Needless to say, I wish I had known the details of this context before I finished my book on religion and Joyce, because both Frazer's book on the Bible and Byron's play are extremely relevant in such a study" (123). This admission is heartening, but falls far short of recognizing Joyce's deep knowledge of the entirety of the Bible—particularly the Lukan narratives and the Book of Revelation—and its significance for all of his work, not just *Finnegans Wake* and bits of *Ulysses*.
9. Lernout, *Help My Unbelief*, 100.
10. Ryken, *The Legacy of the King James Bible*, 213. Ryken draws on Thornton, *Allusions in Ulysses*, for these numbers.
11. See Scholes and Kain, *Workshop of Daedalus*, 264–6.
12. Gillespie, *James Joyce's Trieste Library*, 48.
13. Moseley, *Joyce and the Bible*, vii. Moseley cites Bruni as quoted in Benco, "James Joyce in Trieste," 375–80, and Stanislaus Joyce, *Recollections of James Joyce by His Brother*, 7.
14. Lernout, *Help My Unbelief*, 13, citing Moseley, *Joyce and the Bible*, ix.
15. Moseley, *Joyce and the Bible*, vii; Gottfried, *Joyce's Misbelief*, 63.
16. Letter to Virginia Moseley of June 26, 1954, qtd. in Moseley, "Joyce and the Bible: The External Evidence," 104.
17. McCourt, *The Years of Bloom*, 72, citing Stanislaus Joyce's entry for May 10, 1907 in Stanislaus's *Book of Days: The Triestine Diary*, n.p.
18. Chrétien, *Under the Gaze of the Bible*, 20, quoting Origen, *Homilies on Jeremiah and I Kings 28*, 222.
19. Chrétien, *Under the Gaze of the Bible*, 3.
20. Gillespie, *James Joyce's Trieste Library*, 48; Bender, *Israelites in Erin*, 26.
21. Lernout, *Help My Unbelief*, 108.
22. Alter, *Canon and Creativity*, 159, 154.
23. Gibbons, "'Tarnished Ghosts,'" 1–23.
24. Gottfried, *Joyce's Misbelief*, makes this point, drawing on Thomas E. Connolly's *James Joyce's Books, Portraits, Manuscripts, Notebooks, Typescripts, Page Proofs*, 122 n13.
25. Franke, "James Joyce and the Bible," 638.
26. Pinkerton, *Blasphemous Modernism*, 21. Pinkerton is the latest critic to identify Joyce as a blasphemer, but does so in such interesting, nuanced, and compelling ways that his chapter on Joyce has now become the definitive discussion of Joyce and blasphemy. For a foundational, much earlier statement on Joyce and blasphemy by one of his best critics, see Eco, *The Aesthetics of Chaosmos*, 3: "Joyce abandons the faith but not religious obsession. The presence of an orthodox past reemerges constantly in all his works under the form of a personal mythology and with a blasphemous fury that reveals the affective permanence."
27. Gottfried, *Joyce's Misbelief*, 70.
28. Lawton, *Faith, Text, and History*, 187.

29. Ibid., 187.
30. Ibid., 187.
31. MacDuff, "Joyce's Revelation," 121.
32. McGinn, "Revelation," 523.
33. MacDuff, "Joyce's Revelation," 121. For a thoughtful reading of the presence in *Ulysses* of Revelation, see Terry Reilly, "Apocalyptic Satire: Reading *Ulysses* through Revelation and Frank Kermode's *The Sense of an Ending*." The topic clearly deserves more study: Reilly states at one point that "Allusions to Revelation are so dense, multi-leveled, and ubiquitous that they deserve much more attention than I can give them within the purview of this essay" (304).
34. McGinn, "Revelation," 536.
35. See, for instance, Joyce's admiration for Ibsen throughout his 1900 essay, "Ibsen's New Drama," especially in the opening passage, where he remarks, "his name has gone abroad through the length and breadth of two continents, and has provoked more discussion and criticism than that of any other living man," and muses, "the great genius of the man is day by day coming out as a hero comes out amid the earthly trials" (48). Joyce's great admiration for Parnell as national hero also comes to mind and is a major motif in *Portrait* and in multiple essays.
36. Moseley, *Joyce and the Bible*, 65.
37. MacDuff, "Joyce's Revelation," 124.
38. Blamires, *The New Bloomsday Book*, 192.
39. Exceptions are the chapter "Permutations of Epiphany in *Ulysses*" in Sangam MacDuff's fascinating monograph *Panepiphanal World: Joyce's Epiphanies*, and Richard Kearney, "Epiphanies in Joyce," the latter of which I found after having written this chapter. Kearney identifies specific epiphanies in the novel and argues that "what we have in *Ulysses* is the mature Joyce translating his—and Stephen's—youthful notion of epiphany into a post-romantic literary praxis" that is not "some doctrinal exegesis of epiphany—derived from some grand metaphysical theory—but the performance of epiphany in the text itself. It does not have to be named. It is the very process of naming and writing itself" (254–5). Even more relevant to my argument that the whole novel reveals the message of the Good Samaritan parable, Kearney briefly and brilliantly wonders if "the entire novel itself is an epiphany from beginning to end, with Stephen, Bloom, and Molly serving as three mundane magi—offering us different aspects of a single seed-moment in Joyce's own life: 16 June 1904? Or a trinity of such moments (Hunter's rescue, Nora's kiss, Skeffington's phrase) combined into one? One epiphanic time in one epiphanic space?" (256).
40. Ricoeur, "The Socius and the Neighbor," 100.
41. Kiberd, *Ulysses and Us*, 297.
42. See ibid., 303–4, for instance.
43. The historical theological and literary precedents for reading the Good Samaritan as Christ include these: Origen's 34th Homily from his *Homilies on Luke*; Henri de Lubac's *Catholicism: Christ and the Common Destiny of Man*, 204–5; William Langland's *Piers Plowman*, Passus XIX; Peter Lombard's *The Sentences: On the Doctrine of Signs*, Dist. 1, chapter 1; Lombard's *The Sentences: The Mystery of the Trinity*, Prologue. Grateful thanks to my colleague in the Department of Religion at Baylor, Dr. Natalie Carnes, for this list.

44. Franke, "James Joyce and the Bible," 638.
45. Ibid., 639.
46. Ibid., 640.
47. See, for instance, both the usually careful Denis Donoghue's seeming authoritative contention in "A Plain Approach to *Ulysses*," and Kevin Birmingham's breezy and erroneous assertion about the incident in his well-publicized *The Most Dangerous Book: The Battle for James Joyce's* Ulysses. Donoghue opens his essay, intended apparently for an unpublished edition of *Ulysses*: "Sometime in 1904 James Joyce, much given to drink and dissipation but not to violence, stumbled into a fracas in Dublin. Providentially he was rescued by a man named Alfred H. Hunter" (157). Birmingham attempts to inject even more drama into the fiction: "Once, Joyce's drinking got him into a one-sided fight in St. Stephen's Green. He approached a woman whom he did not realize was accompanied, and [Vincent] Cosgrave simply walked away while the man beat the would-be writer senseless. As Joyce lay bleeding in the dirt, a stranger, a reputedly Jewish Dubliner named Alfred H. Hunter, lifted him up and brushed him off. He steadied Joyce by the shoulders, asked the young man if he was all right and proceeded to walk him home just as a father would have done. Joyce never forgot it" (25–6).
48. See Costello, *James Joyce: The Years of Growth, 1882–1915*, 226, for the assault on June 22, 1904, and 230–1 for the supposed incident in the Monto area of Dublin on September 15.
49. Bowker, *James Joyce: A Biography*, 123–4.
50. Costello, *James Joyce*, 230–1, and Bowker, *James Joyce: A Biography*, 124.
51. Costello, *James Joyce*, 231, and Bowker, *James Joyce: A Biography*, 124.
52. Costello, *James Joyce*, 231, and Bowker, *James Joyce: A Biography*, 124.
53. Killeen, "Myths and Monuments: The Case of Alfred H. Hunter," 48.
54. Ibid., qtd. on 47–8.
55. Ibid., qtd. on 48; my italics.
56. Ibid., 48. See Costello, *James Joyce*, 228, for his discussion of Hunter's Presbyterian background in the North of Ireland.
57. Ibid., 228.
58. Killeen, "Myths and Monuments: The Case of Alfred H. Hunter," 50.
59. Ibid., 49.
60. Ibid., 50.
61. Ibid., 50.
62. Indeed, Joyce's nearly eight months in Rome remain one of the most under-scrutinized aspects of his biography, although Giorgio Melchiori's account of that time in "The Genesis of *Ulysses*," 37–50, makes clear its importance, including his reading about Judaism, socialism, and his feeling more like an exile in Rome than he had in Trieste.
63. Costello, *James Joyce*, 271.
64. Bowker, *James Joyce: A Biography*, 164.
65. Ibid., 165.
66. McCourt, *The Years of Bloom*, 84.
67. Kearney, "The Hermeneutics of Wounds," 31.

3

REWRITING THE GOOD SAMARITAN PARABLE: THE FICTIONAL RESCUE NARRATIVES OF "GRACE" AND "CIRCE"

> But what of the incident the night of June 22, 1904? While references to it have become obligatory in investigations of Joyce's representations of "the Jew," very few thoughts beyond the argument over its mere occurrence have been offered.
>
> Neil R. Davison, *James Joyce, Ulysses, and the Construction of Jewish Identity*, 105

Joyce's affinity for scriptural stories arose again around the time he was conceiving *Ulysses*—and likely stemmed from the almost certainly apocryphal encounter with Alfred H. Hunter, as we have seen, and his later mugging in Rome. Using the Torah as his analogy, Declan Kiberd has convincingly argued that Joyce saw *Ulysses* as a "holy book" replete with "divine wisdom in the text."[1] He posits that "Joyce was someone who snooped around old texts looking for a back door through which to effect an entry. The New Testament was one such text and a major element in the creation of *Ulysses*."[2] No one until Kiberd has made such a succinct and telling statement of the New Testament's influence on the creation of the novel. And yet even Kiberd, despite his clear recognition of Joyce's secular "gospel" inhering in the mandate to love our neighbor, neglects his reiteration of the Good Samaritan parable as epitomizing that message.

After writing short stories and a play and some poetry, Joyce settled upon what we might now call "long-form fiction," the novel, as his preferred genre, and that preference (as well as his having left the Catholic Church) may well have contributed to the refusal of many critics to employ religious interpretations of *Ulysses*. As Justin Neuman has shown, of all genres, the novel has most resisted religious readings. First, the novel's rise as a genre was largely coincident with "European secularization." Moreover, because of the genre's reliance on narratives of ordinary individuals, which repudiated "the transcendental frames of reference within which allegories, romances, and epics forge their meanings," the "question of immanence prompts scholars to differentiate novels from other prose forms." Finally, the tendency of novels to be "rhizomatic, presenting a multitude of voices and styles through which the active reader must negotiate" is a characteristic "at odds with secularist ideas about religious dogmatism and the monolingualism of a divinely authored text."[3] Immanence was often implicit in the ordinary, however, for Joyce, and he certainly seems to have felt that the rhizomatic voices and styles of his masterpiece were compatible with his unorthodox understanding of Scripture.

When Kiberd argues in his reading of "Wandering Rocks" that "[t]he streets teach good lessons, encouraging people to look after one another, to care for the weak (the blind stripling or crippled sailor),"[4] he correctly identifies Joyce's central project in the novel—how care for others can create community, especially in the prominent example of Leopold Bloom and Stephen Dedalus. But he misleads in suggesting that a loose aggregation of characters on the streets of the city care for others in the absence of any underlying mythos. Rather, Joyce shows repeatedly how that care has been taught through Scripture and embodied in such unlikely characters as Bloom. Joyce's own turn to Scripture strikingly shows how holy writ continued to inspire his creative works long after he left the Catholic Church.

Joyce may have been drawn to biblical narratives as he became a prose writer not just because of his rebellion against the magisterium of the Catholic Church, but also because of their literariness and their endorsement of characters' agency, an outgrowth of what Gottfried terms Joyce's turn to Scripture as manifesting his own "independent agency."[5] Alter posits that the authors of the Hebraic texts actually invented this new mode of prose narration because of its "range and flexibility in the means of presentation" and its ability to "liberate fictional personages from the fixed choreography of timeless events," thus transforming "storytelling from ritual rehearsal to the delineation of the wayward paths of human freedom, the quirks and contradictions seen as moral agents and complex centers of motive and feeling."[6] Theologians did not come to read parables as "freely invented stories" until Dan Otto Via, Jr. published *The Parables: Their Literary and Existential Dimension* in 1967,[7] but clearly, Joyce understood them as narrative fictions with plots, characters, setting, and other traditional literary elements long before the theologians did.[8]

Although "parable" might call to mind those stories told by Jesus and collected in the New Testament, there is a long Jewish tradition of parable as well, and indeed the term's original Greek etymology suggests its wide application: *parabole* meant to toss or throw one thing beside another. Mark Turner, in his 1996 study *The Literary Mind*, argues that parables actually structure human thought itself. Turner offers a fairly broad definition: "The essence of parable is its intricate combining of two of our basic forms of knowledge—story and projection."[9] Then, distinguishing between parable as a creative literary convention and parable as a way in which the mind functions, Turner holds that we constantly engage in narrative acts on a daily basis: "Literary works known as parables may reside within fiction, but the mental instrument I call parable has the widest utility in the everyday mind."[10] Parable, we might say, is an inherently human habitus, and for minds steeped in the Christian tradition, as James Joyce's was, the human tendency to place stories alongside each other to make sense of the world leads us back ineluctably to the parables of Christ.

In a little-noticed passage from *My Brother's Keeper*, Stanislaus points out Joyce's affinity for parabolic literature, rightly conceived, arguing that "[i]n our world today, serious literature has taken the place of religion. People with liberty of choice go, not to the Sunday sermon, but to literature for enlightened understanding of their emotional and intellectual problems. And it answers in parables." But he noted that "[m]y brother held that those parables for the most part falsified men, women, and issues—all life, in fact, as it is lived every day or as it is lived in the imagination, and that at best it was a literature of entertainment, the province of men of letters." While Stanislaus is clearly using "parables" in a looser sense than the theological context of these stories, his choice of the word nonetheless freights Joyce's literary attempts with a profound moral and ethical significance, as does his later remark that Joyce scoffed at those writers who "toyed with literature" and "their vacillating, compromising attitude towards literature and the host of issues it raised," their "literary simony." For his brother, "[f]alsity of purpose was the literary sin against the Holy Ghost, and he was vigilant to detect it."[11] Thinking parabolically not only enabled Joyce to reject the literature of his day that he felt was not sufficiently true to either everyday life or the imagination, but it also gave him the ability to create theologically influenced literary characters such as Stephen and Bloom with great agency and freedom, as Alter suggests above. He felt so strongly about his literary "mission" that he even considered other writers' lack of seriousness to be "simony," a selling of their sacred calling as artists.[12]

In this regard, he likely was also drawn to parables because of their coded messages that an elite group could understand, the encoding of which excluded others not in the know. In his essay on Ibsen[13] and throughout *A Portrait of the Artist as a Young Man*, Joyce admires the theory that the artist (Ibsen, Parnell, Byron) was one of a select group able to apprehend divinely revealed or elite messages and communicate them as a prophet figure. He found additional confirmation of parables as prophecy in the Gospels. For instance, in Luke 8:10, two chapters before Luke tells the Good Samaritan parable, Christ relates the purpose of all his parables in response to his disciples' question about the meaning of the parable of the sower, which he has just told in 8:4–8: "To you it has been given to know the secrets of the kingdom of God, but for others they are in parables, so that seeing they may not see, and hearing they may not understand," a passage that Christ expands upon in Matthew 13:11–13 (ESV). Notice Christ's emphasis on his "inner" and "outer" audiences—the inner ring of the disciples, and the outer ring of those at least temporarily excluded from knowing the parables' meanings because not part of this elect group. Christ certainly extended and amplified the message of his parables to this greater audience, but knowing His limited original audience for the parables indicates their secret messages for those who are "given to know the secrets of the kingdom of God." Similarly, Joyce must have enjoyed parabolically disguising the message of some of his short fiction and even *Ulysses*, leaving clues for the discerning reader who would then know the secrets of his fictional kingdom. Given his interest in epiphany and in the Book of Revelation, parables' hidden messages that could be revealed to him and, in turn, to the initiates, likely appealed to him.

My graduate student Harrison Otis brilliantly characterizes Jesus' description of parable in the passage from Matthew as "a kind of glyph, a symbol laden with meaning that can only be understood by someone with the proper key, someone who has (in an important sense) learned to read." Furthermore, he posits that "[t]he tension between the parable seen as glyph and the parable read as meaning is the cognitive dissonance that draws the reader into the participatory moral formation of the narrative," noting that "[t]he moment of transition between these two states is the moment of epiphany."[14] Finally, because revelation is ongoing and dynamic, what Paul Ricoeur terms a "permanent process of opening something that is closed, of making manifest something that was hidden," Joyce was probably drawn to parables' dynamism, to their continual revelation to us. His own reiterations of the Good Samaritan parable in *Ulysses* achieve something of this continuing process as they happen over and over, slowly revealing more about Bloom's charitable nature, for instance.[15]

In her pioneering essay on Joyce's use of parables in *Dubliners* and *Ulysses*, Jill Shashaty has convincingly argued for reading *Dubliners* parabolically, suggesting that "[t]o think of the stories in *Dubliners* as parables—and of readers as their interlocutors—is to recognize the ways in which *Dubliners* invites the same kind of moral reflection process as ancient scriptural parables."[16] Indeed, Joyce himself was thinking of parables on June 10, 1906, when he wrote to urge publication of his story collection to his London publisher Grant Richards, who dragged out the publication of *Dubliners* from 1906 to 1914: "Buy two critics.

If you could do this with tact you could easily withstand a campaign. Two just and strong men, each armed with seven newspapers—*quis sustinebit*? I speak in parables."[17] Joyce here references the last two words from the Vulgate version of Psalm 129 (Psalm 130 in English translations): "*si iniquitates observabis Domine Domine quis sustinebit*," translated in the King James Version as "If thou, Lord, shouldest mark iniquities, O Lord, who shall stand?" This elliptical reference to the psalm suggests that Joyce believed strongly in the moral project that was *Dubliners*—to liberate the souls in Ireland trapped by British imperialism and the Irish Catholic Church—and that he jokingly sought critics in this process who would affirm this parabolic project in the leading newspapers of the day and protect him from the charges of indecency that Richards was already projecting would be made.

My own occasional frustrations—and those of my students—with the elliptical, mysterious endings of these stories over the years that I have taught *Dubliners* can become a productive situation whereby their ambiguities and incongruities lead us into deep moral debates, just as Joyce intended. For instance, the little boy in the conclusion of "Araby" has failed in his mission to acquire an exotic item for the girl he idolizes at the bazaar, but he is given a clear epiphany in the last sentence: "Gazing up into the darkness, I saw myself as a creature driven and derided by vanity; and my eyes burned with anguish and anger" (*D* 35). Will the little boy move forward into his life cognizant of his vanity and seek to become less self-centered, serving others? Or will he instead quit romantic pursuits and settle into a torpor in which he tortures himself with recrimination for his vanity? The answer, like those given in parables, is simply not clear.

The parabolic process that Joyce puts us through in reading *Dubliners* ineluctably leads to a considerably higher burden on the reader than that enacted by reader-response theory, but with more potential: It instead involves a complete reorientation of how and why we read, and if we fully enter into this process, we become not only better readers but also potentially better neighbors to each other. Joyce sought to completely engage us in *Dubliners* and *Ulysses* through this parabolic process by forestalling certain narrative elements we have come to expect in short fiction, as Shashaty points out. Because "parables both foreground conflicts and suspend their resolution," for instance, the "frustration, disappointment, unfairness, embarrassment, or puzzlement this creates then draws audiences into the narrative." In this way, such unresolved plots "connect with audiences on an affective level (empathy), an ethical one (unfairness, injustice), and an intellectual one (bewilderment, disorientation)."[18] For all the considerable criticism on Joyce's plots, insufficient attention has been paid to their affective, ethical, and intellectual impact on the reader, and understanding their parabolic nature is an essential feature of understanding them and how they are deployed.

What Ricoeur elsewhere has called the "essential profaneness" of the parables,[19] their lack of mythology, their utter ordinariness, surely appealed to Joyce as he was continuing to articulate his modernist project of reclaiming the everyday as a fit subject for fiction, much as Virginia Woolf would later. The characters of the parables—ordinary people drawn from all walks of life—were used by Christ to reach his contemporary audiences of everyday men and women. And yet, just as Joyce would later use ordinary scenes and situations to create profound literary epiphanies, there is a moment in each parable that breaks through ordinary time, erupting into the plane of the sacred. Ricoeur posits that the "logic of meaning in the parables" is precisely the presence of "the extraordinary within the ordinary," and further, that much of the presence of the extraordinary derives from a certain "extravagance" common to all the parables.[20] Because the Good Samaritan parable shares this extravagance with other parables, but also because its excessive generosity goes above and beyond those others, it can be considered the most extravagant parable of all, a meditation on excessiveness in a form already suffused with it. Joyce's interest in hospitality thus happily met its generic expression in the parable, particularly this Lukan parable.

Joyce's musing upon the Good Samaritan parable likely arose both from his interest in that specific parable based on the true fiction of Alfred H. Hunter's rescue of him and his reaction to his mugging in Rome, which I discussed in the last chapter, along with his general desire for the "spiritual liberation" of his country in *Dubliners*. He began incorporating rescue narratives in that short-story collection. For instance, one of the early stories in the volume, "Eveline," silently critiques a false rescue narrative, with Frank potentially saving Eveline from her father's abuse, her circumscribed life, and Ireland's stultifying culture. Eveline's refusal to go to Buenos Aires with Frank in the story's conclusion suggests that she may see him as a fraudulent rescuer figure, if not a fake Samaritan character, even if she does not realize that he might sexually traffic her, since many white European women were sold into prostitution there.[21]

Jack Dudley helpfully shows how readings of *Dubliners* are still indebted to Joyce's remarks about paralysis, but he crucially posits that contemporary critics have generally neglected Joyce's earlier statement to Grant Richards: "I have taken the first steps toward the *spiritual* liberation of my country."[22] Noting that Joyce rejected not religion *per se*, but specifically the warped version of Irish Catholicism then dominant in Ireland, Dudley shows that the penultimate story in the collection, "Grace" (originally intended to be the last story), "imagines a kind of 'spiritual liberation,' suggested by the immanent type of grace in the Samaritan encounter between the cyclist and Mr. Kernan."[23] Dudley identifies four groups of religious figures in the story—Father Purdon, who gives the retreat sermon in the conclusion; the Dubliners Cunningham, M'Coy, Power, and Fogarty, who try to lead Kernan into conversion to the Catholic Church; Mrs. Kernan, a faithful Catholic woman; and the young cyclist who washes the blood from Kernan's face and administers brandy. He correctly argues that this fourth religious figure is generally ignored, especially by more contemporary critics such as Margot Norris in her 2003 study, *Suspicious Readings of Dubliners*; and yet the "young man in a cycling-suit" (*D* 151) is just one of several Good Samaritan figures who help Kernan, just as Stephen Dedalus is helped by multiple figures in "Circe."[24]

Joyce first links Bloom to Kernan in the sixth episode of *Ulysses*, "Hades," and he features them in conversation, showing them to have a certain kinship as marginalized figures in rescue stories past and present. Kernan speaks politely to Bloom after Mr. Dedalus breaks down weeping over the death of his wife, saying, "—Sad occasions" (*U* 6.654). We cannot tell if Kernan knows Bloom's own suffering from the past through the death of his father and son Rudy, but his willingness to reach out to Bloom after he has been largely ostracized by his fellow travelers in the funeral carriage (save for Mr. Cunningham) speaks volumes about his own hospitable intentions. Perhaps because he was rescued himself in "Grace," he realizes that Bloom needs some grace and affection, so he attempts to guide Bloom to practice the funeral rituals correctly: "—The others are putting on their hats, Mr Kernan said. I suppose we can do so too. We are the last. This cemetery is a treacherous place" (*U* 6.656–7). Kernan seems aware that hospitality can often be met with treachery, and he may sense that Bloom's hospitable gestures and conversations toward others in the funeral party have been largely rebuffed earlier. So he now rescues Bloom, offering him the sort of hospitable grace that he was offered in "Grace."

Fascinatingly, the narrator simply tells us in response to Kernan's advice to Bloom that they put on their hats—"They covered their heads"—seemingly suggesting that Bloom and Kernan are now both characterized by the sartorial grace of their silk hats (*U* 6.658). In "Grace," Kernan's silk hat, of course, represented his old conception of superficial grace, one that he lost at least temporarily in his drunken fall down the lavatory steps, whereupon he is offered a new grace of care by the young cyclist. But here, Kernan's care for Bloom transforms the symbol of the silk hat into a positive sign of their joint humanity and suffering, a grace he freely offers to Bloom even as he appears drunk once again. As Bloom "nodded gravely looking in the quick bloodshot eyes" (*U* 6.661), he wonders if Kernan is a fellow Mason: "Secret eyes, secretsearching. Mason, I think: not sure. Beside him again. We are the last. In the same boat. Hope he'll say something else" (*U* 6.661–3). Both men are the last mourners in the procession moving through Glasnevin Cemetery, but more than that is signified by Bloom's phrase, "In the same boat." He recognizes that the kindly Kernan also has his troubles—that he has fallen literally and figuratively and that both men are looked down upon by their fellow citizens.

In his ministrations to Bloom, the drunken Kernan thus briefly becomes a Samaritan figure of sorts by seeking him out, getting him to put on a newly re-envisioned symbol of hospitality, and trying to find common religious ground with him—this last by praising the "simpler, more impressive" service "of the [Anglican] Irish church used in Mount Jerome" (*U* 6.665–6). Kernan may know that Bloom was originally baptized Protestant, like himself, and Masonic associations aside, he may see Bloom as a fellow religious traveler. The narrator in "Grace" tells us that "Mr Kernan came of Protestant stock and, though he had been converted to the Catholic faith at the time of his marriage, he had not been in the pale of the Church for twenty years." And moreover, he "was fond" of "giving side-thrusts at Catholicism" (*D* 157). Since the Kernans at the time of "Grace" have been married for a "quarter of a century" (*D* 157), Kernan has likely not attended Mass regularly after the first five years of his marriage. Bloom, himself certainly no regular Mass attender, knows that the Mount Jerome cemetery was predominantly used for burying Protestants at the time and instantly understands Kernan's point, although he obviously does not see himself as Protestant. For instance, after marveling at how many funerals Glasnevin must see every day, he previously thought: "Then Mount Jerome for the protestants" (*U* 6.513–14).

When Kernan says with "solemnity" (*U* 6.669) to Bloom, drawing on the Church of Ireland service at Mt. Jerome, "—I am the resurrection and the life. That touches a man's inmost heart" (*U* 6.670), Bloom simply replies gratefully, "—It does" (*U* 6.671), but he ruminates hilariously in his mind immediately afterward about what happens to bodies in the ground, including Lazarus's, that have been resurrected (*U* 6.672–82). We should not lose sight, however, of what happens to Bloom as a result of his conversation with his Samaritan rescuer: He himself is resurrected temporarily, restored to his fun-loving self, inured for a time to the slings and arrows that Dublin's supposedly respectable citizens would volley at him. Kernan rescues Bloom's profound sense of self, founded on joy and imaginative observation. Thus, through associating Bloom with another figure who has been rescued by a Good Samaritan, who then "rescues" Bloom in turn during "Hades," Joyce prepares us for how Bloom will now, in turn, become transformed from the figure of the beaten traveler in the parable to the Samaritan helper of Stephen Dedalus in the last episodes of the novel by responding to Kernan's Samaritan model and through his own habitus of *caritas*.

Kernan remained on Joyce's mind and, much later in the novel, he strikingly rewrites the opening scene of "Grace" in his depiction of the attack on Stephen and its aftermath in "Circe." We know that Joyce wants us to be thoroughly familiar with his other work when we read *Ulysses*, since previously introduced characters like Kernan and Stephen Dedalus occur again in the novel. But it startles us—or it should—to realize just how closely these events in "Circe" correspond to the initial pages of "Grace," suggesting the continuing importance of the Good Samaritan parable for Joyce's fiction.

Kernan, a stranger of sorts in Dublin since he is a Protestant who married a Catholic, is portrayed at the beginning of "Grace" as "*curled* up at the foot of the stairs down which he had fallen" (*D* 150; my emphasis), with his hat nearby that "*had rolled a few yards away* and his clothes smeared with the filth and ooze of the floor on which he had lain" (*D* 150; my emphasis), and the relevant passage from "Circe" in which Stephen is assaulted by Private Carr reproduces crucial words and phrases from that story. Thus, Stephen, in the brothel, is portrayed in the act of being knocked down, but with strikingly similar language to describe his hat and his bodily posture: "*Stephen totters, collapses, falls, stunned. He lies prone, his face to the sky, **his hat rolling to the wall**. Bloom follows and picks it up*" (*U* 15.4748–50; my emphasis). Shortly thereafter, Stephen is described this way: "(He stretches out his arms, sighs again and *curls* his body. . .)" (*U* 15.4944; my emphasis). Stephen's hat rolls away and shortly thereafter, he curls up—two details that correspond almost exactly with the opening description of Kernan, the fallen Stranger, in "Grace."

Other details in this part of "Circe" correspond almost exactly to those in "Grace." For instance, just as multiple people help Kernan—two gentlemen, a curate, the manager, a constable, the cyclist, and finally Mr. Power—the First and Second Watch, Corny Kelleher, and Bloom help Stephen, although Bloom quickly becomes the main Good Samaritan figure at the end of "Cyclops," continuing into "Eumaeus" and "Ithaca." Bloom whispers quietly to Kelleher, "Simon Dedalus's son. A bit sprung. Get those policemen to move those loafers back" (*U* 15.4808–9), a passage recalling how the injured Kernan is surrounded by a "ring of men" and a "crowd which had followed him [the constable] down the laneway" that "collected outside the door, struggling to look in through the glass panels" (*D* 150, 151). The First Watch in "Circe" asks very similar questions to those posed by the constable in "Grace," who asks "Who is the man? What's his name and address?" (*D* 151). The First Watch, just like the constable, who "produced a small book from his waist" (*D* 150), "takes out his notebook" and asks, "What's his name?", followed by "Name and address" (*U* 15.4799, 4803). The young man in the cycling suit—an early anticipation of Bloom as Good Samaritan—quickly kneels down to help Kernan and thus gets the constable to help and stop asking questions. Bloom, recognizing that Kelleher knows the Second Watch, and that Kelleher has greater social status than him and is more respectable, gets Kelleher to intervene with these two figures of authority, with the result that Kelleher persuades them to not report the incident (*U* 15.4821–30). Kelleher tells them he has a car nearby (*U* 15.4832) and Bloom shakes hands with the policemen and asks them not to publicize the incident, saying "We don't want any scandal, you understand. Father is a wellknown highly respected citizen. Just a little wild oats, you understand" (*U* 15.4839–41). Even though Kelleher asks, "Will I give him a lift home?," and bends over Stephen to ascertain that he is not hurt or robbed, finally proclaiming, "Ah, well, he'll get over it. No bones broken" (*U* 15.4883, 4890–2, 4896), Bloom is already holding his money and hat and stick (*U* 15.4894) and assumes responsibility for the injured Stephen. Kelleher speaks the same phrase as Power does in "Grace" when he takes "his friend by the arm," "No bones broken," adding "What? Can you walk?" (*D* 152). While the cyclist in "Grace" takes "the man by the other arm" (*D* 152) but does not travel along with the injured Kernan and Mr. Power in the car (*D* 153), Kelleher leaves Stephen to Bloom, who starts caring for him at the end of "Circe" and into "Eumaeus," the episode which begins with his redressing Stephen by giving him his hat and ashplant and bucking him up "in orthodox Samaritan fashion."

Notice that, in both of the crucial scenes from "Grace" and "Circe," the rescue of the victim is performed in an atmosphere of squalor and filth, suggesting that Joyce believed that grace could arrive anywhere, at any time, outside the bounds of the Church, carried out by completely ordinary humans who appear out of the blue. Contrast the site of Kernan's rescue, the "filth and ooze" of the pub's lavatory floor, with the respectable Jesuit church in Gardiner Street where Kernan attends a spiritual retreat for his supposed encounter with grace. Unlike the beer-swilling patrons and cyclist who help Kernan up from the filthy floor, Kernan's friends, who are trying to "help" him into grace, are portrayed as clean and proper, and so are their surroundings: The gentlemen at the Jesuit church are "well dressed and orderly," wearing "black clothes and white collars, relieved here and there by tweeds, on dark mottled pillars of green marble and on lugubrious canvasses" (*D* 172). When the congregation kneel, they "produced handkerchiefs and knelt upon them with care" (*D* 173). But Father Purdon, whose name recalls Purdon Street in the former Nighttown district portrayed in "Circe," spectacularly fails to deliver a homily that offers grace as a gift as the young cyclist did to Kernan. One indication of Kernan's refusal to fully enter into or assent to these falsely spiritual proceedings is the way he holds onto the emblem of his sartorial grace, his silk hat: "he held the brim of his hat lightly, but firmly, with the other hand" (*D* 173). When he actually receives the unexpected grace from the cyclist, his hat is "dinged" and "battered" (*D* 151, 152), implying that he has at least temporarily been stripped of his sartorial grace and splendor and yet has received something much more lasting—the unasked-for gift of another's help in a time of crisis.

Perhaps already anticipating that he would develop this motif from "Grace" more fully in "Circe," Joyce recycles his language from the short story in "Hades," reversing the order of Kernan's hat holding and kneeling in his depiction of Bloom at Dignam's funeral:

> The mourners knelt here and there in prayingdesks. Mr Bloom stood behind near the font and, when all had knelt, dropped carefully his unfolded newspaper from his pocket and knelt his right knee upon it. He fitted his black hat gently on his left knee and, holding its brim, bent over piously. (*U* 6.584–8)

Both of these outsider figures, who have been baptized Protestant, then received into the Catholic Church, want to hold onto the trappings of their finery as they watch the insider Catholics kneel and pray. And in the conclusion of "Hades," Joyce shows Bloom "rescuing" John Henry Menton from going about with a "dinge" in his silk hat (6.1015–26), a similar passage to the one about Kernan's hat that is "dinged."

Purdon's sermon in "Grace," couched as it is to an audience mostly of businessmen, lingers uncomfortably on grace as a type of business transaction conducted at least partly by our agency. This, despite his focus on the parable of the unjust steward in Luke 16:8–9: "*For the children of this world are wiser in their generation than the children of the light. Wherefore make unto yourselves friends out of the mammon of iniquity so that when you die they may receive you into everlasting dwellings*" (D 173). Completely ignoring the context of the parable, wherein Christ goes on to admonish his listeners in Luke 17:13, "Ye cannot serve both God and Mammon" (KJV), Purdon instead argues that this parable is "a text for business men and professional men." Christ knows we are "forced to live in the world and, to a certain extent, for the world," and thus, he claims, "He designed to give them a word of counsel, setting before them as exemplars in the religious life those very worshippers of Mammon who were of all men the least solicitous in matters religious" (D 174). Yet Christ does nothing of the sort and actually condemns worshippers of Mammon in successive verses.

While the manager praises the dishonest steward, Christ pointedly says, in his condemnation of the steward and His application of this condemnation to any who are unfaithful in matters of money,

> He that is faithful in that which is least is faithful also in much: and he that is unjust in the least is unjust also in much. If therefore ye have not been faithful in the unrighteous mammon, who will commit to your trust the true riches? And if ye have not been faithful in that which is another man's, who shall give you that which is your own? (Luke 17:10–12, KJV)

Purdon then focuses on his own claim to be the assembled congregants' "spiritual accountant," who understands their temptations, but who then urges them to confess their sins, and "with God's grace, I will rectify this and this. I will set right my accounts" (D 174). But the "true riches" Christ mentions above are the kingdom of heaven, which is freely offered to us, not earned by us.

Joyce consistently rejects this transactional, financial view of grace; recall, for instance, the scene at the opening of chapter 4 in *Portrait*, where the narrator snidely images Stephen as adding up his many acts of self-denial and devotion so that "he seemed to feel his soul in devotion pressing like fingers the keyboard of a great cash register and to see the amount of his purchase start forth immediately in heaven not as a number but as a frail column of incense or as a slender flower" (*P* 148). As Dudley puts it, in Joyce's original conception of concluding *Dubliners* with this story, the volume would open with the simoniac, failed priest of "The Sisters" and would fittingly finish "with a priest prostituting the title of its last story, "Grace," in exchange for monetary and social capital. This would be paralysis to be sure, and spiritual paralysis specifically."[25] Kernan has actually already received grace in the first few pages of the story—crucially outside the bounds of the Irish Catholic Church—and the rest of the story illustrates Joyce's critique of the materialist, transactional grace offered by the Church.[26]

The site of Nighttown in "Circe" echoes the squalor of the lavatory floor upon which Mr. Kernan falls in "Grace": "Rows of grimy houses with gaping doors. Rare lamps with faint rainbow fans. Round Rabaiotti's halted ice gondola stunted men and women squabble" (*U* 15.3–5). The area is filthy, with a "gnome totting among a rubbishtip" who "crouches to shoulder a sack of rags and bones," while "A crone standing by with a smoky oillamp rams her last bottle in the maw of his sack" (*U* 15.28–31). Drunks, prostitutes, police, johns, even children wander through this hellscape.

Whereas "Grace" offers the unexpected grace of a rescue narrative in the midst of filth and critiques the Catholic Church's transactional notion of grace, "Circe" opens with the thoroughly transactional setting of Nighttown wherein no one offers anyone else grace—only what can be cadged, collected, or purchased—and ends with a rescue story. It is clearly a site where Mammon reigns. Notice how both the story and this episode feature as their ostensible climax a Lukan parable—the former, as told and (mis)interpreted by Father Purdon, the latter, as re-enacted by Leopold Bloom and Stephen Dedalus. Contrasting Purdon's misreading of the preached parable of the wise steward in the conclusion of the story and the misleading dialogues featured by the Freudian narrator in the "Circe" episode with both the cyclist's rescue of Kernan in the story's beginning and Bloom's instinctual acting out of the Good Samaritan parable suggests how Joyce privileges in each case the bodily actions of the rescuer over against mere monologue or dialogue that can obfuscate and occlude grace in action.

Grace erupts late in this excessively long episode—and we have to strain and peer fitfully through the haze of narrative obfuscation to see it in action—a simple advertising canvasser who has been vilified all day long rescues a stuck-up, would-be artist who has come to couple with a prostitute named Georgina Johnson (*U* 15.122), upon whom he has previously spent the pound A.E. loaned him (*U* 9.195–6). Joyce reverses the narrative trajectory of "Grace" in "Circe," delaying his restaging of that rescue story until very late in the episode, offering grace in the most unexpected moment possible through an eruption of charity from the "dark" and maligned stranger Bloom.

No one until now has suggested just how thoroughly Joyce borrowed from and rewrote the opening scene of "Grace" in the context of the Good Samaritan parable in these crucial passages from "Circe." Kernan, the first instance of Joyce's stranger from the parable, as Dudley argues, allowed Joyce a trial run at depicting the grace and charity offered by Samaritan figures such as Kelleher. Even more intriguingly, Bloom knows Kernan, the rescued Stranger from "Grace," and he thinks of the tea taster in the "Lestrygonians" episode when he sees Bolton's Westmoreland house, "Tea. Tea. Tea. I forgot to tap Tom Kernan" (U 8.371–2). Even though he sees Kernan here as a potential advertiser he can touch for a possible advertisement, Bloom may well know the story of Kernan's rescue by his Good Samaritans and, at the least, that knowledge could form part of his narrative substrate, along with the parable itself that might condition him to help others. As we have seen earlier in this chapter, Bloom's encounter with Kernan in the "Hades" episode knits them together in their status as outsiders, and Kernan's kind treatment of Bloom in the cemetery restores him to a proper sense of his good-humored self, one that was in danger of ebbing away after the way he has been treated by most of the men in the funeral carriage.

Joyce's interest in and knowledge of the Lukan narrative clearly antedated *Ulysses* and continued after its publication. In "Grace," for instance, he signals his distaste for the priest's sermon, from Luke 16:8–9, the second verse of which states, "Wherefore make unto yourselves friends out of the mammon of iniquity so that when you die they may receive you into everlasting dwellings" (*D* 173), by having him purposely omit the following verse 13: "You cannot serve both God and money" (ESV), a clear rejection of the pursuit of worldly wealth. Moreover, Hugh Kenner suggests that Joyce got some of his plots for *Dubliners* from the Gospels, which were read in Catholic churches every Sunday. He particularly mentions the story that follows the Good Samaritan parable: the story of Mary, who listened to Jesus, and Martha, who bustled around the house while He taught. Kenner cleverly points out how Joyce invokes the roles of the sisters in the Lukan narrative only to invert our expectations of them; he therefore likens the industrious and thus exhausted sister Nannie in "The Sisters" to the listening Mary, and the other, chatty sister Eliza, to the busy Martha.[27] Clearly, Joyce knew this passage well, since Bloom imagines himself as Christ talking to Mary and Martha in the "Lotus Eaters" episode (*U* 5.289–99). Joyce's fascination with Luke never waned: Roy Benjamin has argued for Joyce's privileging of the Gospel of Luke in *Finnegans Wake*, in part because of that writer's skill as a storyteller and "as an arranger of other accounts."[28] Joyce certainly was familiar with Henry Cadbury's *The Making of Luke–Acts*, a landmark and still-cited study of that Gospel published in 1927, which stresses Luke's tendency to disseminate news about Christ over against Mark's penchant for concealment and secrecy.[29]

Joyce must have been pleased to discover not only the suitability of the particularities of the Good Samaritan plot for *Ulysses* but also Luke's literary nature and his narrative gifts, including his embrace of realism. John Drury points out that "[n]either Mark nor Matthew, the previous narrators whose work he builds into his own, enjoyed such calm literary self-confidence and self-consciousness. It is something new." That confidence, reflected in what Drury terms the "magisterial shaping and pacing of the prologue [that] vindicate Luke's claim at 1:3 to be a storyteller perfectly in charge of his matter," would surely have appealed to the famously confident Joyce.[30] Moreover, Luke's ability to write in a variety of forms and styles in both his Gospel and Acts anticipates Joyce's own protean styles beginning in episode 7, "Aeolus." In this regard, Drury notes, "Luke can change styles as time and place demand. In Acts, for example, he manages the official letter, the sermon, and the adventure story."[31] Moreover, other Lukan qualities on display in the parables that were so important to Joyce—distinct from those literary qualities in the Gospels written by Matthew, Mark, and John—seem surprisingly modern, even Joycean, we might say. These include the Lukan parables' "realism, humanism, and more optimistic view of history."[32] Luke "learned his narrative craft, not from apocalyptic seers . . . but from the older [Jewish] realistic historians who rejoiced in the ambiguities of human nature, writ so large in David and Joseph, as the very material with which divine providence worked, rather than as something regrettable awaiting its Doomsday correction."[33] While Joyce was certainly drawn to John's apocalyptic narrative in Revelation, as we have seen, Luke's realism confirmed in him the necessity of grounding his epic in the minutiae of everyday life, as did Luke's much larger vocabulary than that known by the other evangelists with which he expressed that realism.[34]

Luke's ability to write long narrative stretches in the parables must have also appealed to Joyce as he moved into the novel form with *A Portrait of the Artist as a Young Man* and especially *Ulysses* and *Finnegans Wake*. Frank Kermode has held that the relative length of parables like the Good Samaritan and the Prodigal Son suggest "they are about to merge into long narratives, which may also retain some of the qualities of parable."[35] Luke's skill as storyteller surpasses that of the other Gospel writers, and his penchant for developing an epic story about Christ patiently and slowly must have appealed to Joyce as he wrote his meandering epic about the wandering Jew Leopold Bloom. Richard B. Hays points out the epic qualities epitomized by Luke's narration:

> The mode of his narration is not so didactic as Matthew's; nor is it, like Mark's, mysterious and elusive. Instead, the story that he tells has the character of a *dramatic epic*; it is sweeping in scope and measured in pace. . . . Luke takes his time in allowing the plot to unfold on a grand scale. The tone of the narrative is gracious, patient, and confident,

inviting readers to settle back and savor its development, as many different lines and images converge slowly into a complex unity. We might put it this way: Luke's narrative is *symphonic*.[36]

Joyce's long-standing interest in drama, going back to Ibsen, and also in both the epic and music would have found confirmation on Luke's large canvas. And Lukan parables in particular, as Drury puts it, merge the commonplace with the mythical, another model for Joyce's achievement in *Ulysses*. For Drury, the achievement of Luke's parables "may be ranged with what Mozart did for opera with *The Marriage of Figaro*: a grand and basically mythical genre has been transposed into the complexities of the commonplace."[37]

As Joyce with his deep knowledge of Scripture would have known, the Good Samaritan parable appears only in the Gospel of Luke, "who is generally thought of as the most literary as well as the most genial and bourgeois of the evangelists."[38] Joyce's interest in Luke was profound and ongoing, and he likely grasped that "[o]f all the Evangelists, Luke is the most intentional, and the most skillful, in narrating the story of Jesus in a way that joins it seamlessly to Israel's story" since he "highlights God's purpose in fulfilling the promise of redemption for his people Israel."[39] When he turned to the New Testament parable of the Good Samaritan as narrated in Luke as both inspiration for the novel and as plot for many events in its last four episodes, Joyce understood Luke's promises of Christ as the fulfillment of the Old Testament prophecies and used that pattern to undergird his own pattern of Leopold Bloom as fulfilling the charitable activities he has engaged in earlier in the novel by not only becoming a Good Samaritan figure but also the beaten Stranger of the parable. Hays has shown Luke's remarkable repetition of words denoting "fill" and "bring to fullness/fulfillment" throughout his first four chapters, where they "appear no fewer than fifteen times."[40] Bloom's fulfillment as a figure of charity, anticipated by his treatment of the blind stripling, for instance, earlier in the novel, becomes evident once he pursues Stephen in "Oxen of the Sun" at the maternity hospital, at the pub, following him to Westland Row station, then into Nighttown in the next episode, "Circe," as he rescues him in that episode's conclusion, and through his care for Stephen at the cabman's shelter in "Eumaeus" and at his own home in "Ithaca."

Fascinatingly, one of the final passages in the first section of the novel features Stephen, who has "fallen" as an artist with his failed Paris sojourn, invoking a passage describing Satan's fall from heaven as recounted by Christ in Luke, chapter 10, shortly before Christ relates the parable of the Good Samaritan. After the Samaritan village rejects Jesus in Luke, chapter 9, Christ sends out 72 additional followers in advance of His own coming to proclaim the imminence of the kingdom of God. When they return, noting, "Lord, even the demons are subject to us in your name," (Luke 10:17), Christ instantly replies, "I saw Satan fall like lightning from heaven" (Luke 10:18 ESV), affirming their claim. Stephen, who has previously invoked both Lucifer and Dedalus as models, "Old father, old artificer, stand me now and ever in good stead," at the end of *Portrait*,[41] now sees himself as having fallen at the end of "Proteus." He acknowledges his fallen state by referencing both Luke 10:18: "Allbright he falls, proud lightning of the intellect. . ." (*U* 3.486), and Isaiah 14:12: "How art though fallen from heaven, O Lucifer, son of the morning?" (KJV). Clearly, Stephen knows Luke's Gospel well enough to reference it here— not to indicate the demons and Satan's subservience to Christ, but instead to suggest his artistic failure, his fall. Immediately after this Lukan invocation, Stephen thinks, "*Lucifer, dico, qui nescit occasum*" (*U* 3.486-7), which can be translated as "Lucifer, I say, who does not know a fall," or "The morning star, I say, which does not know a setting," a Latin phrase that comes from the Exsultet, St. Ambrose's Holy Saturday prayer, when the deacon admires the flame of the paschal candle, stating, "*Flammas eius lucifer matutinus inveniat, Ille, inquam, lucifer qui nescit occasum,*" translated as "May the morning star find its flame."[42]

Putting the Lukan passage next to the Ambrosian prayer as Joyce has Stephen do suggests that he is torn between admitting something like his overweening Luciferian pride and his eventual fall in Paris in not becoming an artist, and a potentially new Luciferian vow to "find" his flame or passion. The answer to this dilemma comes immediately after these invocations of Lucifer: "No. My cockle hat and staff and hismy sandal shoon. Where? To evening lands. Evening will find itself" (*U* 3.487-8). Stephen now seems to vow to become a pilgrim, looking for either a new basis for his art or a new vocation entirely. In contextualizing this passage in terms of the overarching Good Samaritan parabolic arc of the novel, Joyce employs a passage only seven verses before the start of the parable in Luke 10 to suggest that he is casting Stephen as a type of the traveler from the parable, attacked while on the road from his home. As if to affirm his rejection of a Luciferian identity, Joyce has Stephen think, just a few lines from the conclusion of "Proteus," after he lays a bit of dried snot on a rock, "Behind. Perhaps there is someone" (*U* 3.502). This passage certainly could suggest that Stephen is seeking an audience for this pitiful production of his "art," but it also clearly alludes to a passage from *Portrait* where Cranly recoils from Stephen's avowed Luciferian posture of "*non serviam.*"[43] Now, however, Stephen seems to perceive himself as trying to get away from Lucifer's influence upon him.

After having Stephen meditate on this passage from Luke 10:18 to conclude the first three episodes of the novel, the "Telemachiad," Joyce then references Luke 10:25-37 to open the last three sections, "Nostos," of *Ulysses* in the first sentence of "Eumaeus." He thus places Stephen's fall, mediated by the Lukan passage in the conclusion of "Proteus," in dialogue with his being picked up, rescued, by Leopold Bloom, in the context of another Lukan passage, the Good Samaritan parable, to open "Eumaeus." Joyce therefore suggests the importance of reading Stephen's artistic failure, his fall, through a rejection of Luciferian pride, in conjunction with his rise through his personal rescue by the humble Leopold Bloom in the guise of the Good Samaritan—through two crucial passages from chapter 10 of Luke's Gospel that conclude and begin the first three episodes and last three episodes of the novel, respectively.

Very few critics have dwelt on the implications of the Good Samaritan parable for the novel—if they have noticed its intertextual presence at all—but one who does so, Denis Donoghue, articulates conclusions that are finally disappointing. Donoghue references the supposedly factual precipitating incident for the novel early in his meditation, as we have seen; he then further observes, "Homer's Odysseus was commonly thought of as a man of the world, a voyager, 'the interminable adventurer,' as Wallace Stevens calls him in 'The World as Meditation.' He was also admired as a man of parts, endlessly resourceful. But he was rarely identified with the Good Samaritan." Then, he helpfully remarks,

> Several years later and long after the publication of *Dubliners* [for which Joyce had planned to include a fictionalized version of this "incident" as "Ulysses"], the unwritten story became chapter 16 ("Eumaeus") of a long novel, *Ulysses*. In that chapter Leopold Bloom rescues Stephen Dedalus "in orthodox Samaritan fashion" from a bad night on the town and brings him to the cabman's shelter under the Loop Line Bridge, near Butt Bridge and the Custom House.[44]

But strangely, Donoghue nowhere pursues further the importance of this crucial parable in his fascinating reading of the novel, and puzzlingly, he gradually backs away from his opening declaration of interest in reading the novel parabolically, simply stating this in conclusion:

> Paddy Dignam dies, and Molly Bloom copulates with Blazes Boylan: these events are not to be thought away. But the reality of Dublin for the most part seems to consist of talk, rumination, old songs, the drift of associations idly held in someone's mind. The chapters are replete, but indiscriminate, as if Joyce saw no good reason for preferring one motif to another, one style to another. Whatever comes into Bloom's mind has as much right to be there as anything else: no consideration of relevance is allowed to assert itself.[45]

One might logically ask: "What about Bloom's rescue of Stephen?", identified by Donoghue as an important part of the novel in his opening paragraph—not to mention the parable's inspiration for the novel. All he says later about this crucial aspect of the narrative arc is, blandly, "In certain chapters a recollection of the Prodigal Son or the Good Samaritan is more helpful. But Joyce instructed his first readers to think of Homer."[46] And what about the anti-Semitic treatment of Bloom and his largely pacifist rejection of that treatment? These are all huge subjects for the novel, clearly encompassed by Joyce's retelling of the Good Samaritan parable, which, while recognized early on, is obscured by Donoghue's downbeat, relativistic, even banal and trivial conclusion.

To return to the specific consideration of the role of parable in the novel, certainly it is unhelpful to read episodes such as "Aeolus" or, say, "Scylla and Charybdis" as being solely and specifically structured by the events of the Prodigal Son or Good Samaritan parables, and I certainly will not make that claim here. But Donoghue restricts the Good Samaritan parable's presence only to "Eumaeus," relegating it to the role of what we might term a "micro-narrative," while in fact it is a major macro-narrative for the novel, one that does not compete with the Odyssean parallels, but rather complements and heightens them as Joyce makes his modern-day Ulysses more complex.

Donoghue is surely right to claim that Odysseus is rarely identified with the Good Samaritan—and the bellicose attitude of Odysseus/Ulysses is far from the pacifist attitude of Leopold Bloom[47]—yet Homer's hero is certainly a rescuer in multiple ways, as is Joyce's Bloom. Odysseus saves his men, for example, from the Cyclops and from Circe; moreover, he saves men's lives in Menelaus's story of Odysseus at Troy when he holds them back in the wooden horse when Helen calls them by name to come out as she imitates their wives' voices; and he finally saves Penelope from the depredations, threatened and real, of her suitors. In *Ulysses*, there are still many traces of the Odyssean intertext—the lack of recognition between "father" and "son" just as in Homer, for instance—but the Lukan parable becomes a major, complementary intertext. Bloom is not somehow restored to his former youthful vigor, as Odysseus is when Athena "stroked him with her golden wand," making "the cloak and shirt on his body / fresh and clean," and further, rendering him "taller, supple, young":[48] he simply wears his daylong outfit of ordinary clothes and helps the disheveled Stephen up, then takes him to the cabman's shelter for food and then to his house for lodging. Were Bloom to be made godlike in true Odyssean fashion, such a transformation would not only play into the Circean narrator's mischaracterization of Bloom as a sort of triumphant Christ figure, but it would also capsize Joyce's portrayal of his protagonist as an ordinary man with quotidian desires who nonetheless makes an extraordinary series of hospitable acts toward Stephen Dedalus—and others in the novel throughout the day and into the night and early morning.

Although Brandon Kershner has claimed that "the Homeric parallel" was "nothing but a temporary scaffolding that helped Joyce in his composition while being of little significance to the reader," such a blanket statement does not attend to Joyce's deep interest in Homer and the way in which Homeric concepts can enrich our reading of the novel, including his interest in hospitality or *xenia*, which I discussed in the introduction. A number of Joyce critics have read his appropriations of Homer profitably, including Richard Ellmann in *The Consciousness of Joyce*, Hugh Kenner in *Ulysses*, and, more recently, Leah Flack, in significant chapters from her *Modernism and Homer: The Odysseys of H.D., James Joyce, Osip Mandelstam, and Ezra Pound* and her *James Joyce and Classical Modernism*, along with David Weir in his *Ulysses Explained: How Homer, Dante, and Shakespeare Inform Joyce's Modernist Vision*.[49]

While the putative proprietor of the cabman's shelter, James Fitzharris (AKA "Skin-the-Goat"), represents Homer's loyal swineherd Eumaeus, Joyce changed much else from Book XVI of the *Odyssey*, including, for example, splitting the role of Odysseus between Bloom and the sailor Murphy, likely because Homer's Odysseus was "simultaneously a great strategist and a master storyteller—a liar, even."[50] More important for his parabolic purposes, Joyce also reversed the burden of responsibility put on Telemachus to show hospitality to the stranger, whom Telemachus does not yet know is his father. For instance, when the loyal swineherd Eumaeus asks Telemachus early in that book to care for the stranger, saying, "I'll put him in *your* hands, / You tend to him as you like. / He counts on you, he says, for care and shelter," Telemachus rejects the chance to offer hospitality, asking, "How can I lend the stranger refuge in my house? / I'm young myself. I can hardly trust my hands / to fight off any man who rises up against me."[51] Instead, in Joyce's "Eumaeus," Bloom, the father figure/Odysseus, cares for Stephen, the son/Telemachus. And while Homer's Eumaeus cooks food for Telemachus and Odysseus in the opening scene, and Telemachus and Odysseus reunite at the end of the book over a huge meal,[52] Bloom merely offers Stephen coffee and a roll at the cabman's shelter, both of which the young man turns down.

If the *Odyssey* can be thought of as a study of the pagan concept of *xenia*, or hospitality—despite Odysseus's killing of Penelope's suitors and their women, for instance, in Book XXII, a slaughter that revolted Joyce and which he refused to have Bloom conduct—then *Ulysses* is a study of the Christian concept of hospitality, particularly through the parabolic arc of the Good Samaritan story.[53] In this reading, Stephen Dedalus is the exilic, Samaritan traveler (often identified as "Greek" and outside the Irish tribe) returned to Dublin to be assailed by the verbal volleys of Buck Mulligan, Mr. Deasy, et al. on his daylong journey through woundedness and questioning of his artistic vocation. In turn, Bloom is *both* the wounded stranger, assailed vicariously by Deasy, the representative of Protestantism, and by Stephen's father and other Catholics, including the Cyclops, along with Blazes Boylan, *and* the secular Jewish rescuer, who prepares himself all day to help Stephen in chapters 15–18. And yet we as readers are finally are pressed into service, as it were, when Stephen responds stingily and unhelpfully in "Eumaeus" to Bloom, although he does act as a Good Samaritan to Corley. We "rescue" Bloom through our responsiveness to his re-enactment of the Good Samaritan parable.

The usual way critics read parables in *Ulysses*, if they do so at all, is through the "Parable of the Plums" that Stephen iterates toward the end of "Aelous," but this is at best a spontaneous, even throwaway (with a nod to that ongoing pun in the novel) artistic creation of Stephen's that in no way works as an effective hermeneutical means of reading the novel parabolically. Much more helpful for understanding *Ulysses* would be to trace the parabolic function of the Prodigal Son narrative, which finds its fulfillment in the meeting of Telemachus/Stephen/son with Ulysses/Bloom/father and is introduced early in "Telemachus" with Buck's telling Stephen, "And to think of your having to beg from these swine" (*U* 1.160). It continues in "Circe," with Stephen thinking, "Filling my belly with husks of swine . . . I will arise and go to my" (*U* 15.2495–6). This parabolic reading, also drawing on Luke's Gospel, chapter 15, is promising and deserves further development by Joyce critics.[54] Joyce remained interested in parables, even writing some for *Finnegans Wake*, including the parable of "The Mookse and the Gripes" (*FW* 152–9) and "The Ondt and the Gracehoper" (*FW* 414–19).[55]

A proper understanding of the significance of this passage that opens "Eumaeus," moreover, is crucial to apprehending an important narrative arc that shows Bloom to be a good Samaritan more generally, and attending to that trajectory suggests how Joyce's casting of Bloom and Stephen acting out this parable at the end of "Circe" and directly referencing it at the beginning of "Eumaeus" heightens our sense of Bloom's charity toward others. These last two episodes before Bloom brings Stephen home prominently feature the Samaritan narrative, deployed by Joyce to suggest how pre-existing narratives can color and impinge upon our actions in the present, and enable us to retrospectively perceive Bloom's warmth and charitable attitude toward Stephen earlier in the day, when he sees him while traveling to Paddy Dignam's funeral (*U* 6.39–40). The underlying, loving action of Bloom's rescue of Stephen after the Circean narrator has distorted his character and his continuing attention to Stephen in the face of the clearly anti-Semitic ballad he sings in "Ithaca" suggest just how committed he is to his mercy ministry, despite being attacked verbally periodically throughout the day.

Notes

1. Kiberd, Ulysses *and Us*, 301.
2. Ibid., 296.
3. Neuman, *Fiction beyond Secularism*, 183. For more on the persistent tendency of critics to view the novel as secular, see Jerilyn Sambrooke's analysis of this bias in her "Secularism, Religion, and the 20th/21st Century Novel," 3–6. She is

particularly helpful in showing how Pericles Lewis's groundbreaking study, *Religious Experience and the Modern Novel*, privileges the "persistence of the 'sacred' in the modernist moment," and thus actually retains "the framework of the secularization thesis—even as he resituates modern writers in relation to it," limiting "the kinds of questions he asks" (6).
4. Kiberd, *Ulysses and Us*, 161.
5. Gottfried, *Joyce's Misbelief*, 61.
6. Alter, *The Art of Biblical Narrative*, 28.
7. Via, Jr., *The Parables*, 96, qtd. in Hedrick, *Many Things in Parables*, 77.
8. Both Hedrick, *Many Things in Parables*, 77–83, and Colón, *Victorian Parables*, 9–10, laud Via's study as the major turning point in the interpretive history of parables. Colón notes that "Though he has been fairly criticized for neglecting the parables' historical context altogether, Via's major contribution . . . was to insist on the parables being both aesthetic productions (against biblical scholars of his day who viewed the parables as material from which a 'point' must be extracted) and as having an existential-theological dimension. . . . Right reading of the parables, Via suggested, requires keeping alive the tension between their literary and theological dimensions" (10). For an excellent overview of how parables have been read by both theological and literary scholars starting with Augustine, see Colon, *Victorian Parables*, 7–21. For a helpful brief theological summary of parables, see Hedrick, *Many Things in Parables*, xiv–xv.
9. Turner, *The Literary Mind*, 5.
10. Ibid., 7.
11. Stanislaus Joyce, *My Brother's Keeper*, 109. Careful readers of Joyce will recall that "simony" appears in the first story of *Dubliners*, "The Sisters," which captures the sense of the ecclesiastical failure of the sisters' brother, who is a priest.
12. Ibid., 108. An examination of Stephen Dedalus's contemplation of a priestly calling in chapter 3 of *A Portrait* clearly suggests that Joyce portrayed that calling as a simoniacal temptation and thus has Stephen reject it. The passage in question occurs when Stephen "listened in reverent silence now to the priest's appeal and through the words he heard even more distinctly a voice bidding him approach, offering him secret knowledge and secret power. He would know then what was the sin of Simon Magus. . ." (*P* 159).
13. See Joyce, "Ibsen's New Drama," where he argues about Ibsen's vision that "He sees it steadily and whole, as from a great height, with perfect vision and an angelic dispassionateness, with the sight of one who may look on the sun with open eyes" (65).
14. Otis, "Reading Notebook: James Joyce."
15. Ricoeur, "The 'Sacred' Text and the Community," 72.
16. Shashaty, "Reading *Dubliners* Parabolically," 213.
17. Joyce, *Collected Letters* II, 140.
18. Shashaty, "Reading *Dubliners* Parabolically," 217.
19. Ricoeur, "Manifestation and Proclamation," 57.
20. Ibid., 60.
21. Others have made this point, but Katherine Mullin's *James Joyce, Sexuality, and Social Purity*, 56–82, remains the fullest exploration of the historical situation of "white slavery" that Eveline likely dodges.

22. Dudley, "From 'Spiritual Paralysis' to 'Spiritual Liberation,'" 176, citing Joyce's May 20, 1906 letter to Richards from Trieste in *Letters*, I, 62–3; emphasis Dudley's.
23. Ibid., 177.
24. Ibid., 183. Dudley notes that both Marvin Magalaner in *Time of Apprenticeship: The Fiction of Young James Joyce*, and C. H. Peake, *James Joyce: The Citizen and the Artist*, passingly link the cyclist's action to the Good Samaritan parable. He also cites Norris's statement that "It is, of course, tempting to read the anonymous young man in the cycling-suit as an introduction of the parable of the Good Samaritan—a dispenser of gratuitous assistance or grace—into this parabolic story," which she then troublingly and quickly rejects (Norris, *Suspicious Readings of Dubliners*, 252 n2), not realizing that her focus on the cyclist as a symbol of liberty should be grounded in a realization of the Good Samaritan as a traveler. Joyce approves of the young man's mobility in the context of the paralysis of many other Dubliners, and moreover, he uses this character to signify "spiritual liberation, the marker of an immanent grace that returns theology to the biblical conceptions of community and *caritas*" (Dudley, "From 'Spiritual Paralysis' to 'Spiritual Liberation,'" 184).
25. Ibid., 183.
26. My graduate student Kelly Chittenden has argued in a seminar paper for the complete reversal of the roles of the major figures of the Good Samaritan parable in "Grace," further showing Joyce's parodic intent to take the measure of what he saw as a Church dedicated to keeping concepts of grace within its walls. For instance, Chittenden points out that rather than the priest, Levite, then Samaritan appearing in "Grace," as in the parable, instead the young cyclist as Samaritan appears, followed by the Levitical friends of Kernan who urge Catholicism on him, then finally Father Purdon, who like the priest in the parable who bypasses the beaten traveler, offers no healing ("Parables and Reading Joyce's *Dubliners*").
27. Kenner, "Signs on a White Field," 209–10.
28. Benjamin, "The Third Gospel in *Finnegans Wake*," 102.
29. Ibid., 110.
30. Drury, "Luke," 418, 419.
31. Ibid., 420.
32. Ibid., 432.
33. Ibid., 433.
34. Drury shows that Luke's Good Samaritan parable "is full of visual detail: stripped, wounded, half dead, oil, wine, beast, inn, two pence. The circumstances of the Prodigal Son, both in want and restored to comfort, are similarly vivid. As a result, of the four evangelists Luke has the largest number of words which appear only once in the Gospels. The other evangelists inhabit much less richly stocked worlds" (ibid., 436). Earlier, Drury states fulsomely, "Luke's great parable section has a character quite different from the equivalents of his precursors. It is as full of domestic detail as a Dutch painting, [and] draws its characters with a subtlety rivaled only by John" (434).
35. Kermode, *The Genesis of Secrecy*, 25.
36. Hays, *Echoes of Scripture in the Gospels*, 275.
37. Drury, "Luke," 434.

38. Alter, *The Art of Biblical Narrative*, 34.
39. Hays, *Echoes of Scripture*, 191.
40. Ibid., 192.
41. See *Portrait*, the diary entry from April 27 and the last passage in the entire novel (P 253). Stephen seems to consciously evoke Lucifer as his figurative father and simultaneously also unconsciously casts himself as the fated Icarus when he avers, "Old father, old artificer," not realizing he is projecting his future trajectory as fated.
42. Slote, Mamigonian, and Turner, "Notes," 579.
43. The phrase or variations on it comes up three times in that novel. First, Stephen and his classmates hear the preacher on the retreat sermon in chapter 3 speak on Lucifer's fall, including the "sin of pride, the sinful thought conceived in an instant: *'non serviam': I will not serve"* (P 117). Then, in chapter 5, Stephen avows the English translation of this Latin phrase to Cranly, "I will not serve," then responds to Cranly's observation, "—That remark was made before," musing, "—It is made behind now. . ." (P 239), figuring himself as Lucifer and Cranly as Christ by referencing the beginning of the passage from Matthew 16:23 (KJV): "Get thee behind me, Satan." And one more time, late in this conversation with Cranly, Stephen states clearly, "*I will not serve* that in which I no longer believe whether it call itself my home, my fatherland or my church. . ." (P 246–7; my emphasis).
44. Donoghue, "A Plain Approach to *Ulysses*," 157.
45. Ibid., 169.
46. Ibid., 160.
47. Leah Flack, *Modernism and Homer*, notes that "The slaughter of the suitors—Odysseus' major act of violence in the *Odyssey*—seemed to Joyce 'unUlyssean,' suggesting that he began his novel with an image of an ideal Odysseus on whom Homer's *Odyssey* did not have the last word" (97, citing Frank Budgen's *James Joyce and the Making of Ulysses*, 262).
48. Homer, *The Odyssey*, Book XVI, lines 194, 195–6, 196.
49. Kershner, "Intertextuality," 175. See Ellmann, *The Consciousness of Joyce*, 23–44, for a compelling narrative of Joyce's deep interest in the *Odyssey*, meditations on it, and sequels to it that together influenced his own epic. See Kenner, "Uses of Homer," 19–30, in the revised edition of his *Ulysses*, for a helpful summary of Odyssean-inspired readings of the novel and for the novel's larger pattern. See also Flack's chapter, "'Damn Homer, Ulysses, Bloom and all the rest': 'Cyclops,' Disorder, and Joyce's Monster Audiences," in her *Modernism and Homer*, 95–124, for a comprehensive reading of the ways Joyce both imitated and departed from Odyssean examples, particularly in her reading of the "Cyclops" episode. More recently, see her chapter in *James Joyce and Classical Modernism*, "Joyce, Homer, and the Seductions of Readings," 75–103. And see Weir's chapter, "Homeric Narrative," 15–72, and his "Appendix C: *The Odyssey* and *Ulysses*: Episode and Chapter Comparison," 223–4, in *Ulysses Explained*.
50. Weir, *Ulysses Explained*, 57.
51. Homer, *The Odyssey*, Book XVI, lines 74–6, 79–81.
52. Ibid., lines 56–61, and lines 529–33.

53. I am indebted to Leah Flack for this suggestion.
54. A starting point for an exploration of Joyce's interest in the parable of the Prodigal Son would be Virginia Moseley's "Joyce's *Exiles* and the Prodigal Son." Joyce wrote about the parable in his "Notes by the Author" for *Exiles*: "The elder brother in the fable of the Prodigal Son is Robert Hand. The father took the side of the prodigal. This is probably not the way of the world—certainly not in Ireland: but Jesus' Kingdom was not of this world nor was or is His wisdom" (102). Apart from Moseley's article, such claims are usually only mooted and not explored deeply. See, in this regard, Kathleen Ferris, *James Joyce and the Burden of Disease*, 18, 44, 47–8, 69. Significantly, the passages about the Prodigal Son cited by Ferris occur in "Circe," and thus precede "Eumaeus," where the narrative significance of the Prodigal Son parable seems to fade and be replaced by the Good Samaritan parable. Although his remit is the issue of snobbery in Joyce, Sean Latham argues in passing in *Am I A Snob?* that *Ulysses*' "narrative carefully shies away from the tragic profundity of a Woolf or a Faulkner and moves instead toward a sentimental reunification of the symbolic father with the prodigal son" (148). And yet, as we will see, Joyce abhorred sentimentality and refused to give such a reunification purchase. My former doctoral student, Elizabeth Fredericks, in "'Unfallen but about to Fall': The Influence of Byron's *Cain* on Joyce's *A Portrait of the Artist as a Young Man*," offers a compelling brief reading of Stephen Dedalus as "the prodigal descendant of" Byron's Cain in both *A Portrait of the Artist* and *Ulysses*, noting that he "finds himself living in a state of anguish and rejection amongst swine in the 'Circe' episode of *Ulysses*, which supplies the pigs of both the Greek enchantress and the prodigal son's employer" (570). For a more biographical reading, see Joseph Kelly, "Joyce's Exile: The Prodigal Son," which concludes, "Like the Prodigal Son, he embraced much of the morality that his father represented" (631–2).
55. Edmund Epstein, *A Guide through Finnegans Wake*, describes "The Tale of the Mookse and the Gripes" as a fable instead, drawn from a Javanese model and based on Aesop's fable of the Fox and the Grapes (76). Similarly, Epstein terms Shaun's later story a "fable": see 172–5 for his analysis.

4

BLOOM AS STRANGER AND SAMARITAN IN "CYCLOPS," "OXEN OF THE SUN," AND "CIRCE"

Those few commentators on the use of parable in the novel, such as Donoghue, tend to relegate its presence solely to the "Eumaeus" chapter, but again, it can be thought of as not only inspiring the novel, but helping structure parts of its final four episodes, together comprising over a third of the novel in terms of page count. For instance, even a very rigorous reading of Joyce's clear allusion to the Good Samaritan parable in "Eumaeus" must recognize that its beginning events are narrated in "Circe" when Private Carr attacks Stephen: "(*He rushes towards Stephen, fist outstretched, and strikes him in the face. Stephen totters, collapses, falls, stunned. He lies prone, his face to the sky, his hat rolling to the wall. Bloom follows and picks it up)*" (U 15.4747–50). Already, we can see Joyce reconfiguring Christ's parable: Instead of two travelers who decide not to stop and help the Samaritan, Joyce's Good Samaritan, Bloom, (assisted by Corny Kelleher), who has been rejected earlier in the day by two groups representing the two travelers (Protestantism: Deasy and Crofton, and Catholicism: Simon Dedalus and the Citizen), instantly stoops to help him. Bloom thus fully assumes the role of the Good Samaritan, a role he has enacted throughout the day even as he is himself introduced objectively as a stranger to us and perniciously attacked by others as a Stranger.[1]

Joyce's adoption of a parabolic structuring device for crucial parts of his novel protests the restrictions of Irish Catholicism, signals an affinity with the apostate Jewish Bloom, and reaffirms the radical agency of both his characters and readers. Neil Davison's contention that "[a]lthough [he is] an apostate from Judaism, Bloom's ethnicity parallels Joyce's view of his own anti-Catholic Irishness" helps us begin to apprehend that Joyce's sense of his own marginality as a lapsed Irish Catholic exiled in Europe gave him certain affinities with the similarly exiled Bloom that enabled him to compassionately portray him through his turn to scriptural narratives to help structure his novel.[2]

In regard to Bloom's strangeness and exilic condition, David Pierce makes the simple but profound point that while Stephen Dedalus and Buck Mulligan have nicknames, employed repeatedly by the narrator and other characters, "Bloom is introduced as Mr Bloom, a polite form of address for someone we don't know."[3] After the noisy shenanigans of Mulligan in "Telemachus," and Stephen's intimate reflections in episodes two and three, "When Bloom arrives on the scene . . . we encounter the quietness and the formality of a stranger, whose predicament the novel is going to explore."[4] Nowhere is Bloom's strangeness more highlighted and stereotyped than in the twelfth episode of the novel, "Cyclops," when the Catholic Citizen pointedly says in Bloom's presence, "We want no more *strangers* in our house," a close paraphrase of what Yeats's and Lady Gregory's Cathleen ni Houlihan says in their play of the same name about the British presence in Ireland;[5] and again, "The *strangers*. . . . Our own fault. We let them come in. We brought them in. The adulteress and her paramour brought the Saxon robbers here" (U 12.1150–1, 1156–8; my emphasis). In this passage, Joyce not only recapitulates the Protestant Mr. Deasy's rhetoric back in "Nestor" when he states, "A faithless wife brought the *strangers* to our shore here" (U 2.392–3; my emphasis), but also links Bloom's presence in Ireland as a supposedly interloping Jew with earlier interlopers: the English who came in under Strongbow in 1170 at the behest of Dermot MacMurrough, who had lost his kingdom and pledged himself to Henry II as his vassal in order to recapture it. For the xenophobic Citizen, Jews replicate the mercantilistic attack of the English on Ireland beginning in 1170, and they must be evicted as the strangers they are. Much of this strangeness stems from the Jewishness that not only the virulently hateful Citizen but also others ascribe to Bloom, and which he finally seems to embrace late in the novel. Joyce remarked to Jacques Mercanton when asked if Bloom were Jewish, "Yes because only a foreigner would do. The Jews were foreigners at that time in Dublin. There was no hostility toward them, but contempt, yes the contempt people always show for the unknown."[6] Despite Joyce's claim, as we will see later, Bloom is really not Jewish: While his father was Jewish, his mother was not, and he has been baptized both Protestant (twice) and Catholic (once).

Later, in "Circe," two moments seem to sum up many Dubliners' reactions to Bloom as stranger. First, J. J. O'Molloy, when serving as mock-counsel defending Bloom against Mary Driscoll's hyperbolic accusation in the "Circe" episode that Bloom assaulted her, simply states, "When in doubt persecute Bloom" (U 15.975–6). Soon after this moment, when Bloom appeals to Hynes (who has helped rescue him from the Citizen's attack earlier in "Cyclops") as a character witness, Hynes "*coldly*" says, "You are a perfect stranger" (*U* 15.1195). Bloom's strangeness is profound and ongoing, but Joyce gradually and purposely highlights it as the source and ground of his empathy by depicting his recognition of his own strangeness, as Declan Kiberd notes: "Bloom himself is valued by Joyce to the extent that he can recognize the 'stranger' within himself. He is more Christlike than any of his fellow citizens, being constantly willing to put himself in the other fellow's position."[7] Bloom's sense of his own strangeness therefore enables him to sense when others are feeling marginalized or persecuted and it results in his many (often instantaneous) acts of intimate charity for others that stem from his habitus of care.

Bloom often expresses his charity and love toward others, and he displays this disposition throughout the novel, but he does so ever more clearly beginning in "Cyclops," which exemplifies an anti-hospitality narrative—the opposite of the Good Samaritan parable. The bigotry expressed by both the unidentified narrator and the Citizen in this episode (and even the hatred and treachery expressed by characters formerly sympathetic to Bloom such as Martin Cunningham and Joe Hynes) together characterize the wounded Bloom as Stranger here and in successive episodes, after which he is transformed into the Good Samaritan figure late in "Circe" and throughout "Eumaeus" and "Ithaca."

As a crucial step in fully becoming first the Stranger, and then the Samaritan figure, Bloom embraces the Jewish identity others ascribe to him while under attack from the Citizen, as Neil R. Davison has shown most convincingly. As Davison points out, "From the opening of the episode, the reader is offered a kind of smorgasbord of religious, economic, and nationalistic anti-Jewishness,"[8] and as a result of the way these manifestations of anti-Semitism are eventually visited upon the person of Bloom, he reacts by reclaiming his Jewish identity and, crucially, identifying himself with the pacifist Christ. Ironically, the mixed-heritage Bloom responds to the racial rhetoric based on supposed blood purity promulgated by the Citizen by "becoming" Jewish to himself for perhaps the first time (in the others' eyes he has always been Jewish).

In so doing, Joyce aligns Bloom with the plight of persecuted and murdered black Americans, such as the lynched black man in Omaha, Georgia in the newspaper article recounted by the hateful local narrator of the episode (*U* 12.1324–8). Bloom becomes dark or black in this episode by such associations, including Ned's linking him to this lynched African American with the word "foes" in his description of "the fighting navy . . . that keeps our *foes* at bay" (*U* 12.1329; my emphasis) immediately after this narrated newspaper article, a word that the Citizen has already used of the English but also Bloom: "the *foes* we hate before us" (*U* 12.524; my emphasis). I do not have the space to develop how Bloom becomes "black" in this episode, a quality that emphasizes his Jewishness and his Otherness, but the rhetoric employed by the Citizen, who calls him "kaffir" in *U* 12.1552 (South African dialect for the hateful pejorative "nigger") and likens him to a Cain-figure in *U* 12.1667 who is "Cursed by God," contributes to this identity that is foisted upon him. White preachers in the American South often tried to justify slavery and Jim Crow laws by classing their black brothers and sisters as descendants of Cain, supposedly marked by God as dark in Genesis and doomed to wander the earth, a racist set of characteristics that Joyce employs here to heighten the stereotype of Bloom as the dark, wandering Jew.

Davison argues that Bloom's embrace of this stereotypical Jewish identity shot through with anti-Semitism "may not be the most profound sense of a Jewish identity, but it is nevertheless a revelation for Bloom; recognizing himself to be a Jew whose self-perception as such has been formed greatly through stereotype, Bloom begins his own victory over self-abnegation."[9] When Bloom tells the Citizen, "Your God was a Jew. Christ was a Jew like me" (*U* 12.1808–9), he not only identifies himself with Christ, but affirms Christ as a "political misfit," who "transgressed Hebraic law and considered himself a new, more divinely inspired Jew," epitomizing "Joyce's predilection for heretics."[10] Bloom is the ultimate heretic in *Ulysses*, and his heresy—his departure from the dominant culture of his day, much like Christ's—enables him to cut through hatred and pretension and attend to the needs of others through the activation of his profound, embodied compassion and empathy.

For instance, after the conversation about the Invincibles in "Eumaeus," Bloom recapitulates his riposte to the Citizen in "Cyclops," hoping to impress something of his own mercy and charity on Stephen:

> —He took umbrage at something or other, that muchinjured but on the whole eventempered person declared, I let slip. He called me a jew and in a heated fashion offensively. So I without deviating from plain facts in the least told him his God, I mean Christ, was a jew too and all his family like me though in reality I'm not. That was one for him. A soft answer turns away wrath. (*U* 16.1081–6)

Bloom's preference for such "soft answer[s]" is inherently Christ-like, and again, like his knowledge of the Good Samaritan parable, shows his knowledge of Scripture, as he here cites Proverbs 15:1.[11] Christian pacifism and pacifism generally appealed immensely to Joyce, who had long expressed his aversion to physical force, dating at least back to his essay, "Force," written when he was 16, explored below in my argument about Bloom's habitus of charity. That essay functions almost as pre-writing for Bloom's remarks to the Citizen, quoted here, and suggests how Joyce viewed charity as a heavenly gift through Christian theology.

Joyce emphasizes an ethic of love throughout the novel, and he privileges this ethic by counterposing Bloom's generous love toward others against the warped versions of love espoused by hateful characters, such as the Citizen in "Cyclops." When Bloom is attempting to debate the Citizen, this repulsive character shouts, "—*Sinn Fein*! . . . *Sinn fein amhain*! The friends we love are by our side and the foes we hate before us" (*U* 12.523–4). Joyce critiques this nationalist, exclusive identity (*Sinn Fein* means "ourselves alone") with Bloom's patient, persistent attempts to articulate an inclusive love of country and others in "Cyclops" and elsewhere. I will return to this passage later, but Bloom's simple declaration of "—Love . . . I mean the opposite of hatred" (*U* 12.1485) resonates gently throughout the entire novel. Immediately after this declaration, Bloom pops out of the pub, stating, "I must go now. . . . Just round to the court a moment to see if Martin is there. If he comes just say I'll be back in a second. Just a moment" (*U* 12.1485–7). Why is Bloom so concerned to catch Martin Cunningham at this moment? Because he is anxious to give him the five shillings for the Dignam children he has lovingly pledged in the wake of Patrick Dignam's demise (*U* 10.973–80), whereas in contrast, characters such as Long John Fanning offer no money at all (*U* 10.1017, 1026–30).

This passage from "Cyclops," combining as it does Bloom's abstract idealism with his determined concrete altruism, captures his quasi-intellectual love ethic and his pedestrian (in the best sense of the word) application of his theory to others. His adoption of the Good Samaritan persona periodically throughout *Ulysses*—as when he helps the blind stripling across the street, and later, most movingly, when he rescues Stephen—enables Joyce to reject exclusivist nationalist rhetoric. Kiberd argues that Joyce uses Bloom's mocking introduction as "a new apostle to the gentiles" in this part of the episode such that Bloom embodies Joyce's injunction to "not just embrace traditional enemies of Israel but to include and love them in an expanded definition of community."[12] In so doing, he articulates how a transnational community based upon acts of mercy and rescue first glimpsed in the transcultural help given by the Samaritan to the beaten traveler in Christ's parable might emerge if we reject nationalist abstractions and instead attend to particular others and their claim upon us.

Despite the rampant attacks on Bloom as stingy throughout "Cyclops"— based on his refusal to stand a round of drinks with the other men—at least two of the characters in Barney Kiernan's pub recognize him as a Good Samaritan figure. In contrast to the Citizen's slighting reference to him, "—A new apostle to the gentiles. . . . Universal love" (*U* 12.1489), John Wyse immediately muses, "—Well. . . . Isn't that what we're told. Love your neighbour" (*U* 12.1490). Although the Citizen dismisses this application of the conclusion of Christ's parable about the Good Samaritan to Bloom with "Beggar my neighbour is his motto. Love, moya!" (*U* 12.1491–2), Bloom's invocation of a selfless, Christ-like love based specifically on this greatest of Christ's parables echoes later in the episode. For instance, when the men slander him in his absence, including Lenehan's argument that Bloom is out "Defrauding widows and orphans" (*U* 12.1622), Martin Cunningham quietly insists, "—Charity to the neighbour. . ." (*U* 12.1665).

The Good Samaritan parable has usually been read typologically to signal the future coming of Christ, and although Bloom is really a secular figure, he seems moved by that parabolic narrative and its concern for the neighbor. He prominently asks early in the novel, "Who is my neighbor?" (*U* 5.341), and that phrase of the lawyer to Christ that leads Him to tell the Good Samaritan parable could easily be Bloom's motto. Kermode points out that "'Samaritan' (as Augustine seems to have known) comes from the same root as 'shepherd'; the Samaritan is the Good Shepherd. Moreover, *plēsion*, neighbor, is related to another Hebrew word meaning 'shepherd'. . . . So the lawyer asked a new question and got the answer to an old one: the Good Shepherd, who comforts our distress and will return hereafter."[13] Bloom consistently shepherds others in the novel, comforting them in their distress, and yet he does so out of great hurt and discomfort himself. As the Good Samaritan figure, he is transformed into a finally secular Christ figure, but can also be read as the beaten Stranger, especially through the "Cyclops" episode.

Christ's choice of a Samaritan to exemplify his mercy character should astound us, as I have argued elsewhere: "Portraying this action of mercy by a Samaritan is especially striking and generous of Christ since earlier, He had tried to enter 'a village of the Samaritans. . . . And they did not receive him, because his face was as though he would go to Jerusalem'" (Luke 9:52–3).[14] After Jesus' disciples James and John see the Samaritans' refusal of hospitality to Jesus, they urge that He call down fire from heaven to burn them up (Luke 9:54), but Christ "turned, and rebuked them, and said, 'Ye know not what manner of spirit ye are of. For the Son of man is not come to destroy men's lives but to save them'" (Luke 9:55 KJV). Christ's parable is suffused with grace: He not only refuses to destroy or hate the Samaritans for their rejection of Him, but instead, astonishingly, offers a Samaritan as exemplifying mercy, thus inscribing a fictional story of hope through imagining true neighborliness proffered by a generous Samaritan whose tribe Luke has just linked to a conspicuous lack of kindness and compassion.

Bloom's nearly automatic response in helping Stephen in "Circe" results from what we might call a habitus of generosity and help that Joyce conceived about his character from early on, based on his reading of the original Odysseus/Ulysses as charitable. Ellmann notes that Joyce told Frank Budgen in a letter about Bloom that "he is complete man . . . a good man," and told Paul Suter and Budgen in conversation that "Ulysses was not a god, for he had all the defects of the ordinary man, but was kindly." Using German for Suter's benefit, Joyce claimed that "Ulysses was not 'gut' but 'gutmütig' [decent]. Bloom is the same. If he does something mean or ignoble, he knows it and says, 'I have been a perfect pig'" (*JJ2* 436).[15] Throughout the novel, Joyce portrays Bloom's character as kind and loving: Think of his sympathetic reaction to the cat in "Calypso" (*U* 4.15–32); think of his helping the blind stripling across the street in "Lestrygonians" and his subsequent imagining of what it would be like to be blind (*U* 8.1075–1143); think of his sympathetic reaction to Mina Purefoy's birth pangs at several points in the novel, including in "Lestrygonians" and "Oxen of the Sun" (*U* 8.358, 373–9; 14.1401–2). As Ellmann puts it, "The kindness of Bloom on June 16, 1904, begins with animals and ends with human beings. So he feeds his cat in the morning, then some sea gulls, and in the *Circe* episode a dog." Ellmann's catalog of Bloom's kind acts continues and startles us in its depth and length:

> He remembers his dead son and father, he is also concerned about his living daughter, and he never forgets his wife for a moment. He helps a blind man cross the street. He contributes very generously—beyond his means—to the fund for the children of his friend Dignam who just died; and, when he begins to see Stephen as a sort of son, he follows him, tries to stop his drinking, prevents his being robbed, risks arrest to defend him from the police, feeds him too, and takes him home in what Joyce calls, half-humorously, "orthodox Samaritan fashion." (*JJ2* 372)[16]

Although she does not develop the point, Karen Lawrence makes a similar claim to my own, noting that "[a]s he navigates his home and his hometown, Bloom displays his strategies and tactics for opening himself up to others inhabiting the landscape."[17] Even those men such as Davy Byrne and Nosey Flynn who have a decidedly mixed view of Bloom, noting, positively, that he never gets drunk and, more negatively, hewing to a stereotype of Jews as stingy, never giving a loan, nonetheless observe, "He's been known to put his hand down too to help a fellow" (*U* 8.983–4).

Joyce found additional warrant beyond the hospitality and charity privileged by Homer for his characterization of Bloom's unselfishness and charity in the Christian faith in which he was raised, expressed in his early essay "Force." There, he presages Bloom's own tendencies toward unselfishness and charity. In a long sentence, Joyce praises "the much-maligned, greatest charity, so distinct from animal profusion and reckless liberality, that charitable deeds do not wholly constitute; but which springs from inner wells of gentleness and goodness. . . ." This quality, Joyce continues, "dictates, from emotions of Heaven's giving, the sacrifice of all that is dear, in urgent need. . . ." Finally, he declaims, "this utter unselfishness in all things, how does it . . . call for constant practice and [is] worth fulfilling!"[18] This passage clearly shows how Joyce believed that unselfishness, itself a gift, can be developed through "constant practice." Bloom's charitable behavior in this regard is further illuminated by Paul Ricoeur's convincing reading of the

Good Samaritan parable that "[b]eing a neighbor lies in the habit of making oneself available."[19] If one practices being neighborly repeatedly, then one becomes a neighbor almost as second nature, as Joyce intimates in his essay and as Leopold Bloom does throughout the day in the novel.

Moreover, Bloom's strong desire to be neighborly, even to his enemies, might also stem from a trait Joyce almost certainly drew on in his early reaction against Stanislaus's portrayal of a stoic, duplicitous, and aloof Christ, as well as from his subsequent preference for Luke's depiction of Jesus over the other Gospel writers' portrayals. In their invaluable *The Workshop of Daedalus*, Robert Scholes and Richard Kain reproduce a long passage from an unpublished section of Stanislaus's *Dublin Diary*, a work which Joyce read "often"; the passage features Stanislaus's negative perception of a haughty, prideful Christ, the opposite of Joyce's perception of Him as a warm and humane figure. As they point out, "much of his thinking" about Christ "was influenced not by the Fathers of the Church but by his own younger brother, whose militant atheism was the steel against which Joyce polished his own tolerant skepticism," and certainly Stanislaus's Christ here would be nothing like the humane and suffering Christ that partially inspired Bloom.[20] Instead, Stanislaus posits that Jesus was an intellectual and that "[h]is crises were intellectual, not emotional. He seemed to be absolutely without sentiment." He also states he "whored greatly" and "was a wine-bibber," terming Him "eminently masculine, unflinchingly wise, knowing man's heart and the world."[21] Repeatedly calling him prideful, Stanislaus surprisingly finds all these qualities attractive, concluding his peroration,

> The Catholic Church is, I believe, nearest to an understanding of Jesus, for in its teaching—not what it preaches—and in its poet Dante, it is proud, intellectual and practically contemptuous of morality. If Christianity is to regain its respect in Europe, it will be with such a Christ, and if it tries to regain its hold by turning democrat, it will lose both its power and its respect.[22]

This "proud, intellectual," and immoral Christ, stoically oblivious to the sufferings of those for whom He would later die, reflects a perverse reading of the portrayals of Christ in Scripture and certainly in Catholic teaching as well, Stanislaus's protestations notwithstanding.

Apparently repulsed by his younger brother's portrayal of this aloof, stoic, even aristocratic Christ, Joyce was drawn instead to Christ's humble origins and His desire to be among the commoners of his time as he read and reread Scripture. Luke depicts Christ's lineage as going back to Adam and God, which, as Herbert G. May in his commentary for the *New Oxford Annotated Bible* points out, emphasizes his "common humanity."[23] Moreover, there were particular contemporary depictions of Jesus as humanized, not so much divinized, with which Joyce was familiar and admired. For instance, in chapter 14 of his study *Ecce Homo: A Survey of the Life and Work of Jesus*, entitled "The Enthusiasm of Humanity," a copy of which Joyce had in his Trieste library, John R. Seeley sketches a loving, warm Christ. Seeley opens by arguing for Christ's selfless love in terms apposite to Bloom's actions in the novel, ranging from his ill-treatment by most of the men (save Martin Cunningham to some degree) in the "Hades" episode to the outright attacks on him by the Citizen in the "Cyclops" episode:

> The first method of training this passion that Christ employed was the direct one of making it a duty to feel it. To love one's neighbor as oneself was, he said, the first and greatest *law*. And in the sermon on the Mount he requires the passion to be felt in such strength as to include those whom we have most reason to hate—our enemies and those who maliciously injure us—and delivers an imperative precept, "Love your enemies."[24]

Seeley's humanized, passionate Jesus was appealing to Joyce, who wrote an essay-review of Hungarian painter Mihály Munkacsy's *Ecce Homo* ("Behold the Man") when he was 17 in 1899; his understanding of Jesus as depicted there "enables him to approach the subject of a religious painting from a purely aesthetic point of view," as Mason and Ellmann point out in their introduction to this essay.[25] This became an increasingly common tendency of Joyce: Think of his appropriation of the terms "epiphany" and "epiclesis" from specifically Christian nomenclature and his transformation of these into aesthetic but also finally moral terms for *Dubliners*. Much of *Ulysses*, as these chapters together argue, concerns the gradual revelation of Jesus' message for us to love others as ourselves, an extended "beholding" that likely has its origins in Joyce's reading of this artistic representation of Christ. Joyce never could escape his fascination with Christ; indeed in his Trieste Notebook from 1909, he would muse under the heading "Jesus" that "His shadow is everywhere."[26]

In his essay on Munkácsy's *Ecce Homo*, Joyce praises above all its drama, which he holds to be "the interplay of passions; drama is strife, evolution, movement, in whatever way unfolded." The drama of the painting is created by "the sense of life, the realistic illusion."[27] In other words, the painting exhibited a high degree of verisimilitude in its depiction of ordinary life, a combination that grew increasingly important to Joyce over the years, and is manifested in *Dubliners* but even more so in *Ulysses*. One might even say that Joyce was unwittingly practicing his narrative descriptions of Leopold Bloom and his milieu through his praise of this painting and its subjects. The secularized, humanizing Bloom and his actions in the novel have at least some of their origin in this essay, particularly in such moments as when Joyce states that Munkácsy's "view of the event is humanistic. Consequently his work is drama. Had he chosen to paint Christ as the Incarnate Son of God, redeeming his creatures of his own admirable will . . . it would not have been drama, it would have been Divine Law, for drama deals with man." Munkácsy's Christ has a nose that is "slightly Jewish" and his "whole face is of an ascetic inspired, wholesouled, wonderfully passionate man."[28] This Jewish Christ, a forerunner of the humanized and humanizing Bloom, is "no more than a great social and religious reformer, a personality, of mingled majesty and power, a protagonist of a world drama."[29] In his reading of Joyce's review of the painting, Andrew Gibson argues that while the painting itself "was thought of as the last great work in the tradition of European religious painting," such that people "were often found kneeling in front of the painting in prayer," Joyce instead "*makes* Munkácsy modern" and also "radically secularizes" him.[30] That is, just as he did with Christian texts such as the Lukan narrative of the Good Samaritan, Joyce read Munkácsy's Christ as a secularized, passionate figure of empathy for others, a "character" who clearly prefigures Bloom's secularized empathy for others, grounded on and stemming from, in part, the Lukan narrative of the Good Samaritan.

Along with these characteristics, Bloom's concern for Stephen, beginning in "Oxen of the Sun" and in the Westland Row incident between that episode and "Circe," and finally in his rescue of Stephen at the end of "Circe" and in his actions after that, together reflect his practical nature and the event-oriented parable of the Samaritan, who seemingly does not hesitate but helps the wounded traveler in a series of tersely narrated actions. The crucial recognition scene between Bloom and Stephen occurs early in "Oxen of the Sun" during a passage cast in a prose style similar to Sir Thomas Malory's, when Bloom muses upon Rudy's death, then upon the living Stephen, whom he begins to see as a potential heir:

> But sir Leopold was passing grave maugre . . . as he was minded of his good lady Marion that had borne him an only manchild which on his eleventh day on live had died . . . and now sir Leopold that had of his body no manchild for an heir looked upon him his friend's son and was shut up in sorrow for his forepassed happiness and as sad as he was that him failed a son of such gentle courage (for all accounted him of real parts) so grieved he also in no less measure for young Stephen for that he lived riotously with those wastrels and murdered his goods with whores. (*U* 14.264, 266–7, 271–6)

This passage enfolds three sympathy narratives: Mina Purefoy's present suffering in childbirth, Marion Bloom's suffering in childbirth with Rudy, who died on his eleventh day of life, and Stephen Dedalus's riotous living and sexual promiscuity. Bloom recognizes Stephen as wasting his own opportunity to have children by visiting prostitutes, and later in the episode we realize that Bloom not only sympathizes with Stephen here but also empathizes with him, since he himself was with a prostitute when he was younger. The narrator tells us, "Now he is himself paternal and these about him might be his sons" (*U* 14.1062), and "The wise father knows his own child" (*U* 14.1063), suggesting that he believes the wisdom he has acquired in age has enabled him to recognize Stephen as an heir, in part because Bloom also visited prostitutes like Bridie Kelly (*U* 14.1063–74). He feels now that "No son of thy loins is by thee. There is none now to be for Leopold, what Leopold was for Rudolph" (*U* 14.1076–7), and laments what he sees as his filial infertility. However, Bloom nonetheless crucially begins to see Stephen as a potential heir to replace the dead Rudy, and begins thus to be concerned for his safety and to protect him—first from the raging storm outside, then from his companions when Bloom follows them to the pub, then during the mysterious incident at Westland Row, and finally from the attack by Private Carr at Bella Cohen's brothel in "Circe."

Soon after Stephen's bragging about his sexual conquests, a powerful storm begins, and Bloom's sympathy toward Stephen and growing care for him leads him—upon watching the young man finish his drink "at one draught" to gain some Dutch courage (*U* 14.421–2)—to speak "calming words to slumber his great fear, advertising how it was no other thing but a hubbub noise that he heard, the discharge of fluid from the thunderhead, look you, having taken place, and all of the order of a natural phenomenon" (*U* 14.425–8). Perhaps in a preview of the confusion that attends their meeting in "Circe" and afterwards, Stephen is not calmed down by Bloom's pseudoscientific explanation of the origins of thunder (*U* 14.429–31). Moreover, Stephen is so different from Bloom in temperament and intellectual orientation that he is sufficiently Other to him—yet as we will see, their differences finally are one factor that leads to their eventual partial union as father and son.

Something odd—a lacuna in the narration, perhaps a usually unrecognized aspect of Bloom's rescue narrative—happens between the end of "Oxen of the Sun" and the beginning of "Circe," roughly between 11:00 p.m. and 12:00 a.m, when Bloom follows Stephen and Lynch to Westland Row railway station after they go to the pub toward the end of "Oxen." Haines and Mulligan show up there too, and Hugh Kenner's speculation that Stephen punches Mulligan at the station remains the best explanation of what happens there: a violent incident. Kenner notes that roughly an hour later, in "Circe," Stephen's hand is hurting (*U* 15.3720–1), and he suggests that an early recitation by Stephen of the Paschal Antiphon (*U* 15.77) in that episode—"*Vidi aquam egredientem de templo a latere dextro, Alleluia,*" translated as "I saw water flowing from the temple on the right side"—might well indicate that Stephen hit Mulligan in the right temple at Westland Row after being taunted by him all day, and that he is describing a "satisfying gush from Mulligan's head."[31] Kenner's contention about Stephen's Latin chant convinces, especially because Mulligan opened the novel by chanting a mock Mass as a parody of Stephen's former faith. Now that Stephen "*chants with joy the introit for paschal time*" (U 15.73–4), he may well be celebrating this act of retribution in the "state of high elation" that Kenner perceives, as Stephen has "promoted himself from priest to bishop" with an ashplant as his crozier. Stephen is so drunk, and violence so foreign to his pacifist character, that he might not remember the incident later in "Circe," as Kenner posits in noting Stephen's musing, "Personally, I detest action . . . Hand hurts me slightly" (U 15.4414).[32]

Bloom, who arrives late to the train station, realizes that if Stephen goes back to the Martello Tower later in "Eumaeus," he "won't get in after what occurred at Westland Row station" (U 16.250–1), and although a few lines later he misperceives that Mulligan and Haines were trying to evade Stephen (U 16.262–7), his later perception twice in the same episode that Stephen's hand is hurt (U 16.1296, 1608–9) suggests strongly that, at the least, Bloom realizes that Stephen hurt his hand at the station—even if he likely did not witness Stephen hit Mulligan. This perception of Stephen's physical and emotional distress activates Bloom's care for him such that he feels compelled to follow him into Nighttown so that he does not get into any more trouble.

Although Bloom has always been practical, he has also been assailed by self-doubt and attacked verbally throughout this particular day in his role of Stranger in the parable; now, toward the end of "Circe," he seems reborn into the new role of the Good Samaritan. Before Stephen is attacked by Private Carr, for instance, Bloom, realizing how drunk Stephen is, pays the prostitutes a half sovereign, which enables him to return Stephen's pound note to him (U 15.3589–90); he then picks up Stephen's box of matches and hands that to him (U 15.3597). Right after this, Bloom offers to take care of Stephen's money (U 15.3601–2), and then he throws Stephen's cigarette away, saying, "Don't smoke. You ought to eat" (U 15.3644).

Both the distorting style and the misleading agenda of the "Circean" narrator, however, distract from Bloom's charitable actions in the episode. Kenner argues that

> Bloom at the end of "Circe" seems a changed Bloom, courageous, ready of mind. . . . "Circe"'s rummaging amid the roots of his secret fears and desires has brought forth a new self-possession, and the man who lost his head at the Citizen's taunts and had to be whisked off amid jeers, pursued by a mangy dog and a flying biscuit-box, has managed Stephen's assailants with aplomb.[33]

It is misleading to claim, however, as Kenner and other critics have, that many of the supposedly "secret fears and desires" of Bloom in the episode are truly his; instead, many of these are either projected onto him or exaggerated by the distorting Circean narrator, who is completely dedicated to obsessive Freudian psychology.[34] Kenner's contention that Bloom is a changed man persuades, but the change has likely come from watching the abuse being visited upon Stephen by Private Carr, which he relates to and empathizes with. He is clearly fed up with being attacked himself as a Stranger all day long.

And while he is sufficiently a pacifist not to stand up for himself physically against the Citizen, for example, when he sees Stephen lying prone and the fighting between a nationalist Hag and a Bawd sympathetic to Private Carr, Bloom startlingly "(*shoves them back, loudly*)," and says "Get back, stand back!" (*U* 15.4768). Bloom also manages the aftermath of the attack well, as we saw above in the discussion of the parallels between "Grace" and the end of "Circe," by bringing in Kelleher and getting the policemen not to take down Stephen's name, thus likely preventing him from being jailed for the night. Thornton puts the question well: "If some change is going to take place within Stephen or Bloom, or between them, will it be because of the bogeymen they may have faced—perhaps totally unawares—in their hallucinations, or because of what happens between them during and after their stay at Bella Cohen's whorehouse?" Drawing on Karen Lawrence's claim that Bloom acts in a fatherly way toward Stephen throughout the episode, Thornton correctly holds that "the public acts of Bloom express far more of his real character than do these exaggerated fantasies."[35]

Another way to articulate the view of Bloom offered throughout "Circe" by its Freudian narrator, who projects distortions of his character over against the correct view of Bloom in his helping of Stephen, is to consider Bloom's status as Christ figure. The Good Samaritan is often read as symbolizing Christ, but the Christological reading offered by the Circean narrator contradicts the lowly, helpful, self-denying character of Bloom, the similar figure to the Good Samaritan in the parable, and certainly to that of Christ himself. The narrator repeatedly projects Bloom as desiring glory, for instance, including portraying him as "Lord mayor of Dublin!" (*U* 15.1364) and as a reforming emperor (*U* 15.1398–1710). These depictions are succeeded by a vignette in which Bloom emerges as a triumphal if maligned savior figure who is "pantomime" stoned (*U* 15.1902) at one point; who wears "*a seamless garment marked I.H.S.*" (*U* 15.1935) to signify his status as Christ; who is then bowed down to by "*The daughters of Erin*" (*U* 15.1938–9) who worship him and ask him to pray for them (here he is also the Virgin Mary). After this invocation, "*six hundred voices, conducted by Vincent O'Brien, sing the chorus from Handel's Messiah Alleluia for the Lord God Omnipotent reigneth*," and Bloom is immolated, becoming "*mute, shrunken, carbonized*" (*U* 15.1953–5, 1956). The narrator would have us believe that this vainglorious Bloom, with trappings of pomp and circumstance, desires to be worshipped. In actuality, Bloom is a down-to-earth advertising salesman, embodied to the extent we have already seen him straining to produce a bowel movement in his jakes (4.500–40) and humbly, not pridefully, stepping into the role of Good Samaritan in the final pages of the "Circe" episode. We know that Joyce wrote the messianic scene in "Circe" late in the composition process,[36] as well as the Samaritan opening of "Eumaeus," suggesting that he meant to contrast the narrator's distorted view of Bloom as self-aggrandizing Christ with the suffering, service-oriented Bloom who steps into his Good Samaritan role here in "Circe," and occupies it for the rest of the novel. The Good Samaritan as a figure embodying Christ's best characteristics—humility, helpful service, suffering—thus offers the better way of reading Bloom's desires in this episode—not to obtain vainglory but to humbly serve others.

Stephen's actions too are distorted by the Circean narrator and by several English characters who render him Other and thus expose him to the attack by Private Carr. The Good Samaritan's reaching across cultural and religious barriers echoes in Bloom's rescue of Stephen, who is knocked down by Carr for his anti-monarchical statements about the British king. Even though the spectral figure of Old Gummy Granny, channeling Lady Gregory's and Yeats's drama *Cathleen ni Houlihan*, chants about the British, "Strangers in my house, bad manners to them!" (*U* 15.4586), Stephen is actually the character rendered as Stranger by Carr's taking offense at his remark that "in here [my mind] it is I must kill the priest and the king" (*U* 15.4436–7): "What's that you're saying about my king?" (*U* 15.4447–8). Stephen, trying to be friendly, states simply, "I understand your point of view though I have no king myself for the moment" (*U* 15.4469–70), which makes matters worse since he denies the king's sovereignty over himself as an Irish subject. Shortly thereafter, Carr asks again, "Here. What are you saying about my king?" (*U* 15.4566), and Stephen's dramatic response to this second iteration of Carr's question suggests he is being robbed, an allusion to the Stranger who is robbed while on the road to Jericho in the Good Samaritan parable: "(*throws up his hands*) O, this is too monotonous! Nothing. He wants my money and my life, though want must be his master, for some brutish empire of his. Money I haven't (*he searches his pockets vaguely*) Gave it to someone" (*U* 15.4568–71). Carr is indignant: "Who wants your bleeding money?" (*U* 15.4573), and is not placated by Bloom's pointing out that "We fought for you in South Africa, Irish missile troops. Isn't that history? Royal Dublin Fusiliers. Honoured by our monarch" (*U* 15.4606–7). Partly because of Private Compton's periodically urging him to hit Stephen and because of Cissy Caffrey's insisting again that "He insulted me" (*U* 15.4741), even though she forgives Stephen, Carr finally does hit Stephen in the face.

Caffrey and the British soldiers thus make Stephen sufficiently Other by virtue of their misrepresentations of his comments that Carr feels it is legitimate to visit violence upon him; he is not one of them, they feel, and he must be punished for being different (their seeing him as more educated then themselves does not help either). Joyce thus figures Stephen as a particularly Irish Stranger, a stranger in his own land, we might say, assaulted by forces of the Crown. As Bernard Benstock points out, Stephen's "denial of loyalty to the British monarch becomes an obsession to Carr, despite the otherwise conciliatory tone of Stephen's subsequent remarks." Stephen thus "has resigned himself to being knocked down by Carr, a token act of harassment symbolic of his subject position as an Irishman."[37]

In *Through Peasant Eyes: More Lucan Parables, Their Culture and Style*, Kenneth E. Bailey notes that the traveler's being described as "half dead" is the "equivalent for a rabbinic category of 'next to death,' which meant at the point of death," and furthermore, that if the Jewish priest, freshly purified up in Jerusalem, gets "closer than four cubits to a dead man," he will be defiled, and he would have to "overstep that boundary just to ascertain the condition of the wounded man."[38] The three potential rescuers see each other because of the road's contours and long vista, and Bailey argues that because the Levite "came to the place" (Luke 10:32, ESV), he "may have crossed the defilement line of four cubits and satisfied his curiosity with a closer look," refusing to help not so much out of fear of defilement, but out of fear of the robbers.[39] The Samaritan, however, comes up to the man himself and helps him. The entire sequence thus moves from a distanced view of the traveler, to a closer one, to an up-close, embodied touching and helping of him by the Samaritan. Bloom-as-Samaritan abandons fear of any kind of defilement or public embarrassment and instantly helps Stephen, as does the Samaritan the wounded traveler. He is the literal embodiment of help and freely offers himself to assist the young man.

Clearly, the situation in "Circe" is not exactly parallel to the Lukan parable: Bloom does not simply come upon Stephen and save him but has actively pursued him since "Oxen of the Sun"—to the pub, to Westland Row train station, and now into Nighttown. Moreover, Bloom actively tries to prevent Private Carr from punching Stephen, saying to him, "He doesn't know what he's saying. Taken a little more than is good for him. Absinthe. Greeneyed monster. I know him. He's a gentleman, a poet. It's all right" (*U* 15.4486–8). Soon afterwards, when Carr is annoyed that Stephen has seemingly criticized his king, Bloom again intervenes, saying, "He said nothing. Not a word. A pure misunderstanding" (*U* 15.4600). Right before Carr strikes Stephen, Bloom urges him to walk away after Cissy Caffrey first urges him to leave and says she forgives Stephen for insulting her (*U* 15.4741–2): "Yes, go. You see he's incapable" (*U* 15.4744). And as we have seen, Stephen is not dying, or being robbed, though he performatively claims he is (*U* 15.4568–71).

But soon enough, he is knocked out cold, and Bloom helps prevent further violence to him.

Fascinatingly, although it is passing difficult to term him Jewish in any real sense, Bloom adheres to the Jewish oral tradition of saving life at all costs over against any fear of defilement, as does the Samaritan in the parable. Brad H. Young observes that "[t]he priest and the Levite treated the dying man as if he were already dead. They did not accept the oral tradition concerning the preservation of life at all costs, and they feared their ritual purity was at risk."[40] Intriguingly, Bloom is acutely aware of something like ritual defilement (in his case, public shame for being seen in a red light district), feared by both the Jewish priest and Levite, simply by being in Nighttown, telling Corny Kelleher after the watchmen leave, "I was just going home by Gardiner street when I happened to. . ." (U 15.4866). And yet he overcomes this fear and boldly, publicly, rescues Stephen and encourages others like Kelleher to do the same.

When he hears Stephen sing snatches of Yeats's poem "Who Goes with Fergus" that he sang for his dying mother, our Samaritan Bloom thinks "Poetry. Well educated. Pity," and then "*(he bends again and undoes the buttons of Stephen's waistcoat)*" thinking "To breathe," as "*(he brushes the woodshavings from Stephen's clothes with light hand and fingers)*" (U 15.4936–8). As Bloom recalls the money he held for him, "One pound seven," and which he must now feel on Stephen's body, he thinks, "Not hurt anyhow" (U 15.4938–9). In a stroke, the always practical Bloom has ascertained that Stephen has not been robbed and, more important, that he has no broken bones. Frank Budgen was the first to point out this quality of Bloom in the context of his inability to hate or purposely harm anyone: "for all his prudence, there is in Bloom a strain of impulsive simplicity, as there certainly was in Ulysses, that would probably lead him to speak up just when he ought for his own good to lie low."[41] Compare Bloom's impulsively kind actions here to the original narrative from Luke's Gospel, which features the Good Samaritan also acting quickly and practically. As soon as the Samaritan sees the wounded man, "he had compassion on him, And went to him, and bound up his wounds, pouring in oil and wine, and set him on his own beast, and brought him to an inn, and took care of him" (Luke 10:33–4, ESV).[42] The parataxis of Luke's sentence across these two verses suggests not only the spontaneous, cumulative actions of mercy performed by the Samaritan but also how his compassion was not passive but led quickly and ineluctably to these sequential acts of kindness.[43] Therefore, as subtle and illuminating as Margot Norris's commentary is on this episode as cathartic for both main characters, she misleads when she argues that "Bloom's *caritas*, the individualized implementation of his utopianism, is in full force at the end of 'Circe.'"[44] Norris implies that Bloom consciously helps Stephen in order to implement his notion of the New Bloomusalem, but instead,

Bloom intervenes because of his instinctual, unconscious habitus of *caritas*, which has been formed over the course of the novel and throughout his life by a series of acts of kindness that flow unmediated by any of his fantastical schemes.

While Budgen plays down Bloom's care for Stephen, arguing "[t]here are no tears of recognition, no rescues from shark-infested seas. Bloom cannot even save Stephen from a punch on the jaw," Bloom is no interventionist, no white knight, but a humble figure of the Samaritan.[45] The Samaritan is considered by Jewish society to be thoroughly repulsive and quotidian in the Lukan narrative, and he does not theatrically call attention to his care for the beaten stranger. It is completely against Bloom's nature to literally stop a fight, but it is inherently in his nature to tend to a wounded victim, as he does so well and thoughtfully in the concluding passages of "Circe."

Furthermore, Bloom's spontaneous actions, exemplified and anticipated by those of the Good Samaritan, are illuminated by the actions of those in situations responding to the call of the Other and in situations of gift-giving. Emmanuel Levinas, one of the most convincing philosophers in the last century to write on the subject of the Other, argues in *Alterity and Transcendence* that the dynamism of the Other's call is captured by the personal appeal of the Other's face, which results in an ethical "summons": "It is precisely in that recalling of me to my responsibility by the face that summons me, that demands me, that requires me—it is in that calling into question—that the other is my neighbor."[46] Our ethical response in such situations as Bloom finds himself in, moreover, does not stem from some prior store of knowledge, nor does it flow from the other person's "similarity to me, which I somehow recognize, that calls me toward her."[47] Levinas argues that the Other's call upon us summons us to her aid in a lasting, pre-existing ethical responsibility:

> Thinking the other person is a part of the irreducible concern for the other. Love is not consciousness. It is because there is a vigilance before the awakening that the *cogito* is possible, so that ethics is before ontology. Behind the arrival of the human there is already vigilance for the other. The transcendental *I* in its nakedness comes from the awakening by and for the other.[48]

In this account, care for the other, existing outside of traditional chronology, actually awakens the human response of care, and as we reach out to the Other in unconscious love, we most fully become ourselves. Such a concept gives the lie to the Enlightenment concept of the bounded ego, divorced from responsibility and free from the sort of cultural, religious, political, and emotional constraints that Stephen Dedalus tries to cast off in the conclusion of *A Portrait of the Artist as a Young Man*. Stephen's attempt to do so is not only impossible, it is inherently inhuman—and *Ulysses* slowly, steadily, shows how Bloom's care for him here in "Circe" and into "Eumaeus" and "Ithaca" draws Stephen into caring for others and re-entering human community, haltingly becoming the ethical, embodied self he should be.

Mark Freeman convincingly holds that "[t]he priority of the Other is perhaps most readily recognized in the form of our care for other people. This is not so much a 'decision' we make or the outgrowth of some 'principle' we hold; it is a directly revealed, unassailable reality, issuing from the Other's very presence."[49] This theory suggests that those who reject Bloom in the novel do so consciously and willfully, whereas Bloom's receptivity to others flows organically from him, unchecked and untrammeled. We must work hard to reject others, Joyce implies, and with Bloom's acceptance of others and care for them, we have an embodied example of care-in-action, unmediated by our own selfishness and egotistical needs. Bloom, the least religious person in the novel in many ways—at least in terms of outward observance—ironically most exemplifies the Christian notion of *agape*, the highest form of love because of its unselfishness and sacrificial care for others. *Agape* is never purely mental or emotional, never disembodied, but inherently enfleshed, a concept I develop in the next chapter. As Charles Taylor puts it, "*Agape* moves outward from the guts; the New Testament word for 'taking pity,' *splangnizesthai*, places the response in the bowels."[50]

Bloom's embodied rescue of Stephen arises instantly and organically, prefiguring the actions of our contemporaries who are organ donors, for example. Lewis Hyde has shown how the majority of those who give their kidneys to others in need "volunteer to give as soon as they hear of the need. The choice is instantaneous: there is no time delay, no period of deliberation. Moreover, the donors do not regard their choice as a decision at all!"[51] Such gift-giving, which Hyde contrasts with mere commodity exchange, signifies maturity and can lead to the creation of community: "Instantaneous decision is a mark of emotional and moral life," and moreover, "[a]s an expression of social emotion, gifts make one body of many . . . and when a person comes before us who is in need and to whom we feel an unquestioning emotional connection, we respond as reflexively as we would were our own body in need."[52] Bloom has earlier seen Stephen and pitied him in the "Hades" episode, poignantly being jealous of Simon since he has an heir and Bloom does not since Rudy's death: "Noisy selfwilled man. Full of his son. He is right. Something to hand on. If little Rudy had lived. See him grow up. Hear his voice in the house" (*U* 6.74–6). He has felt this emotional connection to Stephen all day and it has steadily, subterraneously built up over the course of the novel; thus, this connection to Stephen as an unconsciously longed-for replacement for Rudy along with Bloom's habitus of charity coalesce to lead him to this instantaneous, loving action.

Shortly after he brushes Stephen off, Bloom recites part of a Masonic oath pledging not to reveal Masonic secrets while bending over Stephen (*U* 15.4951–4),⁵³ and there is an intriguing possibility that he is not only a Mason but also holds a Masonic degree entitled "The Good Samaritan" that obliges him to help others in need. When musing about the Royal Dublin Fusiliers early in "Lotus Eaters," Bloom thinks of himself, "Never see him dressed up as a fireman or a bobby. A mason, yes" (*U* 5.74–5). Later in "Lestrygonians," Nosey Flynn tells Davy Byrne unequivocally that Bloom is a Mason, noting, "—He's in the craft," and stating that he is a member of the "Ancient free and accepted order. He's an excellent brother" (*U* 8.960, 962–3). As I noted earlier, Flynn muses that "He's been known to put his hand down too to help a fellow," a telling revelation about the community's knowledge of Bloom's habitus of charity (*U* 8.983–4).⁵⁴ Leonard Albert, in the first and still most comprehensive treatment of the subject, argues that "there are forebodings of the Masonic theme in *Ulysses*, beginning with the opening episode. And there is of course, abundant use of the theme after the eighth episode has closed." Albert further argues that "Masonry, as a symbol of 'brotherhood,' is one of the major themes not only of *Ulysses* but of *Finnegans Wake* as well."⁵⁵

It is quite difficult to fully ascertain, however, if Bloom is a Mason, although the evidence points toward his being one. One early commentator suggests that such uncertainty works to Joyce's advantage: "It seems that Joyce intentionally avoids a conclusive answer [about whether Bloom is a Mason] in order to convey some of the mystery and secrecy usually associated with the society."⁵⁶ Joyce obfuscates the issue, perhaps, when he has the hateful Citizen, from whose bigoted judgments we recoil, state baldly in "Cyclops" that Bloom is a "bloody freemason" (*U* 12.300). Yet recently, Sam Slote posited that the Masonic oath Bloom utters bending over the prone Stephen indicates that "Bloom is performing the role of Secret Master and is initiating Stephen as a Mason," a reading based on the addition at the tenth proof level of "Circe" of the passage, "*on guard, his fingers at his lips in the attitude of secret master*" (*U* 15.4955–6). As Luca Crispi points out, however, "These additions provide clear and definite support to the supposedly general Dublin opinion that Bloom is a Mason, though how reliable any information that is provided in 'Circe' is supposed to be is open to question."⁵⁷

One mid-nineteenth-century Masonic expert noted that

> The Good Samaritan is a side degree given to Royal Arch Masons and their wives. Of all the side degrees it is decidedly the most beautiful and impressive. It is founded on the tenth chapter of Luke, 30–35 verses. A Good Samaritan is bound, when duly summoned, to nurse a companion in sickness.⁵⁸

Joyce could have read much of this information in the entry for "Good Samaritan" in the late nineteenth-century volume, *The General History, Cyclopedia, and Dictionary of Freemasonry*, which states that "Good Samaritan" is "[a]n androgynous degree [available to both men and women] in Masonry. It is an impressive and interesting degree, founded on the well-known parable. It is communicated to the wives of Royal Arch Masons."[59] Joyce certainly knew of another similar degree, "The Heroine of Jericho," similarly bestowed on Royal Arch Masons and their wives like the Good Samaritan degree. He references this degree earlier in "Circe," an episode replete with a number of Masonic symbols and gestures, including Bloom making "*a Masonic sign*" to Bella (*U* 15.4298–9). Dolly Gray takes the side of the privates in their argument with Stephen, and Joyce intriguingly portrays her "*giving the sign of the heroine of Jericho*" (*U* 15.4418–19) with her handkerchief, a clear reference to "The Heroine of Jericho" degree.[60]

The 1917 Code of Canon Law, which took effect in 1918, entailed automatic excommunication from the Catholic Church for Masons, and furthermore banned books promoting Freemasonry. The Catholic Church not only recognized that many Masons (many of whom were Protestant) were anti-Catholic, but also believed that the naturalistic deism of Masonry explicitly contradicted Church teachings about Christ's divinity and redemptive mission. As we know, Joyce took delight in thumbing his nose at such proclamations by the Catholic Church, and he certainly could have made Bloom a Mason as a sort of protest by his Catholic-convert protagonist, whose own father converted to Protestantism, against such strictures. More importantly, if Bloom is a Mason with the side degree of "Good Samaritan," that obligation would lead him even more strongly to undertake helping others like Stephen Dedalus.[61]

As "Circe" closes, the apocalyptic events fade and the mercy narrative of the Good Samaritan that Bloom is both starting to re-enact and transmute competes with and is challenged by a finally Circean vision—that of Rudy, "a fairy boy of eleven, a changeling, kidnapped. . ." (*U* 15.4957). Just as the earlier vision of his dying mother had the potential to draw Stephen into a potentially disabling feedback loop of regret ("Agenbite of inwit") and self-flagellation from which he must escape, Rudy's appearance, even more alluring, could catapult Bloom into maudlin thoughts and sorrow such that he neglects the "son" who really needs his help standing right before him. Stephen thought of himself in "Proteus" briefly as "I, a changeling" (*U* 3.307–8), and the reappearance of this narrative, perhaps obliquely transmitted through the fairytale motif of Yeats's "The Stolen Child" (recall that Stephen has just been chanting Yeats's "Who Goes with Fergus?" as he did back in "Telemachus") and privileging Rudy now as changeling, is troubling. Bloom runs the risk of attending for too long to this imaginary, finally maudlin Jewish vision, presented in typically distorted fashion by the Circean narrator, thus becoming mired in the past, ignoring the actual stranger in need at his feet, and being diverted from developing a real relationship with Stephen.

Bloom can do so, however, by assuming the mantle of the Good Samaritan and recovering his complex Jewish heritage as a secular Christ figure, even as he rejects this alluring vision of his dead son.[62] Rudy is clearly presented as Jewish here, as Neil Davison has shown. As he points out, "Rudy's phantom appears to be reading Hebrew" (Joyce "subsequently penciled in the line, 'He reads from *right to left* inaudibly, smiling'") and Rudy then "kisses the page in an imitation of the Jewish ritual of kissing the *siddur*" (U 15.4959–60). Rudy thus has become a *Jewish* "fairy boy of eleven."[63] Davison does not seem, however, to realize the tension between the ghostly Rudy's representation of Jewishness as enclosed and self-referential and Bloom's desire to have an expansive, outward-looking faith predicated upon helping others like Stephen, the living son figure who now wins his attention over the memory of the dead Rudy. That is, Joyce shows Bloom, whose Jewishness is ascribed to him by the local community, to be more attentive to the Christian emphasis on individual freedom through apprehending the narrative possibilities in Scripture such as the parable of the Good Samaritan over against the more orthodox representation of Jewishness figured by his spectral son reading Hebrew from "right to left." Moreover, Davison wrongly locates the line describing how Bloom "watches over Stephen 'in orthodox Samaritan fashion'" to a moment "just before seeing Rudy" (instead of just after, at the beginning of "Eumaeus"); but he helpfully posits that Bloom's reclamation of his Jewishness enables him to become a "Samaritan" figure, a "*mensch,* a mixed-middling who cares for individuals more than doctrines or sectarian solidarity; he is Joyce's Jewish Alfred Hunter aiding the wounded stranger." He is thus "a new kind of Jew to himself: admirably compassionate, masculinely nurturing, active, and worthy of being a Jewish father."[64] Despite my admiration for Davison's reading of Bloom as Samaritan here, my own sense is that Bloom, through becoming this "new kind of Jew," also finally becomes both a kind of secular Christ figure (since the Samaritan is usually thought to represent Christ, who welcomed those of all backgrounds and cultures) and the beaten Stranger of the parable as well, highly influenced by Joyce's being steeped in Lukan narratives such as this parable.

We must remember that Bloom simultaneously plays the role of the beaten Stranger throughout the day, but with a twist: He is known by most of the people who criticize him and his race (save Deasy) and thus their verbal attacks on him are especially disturbing. Bloom, like the beaten stranger in the parable, is rejected by representatives of the two major "tribes" in the novel: Protestants, represented by Mr. Deasy and Crofton, and Catholics/nationalists, represented by Mr. Dedalus, the Citizen, and others. Even as he is being rejected by these characters, though, he is playing the role of the Good Samaritan throughout the day, culminating in his rescue of and care for Stephen, the beaten traveler.

Playing these two roles must be largely unconscious on Bloom's part (and on Stephen's), but our knowledge as readers of the roles enables a deeper sense of the significance of this narrative that they reiterate and reinscribe, and therefore connects their actions to a whole history of archetypes in our minds, placing them in an eternal mythic community. T. S. Eliot's famous review of *Ulysses* in the *Dial* has been cited *ad infinitum* but is worth briefly returning to, especially in the light that Denis Donoghue sheds upon it—and thus upon Joyce's use of mythic narratives in *Ulysses*. Eliot believed that myths lived in communities by virtue of daily repetition, and thus, as Donoghue argues, "An ordinary event becomes significant in the light of the myth it enacts, however residually." Thus, "[i]t acquires a halo of significance when it is seen under a higher perspective, or when it can be shown to participate in a form, a pattern of being, at a certain remove from the level on which otherwise it is merely an event like any other."[65] Who knows how many iterations there have been in life and literature of the Good Samaritan parable? On this day, June 16, 1904, Leopold Bloom's repetitive actions of *caritas* lift him into the serried ranks of those who have protected, helped, and rescued others; he also is verbally attacked all day long, enabling him to play the Stranger of the parable in the moments when he is not helping others. In this regard, Declan Kiberd has argued that Joyce's depiction of Bloom as a modern-day Odysseus in *Ulysses* suggests his "conviction that primitive myths are not impositions of a culture but innate possessions of every single man, who professes to be a unique being but is in fact a copy, consciously or unconsciously emulating the lives of more original predecessors."[66]

Weldon Thornton's early immersion in the allusions of the novel led him to make a similar point that antedates Kiberd's, noting of Stephen's and Bloom's actions that "[t]hough their acts reiterate the acts of earlier men, neither of them seems adequately aware that his individual, seemingly separate existence is given potential form, depth, and meaning by his participation in the perennial, archetypal patterns of man's experience."[67] What might it mean to read the character of Bloom in this way, specifically through his at-times conscious and, more often, unconscious emulation of the Good Samaritan? Both Thornton and Kiberd apprehend that we are connected to others in the past and present through our living out such myths, such archetypes—if we only knew that we were. But Thornton quickly hastens to add that "*aware* is of course the wrong word here, for it implies a high degree of consciousness, and Joyce does not intend that his characters or his readers will begin thinking 'Ah! How like Hamlet was that last gesture of mine!'" Such an awareness would make utterly artificial the connection Joyce desired between Stephen and Bloom: "Too keen a consciousness [of such archetypes] parodies and destroys the needed rapport."[68] In such a situation, we readers then become the necessary, mediating consciousness that reads Stephen and Bloom through earlier myths and narratives, connecting them through a common mythical substrate of which they seem largely unaware.[69]

Joyce's instantiation of various older narratives into the flow of his contemporary novel, what we now call intertextuality, accords with what Charles Taylor has argued about the medieval mind of our predecessors: "The flow of secular time occurs in a multiplex vertical context, so that everything relates to more than one kind of time."[70] And even in our present age, as Eric Gregory and Leah Hunt-Hendrix point out, "Modernity is still marked by kairotic time—we still have festivals and celebrations that remind us of our origins, and we still tell ourselves stories and narratives that shape our identities."[71] As Gregory and Hunt-Hendrix, drawing on Taylor's argument in *A Secular Age*, suggest, in the post-Enlightenment age, "[a]s time takes on a totalizing character, other modes of experience are eclipsed. The multiple notions of time in premodern periods enabled the rupturing of experience, a kind of complementarity to the everyday."[72] But

> In a modernity severed from transcendence and higher times, however, what exists in time is all that is real. Modern morality must be equally totalizing. . . . The flattening of time into a single register corresponds with the reduction of ethics to a code, for in such an ordered world, each moment can be evaluated, each second judged.

With the breaking in of a parabolic narrative to such a flattened and diminished world, however, secular time's code is fractured; the "parable of the Good Samaritan slices through this notion of a timely ethics. Suddenly the code is called into question with the chance arrival of God or the neighbor, the Event."[73]

Taylor argues that contingency is a crucial part of the parable of the Good Samaritan. The answer to the question, "Who is my neighbor?", is, he claims, "the one you happen across, stumble across, who is wounded there in the road."[74] Moreover, as Gregory and Hunt-Hendrix posit in their reading of Taylor's reading of the parable, "Accident and contingency are the venue of love."[75] And yet we know how carefully Joyce planned this encounter with Stephen: everything else in the novel leads up to it in a sense. Bloom and Stephen do not recognize they are now re-enacting the parable of the Good Samaritan. Furthermore, Bloom knows well who Stephen is: he is no stranger.

The strange and violent, hallucinatory, even apocalyptic vision of "Circe" yields to and is a vehicle for the parabolic narrative of "Eumaeus" and beyond. These two episodes together show in microcosm the argument I advanced in Chapter 2—that *Ulysses*, as Joyce's prophetic, apocalyptic "sacred" book, epiphanically reveals his message of loving our neighbor as ourselves. Despite its narrative distortions, the Circean narrator nonetheless manages to articulate

Stephen's breaking of the chandelier in response to his mother's spectral appearance in the brothel as an apocalyptic event, as Beryl Schlossman has argued. His "destructive gesture acts as a cut, a sacrifice, a rupture, actualizing denegation in the form of a catastrophe," and therefore

> Stephen gives himself over to this apocalyptic night, and thus the trial by fire to which he alludes at the end of "Oxen of the Sun" resonates in the last flame of time: "She [Babylon] shall be utterly burned with fire," "There should be time no longer" (Apoc. 18:8; 10:6).[76]

Schlossman continues:

> In Joyce's rewriting of the Revelation of St. John the Divine, Stephen comes face to face with his mother as he awaits her revelation. But the dead mother engages in an institutional battle to save Stephen, who overturns the Revelation of the new Jerusalem (Apoc. 21) by locating Lucifer's refusal ["*Non Serviam*!", U 15.4228] within it.[77]

And yet Schlossman does not recognize that Stephen's true revelation is not so much Bloom's role as paternal figure to his son figure, but the message that Bloom brings to him: to love our neighbor, even if—especially if—he is from another tribe and culture, and even if he does not respond lovingly to our ministrations.[78]

The Good Samaritan parable, which has been termed "a parable *par excellence*,"[79] centrally takes up the question of how we respond charitably and mercifully to our enemies and expresses well the caring attitude Bloom takes to the drunken and exhausted Stephen. Christ's iteration of this parable is provoked by a lawyer, who has just asked him "What shall I do to inherit eternal life?" (Luke 10:25). Christ famously replies to the lawyer, "Thou shalt love the Lord thy God with all thy heart, and with all thy soul, and with all thy strength, and with all thy mind; and thy neighbor as thyself" (Luke 10:27). But the lawyer, who, we are told, wants to "justify himself," cunningly asks Jesus, "Who is my neighbor?" (Luke 10:29 KJV).

Recall that Bloom wonders aloud, "Who is my neighbour?" in "Lotus Eaters" when he enters the Catholic Church (*U* 5.341) as a sort of tourist. Although he conflates this with a chance "to be next some girl" (*U* 5.341), that he nonetheless ponders this question early in the novel suggests that he might know the parable of the Good Samaritan as well, perhaps from his general Masonic training and specifically from his possible Masonic degree of the Good Samaritan. Regardless of whether Bloom himself knows the parable, Joyce certainly expects the reader to recognize this allusion to it. At the end of the "Lotus Eaters," Bloom blasphemously imagines himself as Christ (whom the Good Samaritan prefigures) as well, as he sits in the bath and thinks "This is my body" (*U* 5.566). Earlier he has imagined himself into the passage from Luke 10:38–42 that immediately follows the parable of the Good Samaritan, where Christ sits talking to Martha and Mary (*U* 5.289–99). If Martha and Mary are Jesus' two admirers, Martha and Molly are Bloom's two admirers in the present.

Christ responds to the lawyer's question about who his neighbor is by, as Paul Ricoeur puts it, suggesting that "the neighbor is not a social object but a behavior."[80] Christ replies to the lawyer by relating the parable of the Good Samaritan, in which a priest, followed by a Levite, refuse to help a beaten and robbed traveler. The man is finally helped by a member of a different tribe, a Samaritan. After Christ asks him which one of the three men was a neighbor to the man, the lawyer confesses, "He that shewed mercy to him" (Luke 10:37 KJV). The Jewish lawyer is chastened mainly because Jews then thought Samaritans unclean. A popular saying at the time that Joyce knew held that "a piece of Samaritan bread is the flesh of swine."[81] In a passage I shall return to again from "Eumaeus," Stephen's reaction to Bloom's getting "on his companion's right," to protect "his tender Achilles," and stating "Lean on me," taking his arm, is inexplicable at first: "he thought he felt a strange kind of flesh of a different man approach him, sinewless and wobbly and all that" (*U* 16.1715, 1716, 1720, 1723–4), but it echoes the likely reaction of the beaten victim in Christ's parable to the help of the Good Samaritan. Budgen is again insightful in thinking through this interaction, arguing that "[w]e must suppose that part of Stephen's physical recoil was due to their difference of race," and then strangely, "there exists also a physical chemical repulsion, and this is felt only by the Gentile for the Jewish man."[82] As we will see, despite his initial aversion to Bloom, Stephen receives his help, accepting the difference of the Other in a profound, silent moment of development for their relationship.

The utter physicality of the personal encounters in the parable becomes crucial for our understanding of, first, the disgust of the first two travelers, the Jewish priest and the Levite, who see the wounded man; then, the unexpected reaching out and touching of the wounded man by the Samaritan; next, the contemporary audience's dashed expectations of a Jewish, not Samaritan rescuer; and finally Bloom's reaching out to Stephen, offering him his embodied assistance after he is attacked in the Nighttown brothel. Not only were the Jews hostile to Samaritans, but Samaritans were also hostile to Jews.[83] The man in the ditch, the beaten traveler, along with Christ's Jewish audience, expects "one of their own to show compassion," but as Ian McDonald notes, "the plot of the parable explodes their conventional image of how grace is enacted. The view from the ditch is that of a hated Samaritan face looming above. What can be expected but a final act of hatred?" But in "the reversal of role from stereotypical opponent to supreme helper, the expectation of the Jewish audience is positively assailed."[84]

In his extended reading of the Good Samaritan parable, which he develops from his reading of contemporary philosopher Ivan Illich's *The Rivers North of the Future*, Charles Taylor points out that Illich's understanding of the Samaritan's free response in the parable, "not by some version of 'ought,' but by this wounded person himself," enables him to create

> a new kind of fittingness, belonging together, between Samaritan and wounded Jew. They are fitted together in a dissymmetric proportionality (chapter 17, p. 197 [in Ililch's *The Rivers North of the Future*]) which comes from God, which is that of *agape*, and which became possible because God became flesh.[85]

Taylor terms this newly established and narrated relationship in the parable "a skein of relations which link particular, enfleshed people to each other, rather than a grouping of people together on the grounds of their sharing some important property (as in modern nations, we are all Canadians, Americans, French people; or universally, we are all rights-bearers, etc.)."[86] His reading helps us, along with Bloom, to reject the Citizen's restrictive definition of a nation and to realize that by employing such a parable, Joyce was interested in the bodily or incarnational meetings of human beings that would enable them to establish such hopefully perduring relationships.

Ricoeur suggests powerfully the Samaritan's ability to stand outside of religious tradition and his capacity for invention, much as the marginalized, secular "Jew" Leopold Bloom would stray from his course home and imagine a relationship with Stephen later in the novel: The Samaritan "is not encumbered by his social responsibility, [and is] ready to change his itinerary and invent an unforeseen behavior, available for encounter and the presence of others. The conduct that he invents is the direct relationship of 'man to man.'"[87] Even though we might expect Bloom to be charitable because of his practice of such charitable acts repeatedly earlier in the novel, his extraordinary generosity on a night when he himself is exhausted from the day's travails—the attacks on his person, his wife's unfaithfulness—is nothing less than a stupendous invention in the same sense Ricoeur ascribes to Christ's Samaritan. No one has ever taught Bloom to care for someone in this excessively generous way, but he puts his adman's creative mind to work and comes up with a rescue plan for Stephen that he follows through, bringing both himself and Stephen "home."

In January, 1905, Joyce ordered Ernest Renan's hugely popular *The Life of Jesus* (*SL* 50), first published in 1863, and by the end of February, he would write Stanislaus, "I have read Renan's 'Life of Jesus' . . . it is a model of good writing in many ways: the temper is delightful" (*SL* 55). He read in it about Jesus' emphasis on faith that proceeded from the heart, not from outward observances or mere religious rules. Renan's humanizing of Jesus (but not his insistence on purging Christ of his Jewishness) was likely enormously appealing to Joyce, particularly for his portrayal of the humanist Bloom and in particular for his development of Bloom as a Samaritan character.[88]

Renan's discussion of the physical revulsion the Samaritans occasioned in more dominant and orthodox Jewish sects at the time, and Jesus' interest in and care for this despised group, likely appealed to Joyce as he meditated on the character of Bloom, especially in comparing him to the Good Samaritan. Renan observes, "This poor sect . . . was treated by the Hierosolymites with extreme harshness. They placed them in the same rank as pagans but hated them more. Jesus, from a feeling of opposition, was well disposed toward Samaria, and often preferred the Samaritans to the *orthodox Jews*."[89] Recall the opening sentence of "Eumaeus": "Preparatory to anything else Mr Bloom brushed off the greater bulk of the shavings and handed Stephen the hat and ashplant and bucked him up generally in *orthodox Samaritan fashion* which he very badly needed" (*U* 16.1–3; my emphasis). The crucial phrase here, perhaps echoing but reversing Renan's phrase in his implication that the Samaritans' unorthodox beliefs clashed with those of the "orthodox Jews," is "in orthodox Samaritan fashion." I will examine this phrase and its meaning in my chapter on "Eumaeus," but suffice it to say for now that Joyce likely uses this phrase to signify how Bloom acted charitably, *just like* the original Good Samaritan did, and over against the behavior of the supposedly orthodox believers in the novel (Catholic Christians, save for Father Conmee and, to some degree, Martin Cunningham and Joe Hynes). This opening sentence and other passages where Bloom rejects violence and embraces "mutual equality" suggest how much Joyce endorsed his behavior here.

Renan lavishly praises the Good Samaritan parable, saying, "One of his most beautiful parables was that of the man wounded on the way to Jericho."[90] After summarizing the parable, Renan states that:

> Jesus argues from this that true brotherhood is established among men by charity, and not by creeds. The neighbor who in Judaism was specially the co-religionist, was in his estimation the man who has pity on his kind without distinction of sect. Human brotherhood in its widest sense overflows in all his teaching.[91]

The secular Jewish Bloom epitomizes this overflowing sense of human brotherhood supremely in "Eumaeus," as we shall see.

We know from Ira B. Nadel's pioneering study, *Joyce and the Jews*, that Joyce had several books on Zionism in his Trieste library, including Harry Sacher's 1916 edited volume, *Zionism and the Jewish Future*, in which he likely read Albert M. Hyamson's comprehensive essay "Anti-Semitism," and learned how Jews and former Jews such as his fictional Bloom had been historically discriminated against in various European countries. For instance, one of Hyamson's opening claims suggests that "[t]he Jew in Europe has always been the stranger, different from his environment" and further, that "in the medieval European State, founded on a Christian basis, the Jew was a class by himself, detached from the land, and not naturalized in the city."[92] It would be difficult to find a more accurate description of the roots of Leopold Bloom's uneasy, marginal position in contemporary Dublin as he pads throughout the city on that June day in 1904.[93] And it is precisely because of that dislocated status that he feels so deeply for, even empathizes with, the dispossessed Stephen. Bloom's marginalization both from non-Jewish society and from his own Jewish roots thus gives him a true understanding of what it would be like to function as a Samaritan figure outcast from Dublin society.

Joyce employs this parable because he consistently privileges love, and once we apprehend that the Good Samaritan parable illustrates Bloom's actions earlier in the novel and in the moving scenes with Stephen at the end of "Circe" and throughout "Eumaeus" and "Ithaca," we realize his desire to rescue and tend to the "beaten stranger," Stephen Dedalus, which stems from his habitus of charity. Harry K. Russell even argues that "Bloom's habitual attitude is a merciful understanding of the feelings and needs of others. His empathic response to his inanimate as well as animate environment is so conspicuous that it becomes a kind of immanence."[94]

Such actions taken by a largely secular character contrast sharply with those taken by the Jewish priest and the Levite early in Luke's parable. In Luke 10:31, after the traveler has been attacked and robbed, "by chance there came down a certain priest that way: and when he saw him, he passed by on the other side." This priest, the first of three potential rescuers for the wounded man, walks by him, neglecting Christ's commandment to "Love . . . thy neighbor as thyself" (Luke 10:27, KJV). The Levite does the same, although he gets closer to the traveler, risking defilement. Both might have had sound theological reasons for not helping the traveler, but Christ does not let them off the hook, explicitly contrasting the refusal of these religiously "orthodox" Jews to help the traveler with the marginalized, heretic Samaritan's instant, generous rescue of him.

Robert Funk has argued that Jesus chose the Samaritan as the protagonist of the parable because

> the Samaritan is the one whom the victim does not, could not expect would help, indeed does not want his help . . . the Samaritan is a secular figure; he functions not as an esoteric cipher for a religious faction . . . but in his concrete, everyday significance.[95]

Leopold Bloom is exactly such a "secular figure" in "his concrete, everyday significance." Crucially, Funk points out that the Samaritan's help is not wanted by the victim; nonetheless he offers it, a vital factor for understanding both Stephen's general lack of receptivity to Bloom when he helps him, particularly in "Eumaeus," and even Corley's lack of gratitude to Stephen, who may be turning into a Good Samaritan figure himself when he helps Corley in the same episode. And yet, in another sense, the "everydayness" of our expectations is confounded by Bloom's helping of Stephen, just as the expectations of the hearers of Jesus' parable are shattered. Funk makes this important point when he notes that the entrance of the unexpected Samaritan into the story "shatters the realism, the *everydayness* of the story" (my emphasis) because "[a] narrative begun with all the traits of an experience about which everyone knows, or thinks he knows, is ruptured at the crucial juncture by a factor which does not square with everyday experience." In this way, "[t]he 'logic' of everydayness is broken upon by the 'logic' of the parable."[96] Applying Funk's reading of the parable to Joyce's Samaritan helps us realize that Joyce goes beyond this dynamic by having an everyday, ordinary advertising canvasser appear again and unexpectedly help the wounded Stephen. And yet, as we will see in the next chapter, Bloom's quotidian qualities engender a profound, even ineffable and spiritual—because embodied—relationship with Stephen and with the reader.

Notes

1. Joyce cleverly connects representatives of both groups of Bloom's persecutors—the Protestant Deasy and the Catholic Simon Dedalus—by giving them both a "moustache" that is "angry" (*U* 2.188, 6.72). It should be said that despite their distancing themselves from Bloom earlier in the episode, Martin Cunningham and Joe Hynes *do* finally help him escape from the Citizen. Ellmann points out a fascinating analogy between Cunningham's and Hynes's rescue of Bloom from the Citizen, noting that "Corney Kelleher assists in rescuing Stephen from the Watch (police). Their cooperation is less momentous than Bloom's Good Samaritan act, but suggests that Dublin is not devoid of compassion or good will" (*The Consciousness of Joyce*, 90).
2. Davison, *James Joyce,* Ulysses, *and the Construction of Jewish Identity*, 201.
3. Pierce, *Reading Joyce*, 224.
4. Ibid., 225.
5. See Yeats and Gregory, *Cathleen ni Houlihan*, when the Old Woman is asked by Bridget, "What was it put you wandering?", and she replies, "Too many strangers in the house" (23). Shortly thereafter, when Michael asks her, "What hopes have you to hold to?," the Old Woman repeats the phrase in bellicose language: "The hope of getting my beautiful fields back again; the hope of putting the strangers out of my house" (25).
6. Qtd. in Nadel, *Joyce and the Jews*, 139. In this regard, Margot Norris's point in *Virgin and Veteran Readings of* Ulysses shows how Joyce took pains to emphasize Bloom's humanity in the early episodes of the novel—not his putative Jewishness: "Given that Joyce published *Ulysses* at a time when even his most notable contemporaries displayed little embarrassment about anti-Semitic references and allusions in their work and to their colleagues, he was clearly conscious of a readership

whose response to a Jewish protagonist could not be predicted in advance. The way Leopold Bloom is introduced in *Ulysses* may therefore display a deliberate strategy to guarantee that by having the reader first become immersed in Bloom's personality, an investment in his social and psychological welfare is generated that will maintain sympathy in face of the conflicts the Jewish Bloom will encounter in the later episodes" (102).

7. Kiberd, Ulysses *and Us*, 310.
8. Davison, *James Joyce,* Ulysses, *and the Construction of Jewish Identity*, 215.
9. Ibid., 218.
10. Ibid., 219.
11. Such scriptural knowledge, as well as his knowledge of both Jewish and Christian traditions that predispose Bloom to caring charitably for Stephen, suggest just how misleading are Geert Lernout's claims that "Bloom . . . seems to be in many ways beyond religion" and that "Bloom represents the modern European secularist, who sees religion as a way of oppressing the masses" (*Help My Unbelief*, 187, 189).
12. Kiberd, Ulysses *and Us*, 309. As he continues, "The new covenant must be wholly free of racial or territorial constraint; and on that basis a narrowly nationalist messiah would constitute a defeat for the politics of Exodus" (310).
13. Kermode, *The Genesis of Secrecy*, 38.
14. See Russell, "Parabolic Plots in Bernard MacLaverty's *Lamb*," 27–44.
15. Ellmann quotes Joyce's letter to Budgen of July 11, 1919, reproduced in Joyce, *SL* 239, and then quotes Joyce's unpublished letter to Ezra Pound, April 1, 1918.
16. Thornton, who has long been one of the major advocates for appreciating Bloom's charity, points out Bloom's helping the blind stripling and then his rescuing Stephen later, then adds, "Bloom's human concern and charity are manifested as well in dozens of smaller ways, such as his concealing his revulsion at the scene in the Burton restaurant [in "Lestrygonians"] by pretending to be looking for someone he cannot find" ("The Greatness of *Ulysses*," 27). My graduate student Kelly Chittenden has argued in an unpublished paper for my seminar on Joyce, Beckett, Cormac McCarthy and hospitality in the fall of 2020 that Bloom's attitude toward the cat, including emulating its language, trying to "enter into the cat's sensory perspective," and generously feeding her with warm milk and bits of the kidney he cooks for his breakfast together demonstrate his habitus of generosity. She also makes the intriguing point that had Bloom not been actively concerned for Mina Purefoy's birth pains, he would never have traveled to the maternity hospital and thus would never have met Stephen Dedalus that fateful June night, suggesting that his habitus of generosity "is truly generative, for each act of hospitality leads him to another" ("Parables and Reading Joyce's *Dubliners*").
17. Lawrence, *Who's Afraid of James Joyce?*, 151. Such readings as those advanced by Ellmann, Thornton, and Lawrence, along with the novel's consistent depiction of Bloom as charitable, give the lie to John Cussen's bizarre (and singular, as far as I can tell) claim that Bloom's caring behavior, particularly in "Eumaeus," stems from his drunkenness. Cussen argues, "Although other terms might be used to describe the tenor of the hero's flushed moment—excited, well-intentioned, paternal, solicitous, benevolent, Christian, bewitched, and 'orthodox Samaritan' (*U* 16.3)—none is as thoroughly contextualized by the larger novel as is 'drunk'" ("Bloom's Drunk," 57).

18. Joyce, "Force," 23.
19. Ricoeur, "The Socius and the Neighbor," 99.
20. Qtd. in Scholes and Kain, *The Workshop of Daedalus*, 75.
21. Ibid., 76.
22. Ibid., 77.
23. Qtd. in Benjamin, "The Third Gospel in *Finnegans Wake*," 106.
24. Seeley, *Ecce Homo*, 147.
25. Mason and Ellmann, Introduction to Joyce, "Royal Hibernian Academy 'Ecce Homo,'" 31. I came to this understanding of Joyce's humanistic Christ and its overlap with Renan's and Seeley's portraits of Christ on my own, but I have been pleased to since find Marianna Gula's helpful discussion of this issue in the context of Joyce's appreciation of this painting; see Gula, "'Reading the Book of Himself,'" 56–9. Gula cautions us about drawing too neat a line of influence from Seeley and Renan to Joyce, since we cannot know that he had read Seeley at the time of his review and since he read Renan some six years after the review. "Nonetheless," she argues, "even if it is not possible to unequivocally trace Joyce's unorthodox portrait of Christ in his Munkácsy essay back to the direct influence of any concrete texts, it dovetails neatly with the heterodox portraits of Jesus drawn by Renan and Seeley" (58).
26. Qtd. in Scholes and Kain, *The Workshop of Daedalus*, 101.
27. Joyce, "Royal Hibernian Academy 'Ecce Homo,'" 32.
28. Ibid., 36.
29. Ibid., 37. Thornton long ago made the link between Joyce's essay on Munkácsy's painting *Ecce Homo* and Bloom's use of the phrase in "Lotus Eaters" when he thinks "Not like Ecce Homo. Crown of thorns and cross" (*U* 5.329–30; Thornton, *Allusions in* Ulysses, 82–3). Alessandro Bruni likely did not know Joyce's essay, but his perceptive point that Joyce "only admires completely the unchangeable: the mystery of Christ and the mute drama of the literature that surrounds it" ("Joyce Stripped Naked in the Piazza," 35) captures the essence of Joyce's insistence on Munkacsy's portrait of Christ as essentially dramatic.
30. Gibson, "Thinking Forwards, Turning Back," 69; emphasis Gibson's.
31. Kenner, *Ulysses*, 116.
32. Ibid., 116.
33. Ibid., 127.
34. Thornton, *Voices and Values*, has the most convincing reading of this episode's style and agenda. He posits that "the presenter to whom the episode has been delegated" in "Circe" "has a Freudian view of human nature and especially of the unconscious, and those literary and psychological agendas control the presentation of everything in the episode." Because the "expressionistic/Freudian mode of presentation here is so total and pervasive" (156), many commentators such as Kenner have bought into this deception, believing that we really are seeing Stephen's and Bloom's deepest darkest fears and desires paraded before our eyes. That Stephen really is upset about his inability to be a good Catholic in front of his dying mother, for instance, is unquestionable, but the way in which that memory becomes hallucinatory and threatening suggests it drives almost everything he does and thinks, which is simply untrue. See Thornton, *Voices and Values*, 160–4, for a helpful survey of critical responses to this episode.

35. Ibid., 164. Thornton also quotes Budgen to buttress his argument: "'It is steeped in the atmosphere and governed by the logic of hallucination, but its dominant theme is the fatherly love and care of Bloom for Stephen Dedalus'" (ibid., 164; Budgen, *James Joyce and the Making of* Ulysses, 231).
36. Gabler, "Afterword" to *Ulysses: A Critical and Synoptic Edition*, III, notes, "it is remarkable that the unprecedented addition of entire segments of text to existing chapters, such as the 'Metropolitan Police' addition to 'Cyclops' and the 'Messianic' scene to 'Circe,' should be closely associated with the writing of the finale" (1891).
37. Benstock, "*Ulysses*: The Making of an Irish Myth," 224.
38. Bailey, *Through Peasant Eyes*, 42, 45.
39. Ibid., 47.
40. Young, *The Parables: Jewish Tradition and Christian Interpretation*, 112.
41. Budgen, *James Joyce and the Making of* Ulysses, 284.
42. The oil "served as a salve . . . and the wine as an antiseptic," states Marion Lloyd Soards in her "Commentary on Luke" for the *New Oxford Annotated Bible*, 118.
43. Notice how Bloom's brisk actions here are anticipated by one of the Good Samaritan figures in "Grace," the young cyclist: "He knelt down promptly beside the injured man and called for water. . . . The young man washed the blood from the injured man's mouth and then called for some brandy" (*D* 151).
44. Norris, *Virgin and Veteran Readings of Ulysses*, 181.
45. Budgen, *James Joyce and the Making of Ulysses*, 287.
46. Levinas, *Alterity and Transcendence*, 25, quoted in Freeman, *The Priority of the Other*, 93.
47. Freeman, *The Priority of the Other*, 93, drawing on Levinas, *Alterity and Transcendence*, 27.
48. Levinas, *Alterity and Transcendence*, 98, quoted in Freeman, *The Priority of the Other*, 94.
49. Freeman, *The Priority of the Other*, 84.
50. Taylor, *A Secular Age*, 741. I should add at this point that while much of my argument focuses on the encounter and subsequent ethical implications of Bloom and Stephen late in "Circe," and continuing into "Eumaeus" and "Ithaca," I agree with Ricoeur in his reading of the parable in "The Socius and the Neighbor" that "When I reduce the theology of the neighbor to a theology of the encounter, I miss the fundamental meaning of the Lordship of God over *history*. It is this theological theme which gives to the theme of charity all the extension and breadth of which it is capable" (104). Joyce would certainly not recognize the "Lordship of God over history," but I do.
51. Hyde, *The Gift*, 67.
52. Ibid., 68.
53. Marc Mamogian has pointed out to me that Avery Allyns's *Ritual and Illustrations of Freemasonry* (11–12) is the only publication in which the oath is printed in this exact form.
54. Shortly after this remark, Flynn does mime Bloom signing a document and says, "—Nothing in black and white," a reference to Bloom's refusal to give loans (*U* 8.986, 8.988). While this moment could be interpreted as Flynn's disparaging Bloom's charitable nature right after he praised it, it likely just refers to Bloom's Jewishness and his adherence to the Old Testament prohibition on usury.

55. Albert, "*Ulysses*, Cannibals, and Freemasons," 266.
56. Schneider, "Freemasonic Signs and Passwords in the 'Circe' Episode," 303.
57. Crispi, *Joyce's Creative Process and the Construction of Characters in Ulysses*, 227, citing on 226 Slote, Mamogian, and Turner, "Notes," 812. It is only fair to point out that Albert made this argument first, noting this passage as "evidence for his [Bloom's] actual membership" in the Masons ("*Ulysses*, Cannibals, and Freemasons," 280) and also citing the passage where Bloom is described as having "*his fingers at his lips in the attitude of secret master. . .*": "In the stage-directions which follow [the Masonic Obligation of Secrecy], Joyce makes it quite clear that Bloom knows the secret sign of the secret master-Mason, as well as the obligation," further terming this moment when he sees over Stephen's prone body a vision of his dead son Rudy as evidencing "the importance of the theme of Freemasonry—it is *Joyce's* symbol of fraternal, and paternal love" (283).
58. Mackey, *A Lexicon of Freemasonry*, 426.
59. Macoy, *The General History, Cyclopedia, and Dictionary of Freemasonry*, 342. I am indebted to Marc Mamogian for this reference and also for urging me to investigate possible connections among freemasonry, Bloom, and the Good Samaritan parable.
60. Schneider, "Freemasonic Signs and Passwords in the 'Circe' Episode," 307–8.
61. Joyce had written to Budgen asking him to send reference books, including "[Any little handbook of] British Freemasonry" (*Letters* I, 177), on November 6, 1921, and he added the Masonic references in "Circe" in December 1921 and January 1921, shortly before and then during the time he changed the phrase "good Samaritan" to "orthodox Samaritan," which may suggest that he changed this crucial phrase to disguise not only the Lukan reference but also the Masonic reference.
62. I thus disagree with Ellmann, *Ulysses on the Liffey*, 148, who argues, "The seal upon Bloom's Good Samaritan act is given at the end of the episode by his vision of Rudy." Ellmann likens Bloom's rescue of Stephen, "motivated by *Agape*," to how, "out of love," he "reshapes Rudy's misshapen features and raises him from the grave" (149).
63. Davison, *James Joyce, Ulysses, and the Construction of Jewish Identity*, 228.
64. Ibid., 228. Davison further points out that "each of these attributes are essentials of Jewish manhood as prescribed by the Torah and elaborated on by the Talmud. Corresponding Jewish precepts to Bloom's 'Jewishness' here would include Tzedakah (charitable actions and offerings), Shalom Bayit (the peaceful, nurturing home), the Pirkei Avot (The Ethics of the Fathers), and more" (282 n87).
65. Donoghue, "A Plain Approach to *Ulysses*," 161, 161–2.
66. Kiberd, "Brian Friel's *Faith Healer*," 224.
67. Thornton, "The Allusive Method in *Ulysses*," 246.
68. Ibid., 246. He goes on to add, "What Joyce does wish is that modern man were not so isolated—that he had, if not an awareness, at least a sense that his particular experience is deeply rooted in general, traditional human experience and that this root taps sources of meaning" (246).
69. Without dealing with the question of characters' consciousness of enacting archetypal or mythical roles, James H. Maddox makes a fascinating argument for the revelation "Eumaeus" makes on the subject: "In the earlier chapters of *Ulysses*

Joyce seems content to suggest a *parallel* between mythic times and the modern scene. In 'Eumaeus' it becomes clear to what extent the characters are *reincarnations*— in the sense that they re-enact the deeds of the great men who have preceded them. It is a case of met him pike hoses" ("'Eumaeus' and the Theme of Return in *Ulysses*," 220).

70. Taylor, *A Secular Age*, 57.
71. Gregory and Hunt-Hendrix, "Enfleshment and the Time of Ethics," 234.
72. Ibid., 233.
73. Ibid., 234. Joyce's one-time secretary, Samuel Beckett, strongly grasped this transcendent code of ethics even if he did not always subscribe to it: Think of Didi and Gogot's waiting for Godot in that famous and genre-breaking play. While Godot (or is it God?) never arrives, their neighbors, Pozzo and Lucky, do, as does a boy, and their encounters with these characters gesture toward a timeless code of ethics—treat others as you would want to be treated. When Estragon, who of all the characters in that play should be most sympathetic to the brain-damaged Lucky, begins verbally abusing him, employing brutal language like Pozzo did, we are shocked into a realization that here a real violation has occurred—one human has rejected another.
74. Taylor, *A Secular Age*, 742.
75. Gregory and Hunt-Hendrix, "Enfleshment and the Time of Ethics," 234.
76. Schlossman, *Joyce's Catholic Comedy of Language*, 6.
77. Ibid., 6.
78. Norris, *Virgin and Veteran Readings of* Ulysses, acknowledges something of Stephen's lack of gratitude for Bloom's rescue of him even as early as the conclusion of "Circe" when she notes that Bloom's care for Stephen "remains invisible to its beneficiary," finally musing that while Bloom believes Stephen is in some ways his "changeling" son Rudy returned to him (U 15.4957), "when will Stephen recognize that he has found himself a father surrogate?" (181).
79. McDonald, "Alien Grace," 45. McDonald cites Funk, *Parables and Presence*, 65, who observes, "there is no other parable in the Jesus tradition which carries a comparable punch."
80. Ricoeur, "The Socius and the Neighbor," 99.
81. Mishnah, qtd. in Renan, *The Life of Jesus*, 175.
82. Budgen, *James Joyce and the Making of* Ulysses, 261. A more secularized reading of this passage could be articulated through Julia Kristeva's psychoanalytic reading of ourselves and the Other: "Freud brings us the courage to call ourselves disintegrated . . . in order not to integrate foreigners and even less so to hunt them down, but rather to welcome them to that uncanny strangeness, which is as much theirs as it is ours" (Kristeva, *Strangers to Ourselves*, 192, qtd. in Purcell, "Torn Flesh: Julia Kristeva and the Givenness of the Stranger," 577).
83. McDonald notes that "Samaritan hostility to Jewish pilgrims is even documented in Jocephus [sic]" ("Alien Grace," 40–1).
84. Ibid., 44.
85. Taylor, *A Secular Age*, 738, 739.
86. Ibid., 739.

87. Ricoeur, "The Socius and the Neighbor," 99.
88. Lernout, *Help My Unbelief*, mentions Renan a number of times in passing, but chooses not to focus on any passages in this important biography that Joyce knew and read. In fact, his longest discussion of Renan instead treats Stanislaus's reading of *The Life of Jesus* and notes that "he was not really impressed by what he calls the ex-priest's 'picnic Christianity'" (100). Stanislaus may not have been, but his brother James was impressed by Renan's recovery of a loving, humanized Christ.
89. Renan, *The Life of Jesus*, 174; my emphasis.
90. Ibid., 174.
91. Ibid., 175.
92. Hyamson, "Anti-Semitism," 59, 59–60. See Nadel, *Joyce and the Jews*, 69–84, for a list of these books and a careful exposition of the significance of their content for Joyce's consideration of the somewhat similar plights of the Jews and the Irish.
93. Hyamson only makes one reference to Jews in Ireland—and that in his conclusion. He briefly mentions "the outbreak at Limerick of a few years ago," but puzzlingly terms that "anti-Judaism rather than anti-Semitism," seeing such episodes in Ireland as not exemplifying a comprehensive system of discrimination as in Russia or Germany, but as "almost entirely latent," and which "display[s] itself only in very occasional, local and short-lived outbreaks" ("Anti-Semitism," 86).
94. Russell, "The Incarnation in 'Ulysses,'" 55. Russell argues that while Joyce did not believe "man can know God," he nonetheless believed in the concept of immanence: "Men cannot know the light above, but they can become aware of its irradiation and, like Bruno, Stephen's favorite heretic, see it as the infinite First Cause immanent in the world" (53).
95. Funk, "The Old Testament in Parable: The Good Samaritan," 77. As Colón, *Victorian Parables*, 10, points out, Funk was the "foremost Anglo-American proponent" of the "New Hermeneutics," an approach to the parables that emphasized parables as "'language-events' in which the reader's response is revelatory or formational to and of the reader" (citing Funk, *Language, Hermeneutic, and Word of God*, 51). I believe strongly in Funk's approach in which "Parables can therefore be said to interpret the reader," and yet I share Colón's concern that he overemphasizes this performative aspect of parables and thus "shortchanges the fact that what the parables reveal entails a distinctive ontology and an ethics" (*Victorian Parables*, 10, 11).
96. Funk, *Language, Hermeneutic, and Word of God*, 215.

5

"IN ORTHODOX SAMARITAN FASHION": THE PARABOLIC ENCOUNTER BETWEEN STEPHEN AND BLOOM IN "EUMAEUS"

> All that he [Bloom] does is to hover round him [Stephen] for three or four hours, look after his money, bore him with banal advice, serve him with Epps' cocoa, and invite him to stay the night on an improvised bed. When they take leave of each other we feel certain that they will never meet again. And yet in a measure that no spectacular action could have achieved, we are led from the things done, felt and said to the contemplation of a mystery.
>
> Frank Budgen, *James Joyce and the Making of Ulysses*, 287

Textual Considerations of "Eumaeus"

At the beginning of the "Eumaeus" episode of *Ulysses*, still the most understudied episode in the novel,[1] the narrator describes Leopold Bloom's actions toward Stephen Dedalus, who has been punched by Private Carr in "Circe": "Preparatory to anything else Mr Bloom brushed off the greater bulk of the shavings and handed Stephen the hat and ashplant and bucked him up generally in *orthodox Samaritan fashion* which he very badly needed" (*U* 16.1–3; my emphasis). Given Hugh Kenner's argument that the language of "brushed," "shavings," and "bucked" here returns us to the opening scene of the novel where Buck Mulligan lathers his face and shaves,[2] the new context for this language—Bloom's helping of Stephen—suggests that here, instead of a usurper, a false friend, Joyce now offers Stephen a rescuer, a true friend. Joyce thus reinscribes the Good Samaritan parable in "Circe," "Eumaeus," "Ithaca," and even in "Penelope." But he is also rewriting the first episode, as it were, and bringing Stephen full circle from Buck's attacks on him at 8:00 that morning to Bloom's midnight rescue of him after Private Carr attacks him in "Circe."

There are three other references to the parable in the novel that antedate the reference to it in "Eumaeus." Besides Bloom's pondering of the question, "Who is my neighbor?", in "Lotus Eaters" (5.341), in "Oxen of the Sun", Stephen thinks of the last words of Christ in the parable in the context of a perverted sexual twist on John 15:13: "Greater love than this ... no man hath that a man lay down his wife for his friend" (*U* 14.360–2). Christ utters these words (with the substitution of "life" rather than "wife"!) to the young man who has asked the question Bloom ponders, which leads to His iteration of the parable: "Go thou and do likewise" (Luke 10:37 KJV). And the last two words of Christ's command, "do likewise," appear in "Circe," supposedly uttered by Mrs. Bellingham in the context of illicit sex (*U* 15.1069–70). These other three references differ in tone from the reference to the parable at the beginning of "Eumaeus," since all three connote furtive attempts at illicit sex. The lack of sexual connotation in the phrase about Bloom acting in "orthodox Samaritan fashion" at the beginning of "Eumaeus" signifies a more straightforward allusion to the parable, one that casts Bloom's charity in a favorable light.[3]

Such Lukan language recalls Kiberd's contention regarding how Joyce inserts phrases relating to Christ from the Old Testament into key passages in *Ulysses* about Christ's advent, ministry, death, and resurrection, resulting in a coded prophecy for adepts: "phrases deliberately echoed from the older text in the new one take on an extra charge and depth: they are shot through with prophetic potential, only fulfilled much later in the words and actions of a special man," first Christ, later, presumably Bloom.[4] And yet here Joyce draws directly on a resonant passage from Luke's Gospel in the New Testament, suggesting not only Christ as prophet-figure typologically fulfilling the Old Testament predictions about His coming but more radically the emergence of Bloom as a latter-day suffering prophet who offers a secular message of hospitality and kindness.

The evidence of the existing manuscripts for "Eumaeus" shows clearly, first, that Joyce introduced Bloom as Stephen's rescuer fairly late in the drafting process of the entire novel; second, that when he did so, he cast Bloom's actions directly as done in "good Samaritan fashion"; and then third and finally, that shortly before the novel's publication he changed the phrase to "orthodox Samaritan fashion," partially obscuring his original reference to the parable. Sam Slote has pointed out that the "Eumeo" manuscript that surfaced and was sold at auction in July 2001 was likely "drafted from whatever early (circa 1916) draft had existed," and moreover, that "Eumeo" dates "no later than the second half of 1920, when 'Circe' was being finished" and is the "immediate antecedent to V.A.21," from which the Rosenbach "Eumaeus" was prepared. Slote notes that this "Eumeo" manuscript starts with what we now know as U 16.52–4 with Bloom and Stephen passing the Amiens Street railway terminus and then Talbot Place, and thus, "there is no reference to Bloom picking up Stephen from the ground as we find in the final text."[5] Philip Herring has shown that in BL "Eumaeus" Notesheet 2 for this episode, Joyce referred to Bloom as a "good Samaritan" and then marked out this phrase with blue pencil after he used the version of it we now have, so clearly his characterization of Bloom as this biblical figure came late in the composition process (1921 or later) but was sufficiently important for him to add it at that point.[6] And yet Herring's descriptive essay focused on the Homeric parallels in the "Eumaeus," thus occluding other possible intertexts, such as this parabolic one. Hans Walter Gabler has noted that the "loss of all drafts [from 1914–17] preceding V.A.21 [the final working draft for 'Eumaeus'] no doubt implies a thoroughgoing rewriting, expansion and to some extent even re-conception of the chapter in January–February 1921."[7] Fascinatingly, Joyce may have sought to introduce some confusion about his reference to the parable here by changing "good" to "orthodox" very late in the composition process, just two to three weeks before the novel's publication: Luca Crispi notes that "Joyce changed 'good' to 'orthodox' on the first setting of Proof 36 (Buffalo MS V.C.2.B.25.i; Gabler level 3) sometime between 11 and 16 January 1922."[8]

Certainly, a series of commentators have disagreed about the meaning of the adjective "orthodox," seeing it variously as a sign of Bloom's adherence to the Samaritan's behavior in the parable, as a suggestion of his orthodox Judaism, as a parody of clichéd description, and as an absurdity. Moreover, this reference to Christ's parable has never been fully explained in the context of Bloom's actions in the novel here and elsewhere. Stuart Gilbert, one of the earliest commentators on the novel, notes that "Mr Bloom, indignant at the manner in which Stephen's companions have all deserted him, is determined to play the 'orthodox Samaritan' to the end."[9] This straightforward reading has not always been accepted by later critics. Gifford and Seidman, for instance, point out that the adjective "orthodox" referred originally to those who passed by the injured man and thus, they imply, Bloom is an orthodox Jew as well: The parable "tells of a Samaritan who was willing to help a severely injured man whom the *orthodox Jews ('a certain priest' and 'a Levite') 'passed by' and neglected.*"[10] But Leopold Bloom is nothing like an orthodox Jew in the novel—certainly not like those legalistic Jews Christ criticizes—and seems more culturally Jewish than a believing and practicing Jew; in fact, it is clear that his father converted to Protestantism (U 8.1073–4) and Bloom himself to Catholicism in order to marry Molly, although he muses that they have now left Catholicism: "*Why we left the church of Rome*" (U 8.1074).

More intriguingly, John Porter Houston sees the phrase as an opening example in "Eumaeus" of the "curious ways words are misused," noting, "*In orthodox Samaritan fashion* immediately makes one try to remember whether the Samaritans were orthodox or whether that adjective is even applicable to biblical times," and then helpfully pointing out that such a phrase indicates how "Joyce has managed to make combinations of words of transferred meaning that, though normally dull and mildly unpleasant (*orthodox* for *standard*), here reacquire a literal or original sense."[11] That is, Joyce calls our attention to his use of a seeming synonym for "standard" to focus our attention on the question of how "orthodox" Bloom's behavior really is: It is both typical for him, springing from his habitus of charity, but also "unorthodox" because Bloom's generous, caring behavior toward Stephen singularly contrasts with many other characters' selfish behaviors. By extrapolation, as we will see, Joyce wishes to show the insufficiency of others' rejections of both Stephen (such as Mulligan's usurpation of him) and Bloom (including the Citizen's attack on him), which are "orthodox" because they are standard, happening consistently and regularly. He also thus suggests how Bloom's unorthodox, caring behavior toward Stephen should become exemplary or "orthodox" for other characters, even for us as readers.[12]

Nicholas Fargnoli and Michael Patrick Gillespie puzzlingly claim of this passage that "[t]he Eumaeus episode opens with a sly parody of clichéd description," which "plays off the hackneyed image of the Good Samaritan against the contradictory description of the breakaway Samaritan sect as orthodox." They further posit that starting here, the chapter "signals to attentive readers that it will employ the very misprisions of trite language to create a meaningful and artistically skillful discourse."[13] But the sense of the phrase is not trite at all—while the language in much of the rest of the chapter is—and it surely must mean instead that Bloom acts *exactly* as the Good Samaritan did (and as the kindly Bloom himself has previously done in the novel), in "orthodox Samaritan fashion," by rescuing a downtrodden man. He brushes the shavings off Stephen and gives his hat and ashplant back while also encouraging him and reassuring him—all before trying to feed him and taking him into his own home. Bloom's behaviour thus adheres to the precedent set by the behavior of Christ's Good Samaritan—a now *orthodox* or accepted pattern of behavior exemplified by a decidedly unorthodox, even secularized figure.[14]

The difficult style of "Eumaeus," one of the hardest in the novel to decipher and to describe, has contributed to misunderstandings of this important opening sentence for this chapter and for the "Nostos" as a whole. Richard Ellmann cites this sentence as part of his claim that "Bloom's unassuming decency begins and ends Eumaeus, but is withered a little by the style." Ellmann's statement anticipates a still-prominent claim in criticism on the episode such as Fargnoli and Gillespie's—and more recently, Maud Ellmann's—dismissal of the passage, indeed the entire episode, as clichéd.[15] Because of such misreadings of the style of "Eumaeus" that still persist in a significant strand of Joyce criticism, and because such wrongheaded views tend to prevent commentators from apprehending the significance of the episode, I want to briefly survey the most accurate perceptions about the style here in order both to suggest how well-crafted the episode is, and by extension, how purposefully Joyce employed the Good Samaritan intertext in it.

First, Hugh Kenner's warning should still resonate in our minds here:

> Like "The Oxen of the Sun," the episode has incurred the displeasure of those who don't read closely, and [who] imagine Joyce is conveying the sense of exhaustion by exhausting the reader for fifty pages. . . . On the contrary, Joyce invites close critical attention to the thousands of absurd locutions he employs. The author's mind is working with its usual energy.[16]

Following Kenner, Stanley Sultan misidentifies the narrator as Bloom, and makes a similar point: that there is no indication that Bloom is exhausted like Stephen, and therefore "his" prose here, while clichéd and "pretentious," is also "combined with a more plebeian level of diction to achieve a result that, although ludicrous, is energetic rather than weary."[17] Kenner likewise believes Bloom has essentially "written" this episode; he notes of Bloom that "[t]his is his finest hour," conveyed in a "perfectly awful prose style," yet points out that "'Eumaeus' is not in Bloom's speaking style, true, nor even his thinking style to which we are also privy. But no man writes as he speaks or thinks, but more formally, and generally in longer sentences, and with elegant variations."[18] John Henry Raleigh, author of the fullest commentary on "Eumaeus" besides Christine O'Neill in her book-length study of its style, builds on such contentions, arguing convincingly that despite Joyce's telling Frank Budgen the episode was written in "the language of tired men," Bloom himself "is not tired at all; to the contrary, he is at his liveliest and perkiest of the entire book. And the prose, when examined closely, turns out to be wonderfully energetic and creative in its own peculiar way."[19]

Budgen talked extensively with Joyce as he wrote the novel, and he helpfully points out that despite the obviously bad style of "Eumaeus" (he does not address Joyce's purposes in casting it this way), it nonetheless may be the novel's most poignant in terms of content: "If there are pages of *Ulysses* of a more dazzling virtuosity than those of *Eumaeus* there are certainly none with more insight or tenderness." He continues: "The effect of the slow moving stream of familiar words is comic, till we see emerging out of the dull coloured material a delicate and intimate picture of the relations of a fatherly man to a young man who is a wayward son."[20] More recently, in 1996, O'Neill made clear just this point—that the meandering style can nonetheless convey deep emotion. For instance, she questions Marilyn French's claim in *The Book as World: James Joyce's Ulysses* that "the technique [of "Eumaeus"] is unable to deal with feelings and therefore 'dehumanizing.' For example, the stylistic fumbles can be interpreted as pointing indirectly to Bloom's nervous and gauche endeavors concerning Stephen."[21] And Raleigh identifies the culmination of the passage in which Bloom recounts his encounter with the Citizen as the "most poignant moment of the episode and one of the most poignant moments in the book." Here, after Bloom recalls telling the Citizen that "his God, I mean Christ, was a jew too and all his family like me though in reality I'm not," he adds, "A soft answer turns away wrath" (*U* 16.1084–5, 1085–6), and he is portrayed winsomely: "He turned a long you are wrong gaze on Stephen of timorous dark pride at the soft impeachment with a glance also of entreaty for he seemed to glean in a kind of way that it wasn't all exactly" (*U* 16.1088–90). Raleigh believes that "[i]n *Ulysses* as a whole only Bloom's vision of his dead son at the end of 'Circe' is comparable in pathos: the real son, who was not to be; the 'adopted' son, who will not be."[22] As I argued earlier, Bloom turns away even from his vision of Rudy in the conclusion of "Circe" to pursue Stephen in this rescue narrative adopted from Luke's Gospel, giving it even greater poignancy than Rudy's hallucinatory appearance.

Moreover, the Gabler edition of the novel has cleared up much confusion about the supposedly exhausted style of the "Eumaeus" episode. For instance, Gabler himself points out in his synoptic edition that this episode's style is anticipated late in the earlier episode, "Oxen of the Sun." Joyce had written manuscripts, now lost, between 1914 and 1917,

> as a basis for the final composition of the book's end.... They would seem to have already established the chapter's characteristic style, since the idiom of "Eumaeus" is distinctly anticipated in a passage incorporated in the stylistic conglomerate towards the end of episode 14 ("Oxen of the Sun"; cf. 896.28–898.18).[23]

Significantly, the pre-Gabler editions of the novel generally enervated the style and likely led critics to make claims about it that are somewhat misleading given Gabler's decision to delete excessive commas. William S. Brockman notes that "[a]t least half of the changes to the reading text of *U-G*'s 'Eumaeus' consists of the removal of commas," citing Sultan, who points out that "[t]he energy of the style is a bit more apparent in the Critical Edition, because of the removal of about six hundred spurious commas,' and arguing that "*U-G* [thus] allows Bloom's discursions to continue as fluidly as did his thoughts in earlier episodes."[24]

The Gabler edition of the novel with its newly restored version of a more invigorated "Eumaeus" has spurred several interpretations of the episode that claim this unusual style as purposefully artistic in various ways. For instance, in a significant reading from his 2002 study, *Joyce's Revenge*, Andrew Gibson audaciously sees the style in "Eumaeus" as a then-contemporary and purposeful play on the Irish bull as epitomized in H. P. Kelly's 1919 book *Irish Bulls and Puns*, claiming that the episode "converts blundering—that habit with which the English had long associated the Irish—into a bravura performance, and thus into a form of sustained, cultural triumph" in steering clear of an "elite, Anglo-Irish insistence on the central importance of good English to Irish culture."[25] Further, while not identifying Bloom as the narrator as did Kenner and Sultan, Patrick Colm Hogan argued convincingly in 2014 that this style's redundancy, tendency to exaggeration, and even precision, are part of Bloom's "idiolect" and "sociolect" and that "the narration of 'Eumaeus' is as aesthetically accomplished as that of most other episodes in the book."[26] Moreover, Hogan posits that the "Eumaean sentences are . . . like music," and "repeatedly foster non-anomalous surprise," comprise "instances of beauty," and "convey the story world and story effectively."[27] Thus, despite the persistence of a strand of Joyce criticism that rejects the supposedly exhausted style of "Eumaeus" as not endorsed by Joyce, a critique that makes it more difficult to apprehend Joyce's positioning of Bloom as Good Samaritan in the episode, the critical tide seems to have turned; "Eumaeus" increasingly holds its own as a purposely well-crafted style to express Joyce's message of poignant hospitality, bumbling as some of Bloom's attempts to reach out to Stephen are.

To return to Richard Ellmann's 1972 reading of this opening passage in "Eumaeus" as instancing Bloom's decency despite his belief that the supposedly attenuated style obfuscates this understanding, Ellmann finally leaves room for reading Bloom's actions through this parable: "Since the Samaritans were conspicuously outside orthodoxy, that being important to Christ's meaning, 'orthodox Samaritan fashion' is not only a cliché, but an absurdity. *The use of the word 'Samaritan' nonetheless points up the parabolic quality of Bloom's act.*"[28] Ellmann affirmed this reading in 1984 as part of one of his last statements on Joyce, saying of Bloom, "He . . . fulfills the role of the Good Samaritan when Stephen is knocked down."[29] Fascinatingly, Joyce here has the supposedly Jewish Bloom help the drunken lapsed Catholic Stephen up, and later, minister to him, whereas in the original parable, the Samaritan (heretical in orthodox Jewish eyes) helps the traveler, much to the chagrin of the Jewish lawyer whom Christ chastens by telling this story.

Ernst Renan opens the fourteenth chapter, "Intercourse of Jesus with the Pagans and Samaritans," of his biography *The Life of Jesus*, which Joyce enjoyed so much, with this statement: "Jesus despised all religion which was not of the heart." He continues: "The love of God, charity and mutual forgiveness, were his whole law."[30] Notice that charity, one of Bloom's most appealing characteristics, is number two on this list.

Later, in "Eumaeus," relating his encounter with the Citizen to Stephen, Bloom adds, in an affirmation of his own pronounced charity,

> But with a little goodwill all round. It's all very fine to boast of mutual superiority but what about mutual equality. I resent violence and intolerance in any shape or form. It never reaches anything or stops anything. . . . It's a patent absurdity on the face of it to hate people because they live round the corner and speak another vernacular, in the next house so to speak. (*U* 16.1098–1103).

Many commentators on this episode elide or downplay the clarity of such passages and their moral and emotional thrust by citing what they perceive as the obfuscating, exhausted style or by dwelling upon Stephen's rejection of Bloom's plea for love and tolerance.[31]

Perhaps the most egregious and misleading reading of Bloom's behavior in this episode, however, is advanced by Gerald Bruns, who claimed in his seminal 1974 essay on the episode that Bloom and Stephen's sole connection is "utterly commercial and utterly imaginary."[32] Christine O'Neill cites this passage to challenge it, terming Bruns's reading "too pessimistic," and noting correctly that "Bloom is also impelled by genuine kindness, and Stephen is eventually responsive."[33] Worse, Bruns even mentions Bloom's function as a Good Samaritan figure, but only suspiciously, in his reading of Bloom's plan to manage Stephen's potential singing career. Bruns posits that "Bloom here steps briskly from the Good Samaritan role. . . . If, for example, he appears to seek Stephen's redemption . . . it is because he recognizes in the young man not human but market value."[34] Such a reading, I should add, veers uncomfortably close to anti-Semitism in perceiving Bloom as a predatory Jew interested only in commercial gain. C. H. Peake's reading is more sophisticated and accurate than Bruns's: He points out that

> By the comparatively simple technique of the chapter, Joyce combined Bloom's euphoric and eager officiousness, his underlying weariness, and an ironic exposure of the conceit with which his charitable behavior fills him—and yet at the same time one has to recognize that Bloom is, in fact, being a Good Samaritan.[35]

Peake recognizes the persistence of Bloom's role as Good Samaritan throughout the episode, perceiving him correctly because of the episode's style.

Bloom and Stephen's Parabolic Relationship in "Eumaeus"

Rather than functioning as a minor allusion in the novel, the crucial phrase from this episode's opening sentence—"in orthodox Samaritan fashion"—and its associated parable instead reflect the very inspiration for *Ulysses* and arguably its central question, "Who is my neighbor?," the question posed by the lawyer that prompts Christ's iteration of the Good Samaritan parable. "Eumaeus" answers that question, but does so in inimitably Joycean fashion—through Bloom's care for Stephen in a very unlikely place, the cabman's shelter, and over a small meal (even though only Bloom eats, not Stephen), not the legendary Christmas feast of "The Dead." Neighbors in *Ulysses* can be found in unlikely places, and Bloom's hospitality toward Stephen as he unconsciously re-enacts the role of the Good Samaritan, after helping others all day long, becomes the apotheosis of his charitable actions on that long-ago day in 1904.

At the same time, Bloom also can be read as the stranger who is beaten and helped by the Samaritan in the parable. As I pointed out earlier, he is attacked vicariously by members of other "tribes," including the Protestant Mr. Deasy, who voices vicious anti-Semitism to Stephen in "Nestor," and directly by a series of Catholics in "Hades" and especially in "Cyclops," culminating in the Citizen's shameful abuse of him. Bloom thus oscillates between these two roles—victim and helper—throughout the novel, finally fully claiming his Good Samaritan mantle in "Eumaeus." Despite its deflation of our hopes for a breakthrough conversation, there is nonetheless a significant father and son reunion between Stephen and Bloom that is both somatic and deeply spiritual, and perhaps despite its initially confusing style, "Eumaeus" in many ways works as the climax of the entire novel, although their relationship continues and deepens in the next episode, "Ithaca." Barbara Stevens Heusel suggested as much in 1986 in her exploration of "Eumaeus," when she stated that "the men's linking of arms . . . serves as the climax for all of *Ulysses*."[36] Ellmann even argues that despite their "tentative singleness" and differences from each other, Stephen and Bloom "offer a counterpart, in *Agape* or comradeliness, to the evocation of the *Nausicaa* episode of Eros."[37] Finally, and most recently, although Jack Dudley repeats the false story of Joyce's "rescue" by Alfred H. Hunter in 1904, he nonetheless suggests that "true fiction" (my phrase) inspired what he calls "the central act of *Ulysses*, when Leopold Bloom rescues the fallen Stephen in 'Circe'" and goes on to care for him in subsequent episodes.[38]

Richard Ellmann remains one of the few commentators to point out not only Bloom's rescue of Stephen as a reinscription of the Good Samaritan parable but also its significance for the novel as a whole. He notes that

> Joyce draws upon Christ's parable of the Good Samaritan to make Bloom's unassuming act of comradeliness an instance of *Agape*. . . . Beaten up and friendless, Stephen is helped by a stranger, whose *acte gratuit* redeems the universe from the chilliness of isolated particles and stamps it as irrevocably gregarious. It is timeless and parabolic.[39]

Ellmann's statement suggests that Bloom's Samaritan care for Stephen becomes the apotheosis of the novel, injecting great warmth and community into the chilly universe of isolation that both men have been exposed to throughout. Virginia Moseley, one of the other commentators besides Ellmann and, much later, Margot Norris, to engage with the Good Samaritan parable in the novel, perceives a series of parallels between Bloom and the Samaritan, even though she limits them largely to "Eumaeus." For instance, she points out that Bloom's "solicitude for Stephen and his quoting 'A soft answer turns away wrath' [*U* 16.1085–6] exemplify the compassion of the Good Samaritan in both act and precept."[40] More startlingly, she argues that Stephen is becoming more generous because of Bloom's example, positing, "There are signs that Stephen is becoming a martyr to his 'orthodox' Samaritan's cause and that the mutual need indicated by the ambiguous reference of 'which he very badly needed' in the topic sentence will be met."[41] Later, she suggests, "Gradually turning away from Satanic denial, Stephen is becoming more and more like his 'orthodox Samaritan.' A growing charity is evidenced by his lending a half-crown to Corley (having offered no money to his needy sister during the 'Wandering Rocks' scene)."[42] Compassion can be infectious, and it spreads throughout "Eumaeus" and suffuses this episode with a warm, substantive glow—never saccharine—derived from the continuing intertext of the Good Samaritan parable.

Stephen's charity is even more pronounced than Moseley suggests, since he knows well that Corley has "the customary doleful ditty to tell" (*U* 16.144); the careful Joyce reader also recalls Corley's previous appearance, in "The Two Gallants" from *Dubliners*, and remembers his reputation there for being a "leech" and talking "mainly about himself. . ." (*D* 44, 45). Stephen likely knows Corley's reputation and suspects that the woeful story he now tells him is "a complete fabrication from start to finish" (*U* 16.153). And just as Corley manages to get a gold coin off the girl who works as a skivvy (*D* 55), he now obtains money from Stephen. First, however, in response to Corley's asking him where he could find work, Stephen tells him, "—There'll be a job tomorrow or next day . . . in a boys' school at Dalkey for a gentleman usher, Mr. Garrett Deasy. Try it. You may mention my name" (*U* 16.157–9). While he might suspect that Corley's constitutional laziness will preclude him from taking this job, by offering it Stephen effectively bars himself from returning to the position, further impoverishing himself, at least for now. His generosity here is thus profound, made all the more so by his poignant admission to Corley that "—I have no place to sleep myself" (*U* 16.163). Perhaps because Stephen is also homeless and has been deserted by his friends, he reaches out in empathy to Corley, and as they converse, the narrator tells us, "Though this sort of thing went on every other night or very near it still Stephen's feelings got the better of him in a sense though he knew that Corley's brandnew rigmarole on a par with the others was hardly deserving of much credence"

(*U* 16.172–5). Of course, the "Eumaeus" narrator specializes in repetitions, but for him to tell us twice in the space of less than thirty lines that Stephen really does not believe Corley, and then that he feels sorry for him, is striking. While Stephen only intends to "lend him anything up to a bob or so in lieu so that he might endeavor at all events and get sufficient to eat" (*U* 16.183–4), he cannot find his cash in one pocket at first, but finally finds what he thinks are pennies. When Corley corrects him, telling him they are actually "halfcrowns," the narrator succinctly tells us, "Stephen anyhow lent him one of them" (*U* 16.194, 195–6). This is a real sacrifice for multiple reasons: Stephen must find new lodgings later that day, along with a new job, and furthermore, he knows well that Corley will not repay him. But he laughs it off to Bloom a few minutes later, telling him, "—He is down on his luck" and noting that "I daresay he needs it to sleep somewhere" (*U* 16.233, 43–4).

Despite Margot Norris's insistence that Stephen treats "Corley's interest in finding work" as "bogus," she nonetheless ends up agreeing with Moseley (although she does not cite Moseley's argument published some forty-four years before her own) that in his depiction of Stephen's encounter with Corley, "the narrator turns Stephen into a good Samaritan."[43] Note Norris's consternation and puzzlement at this exchange that stems from her incorrect understanding of the parable, which causes her to believe that someone must really want another's help to be rescued: "the narrative language further makes Corley presumptuous and ungrateful—'But the cream of the joke was nothing would get it out of Corley's head that he was living in affluence and hadn't a thing to do but hand out the needful. Whereas'" (*U* 16.179–81). As she rightly points out, "[t]he 'whereas' points to Corley's mistake in failing to see Stephen as very needful himself," but reading this episode through the Good Samaritan parable, as the narrator suggests we do, reveals that a selfish attitude to being helped or rescued does not decrease the desire of the rescuer to offer that help.[44]

Strikingly, by borrowing Kenner's contention that the Eumaeus narrator is somehow "created" by Bloom, Norris argues compellingly that "[t]he narrator who begins by showing Bloom physically bucking Stephen up 'in orthodox Samaritan fashion' (16.3) now bucks Stephen up morally by turning him into a Samaritan in his own right—notwithstanding the dubious logic of having the homeless help the homeless."[45] Norris does not seem to grasp here that Stephen helps Corley precisely because he is also homeless; he truly empathizes with his plight, even though Corley is better off than him and can get money more easily. Much later in the episode retrospective evidence emerges that Bloom's pity for the now homeless Stephen might even help Stephen reach out in empathy to the temporarily homeless Corley: "To think of him house and homeless, rooked by some landlady worse than any stepmother, was really too bad at his age" (*U* 16.1565–7). Even if one does not agree with Kenner's assertion that the narrator is Bloom, this narrator nonetheless seems to do just what Norris argues—turn "Stephen into a Samaritan in his own right." This must stand as one of the most positive readings of this episode—although, as we will see, Norris shortly and strangely undercuts this entire premise.

Many critics still tend both to believe that Bloom and Stephen's relationship bears no fruit and to concur with Joyce's oft-cited statement to Frank Budgen that "Stephen no longer interests me. . . . He has a shape that can't be changed";[46] clearly, however, Stephen is changing and developing during the hours he spends with Bloom, and despite his semi-inertia and even rudeness, he is already depicted as helping other unfortunates like Corley. Perhaps Joyce had spent so much time in developing Stephen's character in *A Portrait of the Artist* that understandably, at least through most of *Ulysses*, he devoted more time to his new character Bloom, the everyman advertiser. Although there is a long-standing tendency in Joyce studies to focus on Bloom's development, supremely so, perhaps, in Luca Crispi's wonderful study *Joyce's Creative Process and the Construction of Characters in Ulysses*, we should focus on the possibilities for Stephen's development arising from reading his relationship with Bloom parabolically. And perhaps then our old assumptions—even Joyce's own—about Stephen as unchanging in the novel may evolve accordingly.

Significantly, shortly after helping Corley, Stephen thinks with pity of the abject poverty of all the younger children in his family, particularly of his sister Dilly, and thus he might be becoming more empathetic toward them as well. Less than two pages after Stephen lends Corley a half-crown, Bloom tells Stephen that his father is proud of him (U 16.261–2). In response to Bloom's suggestion that he could go back home (U 16.262), Stephen poignantly muses upon

> his family hearth the last time he saw it with his sister Dilly sitting by the ingle, her hair hanging down, waiting for some weak Trinidad shell cocoa that was in the sootcoated kettle to be done so that she and he could drink it with the oatmealwater for milk after the Friday herrings they had eaten at two a penny with an egg apiece for Maggy, Boody and Katey, the cat meanwhile under the mangle devouring a mess of eggshells and charred fish heads and bones on a square of brown paper. (U 16.269–76)

Taken together with his gift of money to Corley, this scene suggests that Stephen is growing more tender toward his younger siblings and is distressed anew by their economic hardship. Recall that over three hundred pages earlier in the novel, in "Wandering Rocks," Stephen also has great pity toward Dilly and wants to save her, but fears she will pull him down with her: "She is drowning. Agenbite. Save her. Agenbite. All against us. She will drown me with her, eyes and hair. Lank coils of seaweed hair around me" (U 10.875–6). One could argue that Stephen imagines this picture of home as a sort of silent riposte to

Bloom's suggestion that he go back to his family—and his detailed images of poverty may imply that he feels he cannot go back to *that*—and yet he could simultaneously be expressing sorrow for his siblings and feeling that if he were to return, he would be one extra mouth to feed and could throw them into further poverty. Stephen seems to be in flux before our very eyes—simultaneously selfish and sympathetic, turned inward and yet slowly turning outward toward others. Joyce himself certainly believed strongly in the potential of human beings—and his own characters—to change. For instance, citing Joyce's deep belief in Aristotelian *potentia*, Hugh Kenner has argued that "[i]n the mind of Joyce there hung a radiant field of possibilities, ways in which a man may go, and corresponding selves he may become, bounding him by one outward form or another while he remains the same person in the eye of God."[47]

Rejecting the false selves previously projected by the Circean narrator enables us to apprehend the burgeoning selves-in-formation of Stephen and Bloom, who both share a quality of charity that Bloom exemplifies for Stephen directly and physically. Crucially, their growth is predicated upon their recognition of their own otherness, which enables them to then reach out to each other, surmounting (especially in Bloom's case) the ego-trap of the modern self.

In Norris's reading of "Eumaeus," she posits that Stephen "has failed Bloom utterly" in his refusal to engage with Bloom's discussion of the Citizen's earlier anti-Semitism and his own socialist mercantilistic plan. Citing Lubomír Doležel, "Communication is an exchange of semiotic acts and, like physical interaction is reciprocal and can be either symmetrical or asymmetrical," she terms their exchange "asymmetrical with Stephen barely listening and consequently unresponsive."[48] And yet she herself suggested that Stephen has indeed "reciprocated" Bloom's re-enactment of the Good Samaritan parable by helping Corley in turn, who is also homeless and penniless. That is, Stephen's relative silence and seeming rejection of Bloom's overtures to him might mask his growing evolution into a charitable figure, a new Good Samaritan figure, modeled on Bloom's charity and compassion.

Robert M. Adams long ago anticipated such critical disappointment in Stephen's inability to respond verbally to Bloom in any substantive way, noting that "nothing has happened to Stephen on June 16, 1904 which could properly cause him to comprehend Bloom—while Bloom's very position in *Ulysses* renders it obvious that he has been comprehended by Joyce."[49] Expecting a former university student and teacher, cosmopolitan and largely cynical, to have an instant verbal rapport with the self-educated, culturally different, generally warm, middle-aged Bloom seems a stretch even on its face. As the narrator tells us at one point, the two are "poles apart as they were both in schooling and everything else with the marked difference in their respective ages. . ." (*U* 16.774–6).

The larger question of epistemology for the entire novel may also have led Joyce to forestall any easy closure (including a definitive answer about the future of the relationship between Stephen and Bloom) in the novel generally. He perceived, as Kenner believed, "the dangers of hermetic closure, of fastening the last rivet in what he seemed to be achieving, the ultimate late-nineteenth-century novel where everything pertinent seems known and accounted for," and he "glimpsed the truly terrible knowingness, and the reductiveness of that." Moreover, "though he loved closed systems he was attracted even more . . . to a mental cosmos founded, as Stephen tells us the church is founded on mystery, 'and founded irremovably because founded, like the world, macro and microcosm, upon the void. Upon uncertitude, upon unlikelihood'" (U 9.841).[50] The Odyssean parallels and the extensive correspondences—among other aspects of the novel—between Stephen and Bloom (different as they are in temperament and outlook) together make *Ulysses* seem definitive, solvable. Some mystery must remain, however, and Joyce likely delighted in subverting readers' expectations that Bloom and Stephen's meeting would lead to an instant rapport and friendship between them and even to a father–son relationship.

Moreover, as John Porter Houston has pointed out, Bloom and Stephen have had few opportunities for normal dialogue in the episodes leading up to "Eumaeus": "As with Bloom, we begin to realize in reading Stephen's remarks [in "Eumaeus"] that he has actually taken part in little ordinary dialogue in recent chapters; in fact, declaiming, as in 'Scylla and Charybdis' or 'Oxen,' has been his more favored expression."[51] Having an actual dialogue with another person is a relatively rare experience for Stephen; among the few are the one he has with the anti-Semitic Deasy that morning, and then later with the men in the National Library in "Scylla and Charybdis" when Buck Mulligan undercuts Stephen's theory of Shakespeare with his masturbatory theory of art.

Joyce's tendency to reject sentimentality also emerges in his refusal to give us some sort of dramatic emotional breakthrough between Stephen and Bloom. He realized that our sentimentalized expectations might actually subtract from the profound nature of their encounter, because Joyce felt that being sentimental "was to deny the body, an offence just as serious as to deny the soul."[52] Joyce found a powerful example of emotional restraint in François de Salignac de la Mothe Fénelon's influential sequel to the *Odyssey*, *Les Aventures de Télémaque*, which was in his Trieste library. Fénelon's book has Telemachus retrace Odysseus's journey, and Joyce not only adapted his structure of only eighteen episodes (instead of Homer's twenty-four books), but also was likely influenced by what Ellmann has termed "the remarkably muffled way" that Fénelon handles the meeting between Telemachus and Ulysses.[53] Telemachus does not realize till after Ulysses has departed that he was speaking to his father, which Ellmann casts as "one of those resonant unfulfilments, like Wordsworth's discovery that he has crossed the Alps without knowing it. Joyce had here an unusual precedent for the equally resonant and yet extremely muted ingathering of Bloom and Stephen."[54]

We would also do well to remember John Henry Raleigh's memorable assessment of their meeting, which, while it does not excuse Stephen's behavior, nonetheless suggests how utterly mismatched the pair are in terms of energy and soberness: "if in 'Eumaeus' Bloom is at his perkiest and most vivacious, he has before him an auditor the least likely of anybody he has conversed with during the day to comprehend him in any consecutive fashion. . . . Glimpses into Dedalus's state of 'mind are rare,'" but we realize that he is in an "alcoholic haze, with a kind of slow movement of its own, through which penetrate, only faintly, stray words or phrases out of the torrent of words that issue periodically from his companion."[55] Stephen is so far gone for most of the episode that, as Raleigh notes, he only hears occasional words or phrases, as, for example, when Bloom has just given a long disquisition on Jewish history, concluding with his socialist scheme for universal income:

> Over his untastable apology for a cup of coffee, listening to this synopsis of things in general, Stephen stared at nothing in particular. He could hear, of course, all kinds of words changing color like those crabs about Ringsend in the morning. . . . Then he looked up and saw the eyes that said or didn't say the words the voice heard said, if you work. (*U* 16.1141–4, 1146–7).

All Stephen hears is "if you work," and all he can manage in reply is "—Count me out. . ." (*U* 16.1148), an individualist reply to the communally oriented Bloom: "The eyes were surprised at this observation because as he . . . observed . . . all must work, have to, together" (*U* 16.1149, 1150, 1150–1). While Stephen was at his liveliest earlier in the novel in episodes such as "Telemachus" and "Scylla and Charybdis," Bloom was at his most sluggish (think of his torpor in "Calypso," for instance). Their conditions are reversed here, an awareness of which should mitigate our hope that there will be some sort of major breakthrough in their conversation.

Beyond realizing Stephen's generally non-receptive state of mind, we should also bear in mind how the style might prevent fuller communication between Stephen and Bloom—at least from the reader's point of view. C. H. Peake makes the reasonable point that "[f]or most of the chapter, even where there are points of similarity or contact [between Stephen and Bloom], they seem minimized by the technique," whereby "Bloom's garrulous enthusiasm contrasts with Stephen's terse ironic detachment."[56] Christine O'Neill posits that it finally undercuts Bloom's ministrations to Steven. For O'Neill, the "Eumaeus" style is hybridized, both Bloomian in language and articulated by a narrative agency that "exaggerates and parodies Bloomian traits and makes him balance uncomfortably between being its victim and its author."[57] Using language borrowed from Bakhtin, she posits that "Bloom's ideas and sensations are evoked in (free) indirect discourse; the quasi-literary style is a third person narrative which is self-conscious and rambling. These two strands are commonly fused in a single sentence." Therefore, "[t]he hybridization through Eumaeus is an encounter between two linguistic consciousnesses which intersect unobtrusively rather than discordantly," so much so that a great deal of the episode "reads like transliterated stream of consciousness."[58] And yet O'Neill argues that the third-person narrative has more agency than Bloom's narration and both mediates and distorts his thoughts, exercising "control largely through hyperbole and irony." Because this superior narrative voice "has introduced into it an opposing semantic intention which forces Bloom's discourse to serve a contrary end," Bloom's rhetoric cannot reach Stephen effectively: "Bloom bores Stephen instead of captivating his attention by mature views and a refined style."[59] In this reading, Bloom's attempts to speak straightforwardly and confidently to Stephen are sufficiently exaggerated and parodied such that the already drunk Stephen cannot take him seriously. Thus, given Stephen's drunkenness and the way the third-person narrator parodies Bloom, there should be little expectation that Stephen would listen carefully to Bloom, much less adopt some of his advice and theories.[60]

Our excessive belief that there will be a major breakthrough between Bloom and Stephen is founded upon our faith in language to effect that breakthrough, but as Declan Kiberd has memorably put it, "in a book which has repeatedly exposed the limits of language, why should the climax be verbal?" After "the real meeting of both men [which] began in 'Circe,' where they shared something as intimate as dream life," how, Kiberd goes on, "could any mere conversation measure up to that?" Finally, as he further observes, "Critics in search of a talking climax may be thinking in terms of a traditional novel and missing the deeper point of the new psychic layers uncovered by *Ulysses*."[61] As we will see later in this chapter, not only do Bloom and Stephen share new "psychic layers," but more importantly, by the end of "Eumaeus," they are profoundly physically connected as Stephen leans on Bloom and receives his flesh in an embodied sense.

Moreover, it is possible to read Stephen's many silences toward Bloom's questions and talk in this episode as fruitfully productive for their eventual union. What Jean-Louis Chrétien terms "the hospitality of silence" is predicated upon listening, and even if Stephen is not actively listening, he nonetheless adopts a posture of potentially passively listening, thereby often checking his own impulses to speak and his own egotism. Chrétien formulates this dimension of silence as nonetheless "still itself speech, an eloquent silence, a place of encounter and mutual presence."[62] Furthermore, although he is thinking of one's silence before God, such a posture also makes us receptive to the Other, as Stephen slowly becomes to Bloom in this episode: "My silence tears me away from myself and leads me to renounce myself so that within me the

Other may come into being and be given birth."⁶³ Theirs, then, is largely a wordless connection—mind and body and spirit—not linguistic, and this silent connection continues into "Ithaca," when they silently gaze together at the stellar beauty of the night sky, decentered and receptive to the other through their joint amazement at the stars' beauty.⁶⁴

There is additionally the problem of Stephen's suffering, which we tend to confine solely to mental and physical anguish, and which Ricoeur indicates is also compounded of a corresponding diminution of agency in a typical relationship between sufferer and rescuer. He observes that not only can agency be reduced in such a scenario, but suffering can also destroy "the capacity for acting, of being-able-to-act, experienced as a violation of self-integrity."⁶⁵ Bloom, in contrast to Stephen, retains the capacity to act and to do so with great compassion despite his suffering mental and physical agonies throughout the day. His capacity for charity, rendered over time into a habitus of caring behavior, provides the effective bulwark behind which he can be shielded from the slings and arrows of a series of other characters.

Despite the charity Bloom offers him, Stephen effectively dispossesses Bloom in one of the few moments of verbal lucidity he seems to have. When he tells Bloom, "Ireland must be important because it belongs to me" (*U* 16.1164–5), Bloom feels marginalized again, and the moment seems a milder version of the Citizen's virulent nationalism back in "Cyclops." The narrator portrays the stunned Bloom as casting around in his mind, trying to take in Stephen's statement: "Mr Bloom, to change the subject, looked down but in a quandary, as he couldn't tell exactly what construction to put on *belongs to* which sounded rather a far cry" (*U* 16.1172–4; my emphasis). Bloom, typical of his attempts to spare other's feelings, even when his own are hurt, looks down so as not to confront Stephen too strongly here, but he is shaken. As Fritz Senn points out, "The patched construction of the sentence imitates Bloom's bewilderment over the construction of" Stephen's nationalistic claim to Ireland.⁶⁶ Furthermore,

> That Bloom would worry over a phrase like "belongs to" is subconsciously linked to his fellow Dubliners' aspersion that he, a stranger, does not belong to Ireland, as was driven home in "Cyclops," where Bloom also contended: "And I belong to a race too . . . that is hated and persecuted. . . . Persecuted. Taking what belongs to us by right" (12.1467, 12.1470–1), with the further irony that he does not quite belong to *that* race either.⁶⁷

Stephen has come back to Ireland at the beginning to the novel, but he has also re-embraced his need to link his art to Ireland, whereas he foreswore that national allegiance famously at the end of *A Portrait of the Artist*. He could not have known that the Citizen had earlier verbally excluded Bloom from his narrow definition of Ireland, but he could not have hit on a worse, more alienating phrase in this moment given Bloom's own use of it in "Cyclops" and his own alienation from both Ireland and Judaism.

Bloom knows that Stephen's language of exclusion here is "rather a far cry" from his own definition of a nation, expressed seemingly simplistically in "Cyclops" as the same people living in the same place and also, diasporically, in different places.[68] Bloom's actions in the novel (not his words), including caring for Stephen, best illustrate his true concept of community as a network of disparate individuals who know, even love, each other. As Declan Kiberd notes, whereas Bloom is "mockingly introduced in 'Cyclops' as a Jew in a gentile city, as a 'new apostle to the gentiles'" (U 12.1489), in fact, "[o]ne of the most innovative injunctions of Jesus concerned this very point—the need not just to embrace traditional enemies of Israel but to include them in an expanded definition of community."[69] For these reasons, Bloom struggles to understand why Stephen, who has himself been made to feel marginalized by the British soldiers in "Circe," makes such a statement. But of course, one reason Stephen verbalizes this assertion is that he knows Ireland *does* belong to him as a native more than it does to the British soldiers, emblems of the colonizer. Telling Bloom that Ireland belongs to himself as a native Irishman thus likely is a delayed riposte to the soldiers, especially Private Carr, who attacks him because of Stephen's comment about "his" king.

A final impediment to Bloom's breaking through into an embodied relationship with Stephen involves Stephen's marked arrogance throughout the novel, which recurs periodically in this episode, even though there are competing signs that Stephen is becoming more empathetic to others. The university-educated Stephen, lover of Parisian culture, cannot at first appreciate the earthy, practical Poldy who desires to help him. As Sean Latham articulates their juxtaposition in his study of the snob in modernist literature, "the intellectual aesthete now emerges as a severely circumscribed snob who cannot match the imaginative freedom and empathy of a modest canvasser."[70] However, Latham's view of Stephen as a snob caught in amber, buttressed by his citation of Joyce arguing that Stephen "has a shape that can't be changed," runs up against the indications in "Eumaeus" and "Ithaca" explored in this and the next chapter whereby Stephen seems to be becoming more charitable toward friends and family.[71]

Bloom recovers his bearings after this exchange and goes on to achieve a profound, enfleshed connection with Stephen by the end of the episode. Actions again speak louder than words—and count more than them. To ascertain the true state of Bloom's relationship with Stephen in the context of the Good Samaritan parable—and to determine whether or not his care for Stephen might have charitable repercussions in Stephen's actions toward others—our focus finally should remain on Bloom's charitable actions toward Stephen and Stephen's charitable actions toward Corley along with his newfound sympathy for the poverty of his siblings at home.

In a provocative reading of the last three "Nostos" episodes of the novel in the *Cambridge Companion to* Ulysses, Maud Ellmann argues that rather than offer a traditionally redemptive ending, instead, "Joyce introduces a throwaway aesthetic in which words outnumber deeds by at least 20:1," further noting, "[w]hereas the traditional novel ends in marriage, *Ulysses* ends with the throwaway encounter of Bloom and Stephen, which is broken off before it has a chance to blossom, followed by the celibate encounter of Bloom and Molly in the conjugal bed."[72] She is taken in, however, by the narrator's love of logorrhea, which can capsize our true apprehension of the depth and profundity of Stephen and Bloom's relationship. Instead, we might say that despite the beauty of some phrases and the emotional charge of others, many of the words in the parade of circumlocutions and fumbling phrasing in "Eumaeus" (and in "Ithaca," for that matter) are the true "throwaway," whereas the actions are what matter, just as Jesus' parable of the Good Samaritan suggests.[73]

I want to linger briefly on Maud Ellmann's point about Bloom and Stephen's allegedly "throwaway" relationship, which seems stunted and shorn of any redemptive potential in her formulation. Her contention echoes that of Thornton and many others such as Donoghue.[74] Ellmann harps on the many instances of waste—literal and more figurative—in these final chapters, but what emerges in a properly parabolic reading of their relationship reveals Bloom's growing prodigality, his excessive generosity, his abundance in caring so warmly and charitably for Stephen, despite the young man's lack of interest and receptivity. In apprehending Bloom's *caritas*, we as readers come to care for him even when no one else seems to for much of the novel. Joyce certainly was much concerned about the reader's response to his novel. He believed, according to Frank Budgen, that "Bloom should grow upon the reader throughout the day," and indeed he does.[75]

While Stephen does not respond gratefully to Bloom and seems largely dismissive (even to the point of replicating the Citizen's exclusionary behavior) for all the reasons outlined above, his response is not really Joyce's point, nor was it the point in Jesus' parable of the Good Samaritan. There, the focus was never on the beaten man's reaction to being rescued, but on the initial response of the traditionally marginalized man—the Good Samaritan—to an unknown traveler whom he stumbles upon. Joyce would have read in the conclusion of chapter 13, "The Christian a Law to Himself," in his copy of John R. Seeley's *Ecce Homo*, this statement, which is startling—especially in the context of Stephen's relative lack of warmth toward his rescuer that Maud Ellmann and others have identified and lamented:

> There is a fellow-feeling, a yearning of kindness, toward a human being as such, which is not dependent upon the character of the particular human being who excites it, but rises before that character displays

itself, and does not at once or altogether subside when it exhibits itself as unamiable. We save a man from drowning whether he is amiable or the contrary, and we should consider it right to do so even though we knew him to be a very great criminal, simply because he is a man."[76]

We might therefore posit that the secular Jew Bloom displays just this "fellow-feeling, a yearning of kindness," toward Stephen Dedalus, and that it "rises before that character displays itself, and does not at once or altogether subside when it exhibits itself as unamiable," as Stephen surely does. This attitude, too, we might think of as leading Bloom to act in "orthodox Samaritan fashion," since no Catholics or other Christians in the novel act in this way, save Father Conmee, whose charitable mission is distorted by the narrator of "Wandering Rocks." The secularized Samaritan Bloom shows the most "fellow-feeling" of anyone in the novel, another instance of how Joyce took the humanized Jesus of Renan and Seeley and incorporated Him both into his protagonist's character and into the narrative arc of the novel. By attending to Bloom's behavior, rather than Stephen's verbal rejection of his charity, we apprehend Joyce's message of the essential conditions for brotherhood and friendship—reaching out to those different from us (the intellectual lapsed Catholic Stephen certainly differs from the instinctual lapsed "Jewish" canvasser Bloom) in charity and kindness.[77]

Seeley's emphasis on rescuing a stranger whether or not he is "amiable" or "unamiable" fruitfully illustrates Joyce's own capacious sense of hospitality toward the Other, which also involves a deep vulnerability and the consequent ability for the rescuer to be hurt by the rescued. In his reading of Jacques Derrida's *On Hospitality*, Joshua Mills-Knutsen identifies vulnerability as being at the heart of ethics and thus the basis of what makes us human. He posits, "At base, we are strangers as much as we are selves; our humanity is essentially vulnerable to the ravages of the monstrous other. To seek to eliminate that vulnerability is to eliminate our very humanity."[78] Attacked by various Dubliners throughout the day in thought, word, and deed, Leopold Bloom nevertheless opens himself vulnerably to Stephen Dedalus by rescuing him and caring for him. Whereas the monstrous Cyclops figure of "The Citizen" most directly attacks him, Bloom is likely wounded just as much or more by Stephen's verbal rejection of him and his singing of the anti-Semitic ballad in "Ithaca," as we shall see. But again, Stephen might be at the same time simultaneously (and unconsciously) attending to and modeling Bloom's generosity by giving money to Corley and offering him his teaching job with Deasy, even as he rejects Bloom's ministrations to some degree.

Stephen might also be, through his encounter with Bloom here, turning into the author he has always wanted to be in front of our eyes and thereby casting Bloom in a charitable light. Margaret McBride argues in her study *Ulysses and the Metamorphosis of Stephen Dedalus* that Stephen actually transforms

Bloom into the book's Odyssean hero in "Eumaeus" and "Ithaca," episodes that "brim with fabulous potencies."[79] Reading the novel as metafictional, McBride brilliantly posits that "Eumaeus" and "Ithaca" show us "the raw fragments that sparked Stephen's epic tale. . . . In the final circumstances of Stephen's day may be found the true genesis of *Ulysses*: the conjoining of Stephen and Bloom is not the story's conclusion but instead its inception."[80] Noting that Joyce drafted the concluding three chapters of the novel first, but oddly neglecting to mention his likely apocryphal story of being assaulted and rescued by Alfred H. Hunter, McBride sees these two episodes as reflecting Joyce fashioning Stephen's artistic transformation of himself and employment of Bloom's narration of the events of his day into "the set of Homeric correspondencies, the 'Analogous scenes' that constitute the novel proper."[81] For McBride, the encounter of Stephen and the stranger Bloom functions as a recognition scene straight out of the *Odyssey*, with Stephen as a modern-day Homer who then transforms this "nobody" into a quotidian but fabulous Odysseus.

In such an analysis, Stephen (not Bloom as Kenner and Norris would have it, nor Bloom and a third-person narrator whose narration merges with Bloom's seamlessly but also undercuts it at crucial moments, as O'Neill argues) as "author" of *Ulysses* is also perfectly capable of employing the Good Samaritan narrative as part of his spinning the novel out into a complete fiction. As I noted earlier, the Odyssean narrative and the Lukan narrative do not compete with each other but complement each other's emphasis on hospitality as a guiding principle. And we must consider strongly the possibility that Joyce called attention to the originating, probably fictitious inspiration for his novel (his 1904 Dublin fight and 1907 Roman mugging and possible rescue) through having Stephen retrospectively narrate the events of the day starting in "Eumaeus" and "Ithaca." The somewhat off-putting style of the two episodes cleverly obfuscates their auto-fictive thrust according to McBride. By starting the entire "Nostos" sequence with the incorporation of Stephen and Bloom into the Good Samaritan intertext he introduces, Joyce casts the concluding passages of "Circe" and all three of the last episodes into this originating narrative, asking them to be read through it.

I want to emphasize this preferred method of reading "Eumaeus," engaging in a continuing dialogue with the episode and the novel as a whole, groping our way toward community with the characters and seeing such provisional communities form in the novel, over against the episode's strident insistence in its middle section, despite the narrator's circumlocutions, that the natural state of human beings is to war with each other. The catalog of fights proffered by the narrator is extremely misleading in this regard. For instance, "Eumaeus" gives us extensive coverage of various disputes, "public and private, actual, impending, or remembered," as John Henry Raleigh has put it.[82] So many disputes and quarrels—between England and Ireland, the Boer War, the Japanese naval victory over the Russians, "eighteenth-century Dublin street fights," along with many "accounts of private quarrels," including Corley and Lenahan's fight, Boylan's anger at Lenehan, Mulligan's betrayal of Stephen, Bloom's estrangement from Molly, Bloom's fight with the Citizen, to name just a few[83]—pervade the pages of "Eumaeus" that readers may feel swamped with such details and caught in a morass with no way out. By focusing on the underlying action of the episode, however, Bloom's rescue of Stephen and his subsequent care and concern for him, I hope this chapter has given a narrative thread through this confusing labyrinth. Moreover, I contend that Joyce is not interested in these disputes, fights, and quarrels that are narrated *ad infinitum*; rather he focuses upon the simple, caring actions of Bloom for Stephen, and even of Stephen for Corley and of the reader for Bloom. This set of actions cuts like a blinding light through the darkness of the hatred endemic to such disputes, illuminating love for the Other as the only way forward if we are to thrive as humans.

While Bloom's ministrations toward Stephen are not very fully verbally reciprocated, Stephen, encouragingly, is becoming outwardly more like the Good Samaritan in his changing attitude toward Dilly Dedalus and especially in his empathy and charity toward Corley; actions, after all, should still count more than mere words. Hence, we at first reject as misleading the ending to the episode supplied by the narrator to "Eumaeus" when the street sweeper watches Stephen and Bloom "walk towards the railway bridge, *to be married by Father Maher*" and "*looked after their lowbacked car*" (U 16.1887–8, 1894). The narrator obfuscates their relationship to such an extent at this point that an inattentive reader might buy into the street sweeper's perspective, but clearly the pair are not going to be married, nor are they in a lowbacked car. Yet Stephen and Bloom do undergo some sort of profound bodily, perhaps even emotional and spiritual union here, which is fumblingly characterized by the narrator as a non-sexual marriage.

Their union stems as well from our recognition of them as a reunited father/son dyad, drawing on Odysseus's reunion with Telemachus at the end of the "Eumaeus" episode in Homer. Joyce purposely delays our recognition of Bloom and Stephen's re-enactment of that mythic meeting until very late in this episode, mirroring Homer's own narrative delay in his telling of it, by virtue of the often obfuscating style, which nonetheless has felicities of its own, as we have seen, and through the appearance of the false epic hero, Murphy, the Irish Odysseus misleadingly presented by the narrator for a time as Stephen's true father figure. But slowly, we recognize, as Joseph Meyer shows, that Murphy's "pursuit of adventure" has "compromised his relationship with both his wife and his son." Thus, "[t]he detachment between Murphy and his son, between epic hero and son, makes Bloom's attachment to Stephen more beautiful, compelling, and real."[84] Joyce's rejection of Murphy's potential paternity for Stephen, what Ellmann termed "falsimilitude"—Murphy's attempted "ambush" of "the verisimilitude that is claimed in *Ulysses*"—compounds the distortions of the Circean narrator and enables a truer picture of Bloom as paternal figure to the filial Stephen to emerge. For Ellmann, Joyce's dismissal of Murphy saves the novel's privileging of the real and sincere: "The rejection of Murphy attests that *Ulysses* is not a confidence trick. Instead the episode is made to register humbly, among the lying sights and sounds, its sincerity."[85]

Having been given sanction to reject Murphy as the false father figure, the reader is thus free to wrestle with the narrator's final description of Stephen and Bloom as deeply individual but finally connected, experiencing a paternal and filial, platonic, if incomplete marriage of minds, bodies, and souls. Distorted as the narrator's view of them as literally married is, nonetheless he grasps that they undergo at least a deep mingling, stemming from a profound receptivity to each other despite their differences—even a communion with each other as a culmination to this hospitality narrative. Ellmann points out that while the rhetoric of marriage is inappropriate and thus enables the narrator to "continue to mock the fusion of Bloom and Stephen," nevertheless "they do fuse, in a manner of speaking: 'Though they didn't see eye to eye in everything,' Bloom reflects, 'a certain analogy there somehow was, as if both their minds were travelling, so to speak, in the one train of thought' [*U* 16.1579–81]."[86]

Moreover, despite the problems created by Stephen's drunkenness and the narrator's fumbling style, their very difference from each other leads Bloom at first, then Stephen, to the other. Because their conversation continues at such length and even at times because of his bizarre replies, Stephen has gradually endeared himself to Bloom as father figure: "The queer suddenly things he popped out with attracted the older man who was several years the other's senior or like his father but something substantial he certainly ought to eat. . ." (*U* 16.1567–9). Therefore, because the intellectual Stephen's sense of self is so utterly Other to Bloom, the pedestrian, humble advertising canvasser is drawn to him: opposites attract. W. H. Auden captures this phenomenon well in his *New Year Letter*, when he muses, "And all real unity commences / In consciousness of differences. . . ."[87]

Finally, while the style might seem to block our apprehension of their developing relationship, its very banality might have finally engendered their connection, as both Frank Budgen and C. H. Peake argued, though they differ on whether or not their new relationship becomes ineffable in any way. Budgen recounts Bloom's rescue of Stephen, stating, "As is usual with Joyce, the simplest incidents are used to convey the deepest things. . . . And yet in a measure that no spectacular action could have achieved, we are led from the things done, felt and said to the contemplation of mystery." That mystery, for Budgen, is "the element of fatherhood in all social devotion."[88] Peake also points out the banality of their relationship but sees nothing profound developing out of it: "This transformation of their relationship has been presented throughout in a manner of deliberate banality, partly because such a manner represents and evaluates Bloom's mood, and partly because it is only at a banal level that the two men can meet."[89] In this reading, the narrator establishes a pedestrian relationship between the two men because of his employment of such a plodding style; and yet Peake does not seem alert to how the style itself seems to change late in the episode, signaling a new transcendent quality to this relationship. I believe instead that the style in these closing paragraphs occasionally becomes Other to its previous manifestation, passing strange and haunting. For instance, when Stephen feels "a strange kind of flesh of a different man approach him, sinewless and wobbly and all that" (*U* 16.1723–4), this newly ineffable style signals considerably more than merely a banal relationship developing between Stephen and Bloom. The banality of much of the episode's style thus meets its Other, sameness approaches difference, and the two are blended, suggesting how the very different Bloom and Stephen meet and mingle.

In a somewhat similar reading focusing mainly on the last paragraph, John Paul Riquelme has pointed out the narrator's inability to separate the "prose discourse mostly in roman type that contains a poetic discourse in italic type," reinforcing the unity of Stephen and Bloom: "Like the full and the lean black figures, they are 'Side by side' (*U* 16.1880) in a '*tête á tête*' (*U* 16.1889), different, and yet strangely linked."[90] In Riquelme's reading, the style in this last passage of the episode draws together prose and poetry, Bloom and Stephen.

As "Eumaeus" draws to a close, Stephen and Bloom come closer together as well, not just shown through how these styles converge but also through their common conversation about the "Sirens' duplicity and about usurpation," which are "two subjects which unite their plights," as Ellmann observes.[91] Riquelme has drawn on the subject of usurpation (and the mythic sirens) to suggest how that subject connects Stephen and Bloom through their common fear of usurpers—implicitly, Bloom's fear of Blazes Boylan and Stephen's of Buck Mulligan—and how memories of this theme from earlier episodes now enable the reader to be connected to both of them. Charles Stewart Parnell's position as a usurper, a major story narrated in "Eumaeus," recalls Stephen's evocation of Shakespeare's situation in "Scylla and Charybdis" (*U* 9.997–1006), itself linked to the usurpation of Hamlet's father by his uncle. Although Riquelme links these references to Buck Mulligan as "usurper" in the last line of the first episode, "Telemachus,"[92] he does not suggest how Buck acts as usurper of Stephen's art with his masturbatory theory of art late in "Scylla and Charybdis," a usurpation interrupted by the fugitive entrance of Leopold Bloom: "A man passed out between them, bowing, greeting" (*U* 9.1203). The promise of hospitality that a strange man offers to Stephen in his exotic dream earlier in "Proteus—"In. Come. Red carpet spread" (*U* 3.368–9)—appears again in the ninth episode, making Stephen now more strongly linked to Bloom as hospitality figure through his brief entrance to the National Library. Bloom's appearance helpfully cuts off Buck's usurpation of Stephen as artist and he offers himself as a potential rescuer figure who might promote Stephen's art: "A creamfruit melon he held to me. In. You will see" (*U* 9.1208). Even though Mulligan graphically warns Stephen to beware "—The wandering jew" (*U* 9.1209), saying that Bloom could somehow impregnate Stephen, in fact Bloom's care for Stephen and later imagining of his career as a singer in both "Eumaeus" and "Ithaca" suggests that Bloom's benign, encouraging presence could become generative for Stephen's artistic development, and effectively replaces Mulligan's squashing of that potential vocation.

Walton Litz was the first to cite Joyce's note about the two main characters' unity in the conclusion of "Eumaeus": "Ul[ysses] and Tel[emachus] exchange unity."[93] The passage I have already cited from "Eumaeus" to suggest Stephen's apprehension at what he perceives as the approach of Bloom's supposedly Jewish flesh nonetheless suggests an interesting bodily rapport between them—and Stephen's receptivity to Bloom's body as a rescuer. At one point, Joyce seems to have pondered whether the two men should hug each other, since he noted that Telemachus and Ulysses do just that in the Butcher and Lang translation of the *Odyssey*, published in 1879: "T[elemachus] and Ul[ysses] embrace."[94] Again, after he asks Stephen to "Lean on me," Stephen "uncertainly" says "Yes . . . because he thought he felt a strange kind of flesh of a different man approach him, sinewless and wobbly and all that" (*U* 16.1720, 1723–4). Karen Lawrence briefly but suggestively traces the start of Bloom's receptive hospitality to Stephen to the younger man's dream of a "Bloom-like figure who makes a gesture of hospitality" in the passage I cited above from "Proteus" (*U* 3.368–9), positing that "the novel enacts hospitality to a different kind of flesh, perceived most intimately by Stephen in 'Eumaeus'" at this moment when Stephen somatically perceives Bloom's "strange kind of flesh" approaching him.[95] This reading suggests that Stephen might have been previously receptive to Bloom's approach at a subconscious level, thus leading him to become more fully receptive here.[96]

Recall that no one has really touched Bloom throughout the day: he must be craving to touch others and to be touched. As Frank Budgen plaintively notes, despite several characters who praise him in the course of the novel, "nobody comes quite near him. It is as if a transparent film cut him off from his surroundings. He can see and be seen, but he can never be touched, and that despite all the apparent amiabilities of discourse."[97] He can also hear and be heard, but remains outcast from this embodied society as he is rendered bodiless, despite all his corporeal affinities—for food, for sex, for companionship, for love. Budgen hammers this point home when he remarks, "Nobody wants to slap him on the back or take hold of his arm. He has another consistency of flesh and a different family odour."[98] So Bloom himself finally initiates that touch in literally reaching out to Stephen, touching him to ascertain he is not seriously injured in "Circe," and then taking hold of his arm in this strange passage from "Eumaeus," in the process transforming himself at least temporarily from neglected and attacked Stranger to Good Samaritan, rescuer of Stephen.

Stephen senses that Bloom has just been reborn in some sense, rendered "sinewless and wobbly" like a new-born colt, perhaps. Why reborn? Because, unlike the false, verbal narrative of Murphy, which the circumlocutious narrator finally admits is not "strictly accurate gospel" (*U* 16.829), the realistic, action-based narrative of the Good Samaritan parable, something very close to the real Gospel truth, slowly emerges here. Bloom has played the role of the Good Samaritan in his ministrations toward Stephen, and he is not received well by Stephen until this point. Linked arm in arm with Bloom now, though, a complete reversal from his shrinking from Mulligan's arm around him in "Telemachus,"[99] Stephen is bodily receptive to Bloom in a way he never is verbally either here or in "Ithaca," unless we accept McBride's auto-fictive argument and agree that Stephen is "author" of "Eumaeus" and "Ithaca." Bloom thus gives his body here to Stephen, conjoined in a profound and ineffable way that the narrator cannot capture but realizes is important. James H. Maddox makes a startling but true claim, largely unrecognized by other critics, about Stephen's reception of Bloom's body here: "this is the whole point of 'Eumaeus': he must be brought to the awareness that his hope of mature equanimity has taken on physical form in Leopold Bloom."[100]

In his reading of Paul Ricoeur's *Oneself as Another*, Constantin V. Boundas shows how if, as Ricoeur claims, Otherness "belongs instead to the tenor of meaning and to the ontological constitution of selfhood," then "Otherness, therefore, must, in a sense, inhabit . . . the Same. The strang(er)ness peculiar to the other person must be anticipated and, in some sense, preceded by the alterity of my flesh, by my suffering, and by the voice of conscience."[101] In such a reading, which develops from Boundas's and Ricoeur's reflections on the Good Samaritan parable, Bloom is already sufficiently Other to himself before he meets Stephen, just as all of us have this component of alterity as a fact of our selfhood. Bloom's growing realization of his internal alterity throughout the day, awakened by the attacks on him by a series of Dubliners, likely actuates that otherness and makes him deeply receptive to Stephen, particularly starting in "Circe" as he sees how Stephen is "othered" by the British soldiers.

Stephen, drunk as he is, has realized earlier in the episode that Bloom is somehow the incarnated fulfillment of Jewish hope, citing the critical part of Romans 9:5 from the Vulgate version of the Bible: "*Ex quibus*, Stephen mumbled in a noncommittal accent, their two or four eyes conversing, *Christus*, or Bloom his name is, or, after all, any other, *secundum carnem*" (*U* 16.1091–3).[102] Translated, Paul's language runs thus: "Whose are the fathers, and of whom as concerning the flesh Christ came, who is over all, God blessed for ever. Amen" (KJV). In this passage, Paul expresses deep anguish for the salvation of his own people, the Jews, and even says in a preceding verse, Romans 9:3, "For

I could wish that myself were accursed from Christ for my brethren, my kinsmen according to the flesh" (KJV).[103] Something of Paul's agonized tone seeps through Stephen's reading of Bloom here as deeply concerned for him through his somatic care for him. This realization of Bloom as a Christ-like, fleshly fulfillment of Jewishness enables Stephen to be properly receptive to Bloom's enfleshed body, a "strange kind of flesh," as he approaches the younger man in the crucial scene later in "Eumaeus."

Here, Bloom mediates between Jews (whom he represents) and Christians (represented by the lapsed Catholic Stephen) through his enfleshed otherness. In a crucial moment from "Circe," the Cap has spoken Pauline language to Stephen in a chiastic phrase, "Jewgreek is greekjew" (U 15.2098–9), semantically signaling Bloom's emergence as a Christ figure through his liminal transcultural and trans-religious role in the novel. Declan Kiberd has suggested that Joyce's approving, proleptic phrase for Bloom exemplifies Paul's letter in Galatians 3:26–9: "There is neither Jew nor Greek; there is neither slave nor freeman; there is no male and female. For you are all one in Christ Jesus."[104]

The act of touching another as Bloom does Stephen can be read as a mediating act consistent with the "carnal hermeneutics" that philosopher Richard Kearney has developed. Drawing on later passages from Aristotle's *De Anima*, Kearney makes the fascinating point that "Aristotle insists on the mediating character of tactility. To be tactile is to be exposed to otherness across gaps, to navigate and negotiate sensitively between other embodied beings."[105] Recall how one of Bloom's major charitable acts in the novel involves helping the blind stripling across the street toward the end of "Lestrygonians."[106] After Bloom "touched the thin elbow gently: then took the limp seeing hand to guide it forward" (U 8.1090–1) and helps the man walk across the street, he immediately begins intuiting, or trying to intuit, elements of the man's life: "Stains on his coat. Slobbers his food, I suppose. Tastes all different for him. Have to be spoonfed first. Like a child's hand, his hand. . . . Sizing me up I daresay from my hand" (U 10.1096–7, 1098). Remarkably, the narrator suggests that the blind man's "limp" hand is also "seeing," and moreover shows Bloom being "read" by the man even as Bloom attempts to read him. Such an interaction perfectly illustrates Kearney's claim about how tactility enables us to mediate between ourselves and others, "to navigate and negotiate between other embodied beings."

Realizing that touch enables the blind man to see in significant ways, Bloom wonders, "How on earth did he know that van was there? Must have felt it. See things in their forehead perhaps: kind of sense of volume. Weight or size of it, something blacker than the dark" (U 10.1107–9). Bloom subsequently imagines himself more deeply into the man's mind by trying to "see" through his touch, were the man to see the "girl passing the Stewart institution" (U 10.1125–6). He supposes that "when he touches her with his fingers must almost see the lines, the curves. His hands on her hair, for instance. Say it was black, for instance. Good. We call it black. Then passing over her white skin. Different feel perhaps. Feeling of white" (*U* 10.1128–31). Finally, he tries out this theory on himself, touching his own belly surreptitiously: "Walking by Doran's publichouse he slid his hand between his waistcoat and trousers and, pulling aside his shirt gently, felt a slack fold of his belly. But I know it's whitey yellow. Want to try in the dark to see" (*U* 10.1140–2). Here he runs up against the limitations of his experiment: unless he were truly blind, he could not apprehend color in this way. But the great imaginative effort involved in this thought experiment, culminating in his somatic attempt to see color, first through imagining the blind man "seeing" the walking girl by touching her, and then by touching his own belly to try to perceive its color, together suggest just how much he has developed his tactile sense over time and how he employs it to greatly sympathize and empathize with others, as he does with Stephen, from first helping him up and loosening the buttons on his waistcoat at the end of "Circe" to now taking his arm and helping him down the street. As he guided the blind stripling, now he guides Stephen, but with an even greater rapport that has built up through conversation between them and is now heightened by this bodily touch. Thus, the encounter with the blind stripling (and undoubtedly others like it that Bloom has initiated earlier in his life) has conditioned him to reach out to Stephen late in the novel across the "gaps" that separate them.

This mediation, this navigation between ourselves and others, continues even after such affective, somatic, even spiritual encounters such as Stephen and Bloom have as he invites Stephen to lean on him in the conclusion of "Eumaeus," in part because a bodily ethic must maintain difference between the bodies touching each other, as not only Kearney but other thinkers such as Norman Wirzba argue. As Wirzba articulates this crucial distinction, citing Graham Ward's contention, "'Only when there is space, where there is distance, where there is difference, can there be the love that desires, that draws, that seeks participation.' Thus, [w]e need the space between self and other so that we can learn to act and share in their joys."[107] Reaching out to and touching the other must not obliterate the other but preserve its essence; in so doing, we heighten our chances of rapport with the other as we reach across the gulf between us with the potential for a future series of hospitable acts toward each other.

The body encompassed both the mind and the spirit for Joyce, and his description of the strange, enfleshed encounter between Stephen and Bloom suggests that trinity of mind, body, and soul, implying how profound their union is, even if temporary. Flesh, as Kearney further posits, drawing on groundbreaking phenomenological work by both Paul Ricoeur and Jean-Louis Chrétien, "first opens me to a radical passivity and passion—naked exposition to the other-than-me, receptive to whomever and whatever exceeds and calls and gives itself to me." Flesh, that is, "inserts me—body and soul—into the flesh of the world. It reveals my radical interdependency as a being who feels both ways—as an embodied consciousness projecting meaning onto others while simultaneously receiving meaning from them."[108] Joyce so focuses on the body of Bloom here because he believed that "a man is not only flesh and blood but a living soul . . . whose habitation is that solid body."[109] Mind is enfleshed as well as soul for Joyce, as Ellmann argued: "For him the mind was profoundly physical, containing all the organs of the body."[110] When Stephen and Bloom touch here, not just their bodies but also their souls and minds commune with each other. Leopold Bloom epitomizes carnal hermeneutics, we might say—anticipates it and models it long before Kearney articulates it, brilliant as his exposition of it is. Inserted bodily into the "flesh of the world" that is Dublin on June 16, 1904, Bloom positively vibrates with the motions of the city, its to-ings and fro-ings, and knows its inhabitants—strangers and friends—intimately through his well-developed tactile apprehension of them.

Chrétien's reading of the body and touch illuminates the spiritual potential for the bodily contact made between Stephen and Bloom late in "Eumaeus," particularly when we bear in mind Bloom's search for love and for a son and how those two quests intertwine in Stephen. For Chrétien, who makes a compelling phenomenological argument for touch in *The Call and the Response* as the most primordial and the most spiritual sense, love can animate touch by giving "the flesh its full bearing of intellect and leads touch to its highest possibility." Moreover,

> touch, in its finitude and based on it, is already open precisely to a presence without image or representation, to an intimate proximity that never turns into possession, to a naked exposure to the ungraspable. The excess over me of what I touch and of what touches me is endlessly attested in the caress.[111]

There is no caress as such between Stephen and Bloom, yet Bloom's invitation to Stephen to lean upon him suggests how the ineffable may enter into this scene, hovering above it, infusing it with love.

Bloom's initially spontaneous, then ongoing and more considered gift of himself to Stephen through a series of hospitable acts establishes what might become an indissoluble bond between them not only because it is bodily but also because it is deeply spiritually enfleshed, based on a likely unconscious recapitulation of the Good Samaritan parable, which like all sympathetic interactions involves a reciprocity, and furthermore recalls Christ's loving gift of Himself to us through his sacrifice on the cross. Lewis Hyde's remarkable work on the subject of gifts illuminates the profound yet strange relationship between Stephen and Bloom. As he points out, "It is the cardinal difference between gift and commodity exchange that a gift establishes a feeling-bond between two people, while the sale of a commodity leaves no necessary connection."[112] Hyde's theory of gifting versus commodity exchange offers the best riposte to Gerald Bruns's contention, cited earlier in this chapter, that Bloom and Stephen's sole connection is "utterly commercial and utterly imaginary."[113] Were it "utterly commercial" it would not even occur, certainly not with the strange and affecting language Joyce employs to describe their union.

Fascinatingly, Bloom's offering of himself to Stephen is not one-sided but reciprocal. Ricoeur argues in *Oneself as Another* that "[i]n true sympathy, the self . . . finds itself affected by all that the suffering other offers to it in return. For from the suffering other there comes a giving that is no longer drawn from the power of acting and existing but precisely from weakness itself."[114] Bloom's desire for companionship is fulfilled through Stephen's weakness and need for help. But crucially, Bloom enters into his relationship with Stephen with no expectation of such companionship, but simply and merely to help save him. His embodied action of love then ramifies out beyond Stephen to us—as we will see—and back to himself.

Hyde discusses gods who become incarnate and offer their bodies to those separated by sin from the god, singling out Christianity as exemplary in this regard: "Christ's body becomes the gift, the vehicle of atonement, which establishes a new covenant between man and God."[115] In the context of Joyce's novel, the secular, earthly Bloom's offering his body to Stephen establishes no such theological covenant, but in its spiritual evocation of Christ's sacrifice through its bodily unselfishness, it nonetheless acquires deep spiritual resonances, enabling Bloom to form likely a lasting bond with Stephen—*whether or not they ever meet again.*[116]

Notes

1. As of November, 2020, the MLA database identifies only 40 articles or book chapters for "Eumaeus," easily the fewest for any single episode of *Ulysses*. Brook Thomas, "The Counterfeit Style of 'Eumaeus,'" commented in 1976 that "it has the privileged status of being the most maligned chapter of the book" (15) and that largely remains the case today. There were welcome developments in criticism of "Eumaeus" such as the work by John Henry Raleigh, Andrew Gibson, Robert Bell, Patrick McGee, and Vicki Mahaffey that Robert Newman, "'Eumaeus' as Sacrificial Narrative," 451, cites in 1993, yet with the exception of the few critics who have done significant work on the episode in the last quarter century since Newman's essay, particularly the work cited in these chapters on *Ulysses* by Christine O'Neill, Fritz Senn, John Paul Riquelme, and Margot Norris, "Eumaeus" criticism continues to languish. This is all the more astonishing since it lays fair claim to being the climax of the novel.
2. Kenner, *Joyce's Voices*, 35.

3. Thornton, *Allusions in* Ulysses, 83, 331–2, 370, 429, lists all these allusions, given here in the order they occur in the novel, from "Lotus Eaters," "Oxen of the Sun," "Circe," and "Eumaeus." He notes that in the reference to the parable in "Circe," "Bloom may be remembering an earlier statement of Stephen's which blends two biblical allusions," alluding, that is, to Stephen's allusion to the parable in the "Oxen of the Sun" reference (370). Here, in this repetition of the last words of Christ's parable, repetition lifts the injunction to "Go and do likewise" into an eternal present, according with Bruce F. Kawin's theory of repetition in *Telling it Again and Again*: "a word can take on more than its ordinary force by virtue of its repeating an earlier use of that word, or [it] can allow a work of art to move as the present moves, beginning again and advancing with the continual youth and power of the present" (93). I explore the admonitory power of that urged action to the reader fully in the last chapter on *Ulysses* and in the coda of this study.
4. Kiberd, *Ulysses and Us*, 304.
5. Slote, "Preliminary Comments on Two Newly Discovered 'Ulysses' Manuscripts," 22.
6. Herring, *Joyce's* Ulysses *Notesheets in the British Museum*, 378. It is difficult to ascertain when the blue pencil-scored phrases were incorporated into "Eumaeus," but it may well follow the general pattern of the next two episodes, "Ithaca" and "Penelope," in which blue-penciled phrases were at "the heart of the Rosenbach Manuscript" for "Ithaca" and in "the first half of the Rosenbach Manuscript" for "Penelope" (Herring, *Joyce's* Ulysses *Notesheets in the British Museum*, 530, citing James Card, "A Textual and Critical Study of the 'Penelope' Episode of James Joyce's *Ulysses*," 29–30). Luca Crispi, "Manuscript Timeline, 1905–1922 [for *Ulysses*]," notes that parts of "Eumaeus" may have been written as early as 1916, pointing out that "In July 1920, when Joyce arrived in Paris he claimed that he had written drafts of the last three episodes, the "Nostos," Part III of *Ulysses*. He may even have written some portion of these episodes as early 1916, evidence of which may be found in the earliest surviving draft of 'Eumaeus'" (16).
7. Gabler, "Afterword," 1863.
8. Crispi, email to the author.
9. Gilbert, *James Joyce's* Ulysses: *A Study*, 349.
10. Gifford and Seidman, Ulysses *Annotated*, 534; my emphasis.
11. Houston, *Joyce and Prose*, 149.
12. "Fashion" also puzzles, since the biblical Samaritan does exactly what is not the fashion; moreover, if a given "fashion" is "orthodox," then making "fashion" part of the phrase concerning Bloom's behavior renders it redundant, which is typical of this narrator's style.
13. Fargnoli and Gillespie, *James Joyce A–Z*, 67.
14. Fritz Senn gets the sense of the phrase exactly right in "Eumaean Titbits," observing, "Any fashion that is 'orthodox Samaritan' is out of the common groove," and stating further, "The parable of the Good Samaritan shows that a member of the 'wrong' faith may well act with more propriety than the orthodox (Jews) did (Luke 10:30–7). The constellation 'in orthodox Samaritan fashion' is scripturally askew, trying to have it both ways, but perversely right in characterizing the Eumaean

style, one of metaphorical inconsonance. The Samaritan of the parable after all also modified a conception of rightness" (179).
15. Ellmann, Ulysses *on the Liffey*, 152. Maud Ellmann, "Endings," contends, "This sentence provides a foretaste of the style of 'Eumaeus,' with its oxymorons ('orthodox Samaritan'), mismatched clichés, labored ironies, and pompous formalities—it is a long time since Poldy has been formally announced as 'Mr Bloom.' Flaccid in construction, the sentence seems afflicted by the narcolepsy that pervades this episode, as if the narrator were stringing words together, too exhausted to attend to syntax or grammar" (99). Well, Bloom is called "Bloom," if not "Mr. Bloom" in both episodes 13, "Oxen of the Sun," and 14, "Circe"—at least in that latter chapter's representation of stage dialogue. One might say that even as this long-winded narrator begins his "wind-up" to his windy narration, he manages to include a core truth about Bloom as an "orthodox Samaritan" in the sense I argue for in this analysis.
16. Kenner, *Dublin's Joyce*, 260.
17. Sultan, *The Argument of* Ulysses, 364.
18. Kenner, *Ulysses*, 130, 129, 130. In his *Voices and Values in Joyce's* Ulysses, Thornton offers up the most pointed and refreshingly brief refutation of Kenner's claim for Bloom's authorship of this episode, noting that "all of the material of the chapter ... undergoes a stylistic recasting that is not simply a third-person mode of Bloom's mentality," while he nonetheless suggests the dialogue does faithfully represent his thinking and can be trusted. Unfortunately, Thornton does not dwell on the significance of such truthful passages of dialogue as I am examining here to think through Stephen and Bloom's relationship in this late episode and focuses on what he sees as the episode's similarity to the "loose, clichéd, enervated prose of much contemporary journalism" (106).
19. Raleigh, "On the Way Home to Ithaca," 14, quoting Budgen, *James Joyce and the Making of* Ulysses, 255.
20. Budgen, *James Joyce and the Making of* Ulysses, 255.
21. O'Neill, *Too Fine a Point*, 29. We can now safely discount Philip Herring's contention in *Joyce's* Ulysses *Notesheets in the British Museum* that "There is ... a distinct possibility that Joyce's own fatigue played a dominant role, for in the 'Eumaeus' notesheets one sees Joyce more dependent than usual on repetitious notes, external structure, and mythological allusion. It is as if his creative imagination were momentarily bankrupt. ... In 'Eumaeus' Joyce plods methodically along, like a horse with blinders" (49–50). There is evidence, for example, from the "Eumeo" manuscript referenced above that Joyce purposely made the style more awkward as he drafted the episode: Slote, "Preliminary Comments," 23, for instance, notes that on this previously unknown manuscript, "revisions made in red to text already drafted in black enhances the awkwardness of style and idiom. In other words, the process of "Eumaeification' is something that evolved over time." See O'Neill, *Too Fine a Point*, 12–41, for a helpful summary and analysis of major critical interpretations of the episode starting in the 1950s with Hugh Kenner's reading of it.
22. Raleigh, "On the Way Home to Ithaca," 80.
23. Gabler, "Afterword," 1863.

24. Brockman, "The New Bloom in 'Eumaeus': The Emendations of *Ulysses: A Critical and Synoptic Edition*," 154, 155, citing on 154, Sultan, "*The Adventures of* Ulysses *in Our World*," 309 n29.
25. Gibson, *Joyce's Revenge*, 218. In his reading of Joyce's style in "Eumaeus" as drawing on the Irish bull's purposeful employment of error and blunder, Gibson terms the language of the episode "a glorious, wicked, delighted perversion of a language . . . that Joyce nonetheless takes to be an unalterable, historical given" (219).
26. Hogan, Ulysses *and the Poetics of Cognition*, 185, 186, 187. Hogan points out that despite the narrator's near-continual recourse to clichés, they are nonetheless deployed in surprising ways, making them vivid and communicative: "Even with the most clichéd phrases, I doubt any reader anticipates just what the narrator is going to say or how he will say it. . . . [I]t is also highly vivid, bringing images and perceptual perspectives to the mind of the reader and conveying information and emotion more effectively than more commonly used alternatives." He then follows with a persuasive analysis in this regard of the "apparently redundant phrase, 'hit upon some drinkables in the shape of a milk and soda or a mineral [U 16.10–11]'" (187, 187–8).
27. Ibid., 188.
28. Ellmann, Ulysses *on the Liffey*, 152; my emphasis. But puzzlingly, on the previous page, Ellmann claims of Bloom, "He appears much reduced [in "Eumaeus"] from that heroic rescuer and artist we saw at the end of the brothel scene" (151). The continuity from the end of "Circe" to the beginning of "Eumaeus" seems immediate.
29. Ellmann, "Prologue: Two Perspectives on Joyce," 3.
30. Renan, *The Life of Jesus*, 170. Joyce was also reading other lives of Christ at this time; Pierce, *Reading Joyce*, notes that he was reading David Friedrich Strauss's *Das Leben Jesus (The Life of Jesus)* (1835) at the same time as he was reading Renan's *La Vie de Jésus* (217). And later, while he was writing *Ulysses*, he certainly also read Léo Taxil's *La Vie de Jésus* (1882), "a scurrilous account of the life of Jesus," which Stephen Dedalus thinks of in "Proteus" (U 3.161–2) (Pierce, *Reading Joyce*, 218).
31. An exception to such readings comes from Declan Kiberd, who properly argues for Joyce's sense of a humanized Bloom as a type reflecting a warmly humanist Christ, but who also largely elides Christ's supernatural identity and renders him merely a revolutionary reformer; see Kiberd, Ulysses *and Us*, 296–312. For instance, soon after Kiberd remarks upon Jesus' "suffering humanity" and the problem of the New Testament writers in presenting "God in a man," he posits that post-Crucifixion, Christ "made a higher evolution in mankind possible, so that all might find it possible to become 'the human form divine,' to partake in God's presence and immortality. The identity of Jesus was really an open space into which people could read whatever they wanted" (311). In this reading, however, Christ as cipher becomes finally too amorphous to carry any ethical weight, much less signify His salvific sacrifice.
32. Bruns, "Eumaeus," 383.
33. O'Neill, *Too Fine a Point*, 18.
34. Bruns, "Eumaeus," 381–2.

35. Peake, *James Joyce*, 278–9.
36. Heusel, "Vestiges of Truth: A Study of James Joyce's 'Eumaeus,'" 403.
37. Ellmann, Ulysses *on the Liffey*, 154.
38. Dudley, "From 'Spiritual Paralysis' to 'Spiritual Liberation': Joyce's Samaritan 'Grace,'" 177.
39. Ellmann, Ulysses *on the Liffey*, 146–7.
40. Moseley, *Joyce and the Bible*, 124.
41. Ibid., 125.
42. Ibid., 129. In *The Argument of* Ulysses, 377, Sultan anticipates Moseley's argument that Stephen is developing compassion toward others, but crucially does not link the change in his behavior to Bloom's having modeled the Good Samaritan parable to him: "The 'loan' to Corley . . . reveals a developed capacity for pity. Unlike Stephen's pupil Sargent in the second chapter, Corley is in no way similar to himself, and he [Stephen] is pointedly no more well off, all in all, than Corley."
43. Norris, *Virgin and Veteran Readings of* Ulysses, 186, 187.
44. Ibid., 187.
45. Ibid., 187.
46. Budgen, *James Joyce and the Making of* Ulysses, 107. For a recent example of this continued tendency, see Matthew Hayward, "Bloom's C.V," 889, who wrongly argues, "For all of Joyce's plans to 'Hellenise' him as Telmachus (1.158), Stephen remains stubborn, and leaves the novel much as he entered it, as Joyce complained to Budgen: 'Stephen no longer interests me. . . . He has a shape that can't be changed.'"
47. Kenner, "The Cubist *Portrait*," 179.
48. Norris, *Virgin and Veteran Readings of* Ulysses, 202, citing Doležel, *Heterocosmica*, 98.
49. Adams, *Surface and Symbol*, 250.
50. Kenner, *Ulysses*, 153.
51. Houston, *Joyce and Prose*, 153.
52. Ellmann, *The Consciousness of Joyce*, 76. And yet he was much drawn to sentimentality and struggled with it most of his life, as Clive Hart has shown in "James Joyce's Sentimentality."
53. Ellmann, *The Consciousness of Joyce*, 31.
54. Ibid., 32. Compare that much more muted, retrospective reaction by Fénelon's Telemachus to the two very emotional reactions in Homer when Odysseus and Telemachus meet. Odysseus's reaction when he reveals himself to Telemachus was clearly far too dramatic and sentimental for Joyce: "Odysseus kissed his son / and the tears streamed down his cheeks and wet the ground, / though before he'd always reined his emotions back" (Homer, *The Odyssey*, Book XVI, lines 215–17). Worse, from Joyce's point of view, would have been when, after initially not believing this stranger to be his father, Telemachus accepts him as such and both men weep uncontrollably: "Telemachus threw his arms / around his great father, sobbing uncontrollably / as the deep desire for tears welled up in both. / They cried out, shrilling cries. . ." (Homer, *The Odyssey*, Book XVI, lines 243–6).
55. Raleigh, "On the Way Home to Ithaca," 80.
56. Peake, *James Joyce*, 279.

57. O'Neill, *Too Fine a Point*, 123.
58. Ibid., 126.
59. Ibid., 132.
60. See Benstock, *Narrative Con/Texts in* Ulysses, however, for a reading that argues that Bloom's immediate, sensible, and direct response to Stephen's questions about why chairs are put upside down on tables at night in cafés (*U* 16.1708–13) begins a new understanding between them, and moreover, establishes a conversation equilibrium that is evident in "Ithaca" as well: "The convoluted intelligence and artistic temperament of Stephen Dedalus are somewhat jarred by the common sense and direct response from Bloom, at this first instance in 'Eumaeus' that Bloom has said anything 'straight off.'" Now, "That Stephen may have come to appreciate an intelligence so different from his own bodes well for a potential writer of Irish life and cuts through the attempts at intellectual conversation that had previously alienated him by its circumlocutions and elliptical assumptions" (12).
61. Kiberd, Ulysses *and Us*, 243.
62. Chrétien, *The Ark of Speech*, 48.
63. Ibid., 53.
64. For an excellent overview of recent attempts to determine whether there is any connection between Bloom and Stephen in this episode, see Johanna Winant, "Empathy and Other Minds in *Ulysses*." Winant is particularly helpful in assessing their relationship through the intellectual history of empathy, and she shows how the philosophies of both Husserl and Wittgenstein, beginning in 1929 and through the 1930s, "established the privacy of other minds" and "radically weakened the conception of empathy" (379). Although she unfortunately does not consider their reciprocal bodily enfleshment in the climactic scene of "Eumaeus" as part of their empathy for each other, Winant's account succeeds in showing how most recent critics who grapple with assessing Bloom and Stephen's relationship do not have an adequate concept or vocabulary of empathy to explain what they sense is its significance: "because we no longer have a concept for a strong sense of empathy, we do not have a vocabulary for it either" (382).
65. Ricoeur, *Oneself as Another*, 190.
66. Senn, "'All Kinds of Words Changing Colour,'" 166.
67. Ibid., 166–7.
68. The usual critical reaction to Bloom's formulation of a nation to the Citizen can unfortunately echo the Citizen's reading of Bloom as an "idealist unfit for the work of constructing the nation-state," as Bryan Yazell, "Irish-Israelism: Reconsidering the Politics of Race and Belonging in 'Cyclops,'" 269 and *passim*, shows. Fascinatingly, although Yazell does not really attend to how Bloom constructs communities of care and love, he at least pushes back against this finally simplistic reading of Bloom's formulation of nationalism that reifies the Citizen's rejection of Bloom, pointing out that "the notion of the 'same people' living in [the] 'same' . . . place . . . suggests instead the need to renegotiate constantly the geographic borders of Ireland," while his addition of "the same people" living in "different places" enables him to "visualize the potential for national affiliations that extend beyond geography" (279).
69. Kiberd, Ulysses *and Us*, 311.

70. Latham, *Am I A Snob?*, 153.
71. Ibid., 154, for this quotation, which he cites from Ellmann, *JJ2*, 459. Note, however, that Latham finally posits that "In consistently contrasting Stephen and Bloom, Joyce interrogates the snobbery not only of the artist but of *Ulysses* itself, and he wagers that the still immature Stephen will eventually overcome the imperious arrogance so integral to the personality of the artist." Yet "[t]he outcome of this gamble . . . depends not on the mystical union ironically passed to us through a catechism but on the reception and acceptance of the novel itself by the very people it claims to represent" (168).
72. Maud Ellmann, "Endings," 96.
73. The observation of McDonald, "Alien Grace," 50, is pithy and appropriate here: "the parabolic image is strong and memorable, but it is what the Samaritan *does*—and the fact that it is he who does it and not the Temple clerics—that matters."
74. See Thornton, "The Greatness of *Ulysses*," 34, where he laments, "In the Eumaeus or cabman's shelter episode . . . it should not take Joyce seventy pages to demonstrate for us the vacuity of the enervated, clichéd, circumlocutory style of that episode, especially when the events . . . are presented through that style. Bloom's taking Stephen under his wing and inviting him to his house could be presented so as to increase our affective engagement with the characters and the *mythos* of the novel." As I have tried to show in these chapters, however, the style of this episode is capable of conveying deep emotion, and certainly late in the episode, the style helps create our "affective engagement with the characters." I take Thornton's larger point, however, that *Ulysses* can sometimes sacrifice narrative on the altar of stylistic excess, particularly in overly long episodes like "Circe"; this is why it is essential to recognize such narrative "through-lines" as the Good Samaritan parable.
75. Qtd. in Budgen, *James Joyce and the Making of* Ulysses, 107.
76. Seeley, *Ecce Homo*, 145.
77. My specific reading of the particular parabolic encounter between Stephen and Bloom is adumbrated by Marian Eide's general insistence in *Ethical Joyce* that, beginning with his viewing of his mother's body after her premature death from cancer, "For Joyce, then, the first ethical obligation is to experience and express sympathy while preserving the differences between oneself and another" (2).
78. Mills-Knutsen, "Becoming Stranger," 532.
79. McBride, Ulysses *and the Metamorphosis of Stephen Dedalus*, 102.
80. Ibid., 99.
81. Ibid., 103.
82. Raleigh, "On the Way Home to Ithaca," 41.
83. Ibid., 41; see 41–54, for Raleigh's extensive discussion of these disputes, including a long and valuable digression on Parnell's fall and its aftermath.
84. Meyer, "Redefining the Epic Hero in Joyce's 'Eumaeus,'" 144–5, 145.
85. Ellmann, Ulysses *on the Liffey*, 155.
86. Ibid., 154.
87. Auden, *Collected Poems*, 241.
88. Budgen, *James Joyce and the Making of* Ulysses, 287.
89. Peake, *James Joyce*, 282.

90. See Riquelme, "'Preparatory to anything else,'" 23.
91. Ellmann, Ulysses *on the Liffey*, 154.
92. Riquelme, "'Preparatory to anything else,'" 23–4, for the usurpation/sirens discussion, and 24 for the "Telemachus" connection, which several other commentators have noticed, including Benstock, *Narrative Con/Texts in* Ulysses, cited below in note 99.
93. Qtd. in Litz, "Joyce's Notes for 'Ulysses,'" 17.
94. Qtd. in Herring, *Joyce's* Ulysses *Notesheets in the British Museum*, 407, citing the sixth notesheet of "Eumaeus."
95. Lawrence, "Close Encounters," 139–40.
96. Lawrence, *Who's Afraid of James Joyce?*, 116, points out how Bloom's advice to Stephen earlier in "Eumaeus" prophesies and lays the groundwork for this union: "'You ought to eat more solid food,' Bloom advises Stephen, 'You would feel a different man' (*U* 16.814). Later Bloom again advises, 'The only thing is to walk then you'll feel a different man' (*U* 16.1719)." Thus, "Bloom's prudent advice, by virtue of the double meaning of the word 'feel,' becomes prophecy—Stephen does feel a different man, and that man is Bloom. Feeling here is physical and emotional; after tactfully maneuvering Stephen through street and conversation, Bloom moves and touches him."
97. Budgen, *James Joyce and the Making of* Ulysses, 280 n1.
98. Ibid., 281. Earlier, Budgen argues of this scene that "There is no moment in *Ulysses* that better exemplifies that indefinite repugnance to Bloom's physical presence, felt by so many throughout the day, than that in which Bloom offers his arm to the weak and still unsteady Stephen" (260).
99. Bernard Benstock makes this point in *Narrative Con/Texts in* Ulysses, 12.
100. Maddox, "'Eumaeus' and the Theme of Return in *Ulysses*," 217.
101. Boundas, "The Good Samaritan, the Philosopher, and the Madman," 181, citing Ricoeur, *Oneself as Another*, 317.
102. Thornton, *Allusions in* Ulysses, 445, cites the allusion.
103. Neil Elliott, "Commentary on Romans," 255–6, points out that "Paul's willingness to be cut off from Christ for the sake of Israel is especially poignant after the assurance in [Romans] 8:39" that nothing can separate us from Christ's love.
104. Kiberd, Ulysses *and Us*, 310.
105. Kearney, "What Is Carnal Hermeneutics?," 103.
106. Note how rudely and carelessly another character, the preposterously named Cashel Boyle O'Connor Fitzmaurice Tisdall Farrell, acts to the stripling two episodes later, exhibiting behavior that clearly contrasts Bloom's own empathic charity in the passage under consideration from "Lestrygonians": "the sway of his dustcoat brushed rudely from its angle a slender tapping cane and swept onwards, having buffeted a thewless body" (*U* 10.1115–18).
107. Wirzba, "The Touch of Humility: An Invitation to Creatureliness," 238, citing Ward, *Christ and Culture*, 145.
108. Kearney, "What Is Carnal Hermeneutics?," 110. Kearney draws on and expands upon the work of Ricoeur, *Freedom and Nature*, and Chrètien, *The Call and the Response*.

109. Budgen, *James Joyce and the Making of* Ulysses, 275.
110. Ellmann, *The Consciousness of Joyce*, 76. Budgen, *James Joyce and the Making of* Ulysses, 108, notes that "Joyce in Zürich was a curious collector of facts about the human body, especially on that borderland where mind and body meet, where thought is generated and shaped by a state of the body." Such a belief, embodied by the physicality of Bloom, suggests how his body shapes his thinking in his care for Stephen, for instance.
111. Chrétien, *The Call and the Response*, 129.
112. Hyde, *The Gift*, 58. Although Lawrence, *Who's Afraid of James Joyce?*, 116–17, does not cite Hyde's seminal book on the subject, drawing instead on Derrida's *Grammatology*, I was pleased to see her recognition of the difference between gift and commercial exchange that Hyde stresses here: "a certain 'receptivity' develops out of the banality of the situation [in "Eumaeus"], a kind of 'gift' that does not compute within the political economy of profits and investments."
113. Bruns, "Eumaeus," 383.
114. Ricoeur, *Oneself as Another*, 191.
115. Hyde, *The Gift*, 60.
116. Indeed, if we follow Ricoeur's explanation of the eschatological nature of the Good Samaritan parable, neither Bloom nor Stephen nor the reader can fully apprehend the significance of the sense of Bloom and Stephen's encounter here until they and/or we meet Christ Himself: "the significance of this encounter does not depend on *any criterion immanent to history* and cannot be definitely recognized by the actors themselves but will be discovered on the last day, like the manner in which I shall have encountered Christ without knowing it" ("The Socius and the Neighbor," 101). For non-believers like Stephen and Bloom, then, recognition of the full significance of their encounter is infinitely delayed, but nonetheless significant, perhaps because of their sense of its inexplicable, ineffable nature.

6

HOME TO "ITHACA" AND "PENELOPE": BLOOM'S HOSPITALITY AND STEPHEN AND MOLLY'S REACTIONS

Bloom's Continuing Samaritan Hospitality to Stephen

Regardless of whether we accept Margaret McBride's auto-fictive account, "Ithaca" continues the events originally iterated in Christ's parable but with a twist: it rewrites the end of the parable when Bloom leads Stephen to his own home, not an inn or hotel like the Good Samaritan did. The Good Samaritan took the beaten stranger to an inn and paid "two denarii," which "would provide approximately two months of lodging in an ancient inn."[1] Yet Bloom goes beyond that hospitality to invite Stephen into his own home and truly make him a neighbor, an act of excessive generosity. Certainly, Bloom wants him to meet Molly and perhaps for him to sing with her eventually, but he is most concerned to care for Stephen.

"Starting united" (*U* 17.2), the two men wander toward 7 Eccles Street, and Bloom's inviting Stephen into his home constitutes an extension of his enfleshed care for the young man. Edward Casey has pointed out that because we have such "increasingly intimate relationships with their material structures, the longer we reside in places, the more bodylike they seem to be. As we feel more 'at home' in dwelling places, they become places created in our own bodily image."[2] Recall the opening of "Calypso," the first episode in the novel in which we meet Bloom. This thoroughly embodied man is preparing his wife's breakfast and is completely at home in his kitchen and house generally. As he wanders home from the butcher's shortly afterwards, the kidney he will soon eat in his pocket, he recoils from what seems like a gray and shrunken world and longs for the embodied world of his home: "To smell the gentle smoke of tea, fume of the pan, sizzling butter. Be near her ample bedwarmed flesh. Yes, yes" (*U* 4.237–9). Molly's concluding affirmations at the end of the novel have rightly garnered more attention, but Bloom's affirmation of his home as an extension of his body—a comfortable and enfleshed place of food and Molly's flesh—deserves more attention and suggests strongly what a generous offer he makes to Stephen when he invites him home in "Eumaeus," then hosts him in "Ithaca" in his continuing role of Good Samaritan. If Casey is correct is arguing that "the elective affinity" we have "between houses and bodies" signifies that "*our very identity is at stake*" in our relationship to our house, then Bloom's offer to Stephen implies a welcoming into the heart of his very identity, which is, after all, predicated on hospitality and helping others, not selfishness.[3] All day long, assailed and marginalized as the Stranger, Bloom wants nothing more than this embodied, domestic comfort. Moreover, as Heffernan points out, "[w]hile Bloom contrives to vanquish Boylan mentally, to drive this unwanted guest from the house of his mind" in earlier episodes because Bloom is a "host whose hospitality, like that of Odysseus, has been grossly abused," he "yearns to make Stephen an almost apostolic guest."[4] That is, he now wants Stephen to have the comforts of home—physical, mental, even spiritual—that Stephen has not had all day after leaving the tower, and that he, Bloom, has not had since the morning and which he pines for. So after touching and helping guide him, arm-in-arm, Bloom leads Stephen home, to an extension of his body, mind, and soul, opening himself further to him.

While I do not agree with Leo Bersani that Stephen and Bloom achieve no lasting connection here or elsewhere in the novel, he correctly points out the impersonal style of "the relentlessly tedious 'Ithaca,' with its nearly unreadable scientific expositions." While he believes this episode's style enforces its message, finally becoming "a kind of Pascalian meditation on the lack of connectedness not only between human beings but also between the human and the cosmos," the cold, clinical style actually brings into relief the moving and warm actions of Bloom and, for much of the chapter until he sings the anti-Semitic ballad, of Stephen as well.[5] Thus Bloom's ministrations toward Stephen as articulated in his re-enactments of the Good Samaritan parable (and even in some of the ways he surpasses the Samaritan's care for the beaten Stranger) are made all the more moving to us because the style's coldness contrasts so greatly with his warm care for Stephen.

Bloom's concern for Stephen continues unabated once they get to 7 Eccles Street: Bloom lays a fire in the grate (*U* 17.126–33), puts a kettle of water on the "now burning coals" (*U* 17.229), washes his hands and tries unsuccessfully to get Stephen to wash his hands too (*U* 17.231–40). He then makes Stephen a lavish cup of cocoa (*U* 17.355–8) and showing "marks of special hospitality" (*U* 17.359), refuses to drink out of his special "moustache cup of imitation

Crown Derby" that his daughter Milly gave him (*U* 17.361–2); instead, "he substituted a cup identical with that of his guest and served extraordinarily to his guest and, in reduced measure, to himself the viscous cream ordinarily reserved for the breakfast of his wife Marion (Molly)" (*U* 17.362–5). We know from "Calypso" and other episodes just how much Bloom loves his creature comforts such as special foods and drink; here, he denies himself some of that comfort in taking a lesser mug identical to that of Stephen and less cream than he offers Stephen. He has additionally already suppressed some helpful admonitions, including not lecturing Stephen on hygiene when he will not wash his hands (*U* 17.241–6) and not lecturing him on diet (*U* 17.249–51). Now, as they "drank in jocoserious silence Epps's massproduct, the creature cocoa" (*U* 17.369–70), the narrator puns on "massproduct," suggesting "the mass in which Bloom is functioning as priest, Stephen as communicant,"[6] adding another theological layer of significance to their ongoing iterations of and additions to the Good Samaritan parable.

Bloom then "contemplated but suppressed" other "marks of hospitality" (*U* 17.371), in the hopes of "reserving them for another and for himself on future occasions to complete the act begun" (*U* 17.372–3). These suppressed acts of hospitality, which he, in typically practical Poldy fashion, stores away, as it were, for another meeting with Stephen, include "The reparation of a fissure of the length of 1½ inches in the right side of his guest's jacket. A gift to his guest of one of the four lady's handkerchiefs, if and when ascertained to be in a presentable condition" (*U* 17.374–6). Bloom likely suppresses these hospitable acts so as not to embarrass Stephen and be too presumptuous in his care for him.

Beyond this scene, the narrator implies that each man engages in a memorable flight of fancy that envisions himself as the other, resulting in the new, partially fused identities of "Blephen" and "Stoom." This birth of blended new names signifies each's profound interest in the other and suggests a powerful, empathetic, even substitutionary relationship (yet one that preserves their individual identities), greatly surpassing what Arnold Weinstein misleadingly claims: "We may wish to regard them as a special pair, but their merging is manifestly achieved by authorial fiat, a marriage of names only, a linguistic tandem that has no truck with human relationship."[7] Such a wrong-headed, even perverse reading ignores all the ways in which the two have been linked directly and indirectly throughout the novel, and certainly much more directly since the events of "Circe." When the coldly impersonal narrator asks, "Did they find their educational careers similar?," we are given this astonishing sentence:

> Substituting Stephen for Bloom Stoom would have passed successively through a dame's school and the high school. Substituting Bloom for Stephen Blephen would have passed successively through the preparatory, junior, middle and senior grades of the intermediate and through

the matriculation, first arts, second arts and degree courses of the royal university. (*U* 17.549–54).

And yet the narrator makes clear very shortly after this moment that each man remains separate: "What two temperaments did they individually represent? The scientific. The artistic" (*U* 17.559–60).

I find Ellmann's reading of this passage in *The Consciousness of Joyce* to be the best and most convincing. Pointing out that the fact that "[t]he two men converge only partially does not diminish the exemplary value of their partial convergence," he argues that Joyce is punning on their names here, and that "[i]n a pun the component parts remains distinguishable, and yet there is a constant small excitement in their being yoked together so deftly and so improperly."[8] Certainly in the Good Samaritan parable, there is no complete fusion of Stranger and Samaritan—part of Christ's point is that each is so Other to the other as to normally preclude any interaction at all, much less a rescue narrative based on empathetic touch and care. But surely the Samaritan must have exercised his imagination to realize the suffering of the Stranger as he lay wounded. And here and elsewhere in these last few episodes, not only Bloom (playing the role mainly of Samaritan but reverting at times back to his role of Stranger) but also Stephen (playing the role of Stranger, then, to some degree, starting to become a Samaritan in his care for Corley's well-being) display such well-developed imaginative powers of empathy—all the more remarkable because of their very different upbringings, natures, and temperaments. As Ellmann continues:

> To the complaint that they do not fuse Joyce would doubtless have answered that the essence of the pun is not complete but incomplete juncture. To have them fuse [fully] would be to abolish the reason for their having been brought together. The parts of the pun keep their identities even while these are demonstrated to be less isolating than they appeared.[9]

More and more connected, yet each still distinctly himself, Stoom and Blephen, Bloom and Stephen, converse incompletely in thought, word, and deed throughout much of "Ithaca," just as they did in "Circe" and "Eumaeus."

Stephen's weakness as suffering Stranger to Bloom's Samaritan is predicated upon their very inequality, as Ellmann suggests, a disparate relationship that nonetheless moves slowly and tentatively toward the type of equalization between sympathizer and sufferer that Paul Ricoeur has articulated in *Oneself as Another*. Ricoeur muses that

> In true sympathy, the self, whose power of acting is at the start greater than that of its other, finds itself affected by all that the suffering other offers to it in return. For from the suffering other there comes a giving

that is no longer drawn from the power of acting and existing but precisely from weakness itself.[10]

We have seen the relative verbal paucity of Stephen's "return" to Bloom for his profligate hospitality, along with the more positive action of Stephen's helping of Corley with the gift of money. Despite their unequal exchange, nonetheless, as Ricoeur observes, "unequal power finds compensation in an authentic reciprocity in exchange, which, in the hour of agony, finds refuge in the shared whisper of voices or the feeble embrace of clasped hands."[11] Bloom, fleeing his "hour of agony," his public humiliation by the Citizen, reaches out in charity to help the beaten Stephen—and in so doing, "finds refuge," his true self in the Other.

All of these actions of hospitality—actual and mentally envisioned—further lead Bloom to care for Stephen as he continues to minister to him, opening his home (and by extension his own body) fully to him and caring for Stephen's bodily and spiritual needs. This embodied *caritas* helps insulate Bloom from Stephen's seeming attack on him when he sings the anti-Semitic ballad (U 17.801–28) immediately after they are again described as having drunk cocoa together (U 17.797–800), a communal act that was not achieved in the cabman's shelter in "Eumaeus" since Bloom drank coffee and ate the roll by himself. The drinking of the luxuriously rich cocoa and the communion it engenders—along with all the other hospitable actions that each has now performed toward the other—must soften the anti-Semitic thrust of the ballad, a fact commentators generally seem to have neglected. More relaxed, more united now than ever, the two men have sufficiently lowered their guards to first chant Irish (Stephen) and Hebrew (Bloom) to each other (U 17.727–30), then write Irish and Hebraic characters for each other's inspection (U 17.733–40), and now, finally, sing to each other.

Two more instances of mutual recognition, both successive, immediately precede Stephen's singing of the anti-Semitic ballad, and these moments also strengthen their relationship sufficiently to mitigate some of the hurt visited upon Bloom by Stephen. Bloom has played the Good Samaritan role across the conclusion of "Circe," all through "Eumaeus" and now through part of "Ithaca" sufficiently that he has taken on a new, symbolic identity—that of a secular Christ, who the Good Samaritan is often thought to represent. Although Harry Blamires reads too many Christian parallels into *Ulysses* at times in his classic study, *The New Bloomsday Book*, his reading of this scene seems unassailable. As Stephen hears Bloom's chanting of the "first distich" of the Hatikvah, "As long as within our hearts the Jewish soul sings" (translation of the Hebrew of U 17.763–4) and Bloom's summary of the rest of the song that conveys the Jewish people's two-thousand-year hope of returning to their homeland, he "heard in a profound ancient male unfamiliar melody the accumulation of the past" (U 17.777–8);

conversely, Bloom sees "in a quick young male familiar form the predestination of a future" (*U* 17.780).

Then, Stephen has a visual epiphany and Bloom an auditory one at virtually the same time of the other's identity: "Visually, Stephen's: The traditional figure of hypostasis, depicted by Johannes Damascenus, Lentulus Romanus and Epiphanius Monachus as leucodermic, sesquipedalian with winedark hair. Auditively, Bloom's: The traditional accent of the ecstasy of catastrophe" (*U* 17.783–6). After noting that Stephen apprehends "the deep wealth of the past" in Bloom's voice, and Bloom "the promise of the future" in Stephen, Blamires suggests that

> Stephen senses in Bloom's appearance the figure of the Christ, the [L]ogos personalized with white skin [leucodermic], dark hair, and a touch of pedantry [sesquipedalian], as He is in the works of the staunch defenders of orthodoxy such as St. John of Damascus (c. 675–749) and St. Epiphanius (c. 315–403). Bloom senses in Stephen's voice the ecstatic note of coming catastrophe.[12]

James H. Maddox convincingly argues that Stephen's recognition of Bloom as a Christ figure here is anticipated by the passage in "Eumaeus" where Stephen thinks of Bloom as "*Christus*" (*U* 16.1092), and he identifies this moment as the point when "he comes closest to recognizing his spiritual father in 'Ithaca'" and perceives "the Incarnation itself."[13] Joyce finally suggests here how completely the true friend Bloom has replaced the false friend Buck Mulligan, who recites the Greek phrase to Stephen from the *Odyssey* in "Telamachus": "*Epi oinopa ponton*," translated as "over the wine-dark sea" (*U* 1.78). Whereas Mulligan's hair is "grained and hued like pale oak" (*U* 1.16), a reference to the treachery of the wooden Trojan horse, Bloom's hair is depicted here as "winedark" to contrast Buck's light-colored hair and connotes his steadfastness and loyalty to Stephen as spiritual protector.

Additionally, whereas Mulligan conducts a mock Mass (*U* 1.4–5, 20–3), invokes the Trinity when he serves breakfast to Haines, Stephen, and himself (*U* 1.349–51), and casts himself when he takes off his clothes to go swimming as Christ being stripped of his garments before He is crucified (*U* 1.510), Bloom, who has attempted to give Stephen food and drink at the cabman's shelter in "Eumaeus" and has now served him cocoa, seems to form part of a trinity with Stephen and Molly, and is perceived by Stephen as Christ. Blamires argues that because St. John of Damascus's theology of the Trinity formulates a concept called "circumincession" to convey the relationship among the three members of the Trinity—Father, Son, and Holy Spirit—and "held a high doctrine of the Blessed Virgin Mary," including her heavenly assumption, Joyce's invoking of him in this second moment of mutual recognition suggests "an apparent instance of circumincession, in that father and son [Bloom and Stephen] exist reciprocally in one another." He even posits that not only this moment but "Ithaca" generally "seems to express the composite nature and will of a 'Stoom' or a 'Blephen' rather than to convey a dialogue," and views Molly, the "'Queen,'" as "present by influence throughout, extending her divine maternity over both."[14] There are problems in such a formulation: Bloom as father figure might be expected to be portrayed by the narrator and seen by Stephen as God and Stephen perceived by Bloom as Christ, but in fact, Stephen perceives Bloom as Christ and Bloom sees Stephen as a catastrophic figure, not as Christ. And Molly as Virgin Mary in such a formulation must be presented ironically, since she has cuckolded Bloom that day; there is precedent and warrant for Joyce's reversal of the Virgin Mary figure in his characterization of Polly, who seduces Bob Doran in "The Boarding House."[15] And yet despite Bloom as secular Christ, Stephen as a figure of catastrophe, and the hovering Molly as ironic Virgin Mary figure, there is a *gravitas* to this vision, even if the possibility of a trinitarian relationship among the three is vexed and will not be finally established.

Joyce precedes Stephen's recitation of the "Ballad of Little Harry Hughes" with these successive scenes of mutual recognition, suggesting that Bloom and Stephen grasp something of the essence of each other, after which, confirmed by the other's hearing and seeing, their relationship can survive even this seeming attack on Bloom. Bloom as a secular Christ figure will forgive Stephen despite his shock at hearing this ballad, while Stephen, as embodiment of "the ecstasy of catastrophe" (either an analeptic reference to the attack on him by Private Carr in "Circe" or a proleptic anticipation of the ballad he is about to sing, which could imperil his relationship with Bloom) in the second mutual recognition moment, steadies himself after singing the ballad and calmly and deliberately embraces his identity as artist, an identity Buck Mulligan has tried to steal from him that day but that Bloom, in another gift to him, seemingly has returned.

Margot Norris's reading of Stephen's singing of the anti-Semitic ballad in *Virgin and Veteran Readings of Ulysses* remains powerfully persuasive. She is alert to and welcomes the possibility that at this moment in the episode, "[r]hetorically, the narrator is here shaping a crescendo of communicative possibility leading to a climax of meaningful understanding and exchange that will take form as a celebration in song." Once the narrator asks, "What anthem did Bloom chant partially in anticipation of that multiple, ethnically irreducible consummation?" (*U* 17.761–2) and Bloom "offers a perfect response with his chant of the anthem of the Zionist movement," we expect Stephen to perhaps sing "an Irish anthem or signature tune, perhaps in Gaelic, in response to Bloom's chanting of Hatikvah"; but instead, "in a stunning fracture of the game, and sabotage of the climax, Stephen sings his anti-Semitic ballad."[16] At this point in the novel, any communion between the two established late in "Circe" and throughout "Eumaeus," including in their linking of arms and strange bodily mingling in the conclusion of that episode, seems gone, the Good Samaritan narrative's efficacy for reading their relationship destroyed; and yet strangely, the two men stay close after this episode, even urinating together shortly before Stephen leaves (*U* 17.1186–1209).

Peake posits that each man's reaction to Stephen's singing of the ballad similarly signals their shared belief in their own different victimhoods: Stephen accepts his artistic destiny and the suffering that it will cause him "in his artistic egoism," never thinking "of the possible effect on Bloom of the ballad of little Harry Hughes," while Bloom is reminded of the whole history of Jewish victimhood and accepts his own suffering as part of that persecution.[17] And yet, despite their being separated by "their essential natures and destinies," this "divergence has nothing to do with a loss of mutual sympathy; on the contrary, the friendliness of the relationship increases, and culminates in Bloom's offer of accommodation and Stephen's amicable and grateful refusal."[18] Zack Bowen's reading of the ballad's effect on both men shares Peake's emphasis on their shared but differing victimhood: "The victim of Stephen's song is both himself, as he exposes himself to Bloom through inadvertence at Bella Cohen's, and through design at the cabman's shelter by consenting to return home with Bloom, and Leopold, who is misled by Stephen, his 'apparition of hope and youth.'" Citing the remaining verses of the ballad unsung by Stephen in which the boy Harry is lured by the Jew's daughter with promises of food, Bowen observes sagely that "Stephen, unlike Harry, will not be seduced with seeming kindness and cocoa." And thus, as we will see, even though we perceive Bloom as both host and now victim, Stephen sees him merely as victim, a shared condition that cements their bond.[19]

There is another way of reading the effect of Stephen's ballad on Bloom, however, and it inheres in understanding it as a sort of prophecy that Bloom thinks Stephen is making for Milly Bloom—not considering it as an anti-Semitic attack on Bloom or as a simultaneous recognition of their differing victimhoods through which their new relationship in part coheres. Bloom, after all, has already explicitly told Stephen that although he became Jewish for the audience in Barney Kiernan's pub, including the vituperative Citizen, telling him "his God, I mean Christ, was a jew too and all his family like me," in fact, "in reality I'm not" (*U* 16.1084–5). Bloom's disavowal of being Jewish here is complicated by the Ithacan narrator's question and answer about his status, though: "What, reduced to their simplest reciprocal form, were Bloom's thoughts about Stephen's thoughts about Bloom and about Stephen's thoughts about Bloom's thoughts about Stephen?" (*U* 17.527–9). The answer is similarly confusing, but can be parsed for sense: "He [Bloom] thought that he [Stephen] thought that he [Bloom] was a jew whereas he [Stephen] knew that he [Bloom] knew that he [Stephen] knew that he [Bloom] was not" (*U* 17.530–1). The verbs are crucial here, and they change from the procession of "thoughts" in the question: In the answer, Bloom previously *thought* that Stephen *thought* he was Jewish, but now, Stephen *knew* that Bloom *knew* that Stephen *knew* that Bloom is not in fact Jewish. Thus Bloom is not Jewish, and does not anymore claim to be, once out of the xenophobic pressure cooker of Kiernan's pub; Stephen knows good and well he is not Jewish, and Bloom knows that Stephen knows that.

There is further evidence in the very next passage in "Ithaca" that Bloom is not Jewish because we are told that his mother and grandmother were both Irish (Jewishness is passed down matrilineally). Bloom is the "only born male transubstantial heir of Rudolf Virag . . . and of Ellen Higgins, second daughter of Julius Higgins (born Karoly) and Fanny Higgins (born Hegarty)" (*U* 17.534, 536–7). Finally, in the succeeding passage we learn, surprisingly, that Bloom has had a Christian baptism three times—once by a Protestant preacher (*U* 17.542–3), once with other people "under a pump in the village of Swords," likely part of a Protestant revival (*U* 17.543–5), and once by the same Catholic priest who baptized Stephen Dedalus, "the reverend Charles Malone C.C., in the church of the Three Patrons, Rathgar" (*U* 17.545–6; see *U* 17.546–7 for Stephen's being baptized by Malone). Taken together, these revelations suggest not only that Stephen knows Bloom is not Jewish—despite popularly being thought so in Dublin—but that he might well perceive Bloom as a fellow (lapsed) Catholic.

This knowledge about each character's religious affiliations and rejections casts Stephen's anti-Semitic ballad in a different light and leads us to consider why else Bloom might be offended by it. In his initial reaction to the ballad, he once again dons the mantle of Jewishness as he did back in "Cyclops," in memory of his father, who was Jewish, and other Jews, but in his second reaction, he might perceive, as the ballad continues, that Stephen is singing a prophecy about his daughter Milly becoming a violent Irish hypernationalist like the Citizen. Consider: When Bloom hears the first part of the ballad, the narrator asks, "How did the son of Rudolph receive this first part?," and then answers, "With unmixed feeling. Smiling, a jew, he heard with pleasure and saw the unbroken kitchen window" (*U* 17.809–11). At first, as the son of the Jewish Rudolph Virag, Bloom has an unalloyed reaction through the eyes of a Jew, hearing the ballad with pleasure and seemingly refusing to believe that little Harry Hughes could break "the Jew's windows all" (*U* 17.807), and certainly not on purpose (Hughes does not break any windows the first time he throws the ball, but he persists in throwing it, which breaks the windows out). Typically of Bloom, who has suffered prejudice throughout the novel, largely as a result of his putative Jewishness, he refuses to think the worst of this little boy, or, for that matter, of the Jew.

But when Stephen sings the next four stanzas of the ballad, which culminate in the "jew's daughter" who is "all dressed in green" (*U* 17.813, 814) finally taking "a penknife out of her pocket" and cutting "off his little head" (*U* 17.825, 826), Bloom is understandably upset. Now, the narrator asks, "How did the father of Millicent receive this second part?", answering, "With mixed feelings. Unsmiling, he heard and saw with wonder a jew's daughter, all dressed in green" (*U* 17.829, 830–1). Now he casts himself as Milly's father and may perceive that Stephen is casting Milly as a type of violent Jewish-Irish nationalist "all dressed in green," who kills a little boy. The phrase "all dressed in green" appears in nationalist ballads as well,[20] and Bloom likely contextualizes this ballad through the earlier scenes in Barney Kiernan's pub, believing that Stephen is warning him that his daughter's Irishness is trumping or overwhelming her Jewish ancestry and could lead her into violence.[21] We have no way of knowing if Bloom knew the Celtic cult of worshiping the severed head, but Joyce certainly knew it, and he suggests here that the daughter dressed in green ritually murders the little boy as a sacrificial, sacred act evoking that practice of the ancient Celts. Because over two pages of Bloom's memories of Milly follow the ballad's recitation and Bloom's reception of it (*U* 17.858–928), we can be assured that Milly's future is on his mind, as it is periodically throughout the novel when he thinks of her at the seaside with Bannon, who knows the lecherous Buck Mulligan well.

But the more traditional interpretation of these passages stems from Bloom's knowledge that Stephen's song, a version of the ancient English ballad "The Jew's Daughter," is based on the supposed murder by a Jew of Hugh of Lincoln (1246–57 AD). This song was circulated to promote the false story of Jewish blood libel, and it raises that specter for Bloom even if he is not really Jewish. Blood libel alleges that Jews need the blood of Christian children to bake their matzos during Passover, and Bloom undoubtedly knows of this horrid, anti-Semitic tradition, as the narrator makes clear in the passages that follow his second reaction to the ballad. For instance, Stephen's condensed commentary speaks of little Harry Hughes, "the victim predestined" (*U* 17.833), being led "to a strange habitation, to a secret infidel apartment, and there, implacable," being "immolate[d]. . ." (*U* 17.836–7). Bloom is then successively characterized as "the host (victim predestined)," as well as "the host (reluctant, unresisting)," and finally as "the host (secret infidel)" (*U* 17.838, 841, 843). In these tags, he is still outwardly the warm and generous Good Samaritan host of the beaten Stranger Stephen, with whom he has now achieved a breakthrough father/son relationship, while also becoming, variously, Little Harry Hughes, both a reluctant and unresisting host to Stephen, and the "secret infidel" or Jew of the ballad whose daughter murders the little boy. Bowen argues that Bloom as both victim and host is recognized more as simply victim by Stephen, thus confirming "his interchangeability with Bloom," which "emphasizes the real consubstantial bonds existing between the two men."[22]

Perhaps Joyce intended both interpretations of this passage, and a blending of the two approaches suggests something like the following outline: Bloom vacillates here between "playing" a Jew (son of Rudy) and being Milly's father, between his own Jewish and Irish identities. Caught in this liminal position, he is equally alert to the possibility of Milly becoming a Jewish-Irish nationalist caught up in violence (and the record shows that there were women, such as Maud Gonne and others, who were committed to using violence to achieve Irish independence from England) and to the continued blood libel slurring of Jews. But, crucially, his identification (three times by Joyce) as "host," in the context of the Good Samaritan parable that arcs across this episode, enables him to overcome his fears of these possible futures (which are rendered parenthetically as we have seen, suggesting that they do not dominate his mind as his identity as host does). He instead attends to Stephen's needs and invites him to spend the night (U 17.931–4), which Stephen declines (U 17.955). Bloom's Samaritan identity even allows him to contemplate the possibility of Stephen marrying Milly someday, a possibility expressed in language recalling that of the ballad Stephen has just sung: He thus wonders whether there could be a "reconciliatory union between a schoolfellow and a jew's daughter?" (U 17.942). Clearly, Bloom has reasons to turn on Stephen after he recites this ballad (perhaps thinking that since Bloom was not really Jewish, he would not mind?), but he chooses to focus on caring for the young man.

At this moment, when we try to understand this seemingly sabotaged climax of a father and adopted son narrative, we would do well to recall James Heffernan's contention about how hospitality works in literature and even sometimes in life. While "hospitality yearns to domesticate the stranger, to take him in as if he were part of the family, to vanquish and absorb his otherness," in reality, "the otherness of the stranger can never be wholly assimilated, and the secular communion wrought by hospitality—the warm, joyful, convivial sharing of board and household—is never wholly safe against subversion." And it is "always vulnerable to one of more of the infinitely variable forms that treachery can take."[23] Rather than being a sheer sentimentalist or a naïve Pollyanna (like the narrator of the "Nausicaa" episode, whom Joyce exposes and undercuts), Joyce understood the possibilities but also the pitfalls of hospitality. We are never shown the saved victim's reaction in the Good Samaritan parable, but he is notably silent throughout and is certainly not portrayed as thanking the Samaritan. Joyce's relatively taciturn, drunk Stephen comports himself similarly: He does not sufficiently appreciate that Bloom has narrowly saved him from both Private Carr and the law.

Bernard Benstock claims that the "conversational balance" between Bloom and Stephen that is created between them late in "Eumaeus" when Bloom responds to Stephen's question about why chairs are put upside down on café tables at night (U 16.1708–13) carries over into "Ithaca" because the "narrational medium mirrors that balance," and he posits further that "even the (presumed) gaucherie on Stephen's part of introducing the anti-Semitic song fails to disturb that equilibrium."[24] This argument stands along with

Peake's and Bowen's even more positive reading as one of the most convincing readings of this awkward, even potentially destructive moment in "Ithaca." If true, and their conversational and bodily, mental, and spiritual union is sufficiently strong at this point for Bloom not to be severely hurt by Stephen's ballad, then his subsequent action in inviting Stephen to spend the night is a natural extension of that relationship. If, on the other hand, he is hurt by Stephen's ballad, then his invitation to spend the night becomes startling, a profligate gesture of generosity offered in response to a wounding blow by the Stranger he has rescued. This invitation, of course, goes well beyond what even Christ's Good Samaritan did in taking the wounded stranger to the inn and paying for his stay there. Fascinatingly, Bloom oscillates between Samaritan and Stranger during this seminal moment, starting as Samaritan and ending as Stranger, perhaps wounded again, after which he again steps back into his role as Samaritan but with a twist: Stephen as potential Good Samaritan now has the opportunity to care for Bloom the Stranger he has just hurt, protecting his reputation in the future by spreading the narrative of his generosity throughout Dublin, as Margot Norris argues.

Norris's speculation that since the ballad prompts "Bloom to think at some length with troubled affection about his daughter Milly, [it] stirs his paternal feelings sufficiently to overcome any sense of offense"[25] convinces, even though, as I have suggested, he might also see this anti-Semitic ballad as a prophecy about Milly's future propensity to violence were she to come under the sway of someone like the Citizen. Bloom's clear affection for Milly, heightened by this disturbing ballad, contextualized by our understanding of how the Good Samaritan's actions did not depend on the rescued victim's response, indicates his habitual *caritas* and attitude of paternal protection combining to insulate him from Stephen's potential offense.

Norris's reading of the ballad in the larger context of the anti-Semitism Bloom has experienced earlier in the day is the most satisfying available, and although she does not yoke this reading to the enactment of the Good Samaritan parable, her interpretation can easily become part of an extension of a parabolic reading that shows how Stephen has the potential in the future as a proleptic Good Samaritan figure to rescue Bloom from vicious rumors that may soon circulate in Dublin about him, or to exacerbate those rumors and condemn Bloom to an isolating future in which he could even become a suicide like his father. Thus Norris's tantalizing suggestion that Stephen might have finally realized the hurt he has just caused Bloom in singing this ballad, and his efforts to qualify and mitigate that harm,[26] might offer a "glimmer of hope that Stephen could yet play an important role in averting a disastrous future for Bloom" since the Cyclops's earlier attack on him as a "greedy, stingy Jew" might have ruined Bloom's reputation, and thus "Bloom needs a friend and defender more than he knows." Hence, "[a] Stephen at last alerted to Bloom's racial vulnerability could literally save Bloom from social devastation by countering such stories [including Alf Bergan's erroneous narration of the Gold Cup story] with his first-hand evidence of Bloom's enormous generosity and kindness."[27] Although Norris cautions that Stephen could certainly still betray Bloom and spread nasty rumors about him that would compound those already circulating, the trajectory of the development of Stephen into a Good Samaritan character, as seen in his care and concern for the dissembling Corley and now, somewhat improbably, after he sings this anti-Semitic ballad to Bloom, suggests otherwise. When Bloom offers his home for Stephen to sleep in that night, Stephen's response is described in a friendly way: "Promptly, inexplicably, with amicability, gratefully it was declined" (U 17.955), suggesting that he might regret having sung the ballad and now appreciates and cares for Bloom. Bloom's lasting gift to Stephen is a burgeoning habitus of *caritas*—exemplified earlier, in "Eumaeus," through Stephen's giving Corley a half-crown and in Stephen's sympathetic imagining of his siblings' wrenching poverty—an attitude that is made all the stronger for Stephen's striving to overcome his moment of anti-Semitism here.[28]

Stephen's evolution toward becoming more charitable and caring toward others is strengthened by a fuller apprehension of what happens when he and Bloom experience at first a somatic, then an extra-somatic, transcendent moment, their well-known moment of parallax in simultaneously staring at the beauty of the heavens. Their parabolic encounter ushers in the condition of receptivity whereby they can apprehend this heavenly beauty and potentially be changed by it. When they emerge into Bloom's garden, they—and even the clinically cold narrator—are momentarily struck by the deep beauty of the heavens: "The heaventree of stars hung with humid nightblue fruit" (U 17.1039). As Bloom offers a disquisition on the constellations in a long and tedious paragraph, the narrator concludes by mentioning "the parallax or parallactic drift of socalled fixed stars, in reality evermoving wanderers from immeasurably remote eons to infinitely remote futures. . ." (U 17.1052–4). As they gaze at the heavens together, both characters enter so fully into the life of the constellations that they temporarily become heavenly bodies themselves, perhaps the high point of their entire relationship as portrayed in the novel.[29]

Projecting themselves away from 7 Eccles Street in Dublin into the heavens involves a tremendous joint act of imagination that further connects them in entering into the lives of stars, which are cold and distant but which ironically illustrate the new warmth and closeness of their relationship. Joyce's famous letter to Frank Budgen containing a description of the episode's style contains a clue that implies his two main characters' closeness in this moment, which contrasts the impersonal and clinical style: "I am writing *Ithaca* in the form of a mathematical catechism . . . so that not only will the reader know everything and know it in the baldest, coldest way, but Bloom and Stephen thereby become heavenly bodies, wanderers like the stars at which they gaze" (*SL* 278). Notice the somatic similitude that Joyce gives Bloom and Stephen as "heavenly bodies" and also how those ethereal bodies transcend time and space; in that transformation, they become ineffable, beyond our ken and beyond the ken of the seemingly all-knowing narrator of "Ithaca." Connected through Bloom's acts of hospitality and their embodied union at the end of "Eumaeus," they are now, temporarily, heavenly bodies with a corresponding deepening of their relationship that outpaces any notions of relationship on earth and moves toward a potential future together. And even though Stephen leaves 7 Eccles Street, Ellmann's claim that Joyce predicates the entire novel upon acts of love, including here, is undeniable:

> Like other comedies, *Ulysses* ends in a vision of reconciliation rather than of sundering. Affection between human beings, however transitory, however qualified, is the closest we can come to paradise. That it loses its force does not invalidate it . . . the word known to all men [love] has been defined and affirmed, regardless of whether or not it is subject to diminution.[30]

Moreover, Ellmann's suggestion that Stephen and Bloom's relationship "loses its force" can be heavily qualified, even revised, by our reconsideration of this famous passage about stellar beauty in "Ithaca." The beauty that breaks through the cold language of that episode via the sentence "The heaventree of stars hung with humid nightblue fruit" suggests powerfully a manifestation of beauty that may signal a breakthrough in Stephen and Bloom's relationship that goes beyond aesthetic appreciation into future continuity. As the philosopher Jean-Louis Chrétien puts it, "the event of beauty" gathers "together to deliver and set free, here and now, the murmuring, singing clarity that it bears within it, giving itself up to its own daylight and opening itself to it."[31] As Chrétien argues further, "The appearance of beauty does not *take place*, it *makes space* . . . it causes this place, *here*, to arise in all its jubilant and heart-rending exclamation."[32] Aesthetician Elaine Scarry has posited similarly that "[s]omething beautiful fills the mind yet invites the search for something beyond itself, something larger or something of the same scale with which it needs to be brought into relation. Beauty . . . causes us to gape and suspend all thought."[33] The narrator's question that precedes the gorgeous phrase "The heaventree of stars hung with humid nightblue fruit" indicates something of the literal and figurative radiance of the moment that suspends "all thought" for Bloom and Stephen as they emerge from the darkened house into the night: "What spectacle confronted them when they, first the *host*, then the *guest*, emerged silently, doubly dark, from obscurity by a passage from the rere of the house into the penumbra of the garden?" (*U* 17.1036–8; my emphasis). Bloom does launch into a long meditation about constellations, but clearly both are first awestruck by this stellar manifestation of beauty.

As both Chrétien and Scarry suggest, beauty's dynamism can move us into exalted states, and Scarry's additional observations about its propulsive power further illuminate this moment of hospitality in the novel. Notice Joyce's language of "host" and "guest" in this regard. Along with arguing that beauty "brings copies of itself into being" as we attempt to verbalize it, draw it, or take pictures of it, which holds great promise for both Bloom's and Stephen's future acts of creativity, Scarry also shows how our perception of beauty "is bound up with an urge to protect it, or act on its behalf, in a way that appears to be tied up with the perception of its lifelikeness."[34] Not only might Bloom and Stephen later try to write (for both are writers of a sort) or describe this moment of stellar beauty to Molly or Stephen's friends, respectively, but also, this joint apprehension of beauty might lead them both into protective postures toward it—and extrapolating from that behavior, toward each other. Bloom is likely going to have his already strong paternally protective feelings toward Stephen enhanced by this moment, and Stephen might be even more inclined to protect Bloom's reputation by spreading the story of his hospitality to combat the noxious narratives that have been told about him all day.

Finally, Scarry holds that the act of perceiving beauty causes us to leave behind our egocentric conception of self and enter into the life of the object or subject whose beauty we apprehend, which Stephen and Bloom both clearly do in this moment, with profound implications for their hospitality toward each other. Scarry believes that "[a]t the moment we see something beautiful, we undergo a radical decentering . . . [w]e cease to stand even at the center of our own world. We willingly cede our ground to the thing that stands before us."[35] Bloom and Stephen's joint viewing of the beauty of heaven in all its strangeness leads, paradoxically, to their reciprocal hospitality toward each other as they welcome beauty's strangeness into their midst.[36] That is, by hospitably welcoming what Chrétien calls "the powerful strangeness of beauty"—the "'here,' wrenched away from the indifference and interchangeability of places—a 'here' on which the furthest distances converge,"[37] the beyondness of their stellar vision leads them into the strangeness of stellar beauty, which then grounds them in the specific place of 7 Eccles Street and their joint intimacy with each other. Formerly strangers to each other, now familiar to each other because of their apprehension of the strangeness of this early morning beauty, their thoughts, minds, bodies, and spirits are knit together—whether or not they ever see each other again.

But crucially, as Scarry suggests, "The three-second call to beauty can have produced the small flex of the mind, the constant moistening, that other objects—large, arcing, flexuous—will more enduringly require."[38] Given this "small flex of the mind" that both Bloom and Stephen have experienced in their joint viewing of the gorgeously rendered stars, they are both likelier to be more receptive to further manifestations of immanently erupting strange beauty—and by extension, to offer hospitality to others—in the future. So not only their enhanced receptivity toward and interest in hospitable acts—whether toward others or toward beauty—but also the ongoingness of their relationship that redounds from this moment become Joyce's lasting gifts to us.

Moreover, as they urinate together in Bloom's garden shortly before Stephen leaves, Joyce suggests how they are reciprocally united and embodied once again; they stand "silent, each contemplating the other in both mirrors of *the reciprocal flesh* of theirhisnothis fellowfaces" (*U* 17.1183–4; my emphasis), yet are still fundamentally different. But we would not want them to somehow fuse and become one character, would we? It seems enough here that their flesh is "reciprocal," and now Stephen fully and vulnerably opens himself up to Bloom at least on a bodily level, grateful for his rescue of him that evening and all his subsequent acts of profound hospitality, including his invitation into his home—an extension of Bloom's body that he first offers to Stephen to lean on toward the conclusion of "Eumaeus," when the young man feels "a strange kind of flesh of a different man approach him, sinewless and wobbly and all that" (*U* 16.1723–4).

These two literally fleshly moments, one from "Eumaeus" and the other from "Ithaca," are profound indications of the *agape* Bloom has for Stephen and Stephen's openness to it, even though he does not spend the night and though they may never meet each other again; certainly they do not in the novel. Apprehending this enfleshed connection that mirrors that articulated by Christ in the parable of the Good Samaritan suggests just how profoundly rich the relationship between Stephen and Bloom has become in a relatively short period of time. Its depth is achieved through Bloom's secular, hospitable opening of his enfleshed self to Stephen in a manner akin to what Paul describes as how Christ "has broken down in his flesh the dividing wall of hostility" between Jew and Gentile in Ephesians 2:14 (ESV).

Bloom is still badly wounded, however, and slips back into the role of the beaten Stranger after ministering to Stephen in his Good Samaritan role. As Heffernan suggests, "Nothing Bloom does all day can hide or heal the wound of knowing that his house has been violated, his wife usurped, and his hospitality betrayed by a grossly presumptuous guest." And the psychic pain of this wound caused by Blazes Boylan is heightened by Bloom's bumping his head on the sideboard that Boylan has apparently left against the door to the front room (*U* 17.1285–8). This physical pain coalesces with the psychic wound of betrayal, prompting Heffernan to argue wittily, "Possibly the only thing worse than a guest who rearranges your furniture in your absence is a guest whose rearrangement literally strikes you in the head."[39] How can our newly wounded Stranger recover and be himself rescued, his wounds bound up?

Molly's Role in Joyce's Samaritan Narrative

While it is beyond the scope of this book to offer a lengthy consideration of "Penelope," the last episode of the novel, narrated in its entirety by Molly Bloom's stream-of-consciousness, that episode too benefits from being read in the context of the Good Samaritan parable that Stephen and Bloom have been re-enacting. After having opened himself bodily to Stephen in various caring ways, including offering him the hospitality of his home, Bloom comes "home" to Molly's body, sufficiently steeped in caring embodiment—and likely depleted by it—to need his own flesh comforted, which he finds in kissing her bottom: "He kissed the plump mellow yellow smellow melons of her rump, on each plump melonous hemisphere, in their mellow yellow furrow, with obscure prolonged provocative melonsmellonous osculation" (U 17.2241-3) and is satisfied, "homed" again.

With the focus now shifting to Molly's consciousness through her embodied musings in "Penelope," one way to think through the lens of the Good Samaritan narrative here involves recognizing that Molly has not practiced hospitality herself—or rather, that she has been too hospitable by inviting strangers such as Blazes Boylan into her bed. Perhaps Molly unconsciously recognizes Bloom as the Odyssean hero that Stephen has created before our eyes in "Eumaeus" and "Ithaca," if we follow Margaret McBride's auto-fictive reading mooted in the previous chapter. Or, on the other hand, Molly may simply apprehend a transformation in Bloom effected through his rescue of Stephen and attempts to care for him. In either case, this "stranger" to her house and her bed who has been exiled all day and usurped by Blazes Boylan returns home, and she somewhat grudgingly recreates their home as a place of hospitality. 7 Eccles Street may be an unlikely inn, but it certainly functions as such in Joyce's contemporary retelling of the parable—first for Stephen, then for Bloom.

In this reading, Molly Bloom functions as innkeeper offering hospitality through her own flesh. Just as Bloom's flesh has met Stephen's, effecting a union between them, Molly's body, her flesh, has served as a site of perverse hospitality for Blazes in her adultery with him, and now could work in that way again, possibly for Stephen, whom she considers seducing. She, like Stephen, has a choice to make about whether or not to care for Bloom, and she seems finally to care again for him, offering her body as an enfleshed "house" for him. She vows to give Bloom "one more chance" (U 18.1498) and let him "kiss my bottom" (U 18.1520) and even ejaculate on her bottom (U 18.1527-8).[40]

But more important than these sexual ministrations—or just as important, anyway—is her concluding memory of lying with Bloom on Howth Head when she decided to marry him. In returning to this enfleshed memory where she recalls "he asked me would I yes to say yes my mountain flower and first I put my arms around him yes and drew him down to me so he could feel my breasts all perfume yes and his heart was going like mad and yes I said yes

I will Yes" (18.1605–9), she belatedly offers Bloom the touch, the embrace, the sacrificial embodiment of another that he has craved all day. Her repeated reaffirmations of her original acceptance of Bloom's offer of marriage contrast with the rough and harsh lovemaking of Blazes Boylan, which she rejects, saying "no," repeatedly: "no thats no way for him has he no manners nor no refinement nor no nothing in his nature slapping us behind like that on my bottom because I didnt call him Hugh. . ." (*U* 18.1368–70). This passage about Blazes's lovemaking also contrasts Molly's approval of Bloom's lovemaking earlier in the episode: "I liked the way he made love then he knew the way to take a woman" (*U* 18.328–9).

Offering himself bodily to Stephen enabled Bloom to play the role of the Good Samaritan, but now Molly's recollection of offering her body and life to Bloom long ago at Howth enables us as readers to see how Bloom the Stranger returns home to the enfleshed, comforting life with his wife (the last Good Samaritan figure of the novel) that he so desperately needs and has been exiled from all day long.[41]

Notes

1. Soards, "Commentary on Luke," 118.
2. Casey, *Getting Back into Place*, 120.
3. Ibid., 120.
4. Heffernan, *Hospitality and Treachery in Western Literature*, 301.
5. Bersani, "Against *Ulysses*," 177. See Thornton, *Voices and Values*, 110–16, for a thoughtful overview of previous critical approaches to this chapter's mechanical, supposedly objective style, and for his own contention that Joyce does not sanction this style, which itself is far from perfect, riddled with error, and even lets a few felicities of style slip through. More important for showing how Bloom re-enacts the Good Samaritan parable by rescuing Stephen, Thornton shows that Stephen and Bloom's conversation continues despite this style and that we can nonetheless make sense of their actions as well. As he argues, "obviously Stephen and Bloom do converse and reflect, and presumably they do so in language that is of a piece with what they have used all day, rather than in the vocabulary of the catechist." Thus, the "catechistic language of the episode exists only as a [limited] perspective on the characters and events, which continue to develop and unfold here as they have in earlier episodes" (112).
6. Gifford and Seidman, *Ulysses Annotated*, 571.
7. Weinstein, *The Fiction of Relationship*, 292.
8. Ellmann, *The Consciousness of Joyce*, 90.
9. Ibid., 91.
10. Ricoeur, *Oneself as Another*, 191
11. Ibid., 191.
12. Blamires, *The New Bloomsday Book*, 222.
13. Maddox, "'Eumaeus' and the Theme of Return in *Ulysses*," 217.
14. Blamires, *The New Bloomsday Book*, 222.

15. Donald Torchiana has even suggested that the entire forced marriage plot in that disturbing work inverts the story of the Virgin Mary, Joseph, and the Immaculate Conception. See Torchiana, *Backgrounds for Joyce's* Dubliners, 109–24.
16. Norris, *Virgin and Veteran Readings of* Ulysses, 206, 207.
17. See Peake, *James Joyce*, 292–3, 292 for the specific passages quoted. Ellmann, *The Consciousness of Joyce*, 68, however, sees both men as artist figures beginning with the "Aeolus" episode and even states they share a "joint aesthetic policy"; see 68–72 for his entire argument about their artistic projects, including Stephen's calling up of his dead mother and Bloom's of his dead son in "Circe" (70–1).
18. Peake, *James Joyce*, 293.
19. Bowen, *Bloom's Old Sweet Song*, 23.
20. As an example, see the Irish ballad about Irish nationalist Henry Munro in Seamus Heaney's play, *Munro*, particularly these lines: "Then up came Munro's sister, *she was all dressed in green* / With a sword by her side that was well sharped and keen. . ." (65; my emphasis).
21. I am grateful to my graduate students, particularly Ray Stockstad, in my seminar on hospitality in Joyce, Beckett, and Cormac McCarthy in the fall of 2020, for spurring me to develop this reading.
22. Bowen, *Bloom's Old Sweet Song*, 24.
23. Heffernan, *Hospitality and Treachery in Western Literature*, 335.
24. Benstock, *Narrative Con/Texts in* Ulysses, 12.
25. Norris, *Virgin and Veteran Readings of* Ulysses, 211.
26. Ibid., 211–12, wonders if Stephen may still be thinking of the Johannes Jeep song that he sang to Bloom about sirens luring men to their death at the end of "Eumaeus," and thus, "tired and muddled," Stephen, "with that earlier song still in his head," might have "selected 'Little Harry Hughes' without malice, as an unthinking variant on the theme of the siren or the dangerous temptress that surfaced previously in the Jeep ballad? Might he then have been startled to recognize in Bloom's vanished smile after the first verse that he has blundered and caused a despicable, if inadvertent hurt? If so, his commentary turning little Harry into a masochistic martyr might be seen as a clumsy effort to save face, to mitigate the ballad's anti-Semitic harm in an effort to restore the geniality the ballad has momentarily destroyed."
27. Ibid., 212.
28. The other major recent interpretation of the ballad scene comes from Sam Slote, who suggests in *Joyce's Nietzschean Ethics*, 104, that Stephen does recognize Bloom's generosity to him in the "condensed version of Stephen's commentary," which "works as an elliptical acknowledgment of Bloom's rescue of Stephen." In this reading, Slote essentially posits a middle way between Norris's two future possibilities of Stephen either spreading the good news of Bloom's generosity to him or slurring Bloom. He argues that Stephen's acknowledgment of Bloom's care for him must be "elliptical" since if it were direct, "Stephen would be in Bloom's debt and thus trapped in one further net, a debt-net, as it were." Thus, "The condensed elaboration [of the ballad] acknowledges the debt without implicating Stephen into a new debt-relationship, thereby maintaining his purported artistic integrity."

29. Here, Bersani's desire to render Bloom as sundered from Stephen is based on a misreading of this passage. He believes that Bloom has a "kind of cosmic lack of linkage, a singleness that can be rendered only by images of his floating in interplanetary space" ("Against *Ulysses*," 176). Certainly, Bloom does feel alone after Stephen leaves and feels "the cold of interstellar space, thousands of degrees below freezing point or the absolute zero of Fahrenheit, Centigrade or Réaumur..." (*U* 17.1246–7). But he feels so alone here precisely because he has just had such a significant metaphysical, somatic, and mental union on earth with Stephen.
30. Ellmann, "Preface," xiv.
31. Chrétien, *The Ark of Language*, 79.
32. Ibid., 79–80.
33. Scarry, *On Beauty and Being Just*, 29.
34. Ibid., 3, 80.
35. Ibid., 111–12.
36. Without dwelling on the question of beauty in such relationships, Ricoeur, *Oneself as Another*, 191, develops this inequality between rescuer and sufferer in terms of a gradual evolution into an "authentic reciprocity in exchange."
37. Chrétien, *The Ark of Language*, 80.
38. Scarry, *On Beauty and Being Just*, 51.
39. Heffernan, *Hospitality and Treachery in Western Literature*, 300.
40. My Baylor English graduate student Harrison Otis has written a brilliant interpretation of Molly's role in "Penelope" that bears repeating here. Otis perceives Bloom's kissing of Molly's bottom when he returns to their bed as a tacit endorsement of her infidelity "through his reverential submission to her physical being," a "revisioning of the Good Samaritan parable from the perspective of the man lying on the road." Thus, "Bloom shows hospitality not only as a Samaritan to a stranger [Stephen], but also as a wounded man to his wounder." He finally sees both readers and Molly as potentially healing Bloom's wounds, becoming his Samaritan, re-enacting that Lukan parable again and rejecting the parable of the wise virgins from Matthew 25:1–13 that Joyce references both for the two old Dublin women who are the subject of Stephen's "Parable of the Plums" in "Aeolus" and for the three prostitutes in "Circe" (*U* 15.2596). That is, Molly could play the wise virgin and keep Bloom relegated to incomplete intercourse or even prostitute herself to him (*U* 18.1522–4). Yet her reaffirmation of both Bloom's kind character and their picnic together at Howth suggests the appeal (however unconscious) of the Good Samaritan parable for their relationship going forward—both for her and for Joyce (Otis, "Reading Notebook: James Joyce").
41. Pinkerton, *Blasphemous Modernism*, 35, while also privileging a fleshly reading of the novel, instead posits "the end of Joyce's Eucharistic project is not the body of Christ but of a genuine Christine, whose incarnation finally arrives in the form of Marion Bloom." In this reading, Joyce's text itself is corporeal, and "[i]ts affinity for an aesthetics of sacrilege is inherent in its own somato-textual form, a form that finds its perfect expression in the novel's final chapter" (31).

7

ENFLESHED ETHICS AND THE RESPONSIBILITY OF THE READER IN THE GOOD SAMARITAN PARABLE AND THE "NOSTOS" OF *ULYSSES*

> There is something special in the way *Ulysses* not only constitutes a journey in terms of a narrative but also embodies a journey for the reader.
>
> David Pierce, *Reading Joyce*, 299

> The import of a text is not exhausted by what it reveals or conceals about the social conditions that surround it. Rather, it is also a matter of what it sets alight in the reader—what kind of emotions it elicits, what changes of perceptions it prompts, what bonds and attachments it calls into being.
>
> Rita Felski, *The Limits of Critique*, 179

Declan Kiberd has argued that Joyce believed *Ulysses* would "invent a new sort of reader, someone who after that experience might choose to live in a different way. He wanted to free people from all kinds of constriction, among them the curse of passive readership."[1] By perceiving Bloom's encounter with Stephen through the intertext of the Good Samaritan parable, with its emphasis on the need for the hearer to respond, we ourselves are expected to respond in some way; in so doing, in connecting with Stephen and Bloom, we help continue the parable's action into the present.[2] Joyce thus expects and depends upon our readerly labors. Arguing that "disconnectedness" is the "anxiety that *Ulysses* massively struggles to transcend," Leo Bersani posits that "Joyce's dependence on his readers is most pronounced, for it is their intra- and extratextual work that reconstitutes his mind as the serene repository of the resources of our language and culture."[3] Much of Joyce's success in conveying his message of hospitality and loving our neighbor depends upon our response, which is unquantifiable finally, but still worth examining. If *Ulysses* exemplifies a particular kind of wisdom literature, as Kiberd argues throughout Ulysses *and Us*, then by so doing, it also seeks to inculcate a new ethical responsibility—and even agency—in readers because of what we have learned about treating those different from ourselves in its pages. In this regard, Virginia Moseley was the first critic to argue for Joyce employing his retelling of the Good Samaritan parable to reach the reader, even to rescue the reader. She reads "Eumaeus" through Jesus' walk to Emmaus, concluding that Joyce himself "'bucks up' his reader 'generally in orthodox Samaritan fashion, which he very badly' needs."[4]

Jill Shashaty's claims about parables in *Dubliners* help us understand the ethical burden offered to the reader encountering the Good Samaritan parable as retold in *Ulysses*. As she shrewdly surmises, if we think of *Dubliners* "as a set of parables, the work serves as a looking-glass that avoids a didactic approach to morality and instead reconnects readers with ancient forms of ethical inquiry that are participatory and dialogic."[5] We know Joyce's great fascination with the question and answer format of the Catholic catechism and that the Maynooth Catechism likely inspired the catechetical structure of "Ithaca." As Shashaty points out, "Unlike the authoritarian structure of moral teaching often associated with the Catholic Church, parables reinstitute moral authority in a dialogic exchange between storyteller and audience. Parables transform moral introspection into a participatory process, not simply a receptive one."[6] Because of his well-documented aversion to the magisterium of the Roman Catholic Church, Joyce likely was much more drawn to employing parabolic discourse, which places the type of participatory burden on the reader that Shashaty identifies. He likely also realized that he needed to engage readers in this way in order for us to truly grapple with the complexities of the novel.[7]

Joyce's literary ethics in *Ulysses* hinge finally on his turn to biblical narrative, specifically the retelling of the Good Samaritan parable for readers, which corresponds to what Derek Attridge describes as the ethical effect of reading literature upon us: "not a generalized obligation but a call coming from the [literary] work itself—the work as a singular staging of otherness."[8] And parabolic literature specifically calls for even more of a response to the "singular staging of otherness." That is, even if Stephen is largely silent, we cannot be, as the long awaited communion between father and son, Stranger and Samaritan, transpires in what Attridge terms "the event" of literature. Moreover, we find ourselves in the position of substituting for Stephen, making up for his relative lack of interest in Bloom's narration to him, listening raptly to Bloom, sympathizing with him, trying to feel his anguish and embarrassment. Put another way, we the readers become Bloom's neighbor, drawn ineluctably to his sense of abandonment first by the citizens of Dublin, then by Stephen. We become Bloom's Good Samaritan, wanting to help him out of the ditch of his embarrassment, desiring even to figuratively dust him off from his rough encounters with others throughout the day.

The unexpectedness of the new role that is suddenly thrust upon us here is nothing if not parabolic. As Eric Gregory and Leah Hunt-Hendrix put it, the "parable offers a different notion of time and of our participation in its unfolding. In the parable, God's time breaks into the present."[9] In the opening moment of "Eumaeus," the narrative, by its recourse to the Good Samaritan parable, makes us pause and consider the grace offered to the stranger by the Samaritan and wonder about our own new role in this narrative. For Joyce, it may not be so much the case that God's time breaks into the present, but that, at the least, the intertextual time "purchased" by the parable erupts into the present, leading us back to the Gospel narrative and then forward to Bloom and Stephen's relationship—forward to our role in that relationship. As Stephen fades away as a potential interlocutor in "Eumaeus"—although he will rouse himself and speak more in "Ithaca"—our role as interlocutor grows.

Now the significance in the Gospel narrative of the victim's lack of identity becomes clearer. Even though some scholars have posited that the "victim is an Israelite from Judea," others have noted that "the social identity of the victim is not important for how the narrative works."[10] Startlingly, as Charles Hedrick shows in his reading of the Greek meaning of "traveler" for the person helped by the Samaritan, we cannot "even be certain that the wounded traveler is male. The person's anonymity is surprising in a story that uses such specific societal markers for some of its characters."[11] Paul Ricoeur anticipates Hedrick's reading of the stranger as indeterminate (except that he does believe he is male), terming him "the man without a past or authentic traditions; impure in race and in piety; less than a gentile; a relapse. He is the category of the non-category."[12] The victim is thus a cipher, a crucial point for Joyce's narrative purposes in instantiating Bloom as victim, then Stephen. Odysseus famously named himself "Nobody" to escape Polyphemus the Cyclops, and Bloom too is a cipher, termed both "Everyman or Noman" by the narrator of "Ithaca" (*U* 17.2008).

As Bloom reassumes the status of victim vacated by Stephen, we fill his former role, but with a twist: We may wonder how we can help and we may listen and read empathetically, but how can we literally help Bloom? We cannot. But the larger burden Joyce is placing on the reader should by now be obvious: Anyone can be a victim, male, female, from any tribe or nation. Conversely, not everyone can be a Samaritan—human nature, selfishness, self-preservation, may hold us back—but everyone listening to or reading Jesus' parable, and now reading Bloom's interaction with Stephen through it, is a *potential* Samaritan.

Without acknowledging this parabolic reading of Stephen and Bloom's relationship, Margot Norris helpfully crystallizes the reader's role in her adroit reading of the aftermath of Stephen's recitation of the ballad of little Harry Hughes, which I explored in the previous chapter. Norris argues that "[a]lertness to the operation and effects of anti-Semitism are critically important, if Stephen is to serve as Bloom's friend and possible savior, and the same alertness is demanded of the reader by the text." She posits further that mere alertness is not sufficient—that "Joyce's acute anatomy of anti-Semitism" actually "requires the reader's active engagement in sorting out its operation and thereby playing an ethical role in its intervention." Norris suggests that our ethical role here as readers "may be why Joyce defrauds the reader of a sentimental climax," and this suggestion convinces, along with Richard Ellmann's contention in his reading of "Eumaeus" that a "guardedness about emotional commitment was a lifelong characteristic [of Joyce] and he did not allow his book to contain so climactic a relation without ample demurrer," which he traces to the difficult-to-apprehend style of that episode.[13]

Luke's refusal to describe the beaten traveler in his narrative focalizes Christ's parable through the Samaritan's actions, and by application, to us as readers and hearers of this parabolic retelling Joyce accomplishes in *Ulysses*. Hedrick suggests that "[i]t is easier for any reader to identify with the wounded traveler beside the road, because this figure lacks social markers of any sort. The first traveler was both nobody and everybody," and thus "[t]aking the anonymity of the first traveler seriously turns the narrative into a story about human concern for a fellow human being of whatever nationality." By extension, rather than acting like Joyce's Citizen, we have the chance, conditioned by Bloom's extravagant acts of generosity throughout the novel, to act like neighbors to anonymous others we may meet in the course of our daily rounds. And yet, as Hedrick reminds us,

> The benevolence of the fourth man [the Samaritan] . . . is so outlandish as to challenge any compromise that readers may have made between their own acts of kindness or charity and the human need that always exists on every side. Few would ever claim to have been the Samaritan as he is portrayed in this narrative.[14]

Thus *Ulysses* and its retelling of the Good Samaritan parable through Bloom's and Stephen's and now our changing role in the narrative finally leads us to realize the great gap between our desire to be more like Bloom and the petty concerns that hold us back. June 16, 1904 stands as a day holding out a radiant, shimmering possibility for us to act like neighbors, not Citizens.

Reaching out to others as neighbors now brings us closer to both Bloom's and Joyce's idea of the nation. As we have seen, when the Citizen asks Bloom what a nation is, Bloom says, rather banally, "The same people living in the same place" (*U* 12.1422–3), but he really has a much broader conception of the nation, one grounded in "Love . . . the opposite of hatred" (*U* 12.1485). In revisiting and refashioning Homer's *Odyssey*, Joyce sought, as Leah Flack argues, to "construct his enduring, modern, cosmopolitan hero, the Jewish-Catholic-Irish-Hungarian-Greek Bloom."[15] And his epic of Dublin was also influenced by Victor Bérard's theory of the nation in the *Odyssey* in his *Les Phéniciens et l'Odyssée*: "a melting pot of the races."[16] Bloom's understanding of what constitutes a nation is more complex than he himself allows given the duress he is under during his encounter with the Cyclops, and his own biography and actions model the notion of the nation as cohering in a diversity of races and cultures. Moreover, Bloom's theory of the nation starts with a proper understanding of who our neighbor is, which is answered by his repeated re-enactments of the Good Samaritan parable in the novel, supremely so with his relationship with Stephen, and with our own role as Good Samaritan, finally, as we have seen. Nations are built up from local communities of care for those often not like us, and that care can be contagious—can spread like wildfire given the right conditions.

The context of the Good Samaritan parable is not complete without our consideration of how the Samaritans figured in the dissemination of Christianity later in the New Testament. The passage that immediately follows the second section of Acts about the martyred Stephen that Joyce copied into his notebooks, concluding with Acts 8:4, concerns Philip's proclamation of Christ to the Samaritans (Acts 8:4–25).[17] Clearly, Joyce knew this section of Acts as well, and likely drew on it and the passage from Luke about the Good Samaritan as he developed his story about Bloom as Samaritan. While Bloom is an outcast in his own city, as a Samaritan figure he is central to Joyce's novel and to spreading its message of love—especially love of the Other—precisely because of his marginalization. Besides the novel's growing attention to Bloom, his centrality to the story is heightened once we realize that many Samaritans were converted to Christianity after Philip's preaching to them, as recounted in Acts 8. One commentator on Acts 8:14–17, on the reception of the Holy Spirit by the believing Samaritans, notes that "[t]he Samaritans were considered racial 'half-breeds,'" and yet "even the Samaritans, whom the Jews usually avoided, were now filled with the Spirit. This extraordinary sign confirmed the truth of Christ's earlier message (1:8) by indicating that Samaritans were now to be included in the church as full members."[18] By extension, Leopold Bloom is now received into the full fellowship—not of Dublin society, not even fully by Stephen—but of Joyce's "church"—his congregation of readers. The Samaritans' hearing and believing the Gospel, which signified that "the first cross-cultural barrier is breached," began the process of its dissemination to all tribes and people.[19] Similarly, Joyce's secular gospel preached by and exemplified by Bloom's love for his fellow man breaches the cultural barrier between Jews and Catholics (and Protestants too) in the novel, when Bloom as Samaritan rescues and gives hospitality to Stephen, even if Stephen receives his message initially in a taciturn way, only then to be shown in the process of becoming charitable himself toward Corley and Bloom.

To read *Ulysses* parabolically is both to come to tentative conclusions and to realize, just as with parables, that they have endings but not final resolutions, because the endings raise new complications for careful readers, which in turn require further resolution. At the least, attending to the way in which the events of the Good Samaritan parable color the final pages of "Circe" and shape Bloom's actions toward Stephen in "Eumaeus" and "Ithaca," and possibly Molly's toward them both in "Penelope," enables us to focus on the actions and words of the characters as they instantiate a fragile, even if short-lived, community among themselves.

Love consists of embodied actions—not sentimental feelings—and Bloom's actions throughout crucial scenes in the novel reach a crescendo with his acting out the love of the Good Samaritan for the Stranger, starting in "Circe" with his pursuit and care for Stephen and continuing through subsequent episodes. In these last episodes, we apprehend what Ellmann pointed out about the project of the entire novel: "The book as a whole ... addresses itself to the validity of egoistic selfhood ... and slowly but surely rejects it. Bloom, with his advocacy of love, tries to put out the Citizen's Cyclopean 'I.'"[20] Once again, both Bloom and Stephen are playing out roles found in the parable, of which embodiment forms a crucial aspect—caring for another's wounds, binding them up, carrying the Stranger. Recall that the Samaritan instantly and bodily "went to him and bound up his wounds, pouring on oil and wine. Then he set him on his own animal" (Luke 10:34, ESV).

This deeply personal ministration epitomizes the Christian message that certainly crosses racial, cultural, and other barriers, as we have seen, but crucially does so through a going out of one's own body toward intimate, non-sexual contact with another's flesh to love that person unconditionally. Eric Gregory and Leah Hunt-Hendrix point out that while "[s]ecular humanism has rallied around one aspect of the parable, which we can define as a spatial orientation: its expansive momentum, which breaks through a narrow ethics confined to one's ethnos, group, or community, and broadens the scope of possible ethical relationships," that ideology tends to obfuscate or downplay the enfleshed ethics of the parable inherent in its Christian context. Joyce, blasphemer or heretic or apostate—pick your term—that he was, nevertheless knew deeply the embodied message of Christ and the call to believers through spoken, embodied narratives such as the Good Samaritan parable and through the ultimate embodied narrative, the celebration of the Eucharist in the Catholic Church. Gregory and Hunt-Hendrix emphasize the Good Samaritan parable's "carnal, enfleshed occurrence, as a relationship that emerges between specific bodies in a specific place." For Christians, the parable is "inextricable from the Incarnation and the Eucharist, and in each of these three moments, what is emphasized is the enfleshment of God, the fact that God takes on a human form, a physical form." Christianity thus "offers an ethic that seeks not to shun the physicality of our world, but rather to embrace it." Citing Charles Taylor's reading of Ivan Illich's *Rivers North of the Future*, which I pondered earlier, Gregory and Hunt-Hendrix convincingly argue that for Taylor and Illich, and, I would argue, by extension for Christians who understand the parable properly and even for someone like Joyce who had left the Church but still grasped the enfleshed ethics of the parable, "the story of the Samaritan is not simply the story of the expansion of love; it is also a story about the tangibility of love, real bodies taking up real space."[21]

And this is a love offered unconditionally in the parable and by Bloom, who even though he later thinks of Stephen as a project who might sing with Molly and potentially make money for them, acts unhesitatingly and lovingly when Stephen is attacked in the brothel toward the end of "Circe." In this sense, Bloom epitomizes J. Stanley's Glen's assessment of Christ's answer to the clever lawyer's question that prompts His iteration of the Good Samaritan parable: "Thus, the objective question, 'Who is my neighbor?' is answered by the recognition that if one acts like a neighbor, one will discover who his neighbor is." That is, bodily enacting neighborliness leads us to recognize the neighbors around us. And thus, love is finally bodily, not merely verbal, since

> Real love never asks who is to be its object, because this implies a conditional approach, a consciousness of the possibility of either giving or withholding itself. Instead, it gives unconditionally and with a strange spontaneity and indiscrimination which by its nature always discovers the object because of its ability to break through the lines of color, class, and creed.[22]

If the question of the novel, read as a hospitality narrative, is "Who is my neighbor?", Bloom's reckless, profligate act of love clearly answers it: Stephen Dedalus, along with anyone else in his path he encounters who needs his help, even readers, although we may also play the Samaritan and "rescue" Bloom.[23]

In this radically incarnational understanding of Bloom and Stephen's encounter—and of Molly's embodied imaginative encounter with both of them in "Penelope"—love, even unanswered, becomes tangible, enfleshed. As Ricoeur reminds us, "charity reaches its object only by embracing a certain suffering body."[24] Bloom's message of loving others, attacked by the Citizen and seemingly ignored by Stephen, ramifies and spreads to Corley, to Stephen, to us. As embodied readers who understand the thoroughgoing enfleshed emphasis of the Good Samaritan parable, we thus should not be content with mere imaginative care for Stephen and Bloom; we should reach out to those Others around us and help them in bodily, tangible ways. Joyce signals our role in this regard by the opening reference to the Good Samaritan parable in "Eumaeus" and its closing references to sirens and usurpers, the style of which, as Riquelme claims, "induces the opposite of forgetting" because it invites us to "remember earlier moments in the episode, in the book, in other works, and in Irish history."[25] Words thus become permanent living sites of dynamic memory, ramifying out from "Eumaeus" throughout the novel and back into Scripture, among other intertexts. Allusions, after all, as Thornton reminds us, always come to us "trailing clouds of glory from some prior existence in art or history."[26]

In a peculiar way, Joyce's insistence on the primacy of his words—but especially words that recapitulate and echo this parable from Luke's Gospel—and of readers' encounters with them in *Ulysses* echoes and reifies a central slogan of the Protestant Reformation—*sola scriptura*. Just as Protestants believe that Scripture alone, the Old and New Testaments, offers the only authoritative source of God's plan for the salvation of believers, Joyce believed that his words alone—in what finally becomes a hospitality narrative, scaffolded here by his allusions to the Lukan narrative (among many other intertexts)—were a sufficient guide for his readers to experience a sort of aesthetic salvation that would ineluctably (and perhaps ironically) lead them out of themselves. They would then move into community with his characters and even into a extra-textual relationship with himself as the book's author—into embodied relationships, incarnated communities, a fundamentally anti-modernist trajectory. As Thornton has argued, "Our realization of the importance of these cultural schemata, Joyce hopes, will save us from the 'atomic individualism' that is one of the most precious and most costly achievements of modern Western culture."[27] Thus, Joyce's emphasis on his words leads ineluctably not to the Living Word (Christ) like the relationship between word and Word in Scripture, but to the embodiments of his words—Leopold Bloom, Stephen Dedalus, and Molly Bloom, and Joyce himself. His thousands of words body them forth and they step toward us, beckoning us to interact with them as good readers and citizens.[28]

In her brilliant reading of how Stephen leads his detached listeners out of their posture of readerly reserve into active interest in his theory of *Hamlet* in the "Scylla and Charybdis" episode, Leah Flack has shown that both "*Ulysses* and the *Odyssey* feature audiences who wish to maintain aesthetic distances from stories and who nevertheless are drawn into the stories they hear."[29] While "Scylla and Charybdis" offers a discrete demonstration of this process by which detached fictional readers are led into affective reading responses, the last four episodes of the novel suggest Joyce's extra-textual move to more fully draw us in as empathetic and hospitable readers through his gift of portraying Stephen and Bloom's relationship through his retelling of the Good Samaritan parable.

Wayne Booth observed in *The Company We Keep: An Ethics of Fiction* that as we process and read stories, we take in "the new selves" offered there, such that "[w]hen a story 'works,' when we like it well enough to listen to it again and to tell it over and over to ourselves and friends . . . it occupies us in a curiously intense way." We are "occupied," that is, "by a foreign imaginary world."[30] And that world that is so foreign to us eventually becomes part of us, taken into us, in a way that it might become a friend. Booth's description of stories as friendship offerings suggests something of what I am arguing here: "the implied authors of all stories, fictional or historical, elevated or vulgar, welcoming or hostile on the surface, purport to offer one or another of these friendships [pleasure, profit, or a reciprocal friendship good for both friends]."[31] Joyce clearly privileges this third kind of friendship through his model of Bloom and Stephen's relationship in *Ulysses*, and, by extension, for us as readers.

We are drawn into the world of *Ulysses* in such an intense fashion whether or not we know the Good Samaritan parable—and further, whether or not we recognize its operation as a major intertext in the last four episodes of the novel. Joyce, as authorial host, invites us into the house of his novel, as it were, making us guests at his feast of words, helping us get comfortable, delighting in letting us live there for a time. As Kenneth Bailey observes, "A parable is an extended metaphor and as such it is not a delivery system for an idea but a house in which the reader/listener is invited to take up residence."[32]

Once in that house of fiction, accustomed as we become to Bloom's habitus of help and hospitality toward others, we are touched and moved when we witness this Stranger metamorphose into Samaritan in front of our eyes. There is something so undeniably affirming, so human about Bloom's instantly stooping to help Stephen and then to minister to him afterwards that we quickly respond ourselves to that encounter. If we have read the Good Samaritan parable before, our responsiveness to their encounter may be activated faster; regardless, Joyce models for us in such encounters how we should respond to his characters, who are in need of our help to rescue them from entrapping narratives in the novel that others have written for them. But while this narrative help leads us into their lives, we can never fully know them—we are finally strange to them and they to us—just as in any loving relationship.

Along with the present of Bloom to Stephen in their relationship, and perhaps a proleptic gift—Stephen's protection of Bloom's reputation in the future—Joyce gives us the gift of being an active, loving interpreter of the novel, a novel the depths of which can finally never be plumbed. Musing on the relationship between Joyce's play *Exiles* and *Ulysses*, Vicki Mahaffey captures well this sense of gift and burden that Joyce imposes on us through a realization of the novel's elusiveness: "to understand a book on a first reading is to destroy all curiosity and wonder in the world. To make understanding difficult but not impossible *is* a gift, but it is not philanthropy. It is a gift of labor that allows the reader the freedom to free herself from self-limiting assumptions."[33] Loving the labor of reading, stemming in part from getting to know and loving Joyce's characters, draws us nearer to what Mahaffey, quoting Yeats in "The Circus Animals' Desertion," terms "Heart-mysteries," and a recognition that "love depends upon a final unknowability of the beloved, although future insight remains both possible and desirable."[34] Careful reading, as she contends, is a kind of active love, one that draws us nearer to characters and the work in which they live and move and have their being, but one that finally can only hover near them, beside them. Their otherness is finally beyond us as witnesses to and participants in their lives. Reading and attending to such characters, we might take on the temporary guise of the Good Samaritan and perform a series of loving acts in our attitudes toward them.

Ulysses finally brings together two modes of narrative from Scripture—the parabolic epitomized by the Lukan story of the Good Samaritan and the apocalyptic vision of John in the Book of Revelation. Whereas Joyce was fascinated by literary epiphany in *Dubliners* and *Portrait*, in *Ulysses* he uses the apocalyptic mode to convey the message of this parable: The apocalyptic and violent hallucinatory vision of "Circe" thus yields to and is a vehicle for the parabolic narrative running through the remainder of "Circe," "Eumaeus," "Ithaca," and "Penelope." A continuity remains between his previous penchant for revealing a moment of insight or inspiration and his new narrative message of *agape*, expressed through his retelling of the Good Samaritan parable in his Book of Revelation. Richard Kearney's phenomenological exploration of Joyce's sacramental imagination in *Ulysses* carries particular weight for my argument here: "[E]piphany, in its original scriptural sense, involved witnesses who come as strangers from afar. This could be read, in terms of a sacramental hermeneutics, as an event of textual openness to new, strange and unprecedented meanings through the textual encounter between author, narrator and, above all, reader." Kearney continues, drawing on Rudolph Gasché's reading of Joyce in Derrida's "*Ulysses* Gramophone": "Such a sacramental reading epitomizes the 'desire to open writing to unforeseeable effects, in other words, to the Other. It is a function of a responsibility for the Other—for managing in writing a place for the Other, saying yes to the call or demand of the Other, inviting a response.'"[35] By the end of our reading of *Ulysses*, we have become the "witnesses who come as strangers from afar," from the pressing concerns of our daily lives, crossing over the boundaries of nation, sex, politics, culture. As witnesses of Joyce's revelation of his secularized message of loving the Other, regardless of the Other's receptivity to our help, we ideally enter the event of the novel, responding to the hurt Bloom, the sneering Stephen, ourselves becoming temporary Good Samaritans and the best kind of citizens in a world of care and concern that transcends 1904 Dublin.[36]

In the process, Joyce's interest in scriptural narratives leads finally to a nonsectarian, ecumenical understanding of charity, of enfleshed love in community. This sort of embodied love, reaching out in friendship and fellowship to others, is available to anyone, he suggests—Protestants, Catholics, Jews, any member of any religious group, atheists—who seeks to make herself another's neighbor through action. While Joyce certainly mocks Bloom's social reforming project, the "new Bloomusalem" (U 15.1544), ushered in through a burst of grandiloquence that certainly does not accord with Bloom's humility but is expressed by the distorting narrator of "Circe," Joyce nonetheless endorses his vision of the "Union of all, jew, moslem and gentile" (U 15.1686) and his emphasis on truly caring love here and elsewhere.[37] Like the Samaritan, without whom "the story would operate entirely within the closed world of Israel as it was," Bloom breaks in upon the staid, claustrophobic world of 1904 Dublin; like the Samaritan, he is "the world shatterer," the "stimulus toward creating a new world."[38]

Bloom's action in saving Stephen—and our potential actions in rescuing others—can be motivated by our immersion in the novel, as Joyce clearly intended. Thornton has argued consistently for such an imaginative experience with the novel that involves our affective response, one called for explicitly, as I hope to have shown in this study, by Joycean hospitality generally and the Good Samaritan parable specifically. Thornton argues that "[r]eading *Ulysses* should be a wholistic [sic] experience that involves readers' emotions and values fully as much as their ideas and concepts; without that affective experience as a *point d'appui*, discussion of the novel floats about unanchored like the island of Laputa."[39] Affect studies are *de rigueur* now, but Thornton consistently argued for incorporating our affective responses to the novel long before the rise of affect theory. Given the persistence in criticism until relatively recently of W. K. Wimsatt and Monroe C. Beardsley's mid-twentieth-century rejection of what they termed the "Affective Fallacy," Thornton's decades-long reclamation of affective reading signals the need for our recognition of the novel's modeling of charity-in-action in the person of Bloom and its development in Stephen.[40] Implicit in Wimsatt and Monroe's rejection of the so-called "Affective Fallacy" is their belief that appreciating the emotion produced in the critic by a given work of literature reduces, even eliminates, its particular, sharply focused formal qualities that render it literature and leads to a sort of general wallowing in inchoate feelings.[41] But emotion forms a critical part of imaginative literary criticism, as major affect theorists have taught us. Ricoeur links imagination and action in his hermeneutics of reading, arguing that "imagination is involved with the very process of motivation. It is imagination that provides the milieu, the luminous clearing, in which we can compare and evaluate motives as diverse as desires and ethical obligations, themselves as disparate as professional rules, social customs, or intensely personal values."[42]

Indeed—but part of *Ulysses*' powerfully affective appeal is grounded in the transcendent, spiritual call of the Other as well. If we do not hear the call of the Other, and if we hear it but do not follow it, we fail as human beings who are inherently spiritual—not just congeries of atoms, bodies floating about with no purpose. Moments of spirituality such as those which occur several times between Stephen and Bloom come unbidden to us, as they do to Joyce's characters. As Mark Freeman argues of such occurrences, "there is an element of surprise, of grace and gift; we cannot ever know what is like until it happens, and when it does, we can be utterly staggered by its sheer improbable, inexpressible presence."[43] Ineffability, beyondness, often coheres in the presence of the hovering Other who, often unexpectedly, beckons us to her side to experience with her all her hopes and dreams—and even her nightmares. The impossibility of ever fully knowing the Other—even if the Other is our beloved—nevertheless ideally spurs us on to greater heights of care and concern for her.

In *The Sense of an Ending*, Frank Kermode argues for the burden of responsibility on the reader to get to know characters, noting that "[t]hose that continue to interest us move through time to an end, an end we must sense even if we cannot know it; they live in change, until, which is never, *as* and *is* are one."[44] It might seem passé to care about literary characters, but recent work, including that by Rachel Bowlby, suggests the problem with valuing actual persons over literary characters. She observes the implicit narrationality of human beings, noting that "[it] is a commonplace of criticism to denounce the mistake of treating fictional characters as if they were real people," and arguing further that

> this objection harbors . . . a mistaken assumption of its own: that real people are real people—prior to how they are imagined, by themselves as well, or to the stories that are told about them . . . we are always, all the time, making people up, inventing them, reading them, and we do this to a large extent with plausible or likely paradigms of character and action and plot: of the kinds of things that people do, the kinds of ways that people act and think.[45]

We thus constantly invent narratives about those we interact with on a daily basis outside of literature, so we should not assume that "real world" humans are any less narrated (and even invented, to some extent) than literary ones. And because of the time and care we invest in getting to know literary characters, they often become very real to us. Furthermore, caring about characters leads us to care more about those who move and have their being in our ordinary ambit—those whose lives we narrate and imagine on a daily basis. Caring about characters thus conditions us to care about the living, breathing Other in front of us.

I hope I have shown just how much—and how positively—Stephen and Bloom's relationship has changed for the better in the "Nostos" section of *Ulysses*, and might keep changing for the better in the imagined future of the novel, the dynamism of which Kermode attempts to articulate above. But readers still troubled by what they see as the seeming lack of development of a relationship between them might take comfort in realizing that the parabolic structure of the novel, as with all parables, which revel in readerly frustration and doubt, settles not for answers, but asks us finally what we would do in such situations, which occur during our reading of the novel and continue after it "ends." That is, rather than complaining about Bloom and Stephen's relationship, we might ask ourselves a series of questions: "What is my relationship to them?" "Would I have helped Stephen were I in Bloom's situation?" "Would I in the future?" "When I read the novel again?" "When I'm just thinking about it?"

Ricoeur describes this process well when he argues that

> it is in the realm of the imaginary that I try out my power to act, that I measure the scope of "I can." I impute my power to myself, as the agent of my own action, only by depicting it to myself in the form of imaginative variations on ... "I could," even "I could have done otherwise, if I had wanted to."[46]

This conditional tense "provides the grammatical projection of imaginative variations on the theme 'I can,'" which "belongs to the tense-logic of the practical imagination," and thus, "I take possession of the immediate certainty of my power only through the imaginative variations that mediate this certainty."[47] Reading Bloom's rescue of Stephen and Stephen's potential future "rescue" of Bloom in warding off pernicious rumors that may well already be circulating in Dublin through Joyce's reading of their relationship through the Good Samaritan parable conditions us not only to read on multiple levels, but with our imaginations so conditioned, to add our own layer to these narratives, perhaps inserting ourselves into them in the hope that we might transcend ourselves as Joyce's main characters have at times.

Paul B. Armstrong has noted that "[i]n a way that has made readers feel exasperated and annoyed, *Ulysses* points out their limits, their inadequacy, their inability to meet its demands," and yet he observes that "it keeps drawing readers even as it frustrates and repels them."[48] Certainly, reading the novel can frustrate us, in part because we simply do not have Joyce's wealth of learning across cultures, languages, literatures, and other fields of study, as Armstrong and others have observed. Like Vicki Mahaffey, however, I believe that "paradoxically, when a text or a lover is less accessible, it kindles the reader's sense of wonder."[49] Thus, the novel's power to draw us may be stronger than its power to repel, and that alluring power may inhere in what Armstrong terms "the emancipatory, self-expanding pleasures it offers by challenging our capacities—extending, enhancing, and liberating the reader's power to mean."[50] And yet Armstrong leaves out another attraction that *Ulysses* exerts upon us: its crucial, *self-transcending* power, whereby we only become our truest selves by attending to another, just as Bloom does, and as perhaps Stephen will in the future.

Joyce takes the measure of such finally selfish endeavors as Armstrong describes by pointing us constantly toward community—even if it is comprised of only one other person besides ourselves. The community that Bloom and Stephen share, short-lived as it is, is grounded precisely in their difference, or, as Ricoeur would put it, in their "nonsubstitutibility." Since the "agents and patients of an action are caught up in relationships of exchange which, like language, join together the reversibility of roles and the nonsubstitutibility of persons," once we value the Other in solicitude, as Bloom comes to value Stephen, "each person is irreplaceable in our affection and our esteem."[51] Cherishing and caring so deeply for another as to realize how he is so unlike us as to be irreplaceable leads ineluctably to even greater care and concern for that person, a process Bloom seems to undergo in the novel. Caring for even one other person in this way—and Bloom has a chance to care in this manner not only for Stephen but also in the conclusion for Molly as well—is sufficient, Joyce seems to say. Caring can only be local, finally; caring for the whole world capsizes charity and renders it abstract and amorphous, utopian.[52]

I am not calling for a utopia—and neither was Joyce, as his rejection of Bloom's "new Bloomusalem" demonstrates—but instead for a recognition of how the particular fiction before us, in this case *Ulysses*, calls us to help the specific human being who faces us. In this sense, I share with Ricoeur his argument in his essay on "Initiative" that "[e]xpectations must be *determinant*, hence finite and relatively modest, if they are to lead to responsible *commitments*." At the same time, as he posits, "we must also resist any narrowing of the space of experience" and thus "fight against the tendency to consider the past simply as completed, unchangeable, over and done with."[53] If we accomplish these twin tasks—the modest goal of the recognition and care of the Other before us, in fiction or in reality, and an open attitude toward the past's mutability—then the past might be revealed to us "as a living tradition" with it "reopened, and the unaccomplished, thwarted[,] even massacred potentialities rekindled."[54] The present, Dublin on the day and night of June 16, 1904—the present of our current lives—is in this sense "the force that gives to our ethical and political aims in the future the strength to reactivate the unfulfilled potentialities of the past transmitted to us."[55] We cannot unwrite Stephen's largely terse replies to Bloom in "Eumaeus" or his singing of the anti-Semitic ballad in "Ithaca," but we can reread them time and again, entering into that narrative past, making it our present, and wondering if we would have done the same thing, all the while keeping in mind that another potential in Stephen—helper, rescuer—may be developing in front of our eyes through his actions.

Citing and developing his reading of *Ulysses* that I explored earlier, Richard Kearney observes that "epiphany implies witnesses that come as strangers from afar," and suggests that, hermeneutically, this concept signifies the "event of textual openness to new, alien, and unprecedented meanings through the perichoretic textual encounter between *author*, *narrator*, and, above all, *reader*."[56] Citing both Rudolphe Gasché's response to Derrida's commentary on Joyce in "*Ulysses* Gramophone," and Derrida's own reading, Kearney concludes that "[t]his notion of *Ulysses* as an open textual invitation to 'refiguration' finds confirmation in Joyce's own repeated appeal to the 'ideal reader': a gesture akin to Proust's appeal to his future readers to discover in his novel the book of their own life."[57] As Joyce reaches out to us through the pages of his generous-minded novel, we witness Bloom's generosity to others and perhaps become more open and generous ourselves.

Notes

1. Kiberd, Ulysses *and Us*, 17.
2. For an interesting, if not wholly convincing outline of how to read a parable, see Hedrick's chapter, "How Does a Parable Resonate? Empowering the Reader," from his *Many Things in Parables*, 89–99. I reject, for instance, Hedrick's very first step, separating the parable from its literary context. Hedrick would separate the parable of the Good Samaritan told by Christ from its framing context (90), the Jewish lawyer's question, "Teacher, what shall I do to inherit eternal life?", from which Christ draws out of him his knowledge of the necessity to love one's neighbor, the heart of the parable (Luke 10:25, ESV).
3. Bersani, "Against *Ulysses*," 177.
4. Moseley, *Joyce and the Bible*, 131.
5. Shashaty, "Reading *Dubliners* Parabolically," 213.
6. Ibid.
7. See also Mahaffey and Shashaty, "Introduction," 14–22, for a further discussion of the usefulness of parables in grappling with *Dubliners*.
8. Attridge, *The Singularity of Literature*, 124.
9. Gregory and Hunt-Hendrix, "Enfleshment and the Time of Ethics," 235.
10. Hedrick, *Parabolic Figures*, 219.
11. Ibid., 221.
12. Ricoeur, "The Socius and the Neighbor," 99.
13. Norris, *Virgin and Veteran Readings of* Ulysses, 213; Ellmann, Ulysses *on the Liffey*, 151–2.
14. Hedrick, *Parabolic Figures*, 228.
15. Flack, *Modernism and Homer*, 97.
16. Ellmann, *The Consciousness of Joyce*, 29.
17. See Scholes and Kain, *Workshop of Daedalus*, 264–6.
18. Holcomb, "Textual Notes" for Acts, 1465 (ESV).
19. Ibid., 1464.
20. Ellmann, *The Consciousness of Joyce*, 67.
21. Gregory and Hunt-Hendrix, "Enfleshment and the Time of Ethics," 228.
22. Glen, *The Parables of Conflict in Luke*, 51–2.
23. Regrettably, two recent examinations of bodies in *Ulysses* simply do not attend to the embodied interaction between Stephen and Bloom and largely deny any sort of transcendence to embodiment. Despite her interest in reading literary bodies through the lens of religion, one of Jean Kane's concluding statements on bodies in

Joyce in her *Conspicuous Bodies: Provincial Belief and the Making of Joyce and Rushdie* seems especially inattentive to the possibility of embodied transcendence in *Ulysses*. Citing Camille McCole's wrongheaded statement in a 1934 review of the novel that "No character in *Ulysses* ever *does* anything: every single one of them is merely the most passive of protoplasms actuated by no principle," Kane claims that Joyce "robs subjects of any transcendental power, epitomized in readers' ability to bracket the body, or at least to select the times and spaces in which they will acknowledge or engage with it" (129, citing McCole, "*Ulysses*," 723). This entire study clearly shows the opposite of McCole's and Kane's claim about the lack of agency by Joyce's characters, especially Stephen and Bloom, and demonstrates how they actually achieve a transcendent union through their bodily meeting. See also Vike Martina Plock's chapter, "Bodies," in the *Cambridge Companion to Ulysses*, which neglects any possibility that bodies can have a transcendent dimension.
24. Ricoeur, "The Socius and the Neighbor," 105.
25. Riquelme, "'Preparatory to anything else,'" 24.
26. Thornton, "The Allusive Method in *Ulysses*," 238.
27. Thornton, "The Greatness of *Ulysses*," 29.
28. Although he does not develop it as thoroughly as I do, Thornton's reading of Joyce's analogies between the priest and artist and between God and the artist form an important foundation for my argument here. Thornton argues that even Joyce's conception of himself as "a priest of the eternal imagination, transmuting the daily bread of experience into the radiant body of everliving life" [P 221] finally falls short in that it leaves out the reader's role. That is, such an analogy "obscures a sense in which the artist's role is analogous not to the priest's but to God's, and it fails to do justice to the activeness of the readers' role in the work of art" (Thornton, "James Joyce and the Power of the Word," 198). Because the artist's creative work is not *ex nihilo* and thus mimics God's creation, it needs a further "selection and interpretation" if "its potentiality for meaning is to be realized. The role of the reader is to act on this multifaceted work of art and form his own interpretation, a role which, especially in modern art, is itself active and creative" (199).
29. Flack, *James Joyce and Classical Modernism*, 88–9.
30. Booth, *The Company We Keep: An Ethics of Fiction*, 138, 139.
31. Ibid., 174.
32. Bailey, *Jesus through Middle Eastern Eyes: Cultural Studies in the Gospels*, 280.
33. Mahaffey, "Love, Race, and *Exiles*," 308–9.
34. Ibid., 309.
35. Kearney, "Sacramental Imaginations," 252, citing Gasché, *Inventions of Difference*, 230.
36. Although I have developed this argument about the role of the ethical reader in *Ulysses* on my own through a robust reading of the Good Samaritan parable as Joyce reconfigures it in his novel, I should note that the general trajectory of my thesis about the privileged role of the reader (significantly, *sans* Joyce's emphasis on hospitality through loving the Other) was anticipated not only by Thornton's "James Joyce and the Power of the Word" and his "Discovering *Ulysses*: The 'Immersive' Experience," but also, much later, and in strikingly different contexts, by both Riquelme, in the essay on "Eumaeus" cited above, and Jean-Michel Rabaté, who

argued in *James Joyce and the Politics of Egoism* about Joyce's later fiction (*Ulysses* but particularly *Finnegans Wake*) and Ezra Pound's *Cantos* especially that "their Modernist epics force the reader to become the 'hero' of a drama involving the editing and deciphering of texts" (194). Rabatè posits that "*Finnegans Wake* is a text which aims at giving birth to a new reader, a reader who has to approach the difficult and opaque language less with glosses and annotations than through the material evidence of the note-books, drafts, [and] corrected proofs reproduced by the James Joyce Archive" (196). Rabaté would finally dethrone the author in favor of the reader, while I contend that Joyce privileged a concept that featured the dynamic interaction of author, characters, and readers.

37. Ellmann, *The Consciousness of Joyce*, 85–6, argues of Bloom's reforming schemes in these moments in "Circe" that "On this plane Bloom appears ludicrous. . . . But clearly Joyce is here exaggerating to the point of absurdity Bloom's kindness and good-hearted civic feeling." Joyce does not endorse sentimentalism, evidenced not only by his rejection of the mawkishly sweet narrator of the first half of "Nausicaa" (rejected universally by Joyce critics as well), but also by his rejection of an overly sentimental meeting between Stephen and Joyce in "Circe," "Eumaeus," and "Ithaca," as we have seen.
38. McDonald, "Alien Grace," 50.
39. Thornton, "Discovering *Ulysses*," 122.
40. W. K. Wimsatt, Jr. and Monroe C. Beardsley, "The Affective Fallacy," 31, argued that "The Affective Fallacy is a confusion between the poem and its *results* (what it *is* and what it *does*). . . . It begins by trying to derive the standard of criticism from the psychological effects of the poem and ends in impressionism and relativism. The outcome . . . is that the poem itself, as an object of specifically critical judgment, tends to disappear." For the best and most cogent response to Wimsatt and Beardsley, see Jane Thrailkill, *Affecting Fictions*, 1–7, 15–17.
41. Thrailkill, *Affecting Fictions*, 15, argues that Wimsatt and Beardsley feared the "Affective Fallacy" because they wrongly thought that "the absolutely certain thing about emotion was that it was not stable: it did not stay still, from moment to moment, person to person, culture to culture. . . . Drawing on evolutionary theory, these emerging accounts suggest [instead] that while the cultural significance of feelings, along with rules about displaying them, may fluctuate over time, the actual corporeal architecture of emotional experience—almost universal to members of a species, and often highly similar across species—has evolved so slowly over the course of millennia as to be, in the limited timeframe of human history, practically stable." For an analysis of modernist criticism that jettisons emotional approaches to literary criticism, see my essay, "Radical Empathy in Virginia Woolf's *Mrs. Dalloway*," 345–7.
42. Ricoeur, "Imagination in Discourse and in Action," 177.
43. Freeman, *The Priority of the Other*, 215.
44. Kermode, *The Sense of an Ending*, 179.
45. Bowlby, "Two Interventions on Realism," 403.
46. Ricoeur, "Imagination in Discourse and in Action," 178.
47. Ibid., 178.
48. Armstrong, *Play and the Politics of Reading*, 148.

49. Mahaffey, "Love, Race, and *Exiles*," 308.
50. Armstrong, *Play and the Politics of Reading*, 148.
51. Ricoeur, *Oneself as Another*, 193.
52. Ricoeur places similitude first in his hierarchy of the exchange between self and the other, noting, "Similitude is the fruit of the exchange between esteem for oneself and solicitude for others. This exchange authorizes us to say that I cannot myself have self-esteem unless I esteem others *as* myself" (Ibid.). "[T]he paradox of the exchange at the very place of the irreplaceable" features an "equivalence" (193) and "Becoming in this way fundamentally equivalent are the esteem of the *other as a oneself* and the esteem of *oneself as an other*" (193–4).
53. Ricoeur, "Initiative," 221.
54. Ibid., 222, 221. Stephen's Aristotelian interest in potential throughout "Proteus" may well suggest Joyce's own interest in this open sense of the past.
55. Ibid., 222.
56. Kearney, "Epiphanies in Joyce," 257.
57. Ibid., 258, drawing on Gasché's *Inventions of Difference*, 230, and on Derrida's "*Ulysses* Gramophone: Hear Say Yes in Joyce," *passim*.

CODA

"GO THOU AND DO LIKEWISE": POSTCRITICAL AND POSTSECULAR READING THROUGH A JOYCEAN HERMENEUTICS OF HOSPITALITY

[T]here's a devotional quality in agreeing to be worked on by a text, a level of attunement and a willingness to yield that might be like worship.
Tracy Fassenden, "A Hermeneutics of Resilience and Repair," 172

[B]oth religious and secular redress need novels to help envision other worlds, to fancy themselves carried farther than they are able to go on their own.
Kevin Seidel, "Beyond the Religious and the Secular in the History of the Novel," 646[1]

Future Avenues for Joyce and Hospitality Studies

While there are many aspects of hospitality to explore in Joyce these lie beyond the scope of this book, but they would prove fruitful for future research endeavors. Hospitality was an abiding concern of Joyce, and aside from his interest in scriptural explorations of it, there are many other avenues of hospitality to consider.

One of these would be Joyce's receptive and hospitable attitude toward language and translation. Deeply interested in languages from an early age, Joyce became proficient in both Italian and French, and he also knew Latin (especially the Latin of the Vulgate translation of the Bible) and some Irish in addition to English. Having lived on the continent, and having immersed himself in its languages and cultures, and having delivered a series of lectures in Italian, Joyce's career proves his openness not only to language but also translation. His works themselves, particularly *Ulysses* and *Finnegans Wake*, can be profitably read as translations into English of the Dublin idiom Joyce knew well, leavened with snatches of other languages, at times becoming a new language for which we as yet have no name.[2]

Hospitality might be considered as part of another dimension of Joyce's aesthetic and creative process: his interest in other writers and literary traditions beyond his own could be profitably explored. By opening himself up to a series of non-Irish writers such as Ibsen, Defoe, Calvino, and Dante, among others, Joyce showed a remarkable receptiveness to authors whose literary agendas differed from his own; yet he learned a great deal from them even if he rejected some of their particular stylistic or thematic approaches or ideologies.

While the present study does not pursue this line of inquiry, a future study of hospitality and Joyce could investigate the colonial condition of Ireland, which complicates the notion of hospitality, since central to the struggle for Home Rule and political independence was the recognition that the Irish were subaltern and did not have ownership of their homes or land. That struggle toward ownership inflects the conditions under which Joyce's characters offer or are unable to offer hospitality.[3]

The theme of hospitality invites too a consideration of what Mark Osteen has called in *The Economy of Ulysses* the marketplace values and capitalist exchanges that underpin life in Dublin in 1904. Among other moments of hospitality, this study examines Bloom's generous donation of five shillings to the Dignam children whose father has just died even as he is attacked by the xenophobic Citizen, and it also considers Stephen's growing generosity, influenced by Bloom's charity toward him, when he gives the homeless Corley a half-crown; but other moments of economic exchange are ripe for future inquiries into Joyce and hospitality.

Furthermore, there are a series of stories in *Dubliners* and scenes in *Ulysses* that are concerned with parsimony, scrupulous meanness, error, failed encounters, the incorporation of monsters, absurdities, and perversions, and aborted hospitality, all of which would benefit from critical exploration. Joyce's concern with such matters and his critique of them reinforces my argument about his own prodigal, generous hospitality and how Leopold Bloom practices that help and warmth toward those whom he encounters, even when he is rebuffed by them.

Finally, attending to the issue of hospitality in Joyce's last major work, *Finnegans Wake*, would involve enlarging the scope of this project to a degree that is untenable. While the *Wake* may celebrate itself excessively and thus continues to run the risk of alienating readers from its linguistic fun, it also promises to be—and is, for many readers—the ultimately hospitable text, since it allows readers purchase through a variety of critical methodologies that grapple with its complexities. The formation and continuance of many reading groups around the world that tackle the *Wake* testifies to how it has brought readers together in community—if nothing else, to figure out its many puns, puzzles, and significations.[4]

Hospitable Reading Practices: Toward Becoming Good Neighbors

Here, I chart a generative, communal critical hermeneutic that grows out of this study, and I further attempt to show how this postcritical hermeneutic can be allied to a postsecular hermeneutic in which matters of faith are respected, even welcomed. First, in becoming the generous readers Joyce hoped we would be through our attention to *Ulysses*, we have an opportunity to revise the still-dominant critical paradigm that Paul Ricoeur has termed the "hermeneutics of suspicion," one that has become thoroughly embedded in modernity, including late modernity.[5] As the trajectory of modernism has shown, it privileges the elevation of the self above all else: Joyce's own *A Portrait of the Artist as a Young Man* superbly criticizes this view of the self in its portrayal of Stephen Dedalus. Furthermore, selves unmoored from the constraints of community are more likely to engage in critical practices that tend toward suspicion, even paranoia, and that reject charitable understandings of others. Driven back upon ourselves, we only see our desires, our needs. "The driving goal of modern thought," as Rita Felski argues in her 2020 study *Hooked: Art and Attachment*, "is to wrest oneself free from a primordial immersion in the given." Indeed, as she posits, "What defines modernity is a sundering of persons from any form of taken-for-granted community or unity," and thus "[t]o be modern is to be ripped free of the bonds of tradition and superstition, to be borne along by shock waves of social upheaval and secular disenchantment."[6] And yet this understanding of modernity needs serious reappraisal, as Felski argues in her compelling study, even noting that "[o]nce we factor in the vast spectrum of nonhuman actors in later modernity . . . we might well conclude that our condition is [actually] one of ever-greater entanglement, of proliferating ties and multiplying dependencies."[7]

I used to believe in the efficacy and appropriateness of Denis Donoghue's advocacy of disinterested reading advanced in *The Practice of Reading*,[8] but I now affirm with Ricoeur and, later, Felski a model of interested, generous reading that emerges from our exposure to the work under consideration and allows it to speak to us in the present. As Felski points out in *The Uses of Literature*, "reading is far from being a one-way street; while we cannot help but impose ourselves on literary texts, we are also, inevitably, exposed to them."[9] Because of historicism's tendency to encourage a focus on the meanings of texts for others, at a particular moment in time, "[o]ne consequence of such historical embedding is that the critic is absolved of the need to think through her own relationship to the text she is reading. . . . To focus only on a text's origin is to side-step the question of its appeal to the present-day reader."[10] How might we consider the appeal of Joyce's fictions such as *Dubliners* and *Ulysses* for us as readers?

In *Hooked*, Felski develops her theory of how literature appeals to us by articulating a rich concept of "attunement," a multifaceted theory that explores the demands an artwork makes upon us over time, the question of art as "an active force in the world," and finally, the ineffable experiences "that we struggle to articulate" in relation to a work of art.[11] For Felski, attunement "alerts us to the messy co-implication of text and reader," and moreover, that attunement inherently involves our understanding that "the artwork cannot act by itself; it needs allies, supporters, helpers. And crucially, that our experience of art as coproduced does not 'take away' from the value of the work but makes it possible."[12] That is, "[m]ediation does not detract from the magic of art but creates it."[13] This study has shown how the particular parabolic cast of Joyce's fictions, especially *Ulysses*, implicates us as readers and calls us to hospitably care for characters such as Bloom and the literary text itself in our mediation of them, just as Joyce made a home in his pages for an unforgettable cast of characters.[14]

Parables such as that told about the Good Samaritan by Christ are, as I have shown, dialogic and participatory for the listener; they bring home to us the ethical problem at hand, just as Joyce's reiteration and recasting of this parable through Stephen and Bloom's relationship does. Parabolic reading of this kind also attends to historical conditions and cultures, since both the parable and *Ulysses* are deeply grounded in specific local cultures but finally lift off from their particular situations by enabling us to relate to the characters through their polyvalency and multiple meanings, especially their care for others. What a gift Joyce has given us—to know the mind, body, and soul of this ordinary advertising canvasser—and to come to know Stephen Dedalus better (although still not as well as we know Bloom) across the course of this wonderfully rich novel.

Moreover, our concern for such characters whom we get to know so well inevitably leads us to consider those who cross our daily paths, and at least ponder entering into their lives imaginatively. Thornton makes this point well when he suggests,

> After coming to know and value Leopold Bloom through *Ulysses*, we find ourselves subtly influenced by Joyce's valuing of him, and it becomes harder for us simply to categorize and dismiss anyone we meet,

in fiction or in life, no matter how "ordinary" they may appear to be, for we cannot help but wonder whether their interior world might not be colored and illuminated by similar problems and similar virtues, if we but had an opportunity to spend a day looking at the world through their perspective.[15]

Attentive, immersive reading of the lives of Stephen and Bloom leads us out of ourselves, and our prolonged care for them may inculcate something like a habitus of *caritas* in us as readers, a habitus that might inform our daily lives.

When, in the midst of recounting his sexual exploits to the assembled medical students in "Oxen of the Sun," Stephen Dedalus humorously says, "Greater love than this, he said, no man hath that a man lay down his wife for his friend. Go thou and do likewise" (*U* 14.360–2), we laugh, then realize the poignancy of this moment both for Stephen and for Bloom (who undoubtedly thinks of Blazes having just been in his bed with Molly earlier that afternoon and evening). Stephen seems to endorse adultery here, but his underlying message bespeaks his need for a true friend after being betrayed by Buck Mulligan in the novel's first episode, when he takes the key to the tower from Stephen, and later, when he undermines Stephen's artistic theory of *Hamlet* in "Scylla and Charybdis." In parodying both John 15:13, with its admonition to sacrifice our lives for our friends, and Christ's instruction to "Go thou and do likewise" the last verse of the Good Samaritan parable (Luke 10:37), to care for the wounded Other, Stephen nonetheless endorses the emphasis on sacrificial love epitomized by Christ, a point emphasized soon after his Gospel references. When Stephen then muses, "Bring a stranger within thy tower it will go hard but thou wilt have the secondbest bed" (*U* 14.365–6), he is blaming Mulligan for bringing the Englishman Haines to the Martello Tower, who, together with Mulligan, effectively renders Stephen a stranger and leads to his exile from his temporary home. Also briefly invoking his theory about Shakespeare's wife Ann Hathaway being given the secondbest bed back in "Scylla and Charybdis," he may be transposing that theory to his own situation and suggesting that Haines now has the secondbest bed in the tower (and Mulligan the best), while he, Stephen, has none.

Stephen's clear recognition of Christ's command at the end of the Good Samaritan parable at this moment in "Oxen of the Sun" stands out as in gold lettering in the midst of his drunken meditation, a clarion call for Bloom, as it turns out, to rescue the stranger Stephen in the succeeding episodes. And this admonition beckons us too as readers, challenging us to be charitable to Others just as Bloom has modeled that charity for us throughout the novel, but especially in its concluding chapters. Just as Christ's original Jewish audience expected one of their own "tribe" to rescue the beaten man in the ditch, but had their expectations completely exploded in the way the parable "juxtaposes to the known world of the hearers an alternative realm of being which challenges and seeks transformation of their life-world,"[16] we have likely been similarly challenged in our expectations of Bloom's behavior in the novel if we have previously bought into the view of Jews, and Bloom specifically, as stingy and selfish, as expressed by Protestant characters such as Mr. Deasy and Catholic characters such as Simon Dedalus and the Citizen. Even if we have not accepted their jaundiced view of Bloom, we might be surprised at the extent and prodigality of his hospitality toward Stephen and, moreover, be challenged by his example. Joyce's parabolic fiction, similarly to the Lukan narrative of the Good Samaritan, seeks to challenge and transform his audience's worldview, offering Bloom to us as an exemplary figure of charity, one who helps automatically, then extensively, with little or no regard for his own person. Bloom *is* trust (even if shot through with self-doubt), rising above the tides of suspicion that threaten to drown him throughout the day. Bloom finds his identity in others, becomes incarnate in reaching out, touching, and helping the Other, not retreating into himself as we are often tempted to do.

Even in 1970, long before the hermeneutics of suspicion became *de rigueur*, Ricoeur was counseling a hermeneutics of faith as an antidote. Not "the first faith of the simple soul," but the second faith of one who has engaged in hermeneutics, "faith that has undergone criticism, postcritical faith." This second faith is "a rational faith, for it interprets; but it is a faith because it seeks, through interpretation, a second naïveté."[17]

This book has generally followed Ricoeur's suggestion for a hermeneutics of religion, though not always his phenomenological approach. My readings thus shadow Joyce's textually inspired prophetic vision stemming from his transcription of Revelation and his appropriation of the Lukan narrative of the Good Samaritan parable. That vision, as I argued at the end of the last chapter, finally imagines a non-sectarian, pluralist, hospitable community achieved between Bloom and Stephen and other characters, and between readers and Joyce's characters, one that might even extend into our treatment of the Other in our daily lives. We glimpse the outlines of this pluralist hospitality in the tentative incorporation of the Protestant Mr. Browne into the otherwise Catholic community of "The Dead," a story that displays the beginnings of Joyce's hospitality ethic, as I showed in my first chapter, but we see it clearly in *Ulysses* as it is fully enfleshed and offered to character and reader alike.

I have sought to model a way of perceiving this great epic's particular ethical contours and, finally, its invitation to us to reach out to its major characters, particularly Stephen Dedalus and Leopold Bloom (and perhaps beyond them to others who beckon for our help in our current lives), through attending to the particularities of the Good Samaritan parable and Joyce's reiteration and recasting of it. I thus see this study as part of the continuing conversation taking place in the field of literature and religion that Mark Knight has aptly characterized in his introduction to *The Routledge Companion to Literature and Religion* as "a conversation between friends, or at least one between those who might become friends," one that "matters, where what is spoken about is seen to be of value by all parties, and where the participants in it work hard to hear and respond to what the other is saying." We remain "committed to" that conversation "even when it takes us in directions that we did not expect or leads us where we did not want to go," and it "acknowledges a debt to the willingness of religious texts including the Hebrew Bible and the Christian New Testament, to introduce the language of friendship in unlikely places."[18] This conversation, I am arguing, should influence and become part of the contemporary project of postcritical reading.

Friendship, or potential friendship, with readers and other critics should be marked by receptivity and generosity, and, just as the subjects of Jesus' parables and Joyce's reimagined parables of the Good Samaritan exhibit generosity, I hope my own criticism here has been marked by a similar generosity. This generosity ideally offers an exemplary contrast to the habitual tone of critique that has become second nature to many of us, which Felski laments and identifies in *The Limits of Critique*. This tone inheres in a posture of "guardedness rather than openness, aggression rather than submission, irony rather than reverence, exposure rather than tact." As she suggests, "The combative idiom of scholarship ('interrogate' is surely the most frayed word in the current lexicon) soaks us in an overall tonal atmosphere that can be hard to change."[19] But a series of readings by scholars such as Eve Sedgwick, particularly her distinction between paranoid and reparative ways of reading, have done much to promote excitement and affective readings of literature, as Felski shows.[20] Felski finally advocates for what she calls "postcritical reading," an amorphous phrase that both signals a continuity with critical reading and departs from a sheerly uncritical way of reading.[21] In this scheme, "[i]nterpretation becomes a coproduction between actors [reader, text, characters] that brings new things to light rather than an endless rumination on a text's hidden meanings or representational failures."[22]

"Credit" and "trust" would be my own watchwords for this new way of reading—crediting the work at hand to reveal itself through our patient attention to it—not probing it to death or imposing our own meanings onto it—and trusting the work, the characters (if not always the narrators, a special issue in *Ulysses*), the author, and ourselves and other readers. Bloom, I would like to suggest, models openness, submission, reverence, and tact, along with perhaps his most important quality—humility. Bloom seems to be an ideal reader in such a hermeneutic of generosity. If Bloom can practice and acquire a habitus of generosity, why can't we? If he can continually open himself to others and other ways of thinking despite being assailed for his real and imaginary faults, why can't we? *Ulysses* and other great works of the imagination call for such readings, beckoning us into their pages and asking us to lay down our presuppositions and enter their *plena*. In reading *Ulysses* in this way, I hope I have shown that we hover on the threshold of a new moment in literary criticism, one similarly inflected with generosity and openness such that religion finally becomes an accepted part of academic discourse in the field.

I find incontrovertible Lori Branch's contention that

> literary theory, not to mention the inexhaustible well of meanings unearthed in criticism and teaching, tells us that literature and religion do converge at the site of belief and meaning-making, but institutional pressures and the epistemologies from which they spring have so far worked to prevent our living up to the implications of those insights.[23]

Branch's account of these institutional pressures and associated epistemologies has become required reading for those who would seek to understand how literary study has invited so many other disciplines into the contemporary English department while largely attempting to draw a *cordon sanitaire* around religion so that it might not "contaminate" literature. Branch correctly draws our attention to how the "indeterminacy of language and literature . . . always unsettles the knowledge-producing mechanisms of our discipline," and how "texts (thankfully, like students), in their openness, always contain possibilities that these [now dominant models of literary inquiry such as critical theory, political criticism, and "cultural-materialist inquiry"] approaches neither exhaust nor extinguish."[24] Branch calls us to recognize "uncertainty not as indicating ignorance or lack of knowledge," but "rather [to] validate it 1) as the very condition of possibility for freedom and meaning and 2) as the prime concern of our scholarly and pedagogical endeavors." As she concludes, "Far from [constituting] the downfall of our discipline, this exploration and defense of faith as fragile, contingent, and part-and-parcel of the linguistic condition is . . . grounds for advocating for the role of the humanities in culture and education." Thus,

> Religious concerns—especially as to the nature of belief, knowledge, and their relation, particularly as they concern questions of goodness, non-violence, right relation with others, and shaping a self capable of such communion—are not just the parochial concerns of a few among us; rather, they are questions of language and of living in the world as beings who speak, read, and write: who *make meaning*.[25]

A forum on Felski's *The Limits of Critique* in a special issue of *Religion and Literature* suggests the fruitfulness of her postcritical approach to literary studies, even as Felski herself offers some caveats to these scholars' use of her book in their own approaches to reading literature through religious viewpoints.[26] Branch, for instance, offers a helpful image of literary studies' "insistent refusal of the religious" as a type of wound:

> the vulnerability of belief—the profound provisionality of every reading and speech act and prayer—that language continually faces us with, and the history of our discipline is in large part a story of reapplying a new bandage over this cut when the old one stops sticking, a process I call the ritual of our re-secularization.[27]

Branch tentatively sees Felski's work as a way to bridge the postcritical and the postsecular, as I hope my own book has done. As Branch points out,

> Free from reflex secularism, the postcritical and postsecular are potentially great allies, not least when we articulate their common ground and differences, letting postcritique help us speak, for instance, about the extra-virtual openness of religious and spiritual experience, about what it means to suspend one's disbelief not only in a temporary or provisional way.[28]

Joyce's *Ulysses* seems to bridge the postcritical and the postsecular: it works against the hermeneutic of suspicion long ago identified by Ricoeur and not only gestures toward generosity and openness but also models those virtues. And it anticipates the rise of postsecular criticism since it recovers the New Testament parable of the Good Samaritan as the foundation of what we might term a postcritical ideology and instantiates it as a narrative site at which people—characters within the novel and readers of it—of varying beliefs and even of no belief might meet, mingle, and converse, groping toward some profound awareness of how to understand ourselves and the persistent, unflagging demands that the Other makes upon us.

If we think the true audience of this parable is limited to the skeptical lawyer—or to Stephen Dedalus—we fail our hermeneutical responsibility in reading the parable and, frankly, in reading and responding to Joyce's fiction. Through its iterations of this parable, *Ulysses* awakens what Derek Attridge argues is our responsibility to the other: "the other is also vulnerable, in need of my protection, 'destitute,' to use Levinas's word. Its power lies in its weakness. Literature, for all the force which it is capable of exercising, can achieve nothing without readers—responsible readers."[29]

Part of *Ulysses*' power to bridge the postcritical and the postsecular lies in its appeal to our rethinking the question of authority—both the Bible's authority, which of course it often undermines, and its own authority, which it undermines as well, but in ways that tend to affirm the text's protean capacity to cover all manner of knowledge and styles. Many literary scholars who still practice critique, founded on the hermeneutics of suspicion, would instantly be skeptical, unlike Joyce, of attributing any authority to the Bible. That is, they likely know too well (or have experienced) its being "wielded as a book of absolute divine judgements ... especially against its doubters and critics"; however, as Kevin Seidel points out, that "is not the only way or even the most common way its authority is experienced by those who read it religiously, whether for study, guidance, consolation, prayer, or meditation."[30] Indeed, as he holds,

> In none of these practices is the Bible thought the voice of a tyrant, yet it remains authoritative. Learning to recognize and describe the complex, manifold authority of the Bible might prove a first step in rethinking the authority of literary texts generally, so that instead of decrying every manifestation of textual power, critics could distinguish between forms of power, and then argue about which ones are legitimate, which work to the reader's good, and which ones do not.[31]

Engaging in such a process might involve our "agreeing to be worked on by a text, a level of attunement and a willingness to yield that might be like worship," as Tracy Fassenden articulates the matter in the first epigraph to this coda. But while I have no doubt that Joyce intended (somewhat sacrilegiously) exactly this for himself and for our reading of *Ulysses*—despite its altruistic concerns in forming neighbors out of strangers, in and out of the text—such a worshipful posture toward a work (perhaps especially toward the Bible) would be a step too far for most current literary critics. Perhaps we might settle for our "agreeing to be worked on by a text," and having "a level of attunement" to it. Such a posture would at least decenter our own rigidly authoritative, skeptical self-worship for a time. If we adopt such a reading practice, we have the hope of entering into the world of *Ulysses* sufficiently to not only care about its characters but also to come "home" to ourselves, braced and girded by knowledge of the Other and ultimately ourselves.

Our response to *Ulysses* as a hospitality narrative inspired by and structured, particularly in "Circe," "Eumaeus," "Ithaca," and even "Penelope," by Joyce's beating in 1904 Dublin and mugging in 1907 Rome as well as the Good Samaritan parable might mirror the response of hearers and readers of New Testament parables as articulated by Sallie McFague TeSelle: "The spectators must participate imaginatively, must so live in the story that insight into its strangeness and novelty come home to them."[32] Living in Bloom's rescue of Stephen, in Stephen's possible proleptic rescue of Bloom from vicious anti-Semitic rumors, in our own desire to help Bloom and even Stephen, gives us, Odysseus-like, our own kind of homecoming to the novel and to ourselves, since the most significant, perduring, meaningful aspects of the self inhere in knowing and reaching out to others. As

Mark Freeman articulates, "the experiences and things that generally provide the greatest yield of meaning of existential 'nourishment' have little to do with our selves. They derive instead from what is other to self, outside of it."[33] Joyce's novel works against what Charles Taylor terms the modern, "buffered" self and offers instead something like the pre-Enlightenment "porous" self, a self not characterized by interiority but by outwardness and its ability to be influenced by others.[34]

I should hasten to add, though, that I do not share Taylor's insistence here and elsewhere that the Protestant Reformation and its emphasis on the individual believer's relationship with God led ineluctably to the rise of this finally selfish, buffered self. Indeed, these chapters on *Ulysses* have striven to shown how Joyce has reached his readers through a secular insistence on attending closely to the words in his epic just as the Reformation insisted on *sola scriptura* as the guide to salvation. Joyce's conception of the porous self is thus radically unlike Taylor's caricature of the way in which he believes the Reformation led to our sense of disenchantment in the world—the way he thinks we have evacuated mystery from it. Joyce's sense of the necessity of individual freedom finds a natural accord with the Reformation's insistence on such freedom. By embracing our agency, Joyce, and his Stranger/Samaritan characters like Bloom, envision and embody our responsibility to the Other, freely chosen but inherently part of ourselves. Such a process leads inevitably to a re-enchantment of the world and a re-embrace of the porous self.

Make no mistake—this is inherently a spiritual process. Jack Dudley, who was the first to treat the Good Samaritan theme in any depth in Joyce's work in his examination of "Grace" from *Dubliners*, argues that "Joyce's Samaritan grace, enacted both in *Dubliners* and in *Ulysses* as that work's core event, demonstrates that the central idea of redemption and liberation for Joyce was a spiritual one, framed and described out of the material of his religious upbringing, set to new but, nonetheless, transcendent purposes."[35] Joyce may have left the Catholic Church, but its promulgation of the persistence of the immanent and transcendent in the everyday world never left him.

Since, as TeSelle shows, this kind of parable is not "*primarily* concerned with knowing but with doing," therefore, we "must not forget that the goal of a parable is finally in the realm of willing, not of knowing."[36] Susan Colón's argument about the embodied nature of parables accords perfectly with my own argument in these chapters regarding *Ulysses*. She posits that parables "demand an embodied response to the challenge they pose," going on to assert that "[t]he invitation to think very differently about something one thought one knew carries with it an invitation to act very differently, according to a new construal of reality."[37] Jesus employs the parable of the Good Samaritan, as David Lawton points out, "to redefine the word 'neighbour' so that it is no longer geographical, opposed to 'outsider' or 'foreigner,' but social."[38] Notably, the lawyer does not answer Christ's question about who the wounded man's neighbor is by terming his rescuer "a Samaritan"; instead, as Lawton shows, "he replies, abandoning narrative detail for discursive relevance, 'he that shewed mercy on him.'" So the story not only shows the vacuity of biases, but also, in front of our eyes, demonstrates the transformation of the lawyer: "Jesus gets the lawyer to acquire for himself, by the act of interpreting the parable of the Good Samarian, the competence that leads from knowledge through desire to action, and produces the equivalence suggested by the parable itself. To Love equals To Do."[39] Joyce similarly wants us to undergo an interpretive experience in reading *Ulysses* and to begin loving his characters by our active reading of and entering into their world—and that of those around us as well.

At the same time, although we might have identified as the Stranger or even as the ones who did not rescue the Stranger, we must be careful in fully claiming to ourselves the role of Samaritan. Recall Charles Hedrick's observation: "[t]he benevolence" of the Samaritan is "so outlandish as to challenge any compromise that readers may have made between their own acts of kindness or charity and the human need that always exists on every side. Few would ever claim to have been the Samaritan as he is portrayed in this narrative."[40] Or in Joyce's novel, we might add. Thus we must move out into the world in actively and bodily loving the Other, not merely tolerating her presence and congratulating ourselves for doing so, all the while recognizing that we almost certainly cannot match the Samaritan's or even Bloom's prodigal generosity. And yet knowing that near-impossibility should not foreclose our trying to live out an enfleshed ethics. James Joyce's epic asks that we make an effort to understand it by deeply dwelling within its words. By apprehending its parabolic nature, we might yet move toward becoming truly neighborly.

Notes

1. Seidel extrapolates here from Hans Frei's *The Eclipse of Biblical Narrative: A Study in Eighteenth and Nineteenth Century Hermeneutics*, particularly his pointing readers to the "curious, unmarked frontier between history and realistic fiction" (150).
2. For a recent example of scholarly inquiry into Joyce, hospitality, and translation, see Maria Teresa Cabrera, "Joyce, Hospitality, and the Foreign Other." Besides observing actual moments of translation in *Ulysses*, for instance when Stephen speaks in Irish and translates for Bloom, and Bloom does the same from Hebrew for Stephen (*U* 17.724–30) and when Molly imagines translating Spanish for Stephen and his translating Italian for her (*U* 18.1476), Cabrera also convincingly develops Alexis Nouss's argument that translation is a "special form of hospitality between languages and cultures," and that "to translate should always mean to receive the foreigner, who takes refuge in one's language, as one simultaneously takes refuge *in the other's*" (270, citing Nouss, "Translation and Métissage," 227).
3. But see Kevin Barry, "James Joyce, Misunderstanding, and the City of Refuge," who argues, drawing on Derrida's reading in his essay *On Cosmopolitanism*, that Dublin functions as a city of refuge and "recognizes that hospitality is culture; that

ethics is hospitality (Derrida 2001: 16)." Barry extrapolates from his reading of Derrida to posit that Dublin has an "unsentimental capacity . . . to allow a sense of belonging, to allow enough misunderstanding so that even the slighted are secure, to allow that if one man flings a biscuit tin at your head another may be there to rescue you from trouble," and thus, "this internal spaciousness of the city is the saving of Bloom and his possibility of being foreign and at ease" (46).
4. See "Directory of *Finnegans Wake* Reading Groups" for a list of these groups.
5. Ricoeur, *Freud and Philosophy, passim*. While I cannot find the exact phrase in this work, "hermeneutics" and "suspicion" are linked closely in longer phrases and sentences throughout. For an excellent anecdoctal account of the prevalence of the hermeneutic of suspicion in prestigious English (and Religion) graduate schools in the 1980s and 1990s, see Fassenden, "A Hermeneutics of Resilience and Repair," 167–9. She concludes that even as such doctoral graduates moved into a market in which tenure-track jobs were fast disappearing, "Still the hermeneutics of suspicion prevailed as the most satisfying diagnosis of our own marginality. Grievance afforded a method and a *raison d'etre*. Feeling misunderstood made us more like the writers we admired for their opacity, their inscrutability to the world that made them marginal" (169). Like Fassenden, Alan Jacobs articulates the dominance of critique in the 1980s, but unlike her appreciation for how Eve Kosofsky Sedgwick's emphasis on reparative reading has helped erode some of critique's dominance, he says flatly, "I tend to see that period [the 1980s] as the one in which critique assumed the dominance in my profession it has not yet yielded" ("Vulnerabilities and Rewards," 174). Jacobs helpfully shows how critique mimics the scientific method and thus tries to justify itself over and against readers who only seek pleasure from literature and are thus viewed—along with their method of non-critical reading—as frivolous: "Critique is anything but frivolous: it is, one might say, the moral equivalent of the scientific method. . . . Critique distinguishes itself from the powers and strategies of the literary, and puts the text on the rack to extract, with whatever force is required, its secrets" (176).
6. Felski, *Hooked: Art and Attachment*, 9.
7. Ibid., 10.
8. See Donoghue, *The Practice of Reading*, especially when he advocates for "a recovered disinterestedness. If we can't or won't sequester our immediately pressing interests, put them in parentheses for the time being, we have no hope of reading literature" (78).
9. Felski, *The Uses of Literature*, 3.
10. Ibid., 10.
11. Felski, *Hooked: Art and Attachment*, 53.
12. Ibid., 77, 78.
13. Ibid., 78.
14. In this regard, I am taken by the description by Mike Marais in his study of J. M. Coetzee and hospitality, *Secretary of the Invisible*, of how Coetzee welcomes the Other into his fiction: "The text must host the other and so enable it to interrupt history. Indeed, the notion of hospitality implicit here is directly related to the process of writerly inspiration: to be a secretary of the invisible is precisely to become a home for the other and then to try to make for it a home of language, of the text" (xv–xvi).
15. Thornton, "The Greatness of *Ulysses*," 28.

16. McDonald, "Alien Grace," 44.
17. Ricoeur, *Freud and Philosophy*, 28.
18. Knight, "Introduction," 7.
19. Felski, *The Limits of Critique*, 21.
20. Ibid., 29–30. See Sedgwick, "Paranoid Reading and Reparative Reading."
21. Felski, *The Limits of Critique*, 173. She memorably posits, "These are some of the things that a postcritical reading will decline to do: subject a text to interrogation; diagnose its hidden anxieties; demote recognition to yet another form of misrecognition; lament our incarceration in the prison-house of language; demonstrate that resistance is just another form of containment; read a text as a metacommentary on the undecidability of meaning; score points by showing that its categories are socially constructed; brood over the gap that separates word from world."
22. Ibid., 174.
23. Branch, "The Rituals of Our Re-secularization: Literature between Faith and Knowledge," 10.
24. Ibid., 24.
25. Ibid., 28.
26. See Felski, "Entanglement and Animosity: Religion and Literary Studies," 189–95.
27. Branch, "Postcritical and Postsecular: The Horizon of Belief," 161.
28. Ibid., 165.
29. Attridge, *The Singularity of Literature*, 131.
30. Seidel, "Beyond the Religious and the Secular in the History of the Novel," 645.
31. Ibid., 646.
32. TeSelle, *Speaking in Parables*, 71.
33. Freeman, *The Priority of the Other*, 4–5.
34. For Taylor's own capsule history of this process in his magisterial work, see *A Secular Age*, 539–41.
35. Dudley, "From 'Spiritual Paralysis' to 'Spiritual Liberation': Joyce's Samaritan 'Grace,'" 189.
36. TeSelle, *Speaking in Parables*, 71, 79–80.
37. Colón, *Victorian Parables*, 6–7.
38. Lawton, *Faith, Text, and History*, 149.
39. Ibid., 150.
40. Hedrick, *Parabolic Figures*, 228.

WORKS CITED

Adams, Robert M. *Surface and Symbol: The Consistency of James Joyce's Ulysses*. New York: Oxford University Press, 1962.
Albert, Leonard. "*Ulysses*, Cannibals, and Freemasons." *A.D.* (1951): 265–83.
Alter, Robert. *The Art of Biblical Narrative*. Revised and updated ed. New York: Basic Books, 2011.
—. *Canon and Creativity: Modern Writing and the Authority of Scripture*. New Haven, CT: Yale University Press, 2000.
Armstrong, Paul B. *Play and the Politics of Reading: The Social Uses of Modernist Form*. Ithaca, NY: Cornell University Press, 2005.
Arnold, Matthew. *On the Study of Celtic Literature*. London: Smith, Elder, and Co., 1867.
Attridge, Derek. *The Singularity of Literature*. New York: Routledge, 2004.
— and Marjorie Howes, eds. *Semicolonial Joyce*. Cambridge: Cambridge University Press, 2000.
Auden, W. H. *Collected Poems*. Ed. Edward Mendelson. New York: Vintage, 1991.
Avery, Bruce. "Distant Music: Sound and the Dialogics of Satire in 'The Dead.'" In James Joyce, *Dubliners: Text, Criticism, and Notes*. Ed. Robert Scholes and A. Walton Litz. New York: Penguin, 1996. 408–20.
Bailey, Kenneth E. *Jesus through Middle Eastern Eyes: Cultural Studies in the Gospels*. Downers Grove, IL: IVP Academic, 2008.
—. *Through Peasant Eyes: More Lucan Parables, Their Culture and Style*. Grand Rapids, MI: Eerdmans, 1980.

Balsamo, Gian. *Joyce's Messianism: Dante, Negative Existence, and the Messianic Self.* Columbia, SC: University of South Carolina Press, 2004.

Barrs, Jerram. *Learning Evangelism from Jesus.* Wheaton, IL: Crossway, 2009.

Barry, Kevin. "James Joyce, Misunderstanding, and the City of Refuge." *Canadian Journal of Irish Studies* 35.2 (2009): 42–7.

Benco, Silvio. "James Joyce in Trieste." *The Bookman* LXXII (December 1930): 375–80.

Bender, Abby. *Israelites in Erin: Exodus, Revolution, and the Irish Revival.* Syracuse, NY: Syracuse University Press, 2015.

Benjamin, Roy. "The Third Gospel in *Finnegans Wake*." *Journal of Modern Literature* 31.4 (2008): 102–15.

Benstock, Bernard. *Bloom's Old Sweet Song: Essays on Joyce and Music.* Gainesville, FL: University of Florida Press, 1995.

—. *Narrative Con/Texts in* Ulysses. Urbana, IL: University of Illinois Press, 1991.

—. "*Ulysses*: The Making of an Irish Myth." In *Approaches to* Ulysses: *Ten Essays*. Ed. Thomas F. Staley and Bernard Benstock. Pittsburgh: University of Pittsburgh Press, 1970. 199–234.

Bersani, Leo. "Against *Ulysses*." *The Culture of Redemption.* Cambridge, MA: Harvard University Press, 155–78.

Birmingham, Kevin. *The Most Dangerous Book: The Battle for James Joyce's* Ulysses. New York: Penguin, 2014.

Blamires, Harry. *The New Bloomsday Book: A Guide through* Ulysses. 3rd ed. New York: Routledge, 1996.

Booth, Wayne C. *The Company We Keep: An Ethics of Fiction.* Berkeley, CA: University of California Press, 1988.

Boundas, Constantin V. "The Good Samaritan, the Philosopher, and the Madman." In *The Hermeneutics of Charity: Interpretation, Selfhood, and Postmodern Faith*. Ed. James K. A. Smith and Henry Isaac Venema. Grand Rapids, MI: Brazos Press, 2004. 171–84.

Bowker, Gordon. *James Joyce: A Biography.* London: Weidenfeld and Nicolson, 2011.

Bowlby, Rachel. "Two Interventions on Realism: Untold Stories in *Mrs. Dalloway* and Versions of Realism in George Eliot's *Adam Bede*." *Textual Practice* 25.3 (2011): 395–436.

Boyle, Kevin. *James Joyce's Pauline Vision: A Catholic Exposition.* Carbondale, IL: Southern Illinois University Press, 1978.

Brady, Tom. "Suspect Quizzed after 'Good Samaritan' Stabbed to Death." *Irish Independent*, July 24, 2010, <http://www.independent.ie/irish-news/suspect-quizzed-after-good-samaritan-stabbed-to-death-26666045.html>. Accessed March 14, 2022.

Brannigan, John. *Race in Modern Irish Literature and Culture.* Edinburgh: Edinburgh University Press, 2009.

Branch, Lori. "Postcritical and Postsecular: The Horizon of Belief." *Religion and Literature* 48.2 (2016), Special Forum on "Possibilities beyond Critique," 160–6.

—. "The Rituals of Our Re-secularization: Literature between Faith and Knowledge." *Religion and Literature* 46.2–3 (2014): 9–33.

Brockman, William S. "The New Bloom in 'Eumaeus': The Emendations of *Ulysses: A Critical and Synoptic Edition*." *James Joyce Quarterly* 28.1 (1990): 153–68.

Bruns, Gerald L. "Eumaeus." In *James Joyce's* Ulysses: *Critical Essays*. Ed. Clive Hart and David Hayman. Berkeley, CA: University of California Press, 1974. 363–84.

Budgen, Frank. *James Joyce and the Making of* Ulysses *and Other Writings*. Oxford: Oxford University Press, 1991 [1930].

Cabrera, Maria Teresa Caneda. "Joyce, Hospitality, and the Foreign Other." In *James Joyce: Whence, Whither, and How: Studies in Honor of Carla Voglio*. Ed. Giuseppina Cortese, Giuliana Ferreccio, Maria Teresa Giaveri, and Teresa Prudente. Alessandria: Edizioni dell'Orso, 2015. 269–78.

Card, James. "A Textual and Critical Study of the 'Penelope' Episode of James Joyce's *Ulysses*." Ph.D. diss., Columbia University, 1964.

Casey, Edward. *Getting Back into Place: Toward a Renewed Understanding of the Place-World*. 2nd ed. Bloomington, IN: University of Indiana Press, 2009.

Chittenden, Kelly. "Parables and Reading Joyce's *Dubliners*." Paper given at the fall 2020 graduate seminar with Richard Rankin Russell at Baylor University: "Hospitality in Joyce, Beckett, and Cormac McCarthy."

Chrètien, Jean-Louis. *The Ark of Speech*. Trans. Andrew Brown. New York: Routledge, 2004.

—. *The Call and the Response*. Trans. Anne A. Davenport. New York: Fordham University Press, 2004.

—. *Under the Gaze of the Bible*. Trans. John Marson Dunaway. New York: Fordham University Press, 2015.

Colón, Susan. *Victorian Parables*. London: Continuum, 2012.

Colum, Mary and Padraic. *Our Friend James Joyce*. Garden City, NY: Doubleday, 1958.

Connolly, Thomas E. *James Joyce's Books, Portraits, Manuscripts, Notebooks, Typescripts, Page Proofs*. Lewiston, NY: Edwin Mellen Press, 1997.

—. *The Personal Library of James Joyce: A Descriptive Bibliography*, 2nd ed. Buffalo, NY: University Bookstore of University of Buffalo, 1957.

Costello, Peter. *James Joyce: The Years of Growth, 1882–1915*. London: Papermac, 1994.

Crispi, Luca. *Joyce's Creative Process and the Construction of Characters in* Ulysses: *Becoming the Blooms*. Oxford: Oxford University Press, 2015.

—. "Manuscript Timeline, 1905–1922 [for *Ulysses*]," *Genetic Joyce Studies* 4, 2004, www.geneticjoycestudies.org/articles/GJS4/GJS4_Crispi.
Cussen, John. "Bloom's Drunk: A Rereading of the 'Eumaeus' Episode in James Joyce's *Ulysses*." *CEA Critic* 63.2 (2001): 56–74.
Davison, Neil R. *James Joyce, Ulysses, and the Construction of Jewish Identity: Culture, Biography, and "The Jew" in Modernist Europe*. Cambridge: Cambridge University Press, 1996.
Derrida, Jacques. *On Cosmopolitanism*. London: Routledge, 2001.
—. "Hostipitality." In *Acts of Religion*. Ed. Gil Anidjar. New York: Routledge, 2002. 358–420.
—. "*Ulysses* Gramophone: Hear Say Yes in Joyce." In *Acts of Literature*. Ed. Derek Attridge. New York: Routledge, 1992. 253–309.
Derrida, Jacques, and Anne Dufourmantelle. *Of Hospitality: Anne Dufourmantelle Invites Jacques Derrida to Respond*. Trans. Rachel Bowlby. Palo Alto, CA: Stanford University Press, 2000.
"Directory of *Finnegans Wake* Reading Groups." <http://finneganswake.org/ReadingGroups.shtml>. Accessed October 15, 2018.
Doležel, Lubomír. *Heterocosmica: Fiction and Possible Worlds*. Baltimore, MD: Johns Hopkins University Press, 1998.
Donoghue, Denis. "A Plain Approach to *Ulysses*." In *Irish Essays*. Cambridge: Cambridge University Press, 2011. 157–69.
—. *The Practice of Reading*. New Haven, CT: Yale University Press, 1998.
Drury, John. "Luke." In *The Literary Guide to the Bible*. Ed. Robert Alter and Frank Kermode. Cambridge, MA: Harvard University Press, 1987. 418–39.
Dudley, Jack. "From 'Spiritual Paralysis' to 'Spiritual Liberation': Joyce's Samaritan 'Grace.'" In *Rethinking Joyce's Dubliners*. Ed. Claire A. Culleton and Ellen Scheible. New York: Palgrave, 2017. 175–94.
Eco, Umberto. *The Aesthetics of Chaosmos: The Middle Ages of Joyce*. Tulsa, OK: University of Tulsa Press, 1982.
Eide, Marian. *Ethical Joyce*. Cambridge: Cambridge University Press, 2002.
Elliott, Neil. "Commentary on Romans." In *The New Oxford Annotated Bible*, 3rd ed. New Revised Standard Version with the Apocrypha. Ed. Michael D. Coogan. Oxford: Oxford University Press, 2001.
Ellmann, Maud. "Endings." In *The Cambridge Companion to Ulysses*. Ed. Sean Latham. Cambridge: Cambridge University Press, 2014. 95–109.
Ellmann, Richard. *The Consciousness of Joyce*. Oxford: Oxford University Press, 1977.
—. *James Joyce*. New and revised ed. New York: Oxford University Press, 1982.
—. "Preface." In James Joyce, *Ulysses*. Ed. Hans Walter Gabler. New York: Vintage, 1986. ix–xiv.
—. "Prologue: Two Perspectives on Joyce." In *Light Rays: James Joyce and Modernism*. Ed. Heyward Ehrlich. New York: New Horizon Press, 1984. 1–10.

—. *Ulysses on the Liffey*. Oxford: Oxford University Press, 1972.
Fargnoli, A. Nicholas, and Michael Patrick Gillespie. *James Joyce A–Z: The Essential Reference to His Life and Writings*. Oxford: Oxford University Press, 1996.
Fassenden, Tracy. "A Hermeneutics of Resilience and Repair." *Religion and Literature* 48.2 (2016), Special Forum on "Possibilities beyond Critique," 167–73.
Felski, Rita. "Entanglement and Animosity: Religion and Literary Studies." *Religion and Literature* 48.2 (2016), Special Forum on "Possibilities beyond Critique," 189–95.
—. *Hooked: Art and Attachment*. Chicago: University of Chicago Press, 2020.
—. *The Limits of Critique*. Chicago: University of Chicago Press, 2015.
—. *The Uses of Literature*. Malden, MA: Blackwell, 2008.
Fénelon, François de Salignac de la Mothe. *Les Aventures de Télémaque*. Paris: Flammarion, n.d. [1699].
Ferris, Kathleen. *James Joyce and the Burden of Disease*. Lexington, KY: University of Kentucky Press, 1995.
Fish, Stanley. "One University under God?" *The Chronicle of Higher Education*, January 7, 2005. https://www.chronicle.com/article/One-University-Under-God-/45077. Accessed June 7, 2018.
Flack, Leah. *James Joyce and Classical Modernism*. London: Bloomsbury, 2020.
—. *Modernism and Homer: The Odysseys of H.D., James Joyce, Osip Mandelstam, and Ezra Pound*. Cambridge: Cambridge University Press, 2015.
Franke, William. "James Joyce and the Bible." In *The Blackwell Companion to the Bible in English Literature*. Ed. Rebecca Lemon, Emma Mason, and Jonathan Roberts. Malden, MA: Wiley-Blackwell, 2009. 638–49.
—. *Secular Scriptures: Modern Theological Poetics in the Wake of Dante*. Columbus, OH: Ohio State University Press, 2015.
Fraser, James. *Joyce and Betrayal*. Basingstoke: Palgrave Macmillan, 2016.
Freeman, Mark. *The Priority of the Other*. Oxford: Oxford University Press, 2014.
Frei, Hans. *The Eclipse of Biblical Narrative: A Study in Eighteenth and Nineteenth Century Hermeneutics*. New Haven, CT: Yale University Press, 1974.
Funk, Robert W. *Language, Hermeneutic, and Word of God*. New York: Harper and Row, 1966.
—. "The Old Testament in Parable: The Good Samaritan." In *Funk on Parables: Collected Essays*. Ed. Bernard Brandon Scott. Santa Rosa, CA: Polebridge Press, 2006. 67–84.
—. *Parables and Presence: Forms of the New Testament Tradition*. Philadelphia: Fortress Press, 1982.

Gabler, Hans Walter. "Afterword." In *Ulysses, Vol. III, Episodes 16 through 18, A Critical and Synoptic Edition*, prepared by Hans Walter Gabler with Wolfhard Steppe and Claus Melchior. New York: Garland, 1984. 1859–1907.

Gasché, Rudolphe. *Inventions of Difference: On Jacques Derrida*. Cambridge: MA: Harvard University Press, 1994.

Gibbons, Luke. "'Famished Ghosts': Bloom, Bible Wars, and 'U.P. UP' in Joyce's Dublin." *Dublin James Joyce Journal* 2 (2009): 1–23.

Gibson, Andrew. *Joyce's Revenge: History, Politics, and Aesthetics in* Ulysses. Oxford: Oxford University Press, 2002.

—. "Thinking Forwards, Turning Back: Joyce's Writings 1898–1903." In *James Joyce in the Nineteenth Century*. Ed. John Nash. Cambridge: Cambridge University Press, 2013. 61–74.

Gifford, Don, and Robert J. Seidman. Ulysses *Annotated: Notes for James Joyce's* Ulysses. Revised and expanded ed. Berkeley, CA: University of California Press, 1989.

Gillespie, Michael Patrick, with the assistance of Erik Bradford Stocker. *James Joyce's Trieste Library: A Catalogue of Materials at the Harry Ransom Humanities Research Center, The University of Texas at Austin*. Austin, TX: Harry Ransom Humanities Research Center, University of Texas, 1986.

Gilbert, Stuart. *James Joyce's* Ulysses: *A Study*. New York: Vintage, 1958.

Glen, J. Stanley. *The Parables of Conflict in Luke*. Philadelphia: Westminster Press, 1952.

Gottfried, Roy. *Joyce's Misbelief*. Gainesville, FL: University Press of Florida, 2008.

Gregory, Eric, and Leah Hunt-Hendrix. "Enfleshment and the Time of Ethics: Taylor and Illich on the Parable of the Good Samaritan." In *Aspiring to Fullness in a Secular Age: Essays on Religion and Theology in the Work of Charles Taylor*. Ed. Carlos D. Colorado and Justin D. Klassen. Notre Dame, IN: University of Notre Dame Press, 2014. 217–39.

Gula, Marianna. "'Reading the Book of Himself': James Joyce on Mihály Munkásy's Painting 'Ecce Homo.'" In *Joycean Unions: Post-Millennial Essays from East to West*. European Joyce Studies. Amsterdam: Rodopi, 2013. 47–60.

Harkness, Marguerite. *The Aesthetics of Dedalus and Bloom*. Lewisburg, PA: Bucknell University Press, 1984.

Hays, Richard B. *Echoes of Scripture in the Gospels*. Waco, TX: Baylor University Press, 2016.

Hayward, Matthew. "Bloom's CV: Mimesis, Intertextuality and the Overdetermination of Character in *Ulysses*." *English Studies* 97.8 (2016): 877–91.

Heaney, Seamus. *Munro*. *Everyman: An Annual Religio-Cultural Review* 3 (1970): 58–65.

Hedrick, Charles. *Many Things in Parables: Jesus and His Modern Critics.* Louisville, KY: Westminster John Knox Press, 2004.

—. *Parabolic Figures or Narrative Fictions? Seminal Essays on the Stories of Jesus.* Eugene, OR: Cascade Books, 2016.

Heffernan, James A. W. *Hospitality and Treachery in Western Literature.* New Haven, CT: Yale University Press, 2014.

Herring, Philip. *Joyce's Notes and Early Drafts for* Ulysses: *Selections from the Buffalo Collection.* Charlottesville, VA: Bibliographical Society of the University of Virginia.

—. *Joyce's* Ulysses *Notesheets in the British Museum.* Charlottesville, VA: University of Virginia Press, 1972.

Heusel, Barbara Stevens. "Vestiges of Truth: A Study of James Joyce's 'Eumaeus.'" *Studies in the Novel* 18.4 (1986): 403–14.

Hinojosa, Lynne. *Puritanism and Modernist Novels: From Moral Characters to the Ethical Self.* Columbus, OH: Ohio State University Press, 2015.

Hogan, Patrick Colm. Ulysses *and the Poetics of Cognition.* New York: Routledge, 2014.

Homer. *The Odyssey.* Trans. Robert Fagles. New York: Penguin, 1996.

Holcomb, Justin S. "Textual Notes" for Acts. In *Gospel Transformation Bible. ESV [English Standard Version].* Wheaton, IL: Crossway, 2011. 1449–97.

Holy Bible. King James Study Version. Nashville, TN: Thomas Nelson, 1999.

Houston, John Porter. *Joyce and Prose: An Exploration of the Language of* Ulysses. Lewisburg, PA: Bucknell University Press, 1989.

Hungerford, Amy. *Postmodern Belief: American Literature and Religion since 1960.* Princeton, NJ: Princeton University Press, 2010.

Hyamson, Albert M. "Anti-Semitism." In *Zionism and the Jewish Future.* Ed. H. Sacher. London: John Murray, 1916. 59–86.

Jacobs, Alan. "Vulnerabilities and Rewards." *Religion and Literature* 48.2 (2016), Special Forum on "Possibilities beyond Critique," 173–9.

Jervis, Ann. "Commentary on Romans." In *The New Oxford Annotated Bible*, 5th ed. New Revised Standard Version with the Apocrypha. Ed. Michael D. Coogan. Oxford: Oxford University Press, 2018.

Joyce, James. *Dubliners: Text, Criticism, and Notes.* Ed. Robert Scholes and A. Walton Litz. New York: Penguin, 1969.

—. *Finnegans Wake.* Ed. Robbert-Jan Henkes, Erik Bindervoet, and Finn Fordham. Oxford: Oxford World's Classics, 2012.

—. "Ibsen's New Drama." In *James Joyce: The Critical Writings.* Ed. Ellsworth Mason and Richard Ellmann. New York: Viking, 1959. 47–67.

—. *Letters of James Joyce*, Vol. I. Ed. Stuart Gilbert. New York: Viking Press, 1966 [1957].

—. *Letters of James Joyce*, Vol. II. Ed. Richard Ellmann. New York: Viking Press, 1966.

—. *A Portrait of the Artist as a Young Man: Text, Criticism, and Notes*. Ed. Chester G. Anderson. New York: Viking, 1968.
—. "Royal Hibernian Academy 'Ecce Homo.'" In *James Joyce: The Critical Writings*. Ed. Ellsworth Mason and Richard Ellmann. New York: Viking, 1959. 31–7.
—. *Selected Letters of James Joyce*. Ed. Richard Ellmann. New York: Viking, 1975.
—. "She Weeps over Rahoon." In *James Joyce: Poems and Shorter Writings*. Ed. Richard Ellmann, A. Walton Litz, and John Whittier-Ferguson. London: Faber and Faber, 1991. 54.
—. *Ulysses*. Ed. Hans Walter Gabler. New York: Vintage, 1986.
Joyce, Stanislaus. *Book of Days: The Triestine Diary*, Richard Ellmann Collection, McFarlin Library Special Collections, University of Tulsa, Oklahoma.
—. *My Brother's Keeper: James Joyce's Early Years*. Ed. Richard Ellmann. New York: Viking Compass, 1969 [1958].
—. *Recollections of James Joyce*. Trans. from the Italian by Ellsworth Mason. New York: The James Joyce Society, 1950.
Kane, Jean. *Provincial Belief and the Making of Joyce and Rushdie*. Columbus, OH: Ohio State University Press, 2014.
Kaufmann, Michael W. "The Religious, the Secular, and Literary Studies: Rethinking the Secularization Narrative in Histories of the Profession." *New Literary History* 38.4 (2007): 607–27.
Kawin, Bruce F. *Telling It Again and Again: Repetition in Literature and Film*. Ithaca, NY: Cornell University Press, 1972.
Kearney, Richard. "Epiphanies in Joyce." In *Voices on Joyce*. Ed. Anne Fogarty and Fran O'Rourke. Dublin: University College Dublin Press, 2015. 239–59.
—. "The Hermeneutics of Wounds." In *Unconscious Incarnations: Psychoanalytic and Philosophical Perspectives on the Body*. Ed. Brian W. Becker, John Panteleimon Manoussakis, and David M. Goodman. New York: Routledge, 2018. 21–42.
—. "Sacramental Imaginations: Eucharists of the Ordinary Universe." *Analecta Hermeneutica* 1.1 (2009): 240–88.
—. *Strangers, Gods, and Monsters: Interpreting Otherness*. New York: Routledge, 2003.
—. "What Is Carnal Hermeneutics?" *New Literary History* 46.1 (2015): 99–124.
Kelly, Joseph. "Joyce's Exile: The Prodigal Son." *James Joyce Quarterly* 48.4 (2011): 603–35.
Kenner, Hugh. *Dublin's Joyce*. Bloomington, IN: Indiana University Press, 1956.
—. *Joyce's Voices*. Berkeley, CA: University of California Press, 1978.
—. "Signs on a White Field." In *James Joyce: The Centennial Symposium*. Ed. Morris Beja, Phillip Herring, Maurice Harmon, and David Norris. Urbana, IL: University of Illinois Press, 1986. 209–19.

—. *Ulysses*. Rev. ed. Baltimore, MD: Johns Hopkins University Press, 1987.
Kermode, Frank. *The Genesis of Secrecy: On the Interpretation of Narrative*. Cambridge, MA: Harvard University Press, 1979.
—. *The Sense of an Ending: Studies in the Theory of Fiction*. Oxford: Oxford University Press, 1967.
Kershner, R. Brandon. "Intertextuality." In *The Cambridge Companion to Ulysses*. Ed. Sean Latham. Cambridge: Cambridge University Press, 2014. 171–83.
Kiberd, Declan. "Brian Friel's *Faith Healer*." In *Brian Friel: A Casebook*. Ed. William Kerwin. New York: Garland, 1997. 211–25.
—. *Ulysses and Us: The Art of Everyday Life in Joyce's Masterpiece*. New York: Norton, 2009.
Killeen, Terence. "Myths and Monuments: The Case of Alfred H. Hunter." *Dublin James Joyce Journal* 1 (2008): 47–53.
Knight, Mark. "Introduction." In *The Routledge Companion to Literature and Religion*. Ed. Mark Knight. New York: Routledge, 2016. 1–11.
Knight, Mark, and Emma Mason. "Saving Literary Criticism." In *Religion, Literature, and the Imagination: Sacred Worlds*. Ed. Mark Knight and Louise Lee. New York: Continuum, 2009. 150–61.
Kristeva, Julia. *Strangers to Ourselves*. Trans. Leon S. Roudiez. New York: Columbia University Press, 1991.
Langland, William. *Piers Plowman: A New Annotated Edition of the C-Text*. Ed. Derek Pearsall. Exeter: University of Exeter Press, 2008.
Latham, Sean. *Am I A Snob? Modernism and the Novel*. Ithaca, NY: Cornell University Press, 2003.
Lawrence, Karen. "Close Encounters." *James Joyce Quarterly* 41.1/2 (2003–04): 127–42.
—. *Who's Afraid of James Joyce?* Gainesville, FL: University Press of Florida, 2010.
Lawton, David. *Faith, Text, and History: The Bible in English*. Charlottesville, VA: University of Virginia Press, 1990.
Lernout, Geert. *Help My Unbelief: James Joyce and Religion*. New York: Continuum, 2010.
Levinas, Emmanuel. *Alterity and Transcendence*. New York: Columbia University Press, 1999.
Litz, Walton. "Joyce's Notes for the Last Episodes of 'Ulysses.'" *Modern Fiction Studies* 4.1 (1958): 3–20.
Lombard, Peter. *The Sentences: The Mystery of the Trinity*. Toronto: Pontifical Institute of Medieval Studies, 2007.
—. *The Sentences: On the Doctrine of Signs*. Toronto: Pontifical Institute of Medieval Studies, 2010.
McBride, Margaret. *Ulysses and the Metamorphosis of Stephen Dedalus*. Lewisburg, PA: Bucknell University Press, 2001.

McClure, John. *Partial Faiths: Postsecular Fiction in the Age of Pynchon and Morrison*. Athens, GA: University of Georgia Press, 2007.

McCole, Camille. "*Ulysses*." Review of *Ulysses*, by James Joyce, *Catholic World*, March 1934. 722–6.

McCourt, John. *The Years of Bloom: James Joyce in Trieste, 1904–1920*. Madison, WI: University of Wisconsin Press, 2000.

McDonald, J. Ian H. "Alien Grace (Luke 10:30–36): The Parable of the Good Samaritan." In *Jesus and His Parables: Interpreting the Parables of Jesus Today*. Ed. V. George Shillington. Edinburgh: T. and T. Clark, 1997. 35–51.

MacDuff, Sangam. "Joyce's Revelation: 'The Apocalypse of Saint John' at Cornell." *European Joyce Studies* 28 (2018): 118–26. Special issue "James Joyce and Genetic Criticism: Genesic Fields." Ed. Genevieve Sartor.

—. *Panepiphanal World: Joyce's Epiphanies*. Gainesville, FL: University of Florida Press, 2020.

Macé, Marielle. *Façons de lire, manières d'être*. Paris: Gallimard, 2011.

McGinn, Bernard. "Revelation." In *The Literary Guide to the Bible*. Ed. Robert Alter and Frank Kermode. Cambridge, MA: Harvard University Press, 1987. 523–41.

Mackey, Albert Gallatin. *A Lexicon of Freemasonry: Containing a Definition of All Its Communicable Terms, Notices of Its History, Traditions, and Antiquities, and an Account of All the Rites and Mysteries of the Ancient World*, 3rd ed. Philadelphia: Moss and Brother, 1856.

Macoy, Robert. *The General History, Cyclopedia, and Dictionary of Freemasonry*. New York: Masonic Publishing and Manufacturing Company, 1872.

Maddox, Jr., James H. "'Eumaeus' and the Theme of Return in *Ulysses*." *Texas Studies in Language and Literature* 16.1 (1974): 211–20.

Magalaner, Marvin. *Time of Apprenticeship: The Fiction of Young James Joyce*. London: Abelard-Schuman, 1959.

Mahaffey, Vicki. "Love, Race, and *Exiles*: The Bleak Side of *Ulysses*." In *Exiles: A Critical Edition*. Ed. A. Nicholas Fargnoli and Michael Patrick Gillespie. Gainesville, FL: University Press of Florida, 2016. 294–310.

—. *States of Desire: Wilde, Yeats, Joyce, and the Irish Experiment*. Oxford: Oxford University Press, 1998.

— and Jill Shashaty. "Introduction." In *Collaborative* Dubliners: *Joyce in Dialogue*. Ed. Vicki Mahaffey. Syracuse, NY: Syracuse University Press, 2012. 1–22.

Mahon, Peter. *Imagining Joyce and Derrida*. Toronto: University of Toronto Press, 2007.

Marais, Mike. *Secretary of the Invisible: The Idea of Hospitality in the Fiction of J.M. Coetzee*. Amsterdam: Rodopi, 2009.

Mason, Ellsworth, and Richard Ellmann, Introduction to Joyce, "Royal Hibernian Academy 'Ecce Homo.'" In *James Joyce: The Critical Writings*. Ed. Ellsworth Mason and Richard Ellmann. New York: Viking, 1959. 31.

Melchiori, Giorgio. "The Genesis of *Ulysses*." In *Joyce in Rome: The Genesis of Ulysses*. Ed. Giorgio Melchiori. Rome: Bulzoni Editore, 1984. 37–50.

Meyer, Joseph Matthew. "Redefining the Epic Hero in Joyce's 'Eumaeus.'" *Midwest Quarterly: A Journal of Contemporary Thought* 50.2 (2009): 137–48.

Miller, J. Hillis. "The Critic as Host." In *Deconstruction and Criticism*. Ed. Harold Bloom et al. London: Routledge and Kegan Paul, 1980. 217–53.

Mills-Knutsen, Joshua. "Becoming Stranger: Defending the Ethics of Absolute Hospitality in a Potentially Hostile World." *Religion and the Arts* 14.5 (2010), Special Issue on "Hospitality," ed. Chris Yates, 522–33.

Mitchell, Andrew J., and Same Slote, eds. *Derrida and Joyce: Texts and Contexts*. Albany, NY: State University of New York Press, 2013.

Morse, J. Mitchell. *The Sympathetic Alien: James Joyce and Catholicism*. New York: New York University Press, 1959.

Moseley, Virginia. *Joyce and the Bible*. DeKalb, IL: Northern Illinois University Press, 1967.

—. "Joyce and the Bible: The External Evidence." In *Ulysse: cinquante ans aprés. Témoignages franco-anglais sur le chef-d'oeuvre de James Joyce*. Ed. Louis Bonnerot. Paris: Didier, 1974. 99–110.

—. "Joyce's *Exiles* and the Prodigal Son." *Modern Drama* 1 (1959): 218–27.

Mullin, Katherine. *James Joyce, Sexuality, and Social Purity*. Cambridge: Cambridge University Press, 2003.

Neuman, Justin. *Fiction beyond Secularism*. Evanston, IL: Northwestern University Press, 2014.

The New Oxford Annotated Bible, 3rd ed. New Revised Standard Version with the Apocrypha. Ed. Michael D. Coogan. Oxford: Oxford University Press, 2001.

Nadel, Ira B. *Joyce and the Jews*. Iowa City: University of Iowa Press, 1989.

Newman, Robert D. "'Eumaeus' as Sacrificial Narrative." *James Joyce Quarterly* 30.3 (1993): 451–8.

Nolan, Emer. *Catholic Emancipations: Irish Fiction from Thomas Moore to James Joyce*. Syracuse, NY: Syracuse University Press, 2007.

Noon, William T. *Joyce and Aquinas*. New Haven, CT: Yale University Press, 1963.

Norris, Margot. "Words to 'The Lass of Aughrim.'" In *Dubliners: A Norton Critical Edition*. Ed. Margot Norris. New York: Norton, 2006. 247–8.

—. *Virgin and Veteran Readings of Ulysses*. New York: Palgrave, 2012.

Nouss, Alexis. "Translation and Métissage." In *Translation, Reflections, Refractions, and Transformations*. Ed. Paul St-Pierre and Prafulla C. Kar. Amsterdam: John Benjamins, 2007. 221–8.

O'Brien, Darcy. *The Conscience of James Joyce*. Princeton, NJ: Princeton University Press, 2015 [1968].
O'Connor, Frank. *The Lonely Voice: A Study of the Short Story*. London: Macmillan, 1963.
O'Neill, Christine. *Too Fine a Point: A Stylistic Analysis of the Eumaeus Episode in James Joyce's* Ulysses. Trier: Wissenshaftlicher Verlag Trier, 1996.
Origen. *Homilies on Jeremiah and I Kings 28*. Trans. John Clark Smith. Washington, D.C.: Catholic University of America Press, 1998.
—. *Homilies on Luke*. Ed. and trans. J. T. Lienhard, S.J. Vol. 94, Fathers of the Church. Washington, D.C.: Catholic University of American Press, 1996.
Osteen, Mark. *The Economy of* Ulysses: *Making Both Ends Meet*. Syracuse, NY: Syracuse University Press, 1995.
Otis, Harrison. "Reading Notebook: James Joyce." Fall 2020 graduate seminar with Richard Rankin Russell at Baylor University: "Hospitality in Joyce, Beckett, and Cormac McCarthy."
Owens, Cóilín. "Au Contraire." Review of Mark Gottfried, *Joyce's Misbelief*. *James Joyce Literary Supplement* 22.2 (2008): 14–15.
—. "Religion and Irish Studies." *Irish Literary Supplement* 27.1 (2007): 2–3.
Peake, C. H. *James Joyce: The Citizen and the Artist*. Stanford, CA: Stanford University Press, 1977.
Pecora, Vincent P. "'The Dead' and the Generosity of the Word." *PMLA* 101.2 (1986): 233–45.
—. "The Inkbottle and the Paraclete." In *Collaborative* Dubliners: *Joyce in Dialogue*. Ed. Vicki Mahaffey. Syracuse, NY: Syracuse University Press, 2012. 344–59.
—. *Self and Form in Modern Narrative*. Baltimore, MD: Johns Hopkins University Press, 1989.
Pierce, David. *Reading Joyce*. Harlow: Pearson, 2008.
Pinkerton, Steve. *Blasphemous Modernism: The 20th-Century Word Made Flesh*. Oxford: Oxford University Press, 2017.
Plock, Vike Martina. "Bodies." In *The Cambridge Companion to* Ulysses. Ed. Sean Latham. Cambridge: Cambridge University Press, 2014. 184–99.
Power, Father Colum. *James Joyce's Catholic Categories*. Belmont, NC: Wiseblood Books, 2017.
Power, Mary. "A Note on Hospitality and 'The Dead.'" *James Joyce Quarterly* 13.1 (1975): 109.
Purcell, Elyse. "Torn Flesh: Julia Kristeva and the Givenness of the Stranger." *Religion and the Arts* 14.5 (2010), Special Issue on "Hospitality," ed. Chris Yates. 572–88.
Rabatè, Jean-Michel. *James Joyce and the Politics of Egoism*. Cambridge: Cambridge University Press, 2001.

Raleigh, John Henry. "On the Way Home to Ithaca: The Functions of the 'Eumaeus' Section in *Ulysses.*" *Irish Renaissance Annual* II (1981): 13–114.

Reece, Steve. *The Stranger's Welcome: Oral Theory and the Aesthetics of the Homeric Hospitality Scene.* Ann Arbor, MI: University of Michigan Press, 1993.

Reilly, Terry. "Apocalyptic Satire: Reading *Ulysses* through Revelation and Frank Kermode's *The Sense of an Ending.*" *In-Between: Essays and Studies in Literary Criticism* 12.1–2 (2003): 301–9.

Renan, Ernest. *The Life of Jesus.* London: Kegan, Paul, 1891.

Ricoeur, Paul. "Ethical and Theological Considerations on the Golden Rule." In *Figuring the Sacred: Religion, Narrative, and Imagination.* Trans. David Pellauer. Ed. Mark I. Wallace. Minneapolis, MN: Fortress Press, 1995. 293–302.

—. *Freedom and Nature: The Voluntary and the Involuntary.* Evanston, IL: Northwestern University Press, 1966.

—. *Freud and Philosophy: An Essay on Interpretation.* New Haven, CT: Yale University Press, 1970.

—. "Imagination in Discourse and Action." In *From Text to Action: Essays in Hermeneutics*, II. Trans. Kathleen Blamey and John B. Thompson. Evanston, IL: Northwestern University Press, 1991. 168–87.

—. "Initiative." In *From Text to Action: Essays in Hermeneutics*, II. Trans. Kathleen Blamey and John B. Thompson. Evanston, IL: Northwestern University Press, 1991. 208–22.

—. "Manifestation and Proclamation." In *Figuring the Sacred: Religion, Narrative, and Imagination.* Trans. David Pellauer. Ed. Mark I. Wallace. Minneapolis, MN: Fortress Press, 1995. 48–67.

—. *Oneself as Another.* Trans. Kathleen Blamey. Chicago: University of Chicago Press, 1992.

—. "The 'Sacred' Text and the Community." In *Figuring the Sacred: Religion, Narrative, and Imagination.* Trans. David Pellauer. Ed. Mark I. Wallace. Minneapolis, MN: Fortress Press, 1995. 68–72.

—. "The Socius and the Neighbor." In *History and Truth.* Evanston, IL: Northwestern University Press. 1965. 98–109.

Riquelme, John Paul. 'Preparatory to anything else': Joyce's Styles as Forms of Memory—The Case of 'Eumaeus.'" In *Ulysses in Critical Perspective.* Ed. Michael Patrick Gillespie and A. Nicholas Fargnoli. Gainesville, FL: University Press of Florida, 2006. 9–34.

Roughley, Alan. *Reading Derrida Reading Joyce.* Gainesville, FL: University of Florida Press, 1999.

Russell, H.K. "The Incarnation in *Ulysses.*" *Modern Fiction Studies* 4.1 (1958): 53–61.

Russell, Richard Rankin. "Irish Unionism, North of Ireland Protestantism, and the Home Rule Question in Joyce's *Dubliners*." *Joyce Studies Annual* (2013): 62–94.

—. "Parabolic Plots in Bernard MacLaverty's *Lamb*." In *Bernard MacLaverty: New Critical Readings*. Ed. Richard Rankin Russell. New York: Bloomsbury, 2014. 27–44.

—. "Radical Empathy in Virginia Woolf's *Mrs. Dalloway*." *Genre* 48.3 (2015): 341–81.

—. "'Who is my Neighbor'? Leopold Bloom and the Parable of the Good Samaritan." *Dublin James Joyce Journal* 10 (2017): 22–43.

Ryken, Leland. *The Legacy of the King James Bible: Celebrating 400 Years of the Most Influential English Translation*. Wheaton, IL: Crossway, 2011.

Saint-Amour, Paul. "'Christmas Yet to Come': Hospitality, Futurity, the *Carol*, and 'The Dead.'" *Representations* 98 (May 2007): 93–117.

Sambrooke, Jerilyn. "Secularism, Religion, and the 20th/21st Century Novel." *Literature Compass* 15.1 (2008): 1–13.

Scarry, Elaine. *On Beauty and Being Just*. Princeton, NJ: Princeton University Press, 1999.

Scholes, Robert A., and Richard M. Kain, eds. *The Workshop of Daedalus*. Evanston, IL: Northwestern University Press, 1965.

Schneider, Ulrich. "Freemasonic Signs and Passwords in the 'Circe' Episode." *James Joyce Quarterly* 5.4 (1968): 303–11.

Schlossman, Beryl. *Joyce's Catholic Comedy of Language*. Madison, WI: University of Wisconsin Press, 1985.

Sedgwick, Eve Kosofsky. "Paranoid Reading and Reparative Reading, or, You're So Paranoid, You Probably Think This Essay is About You." In *Touching Feeling: Affect: Pedagogy, Performativity*. Durham, NC: Duke University Press, 2003. 123–51.

Seeley, John R. *Ecce Homo: A Survey of the Life and Work of Jesus*. London: Macmillan, 1890.

Seidel, Kevin. "Beyond the Religious and the Secular in the History of the Novel." *New Literary History* 38 (2007): 637–47.

Senn, Fritz. "'All Kinds of Words Changing Colour': Lexical Clashes in 'Eumaeus.'" In *Inductive Scrutinies: Focus on Joyce*. Ed. Christine O'Neill. Baltimore, MD: Johns Hopkins University Press, 1995. 156–75.

—. "Eumaean Titbits—As Someone Somewhere Sings." In *Inductive Scrutinies: Focus on Joyce*. Ed. Christine O'Neill. Baltimore, MD: Johns Hopkins University Press, 1995. 176–96.

Shashaty, Jill. "Reading *Dubliners* Parabolically." *James Joyce Quarterly* 47.2 (2010): 213–29.

Sheery, Eugene, William G. Fallon, Padraic Colum, and Arthur Power. *The Joyce We Knew: Memoirs*. Ed. Ulick O'Connor. Cork: Mercier Press, 1967.

Shepherd, Andrew. *The Gift of the Other: Levinas, Derrida, and a Theology of Hospitality*. Eugene, OR: Pickwick/Wipf and Stock, 2014.

Slote, Sam. *Joyce's Nietzschean Ethics*. New York: Palgrave, 2013.

—. "Preliminary Comments on Two Newly Discovered 'Ulysses' Manuscripts." *James Joyce Quarterly* 39.1 (2001): 17–28.

—, Marc A. Mamigonian, and John Turner. "Notes." In James Joyce, *Ulysses: Based on the 1939 Odyssey Press Edition*. Revised and corrected ed. Richmond, UK: Alma Classics, 2015.

Soards, Marion Lloyd. "Commentary on Luke." In *The New Oxford Annotated Bible*, 3rd ed. New Revised Standard Version with the Apocrypha. Ed. Michael D. Coogan. Oxford: Oxford University Press, 2001.

Sullivan, Kevin. *Joyce among the Jesuits*. New York: Columbia University Press, 1958.

Sultan, Stanley. "The Adventures of *Ulysses* in Our World." In *Joyce's* Ulysses: *The Larger Perspective*. Ed. Robert D. Newman and Weldon Thornton. Newark, DE: University of Delaware Press, 1987. 271–310.

—. *The Argument of* Ulysses. Middletown, CT: Wesleyan University Press, 1987 [1964].

Tate, Allen. "The Dead." In James Joyce, *Dubliners: Text, Criticism, and Notes*. Ed. Robert Scholes and A. Walton Litz. New York: Penguin, 1969. 404–9.

Taylor, Charles. *The Secular Age*. Cambridge, MA: Harvard University Press, 2007.

—. *Sources of the Self: The Making of the Modern Identity*. Cambridge, MA: Harvard University Press, 1989.

TeSelle, Sallie McFague. *Speaking in Parables: A Study in Metaphor and Theology*. Philadelphia: Fortress Press, 1975.

Thomas, Brook. "The Counterfeit Style of 'Eumaeus.'" *James Joyce Quarterly* 14.1 (1976): 15–24.

Thornton, Weldon. *Allusions in* Ulysses. Chapel Hill, NC: University of North Carolina Press, 1968.

—. "The Allusive Method in *Ulysses*." In *Approaches to* Ulysses: *Ten Essays*. Ed. Thomas F. Staley and Bernard Benstock. Pittsburgh, PA: University of Pittsburgh Press, 1970. 235–48.

—. "Discovering *Ulysses*: The 'Immersive' Experience." In *Approaches to Teaching Joyce's* Ulysses. Ed. Kathleen McCormick and Erwin R. Steinberg. New York: Modern Language Association, 1993. 122–8.

—. "The Greatness of Ulysses." *New Hibernia Review* 7.3 (2003): 26–37.

—. "James Joyce and the Power of the Word." In *The Classic British Novel*. Ed. Howard M. Harper, Jr. and Charles Edge. Athens, GA: University of Georgia Press, 1972. 183–201.

—. *Voice and Values in Joyce's* Ulysses. Gainesville, FL: University Press of Florida, 2000.

Thrailkill, Jane. *Affecting Fictions*. Cambridge, MA: Harvard University Press, 2007.
Thurston, Luke. *Literary Ghosts from the Victorians to Modernism: The Haunting Interval*. New York: Routledge, 2012.
Toíbín, Colm. *Mad, Bad, Dangerous to Know: The Fathers of Wilde, Yeats, and Joyce*. New York: Scribner's, 2018.
Torchiana, Donald. *Backgrounds for Joyce's* Dubliners. Boston: Allen and Unwin, 1986.
Turner, Mark. *The Literary Mind*. New York: Oxford University Press, 1996.
Van Mierlo, Chrissie. *James Joyce and Catholicism: The Apostate's Wake*. London: Bloomsbury, 2017.
Via, Dan Otto Jr. *The Parables: Their Literary and Existential Dimension*. Philadelphia: Fortress Press, 1967.
Walzl, Florence. "Gabriel and Michael: The Conclusion of 'The Dead.'" In James Joyce, *Dubliners: Text, Criticism, and Notes*. Ed. Robert Scholes and A. Walton Litz. New York: Penguin, 1969. 423–43.
Weinstein, Arnold. *The Fiction of Relationship*. Princeton, NJ: Princeton University Press, 1988.
Weir, David. Ulysses *Explained. How Homer, Dante, and Shakespeare Inform Joyce's Modernist Vision*. New York: Palgrave, 2015.
Wimsatt, Jr., W. K., and M. C. Beardsley. "The Affective Fallacy." *The Sewanee Review* 57.1 (1949): 31–55.
Winant, Johanna. "Empathy and Other Minds in *Ulysses*." *James Joyce Quarterly* 55.3–4 (2018): 371–89.
Wirzba, Norman. "The Touch of Humility: An Invitation to Creatureliness." *Modern Theology* 24.2 (2008): 225–44.
Yates, Christopher. "Introduction, Hospitality: Imagining the Stranger." *Religion and the Arts* 14.5 (2010), Special Issue on "Hospitality," 515–20.
Yazell, Bryan. "Irish-Israelism: Reconsidering the Politics of Race and Belonging in 'Cyclops.'" *James Joyce Quarterly* 53.3–4 (2016): 269–85.
Yeats, William Butler. *The Collected Poems of W. B. Yeats*. Ed. Richard J. Finneran. New York: Macmillan, 1989.
— and Lady Gregory. *Cathleen ni Houlihan. W.B. Yeats: Selected Plays*. Ed. Richard Allen Cave. London: Penguin, 1997. 19–28.
Young, Brad H. *The Parables: Jewish Tradition and Christian Interpretation*. Peabody, MA: Hendrickson, 1998.

INDEX

Adams, Robert M., 134
aesthetic dimensions of text, 4
affective engagement with text/
 characters, 3, 67, 157n74, 187,
 190, 204
Affective Fallacy, the, 190, 196n40
 critique of, 196n41
affect studies, 16n15, 190
agape, 13, 104, 112, 119n62, 130, 175,
 189
Albert, Leonard, 105
alterity, 8–9, 34, 103, 147
Alter, Robert, 11, 42–3, 47, 64–5
Altizer, Thomas J. J., 52
Ambrose, Saint, 78
anti-Catholic *see* Catholic Church
Antichrist, 50
anti-Semitic, 13, 80, 82, 115n6, 135,
 141, 164, 166–8, 170–2, 178n26,
 193, 207
Apocalypse *see* Book of Revelation
apocalyptic, 2, 49–50, 52, 61n33, 76,
 106, 109–10, 189
"A Portrait of the Artist," 13

A Portrait of the Artist as a Young Man,
 1–2, 38, 44, 49–50, 53, 61n35, 65,
 73, 76, 78, 85n43, 103, 133, 138,
 189, 200
archetypes, 108
Argentina, 20
Aristotle, 148
Armstrong, Paul B., 192–3
Attridge, Derek, 2–3, 181, 206
attunement, 201, 207
Auden, W. H., 144
Augustine, 52
authority, 6, 15, 43, 45, 48–9, 71, 181,
 206–7
 of Christ, 48
 of Scripture, 43, 206–7
 of the Catholic Church, 45, 49
Avery, Bruce, 34
awakening *see* conversion

Bailey, Kenneth E., 101, 188
Bakhtin, Mikhail, 136
"Ballad of Little Harry Hughes," 164,
 166–72, 178n26, 183

Bannon, 169
Barnacle, Nora, 12, 30–2, 40n25, 43, 57–8, 61n39
Barry, Kevin, 209n3
Beardsley, Monroe C., 190
beasts of the Apocalypse, 50
beauty, 13, 138, 140, 172–5
  theory of, 13, 173–4
Beckett, Samuel, 17n21, 120n73
  ethics in *Waiting for Godot,* 120n73
Belfast, 55
Bellingham, Mrs, 123
Bender, Abby, 46
Benjamin, Roy, 75
Benstock, Bernard, 101, 156n60, 170
Bergan, Alf, 172
Bersani, Leo, 161, 179n29, 180
betrayal, 28, 30, 37, 40n25, 143, 175
Bible/biblical text, 2, 11, 15, 16n16, 18n46, 42–9, 52, 60n8, 64, 83n8, 84n24, 94, 124–5, 147, 152n3, 152n12, 181, 199, 204, 206–7; *see also* Scripture
biblical narratives *see* Scripture
Birmingham, Kevin, 62n47
Blake, William, 49, 52
Blamires, Harry, 51, 164–5
blind stripling, the, 64, 77, 91, 93, 116n16, 148–9, 158n106
Bloom, Father, 55, 106
Bloom, Leopold, vi, 6, 13, 15, 38, 48, 50–1, 54–5, 61n39, 64–6, 69–72, 74–5, 79–82, 87–9, 91–100, 102–4, 108, 110–15, 116n11, 116n16, 116n17, 117n34, 122, 124–8, 131–6, 140–3, 145–6, 148–50, 156n68, 162, 164–9, 171–6, 182, 188–91, 193, 201–3, 207–8, 209n2, 210n3
  agape love for Stephen, 175, 186
  as artist, 178n17
  as black American, 89
  as Catholic, 52, 70, 88, 106, 168
  as Christ figure, 30, 37, 75, 80, 89–90, 92, 96, 99–100, 107, 110, 147–8, 151, 154n31, 164–6

  as embodiment of Joyce's words, 187
  as exile, 88, 139, 176–7, 184
  as father to Stephen, 81, 97, 99, 110, 118n35, 120n78, 126–7, 130, 135, 143–4, 150, 165–6, 169–71, 174, 181
  as God, 166
  as Good Samaritan, 14, 51, 58–9, 70–4, 77, 82, 87, 91–3, 96, 98–103, 107–10, 113–15, 115n1, 118n43, 124–5, 128–31, 134, 139, 141, 145, 147, 162–4, 169–71, 175, 177, 181, 184–5, 188, 208
  as heavenly body, 173
  as heretic, 37, 90
  as hero of *Ulysses,* 184
  as host, 161–2, 164, 169–70
  as ideal reader, 204
  as Jewish, 10, 12–13, 23, 52, 76, 80–1, 87–90, 93, 96, 102, 107, 110, 112–13, 115n6, 118n54, 119n64, 124, 127–9, 139, 141, 146–8, 166–70, 203
  as Mason, 105–6, 110, 119n57, 119n61
  as model of humility, 204
  as narrator of "Eumaeus," 125–6, 128, 132, 136–7, 153n18
  as Odysseus, 80–2, 108, 135, 142–3, 146, 176, 182
  as Other, 90, 148
  as priest, 162
  as prophet, 123
  as Protestant, 70, 88, 168
  as reborn, 147
  as received by Joyce's "congregation of readers," 184
  as secular character/as secular savior, 12, 51, 81, 92, 95, 107, 112–14, 116n11, 123, 125, 141, 151, 164, 166, 175
  as spiritually, mentally, or physically united to Stephen, 143–51, 158n96, 161–2, 166, 169, 171, 173–4, 176

Bloom, Leopold (*Cont.*)
  as Stranger, 14, 46, 51, 74, 76–7, 81, 87–9, 92, 98–9, 114, 130, 138, 142, 146–7, 163, 171, 175, 177, 188, 208
  as victim, 182
  as Virgin Mary, 99
  bringing Stephen into his home, 160–1, 164, 167, 172, 175–6
  care for Stephen as a function of drunkenness, 116n17
  concept of a nation, 184
  deceased son, Rudy, 12, 69, 96–7, 104, 106–7, 119n57, 120n78, 127, 169; as Jewish, 107
  epiphany about/with Stephen, 165–6
  fear of usurpers, 145, 176
  fused identity with Stephen, 162–3, 175
  giving of himself to Stephen, 150–1, 161, 176
  habitus of care, esp. for Stephen, 138–41, 143, 146, 161–2, 164, 170, 193, 199
  habitus of charity, 103–5, 108, 113–14, 116n16, 123, 125, 128–9, 134, 138, 140, 164, 171–2, 184, 186, 199, 202
  habitus of generosity, 116n16, 125, 140–1, 161, 171–2, 183, 188, 194, 203–4, 209
  his home as an extension of his body, 161, 164, 175–6
  idiolect of, 128
  knowledge of Scripture, 116n11
  practice of hospitality, 23, 36, 92, 94, 123, 130, 145–6, 149–50, 160–2, 164, 173–6, 185, 203
  reception of the "Ballad of Little Harry Hughes," 164, 166–9
  reader as Bloom's neighbor, 181
  rescued by Cunningham and Hynes, 115n1
  rescued by Molly, 176
  rescue of Stephen, vii, 2–3, 12–13, 51, 54, 58–9, 70–2, 74, 79, 81–2, 87, 91–2, 96–104, 106–7, 110–11, 114–15, 116n11, 116n16, 119n62, 120n78, 122–3, 125, 130–2, 136–7, 140–1, 143–7, 149–50, 159n110, 159n116, 160, 175–6, 180, 185–6, 188, 190, 192, 202, 207
  transcendent moment with Stephen looking at the heavens, 172, 174–5
Bloom, Milly, 162, 167–71
  as violent Irish nationalist, 168–70
Bloom, Molly, 13–14, 55, 61n39, 79, 96, 111, 124, 140, 143, 160–2, 165–6, 174, 176–7, 185–6, 193, 202, 209n2
  as embodiment of Joyce's words, 187
  as Good Samaritan, 177
  as hospitable, 176
  as inhospitable, 176
  as innkeeper, 176
  as ironic Virgin Mary, 166
  giving her body to Bloom, 177
  role in "Penelope," 179n40
Bodkin, Michael "Sonny," 30–2, 40n25
Boer War, the, 142
Book of Common Prayer, 47
Book of Exodus, the, 47
Book of Revelation, the, 11, 17n21, 43, 48–52, 60n8, 61n33, 66, 76, 110, 189, 203
Booth, Wayne, 187
Boundas, Constantin V., 147
Bowen, Zack, 167, 169, 171
Bowker, Gordon, 53–4, 58
Bowlby, Rachel, 191
Boylan, Blazes, 14, 79, 81, 143, 145, 161, 175–6, 202
Branch, Lori, 15, 205–6
Brannigan, John, 9
British
  colonialism, 6, 22, 88, 147
  imperial state, 21, 67, 142
  monarchy, 101
  view of Irish, 129
Brockman, William S., 127
Browne, Mr, 203
Bruni, Alessandro, 117n29

Bruno, Giordano, 57
Bruns, Gerald, 129, 151
Budgen, Frank, 92, 102–3, 111, 116n15, 118n35, 119n61, 122, 126, 133, 140, 144, 146, 158n98, 159n110, 172
Buenos Aires, 20
Byrne, Davy, 93, 105
Byron, Lord George Gordon, 44, 49, 65

Cabrera, Maria Teresa, 209n2
Cadbury, Henry, 75
Caffrey, Cissy, 100–1
Calvinist/Calvinism, 50
Calvino, Italo, 199
caritas see charity
carnal hermeneutics, 148, 150
Carnes, Natalie, 61n43
Carr, Private, 71, 87, 97–101, 122–3, 139, 166, 170
Casey, Edward, 160–1
Catholic Church/Catholicism, 4–6, 10, 17n21, 21, 43–5, 49, 52, 55–7, 59, 64, 67–8, 70, 72–5, 81, 87–8, 94, 106–7, 110, 113, 115n1, 117n, 124, 128, 130, 168, 181, 184–6, 190, 203, 208
  being Catholic, 14, 48, 70, 113, 141, 148
  Mass, 46, 70, 98, 162, 165, 185–6
  teaching of, 94, 106, 181
Cemetery, Rahoon, 31
charity/charitable, vi, ix, 10, 13–14, 22, 59, 66, 70, 74–5, 77, 82, 84n24, 89–90, 92–3, 98, 102–5, 108, 110, 112–14, 116n11, 116n16, 116n17, 118n50, 119n64, 123, 125, 128–31, 134, 138–41, 143, 148, 158n106, 164, 171–2, 183, 185–6, 189–90, 193, 199–200, 202–3, 209
chiasmus, 29, 37
Chittenden, Kelly, 84n26, 116n16
Chrétien, Jean-Louis, 13, 46, 137, 149–50, 173–4
Christianity/Christian, 7–8, 16n16, 17n21, 18n46, 24, 37, 44–8, 51–2, 65, 81, 90, 93–6, 104, 107, 113–14, 116n11, 116n17, 121n88, 140–1, 148, 151, 164, 168–9, 184–6, 204
  Communion, 30
  concept of/ethic of sacrifice, 24, 37
  theology, 48, 90
Christ, Jesus, viii, ix, 1, 2, 8, 13–14, 30, 37, 41n41, 42, 45, 48, 51–2, 61n43, 65–6, 68, 73, 75–7, 80, 85n43, 87, 90, 92, 94–6, 99, 100, 106–7, 110–14, 117n25, 117n29, 123–5, 127–8, 139, 147–8, 150–1, 154n30, 154n31, 158n103, 159n116, 163–7, 175, 179n41, 182, 184–7, 194n2, 201–2, 208
  advent of, 123
  as Good Samaritan, 99–100, 107, 110
  as Good Shepherd, 92
  as haughty and prideful, 94
  as human and warm, 95, 112
  as incarnate Son of God, 96, 112
  as Jewish, 96, 113, 127
  as Living Word, 187
  as political misfit/reformer, 90, 154n31
  as prophet, 123
  betrayal of by Judas, 30
  body of, 18n33, 52, 151
  Christ figure, 30, 80, 85n43, 89–90, 110
  cross of, 37, 41n41, 150, 165
  death of, 123, 154n31, 165
  fulfillment of Old Testament prophecy, 77
  hermeneutic of hospitality, 37
  love of, 95
  ministry of, 123
  new covenant, 151
  parables of, 42–3, 48, 65, 68, 87, 91–2, 110–11, 115, 124, 128, 130, 140, 160, 175, 182–3, 185, 202, 204, 208
  resurrection of, 52, 70, 123
  Second Coming of, 50, 92

Christ (*Cont.*)
  suffering/sacrifice of, 37–8, 41n41, 94, 150–1, 154n31, 165
  teachings of, 15, 42, 46, 73, 111, 113–14, 139, 184, 202
  walk to Emmaus, 181
Christological symbols, 11, 25, 28, 37
Citizen, the, 87, 89–91, 95, 98–9, 105, 107, 112, 115n1, 125, 127, 129–30, 134, 138, 140–1, 143, 156n68, 164, 167–8, 171, 183, 185–6, 199, 203
Clare, Angel, 35
Coetzee, J. M., 210n14
Cohen, Bella, 50, 97, 99, 106, 167
Colón, Susan, 83n8, 208
communion, 15, 28, 32, 143–4, 150, 164, 166, 170, 181, 205
  with the dead, 28, 32
community, 1–2, 4–6, 9, 14–15, 23, 28, 35, 43, 48, 64, 84n24, 91, 104–5, 107, 131, 139, 142, 156n68, 184–5, 187, 189, 193, 200, 203
  eternal mythic community, 108
  reading community, 200, 203
Compton, Private, 100
Conmee, Father, 113, 141
Conroy, Gabriel, 11, 19, 21–38, 39n13, 40n19, 40n26, 59
Conroy, Gretta, 22–3, 25, 27–38, 40n19, 41n41, 59
conversion, 27, 30, 32, 35–6
Corelli, Marie, 39n7
Corley, 13, 82, 115, 131–4, 139, 141, 143, 163, 172, 185–6, 199
Cosgrave, Vincent, 53–4
Costello, Peter, 53–5, 58
Cranly, 78, 85n43
Crispi, Luca, 105, 124, 133, 152n6
Crofton, 87, 107
Cunningham, Martin, 68–9, 89, 91–2, 95, 113, 115n1
Curran, Constantine P., vii, 53
Cussen, John, 116n17
cyclist, the kindly, 19, 68–9, 71–2, 74, 84n24, 84n26, 118n43

Dante Alighieri, 45, 52, 94, 199
D'Arcy, Bartell, 28, 29, 36
Davison, Neil R., 63, 87, 90, 107, 119n63
dead, the, 27–8, 30–4, 38, 97; *see also* ghost
Deasy, Garrett Mr., 81, 87–8, 107, 115n1, 130–1, 135, 203
Dedalus, Dilly, 133, 143
Dedalus, Simon, 38, 69, 71, 87, 104, 107, 115n1, 133
Dedalus, Stephen, vi, 6, 13, 15, 20, 38, 48, 50–1, 54, 57–9, 61n39, 64–5, 69–74, 77–82, 83n12, 85n41, 85n43, 87–8, 90, 93, 96–9, 100–3, 105–6, 108, 110–11, 114–15, 115n1, 117n34, 122, 124–40, 142–3, 145, 147–9, 154n30, 160–2, 164–76, 182–3, 186, 189–91, 193, 200–3, 206–7, 209n2
  artistic failure of, 77–9
  artistic transformation of, 142, 167
  as artist, 146, 156n60, 157n71, 166, 178n17
  as "author" of *Ulysses,* 142, 147
  as Bloom's savior, 183, 207
  as Bloom's son, 97, 99, 104, 110, 119n57, 120n78, 126, 130, 135, 143, 165, 167, 169–70, 181
  as catastrophic figure, 166
  as changeling, 106, 120n78
  as Christ, 166
  as embodiment of Joyce's words, 187
  as exile, 81, 114, 202
  as Good Samaritan, 115, 131–4, 143, 163–4, 171–2
  as heavenly body, 173
  as Homer, 142
  as lapsed Catholic, 128, 148, 168
  as Murphy's son, 143–4
  as Other, 100–1
  as Prodigal Son, 82, 86n54, 97
  as Samaritan rescuer, 81, 133, 193
  assault of Buck Mulligan, 97–8

as spiritually, mentally, or physically united to Bloom, 143–6, 148–51, 158n96, 162, 166, 169, 171, 173–4
as Stranger, 100–1, 109, 114, 163, 169, 181, 202
as Telemachus, 80–2, 135, 143, 146
as victim, 182
becoming like Bloom, 131–2, 134, 139, 141, 143, 155n42, 172, 185, 199
charity of, 131, 139, 143, 172
concern for younger siblings, 133, 139, 172
elliptical acknowledgment of Bloom's care, 178n28
encounter with/helping Corley, 131–2, 139, 141, 143, 163–4, 172, 185
epiphany with Bloom, 165
fear of usurpers, 145
fused identity with Bloom, 162–3, 175
generosity of, 131–2, 141, 199
hospitality of silence, 137
Joyce's interest in, 133
notion of hyper-elitist artistic predestination, 1
potential singing career, 129
poverty of, 131–4
rejection of Bloom, 129, 134, 137, 140–1, 158n98
relationship with Bloom read parabolically, 74–175, 177–97, 201–2
suffering of, 138, 167
theory of Shakespeare, 135, 202
transcendent moment with Bloom looking at the heavens, 172, 174–5
transformation into an author, 141, 174
Defoe, Daniel, 199
Derrida, Jacques, 4, 7–9, 35–7, 41n38, 141, 159n112, 189, 194, 209n3, 210n3
and hospitality, 8–9, 17n24, 35–7, 41n38, 141
Devlin, Denis, 17n21

Dial, The, 108
diction, 29
Dignam, Paddy, 72, 79, 82, 91, 93, 199
Doležel, Lubomir, 134
Donoghue, Denis, 62n47, 79–80, 87, 108, 140, 200, 210n8
Doran, Bob, 21, 166
Drury, John, 76–7, 84n34
Dublin/Dubliners 21–2, 28, 30–1, 47, 54, 56, 58–9, 70, 79, 81, 88, 99, 105, 114, 115n1, 138, 141, 143, 147, 150, 168, 171–2, 179n40, 182, 184, 189–90, 192–3, 199, 209n3, 210n3
Dubliners, vii, 1–3, 9–11, 19–21, 30, 50, 53, 59, 66–9, 74–5, 79, 95, 131, 181, 189, 199, 201, 208
"Araby," 20, 22, 67
"Boarding House, The," 20, 22, 166
"Counterparts," 21–2
"Dead, The," 11, 19–24, 29, 30, 34–8, 40n25, 41n41, 59, 130, 203
"Eveline," 20, 22, 68
"Grace," 12, 19–20, 36, 59, 63, 68–75, 99, 118n43, 208
"Ivy Day in the Committee Room," 41n41
"A Painful Case," 22
"Sisters, The," 20, 22, 74–5
"Two Gallants," 131
Dudley, Jack, 10, 43, 68, 74–5, 84n24, 130, 208
Duffy, James, 22

"Ecce Homo," 52
Eccles Street, number 7, 160–1, 172–4, 176
as the inn, 176
Eco, Umberto, 60n26
Eide, Marian, 18n46
Eliot, T. S., 108
Eliza (in "The Sisters"), 75
Elliott, Neil, 158n103
Ellmann, Maud, 125, 140, 153n15

Ellmann, Richard, 21, 30–1, 37–8, 41n41, 44, 53–8, 81, 92–3, 95, 115n1, 119n62, 125, 128, 130–1, 135, 143–5, 150, 163, 173, 178n17, 183, 185
embodiment/embodied, 13, 16n10, 28, 37, 51–2, 64, 90–1, 100–1, 104, 111, 115, 137, 139, 146, 148, 150, 160–1, 164, 175–7, 185, 187, 189, 194n23, 208
 and transcendence, 195n23
empathy/empathetic, ix, 12, 16n15, 19, 25, 28, 32, 36–8, 89–90, 96–7, 99, 114, 131–3, 139, 143, 149, 156n64, 158n106, 162–3, 182, 187
enfleshment/enfleshed, 13–14, 28, 48, 104, 112, 139, 146, 148–50, 156n64, 160–1, 175–7, 180, 185–6, 189, 203, 209
English *see* British
Epiphanius, Saint, 165
epiphany/epiphanies, 49–52, 61n39, 66–8, 95, 109, 165, 189, 193
epistemology, 134, 205
ethic/ethical/ethics, 3, 6, 10–11, 14, 16n10, 18n46, 24–5, 28, 34, 37, 42, 65, 67, 91, 103–4, 109, 118n50, 120n73, 121n95, 141, 149, 154n31, 157n77, 180–1, 183, 185–7, 190, 193, 195n36, 201, 203, 209, 210n3
Eucharist, 52, 185–6
Eumaeus, 81
"Eumeo," 123–4, 153n21
Europe/European, 114
exile, 1, 10–11, 45–6, 50, 56, 62n62, 81, 176–7, 202
Exiles, 40n25, 86n54, 188

Fanning, Long John, 91
Fargnoli, Nicholas, 125
Farrell, Cashel Boyle O'Connor Fitzmaurice Tisdall, 158n106
Farrington, 21
Fassenden, Tracy, 15, 198, 207, 210n5
Father Purdon, 68, 72–4

Faulkner, William, 42
Feeney, Michael, 31, 40n25
Felch, Susan, 5
"fellow feeling," 141
Felski, Rita, viii, 3, 15, 180, 200–1, 204–6, 211n21
Fénelon, Francois de Salignac de la Mothe, 135, 155n54
Finnegans Wake, 50, 52, 60n8, 75–6, 82, 105, 196n36, 199–200
 as the ultimately hospitable text, 200
Fish, Stanley, 4
Fitzharris, James, 81
Flack, Leah, 81, 85n47, 184, 187
Flynn, Nosey, 93, 105
Fogarty, Mr, 68
"Force," 93
France, Anatole, 41n41
Francini-Bruni, 45
Franke, William, 5, 47, 52
Fraser, James Alexander, 30
Frazer, James, 60n8
Fredericks, Elizabeth, 86n54
Freeman, Mark, 104, 191, 208
French, Marilyn, 127
Freud/Freudian, 35, 74, 99, 117n34, 120n82
friendship, 9, 33, 135, 141, 188–9, 204
 in marriage, 33
Funk, Robert, 114–15, 121n95
Furey, Michael, 11, 22, 25, 27–38, 40n19, 59

Gabler, Hans Walter, 118n36, 124, 127
Galway, 30, 31, 32
Gasché, Rudolph, 189, 194
Gawain, 35
generous/generosity, viii, 13–15, 22–5, 27–8, 30, 32–3, 35–8, 39n10, 40n19, 40n20, 68, 91–3, 112, 114, 116n16, 125, 131, 140–1, 160–1, 169, 171–2, 178n28, 183, 194, 199–200, 204–6, 209
 hermeneutic of, 204
Gentile, 91, 111, 139, 175, 182, 190

ghost
  of Michael Furey, 28–30, 35, 36
  see also the dead
Gibbons, Luke, 47
Gibson, Andrew, 96, 128
Gifford, Don, 124
Gilbert, Stuart, 124
Gillespie, Michael Patrick, 125
Glasnevin Cemetery, 69
Glen, J. Stanley, 186
God, 10, 46, 52, 73, 75, 90, 99, 109–10, 112, 118n50, 127, 134, 137, 151, 154n31, 166–7, 182, 185–6, 195n28, 208
Gogarty, Oliver St. John, 57
Gonne, Maud, 170
Good Samaritan, 1, 8, 11, 13, 15, 20, 51, 59, 68–72, 75, 79, 81, 87, 89, 91, 96, 98–103, 105–6, 110–13, 119n, 123–5, 128–32, 134, 140, 143, 147, 157n73, 160–1, 164, 169, 171–2, 175, 177, 182, 184–5, 189, 203, 206, 208
  Leopold Bloom as *see* Bloom
Good Samaritan parable (Luke 10:25–37), 3, 11, 14, 16n10, 19, 24, 38, 42, 48, 51–3, 56, 59, 63, 66, 68, 70, 74–82, 84n34, 87, 89–92, 94, 96, 98–100, 102–3, 107–12, 114, 122–3, 126, 130–2, 134, 139–40, 142, 147, 150, 152n14, 155n42, 159n116, 160–3, 167, 170–1, 175–6, 177n5, 179n40, 180–90, 192, 195n36, 201–3, 206–9
Good Shepherd *see* Christ
Gospel *see* Scripture
Gospel of Luke *see* Luke
Gottfried, Roy, 5, 17n21, 43, 45, 48–9, 64
grace, 68–9, 72–5, 84n24, 84n26, 92, 111, 182, 191, 208
Gray, Dolly, 106
Greene, Plunket, 31
Gregory, Eric, 109, 182, 185
Gregory, Lord, 29

guest, 6–7, 20–1, 27–8, 30, 32–7, 39n13, 161–2, 173–5, 188
Gula, Marianna, 117n25

habitus, vii–viii, 8, 23, 25, 30, 65, 70, 89–90, 92, 94, 103–5, 114, 116n16, 125, 138, 171–2, 188, 202, 204
Haines, 2, 57, 97–8, 165, 202
"halo of significance," 108
Hamlet/*Hamlet*, 108, 145, 187, 202
Hammond, Meghan Marie, 16n15
Hardy, Thomas, 35
Hart, Clive, 155n52
haunting, 29, 32, 34
Hays, Richard B., 76
Hedrick, Charles, 83n8, 182–3, 194n2, 209
Heffernan, James A. W., 6–8, 23, 30, 35, 40n19, 161, 170, 175
Herbert, Christopher, 5
heretic/heretical, 5–6, 12, 37, 90, 114, 121n94, 128, 185
hermeneutic/hermeneutics, 189, 193, 198, 200, 204, 210n5
  communal, 200
  generative, 200
  "of faith," 203
  of religion, 203
  "of suspicion," 200, 203, 206–7, 210n5
  postcritical, 200, 203–07
  postsecular, 200, 206–07
Herring, Philip, 124, 152n6, 153n21
Heusel, Barbara Stevens, 130
Hinojosa, Lynne, 5
history, as under the Lordship of God, 118n50
Hogan, Patrick Colm, 128
home, 2, 8, 13, 20–3, 29, 31, 35, 44, 54, 56, 58–61, 62n47, 71, 77–8, 82, 85n43, 93, 102, 112, 119n64, 125, 132–3, 138–9, 146, 160–1, 164, 167, 172, 175–7, 199, 201–2, 207, 210n14
  as extension of one's body, 161, 164, 175–6

Homer, 7, 79, 81, 135, 143, 155n54, 184
hospitality, viii, ix, 1, 3–4, 6–15, 16n10, 16n15, 17n24, 19, 20–30, 33–8, 39n7, 39n13, 40n19, 41n26, 41n38, 42, 48, 51, 57–9, 68–9, 80–1, 89, 92–3, 116n16, 123, 128, 130, 137, 141–2, 144–6, 149–50, 160–2, 164, 170, 173–6, 179n40, 181, 185–8, 190, 195n36, 198–200, 203, 207, 209n2, 209n3, 210n14
    abuse of/false versions of/anti-hospitality, 20–1, 25–6, 29, 39n7, 89
    Christian concept of, 8, 18n33, 37, 41n38, 48, 81, 93
    ethical dimensions of/ethic of, 34, 42, 141, 181
    etymology of, 6, 9
    generative, 21, 200
    hermeneutics of, 198
    narratives of, 3, 33–4, 144
    of Dublin/of Ireland, 1, 10, 19, 21–2, 24–7
    of silence, 137
    reading hospitably, 3–4, 15
    reverse of as betrayal or treachery, 30, 69, 175, 202
    theme of, 20
    theory of, 35, 37, 41n38
    translation as, 209n2
host, *hostia*, 6–7, 11, 20, 23–7, 30, 32–6, 39n13, 161, 167, 169–70, 173–4, 188, 210n14
    double meaning of, 20
    sovereignty of, 39n13
Houston, John Porter, 125, 135
human beings as narrational, 191
Hungerford, Amy, 5
Hunter, Alfred Henry, 53–6, 58–9, 61n39, 63, 68, 107, 130, 142
Hunt-Hendrix, Leah, 109, 182, 185
Hurley, Michael, 5
Huxley, Aldous and Maria, 42
Hyamson, Albert M., 113–14, 121n93

Hyde, Lewis, 104, 150
Hynes, Joe, 89, 113, 115n1

Ibsen, Henrik, 61n35, 65, 77, 199
Illich, Ivan, 112, 186
Immaculate Conception, 21, 178n15
immanence, 64, 68, 84n24, 114, 121n, 159n116, 175, 208
immortality, 50
incarnation/Incarnation, 8, 16n10, 36, 41n38, 51–2, 112, 147, 151, 165, 179n41, 185–7, 203
incarnational ethics, 16n10
"in orthodox Samaritan fashion," vi, 72, 79, 107, 113, 122, 125, 129, 132, 141, 152n14, 153n15, 181
interpretation as coproduction between reader, text, and characters, 204
intertext/intertextuality, 13, 16n16, 22, 43, 47, 79–80, 109, 124, 126, 131, 142, 180, 182, 187–8
Ireland/Irish, 21–2, 26, 36, 45, 50, 55, 67–8, 88, 100–1, 121n93, 128, 138–9, 142, 156n68, 164, 166, 168–70, 184, 187
    Catholicism *see* Catholic Church
    culture, 128, 156n68
    Famine, 24
    Home Rule, 22–3, 199
    hospitality *see* hospitality
    Independence, 49, 199
    language, 199
Ivors, Miss, 22, 24–7

Jacobs, Alan, 210n5
jealousy, 35, 40n25
Jew/Jewish/Jewishness/Judaism, vii, 3, 10–14, 23, 44, 52–6, 59, 62n47, 63, 65, 76, 80–2, 87–90, 93, 96, 101–3, 106–7, 110–14, 115n6, 116n6, 116n11, 118n54, 119n64, 120n83, 121n92, 124, 127–30, 134–6, 139, 141, 146–8, 152n14, 161, 164, 166–71, 175, 183–4, 190, 193, 194n2, 202–3, 207

John of Damascus, Saint, 165
Johnson, Georgina, 74
Joyce, Georgie, 57–8
Joyce, James/Joyce's, 15, 17n21, 19–22, 24, 26, 28, 30–7, 41n41, 42–50, 52–8, 61n35, 61n39, 63, 66–7, 69–70, 73–81, 87, 89–91, 93–6, 100, 104, 106–7, 109–115, 115n1, 116n16, 122, 125–6, 128, 130, 134–5, 139–40, 142, 144, 146, 148, 150–1, 165–6, 169, 173–6, 180–5, 187–94, 198–201, 203, 206–9, 209n2
    admiration for the mystery of Christ, 117n29
    "aesthetics of sacrilege," 179n41
    and Homer, 7, 35, 47, 80–1, 93
    anti-clericalism of, 45
    apocalyptic vision of, 52, 109, 203
    as apostate, 185
    as blasphemer, 60n26, 185
    as exile, 88
    as heretic, 185
    as host to his readers, 188
    as "priest of the eternal imagination," 195n28
    assaulted in Dublin and Rome, vii, 1, 12, 38, 42, 53–9, 68, 142, 207
    as Stephen Daedalus, 53
    aversion to magisterium of Catholic Church, 181
    belief in Aristotelian *potentia*, 134
    concept of nation, 183–4
    critique of nationalism, 91, 183
    dependence on his readers, 180–1
    development of Bloom's character, 133
    development of Stephen's character, 133, 155n46
    ethics of, 18n46, 91, 118n50, 120n73, 157n77, 181, 186, 203
    "Eucharistic project" in *Ulysses*, 179n41
    fascination with Catholic catechism, 181
    fictional practitioner of hospitality, 38
    hermeneutics of hospitality, 198
    humanistic portrayal of Christ, 117n25, 121n88, 141, 154n30, 154n31
    interest in Christ, 94–6
    interest in drama, 77
    interest in hospitality, 4, 19–26, 30, 38, 39n10, 56, 68, 81, 93, 128, 141, 143, 174, 190, 198–9; *see also* hospitality
    interest in incarnational meetings of human beings, 112, 143, 150
    interest in languages and translation, 199, 209n2
    interest in Lukan narrative forms, 75–7, 176, 181, 185, 189, 203
    interest in parables/parabolic turn of mind, 43, 65–6, 82, 86n54, 87, 90, 114, 181, 183, 201, 203
    interest in puns, 163, 200
    interest in reader's care for Bloom, 143, 188, 201, 209
    interest in religion and in Christianity, 44, 47, 51, 63, 75, 185
    knowledge of Scripture, 45, 47, 56, 60n8, 75, 77, 90, 116n11, 189
    leaving the Catholic Church, 6, 44–8, 64, 88, 186, 208
    motive for using the phrase "orthodox Samaritan," 119n61
    narrative purposes, 14–15, 182
    notion of epiphany, 61n39, 109, 189
    Paris library of, 47
    placing ethical burden on the reader, 181–3, 188, 192–3
    predilection for heretics, 90
    rebellion against institutions, 10, 43–4, 48–9, 88, 181
    receptivity to authors, 199
    rejection of sentimentality, 39n10, 135, 155n52, 155n54, 170, 183
    relationship to his readers, 14, 180
    "rescue" by Hunter, vii, 42, 53–6, 58–9, 61n39, 62n47, 63, 68, 107, 130, 142

Joyce, James/Joyce's (*Cont.*)
  retelling Good Samaritan parable in *Ulysses,* 176, 181, 183, 187, 189, 192, 201, 203–4
  reversal of Virgin Mary figure, 166
  sacramental imagination of, 189
  secular gospel of, 184
  skepticism regarding the knowledge of God, 121n94
  spiritual idealism, 10
  stances in religion and politics, 5, 44, 49, 91
  subverting reader expectations, 135–6, 183
  theory of/ethic of hospitality, 7, 10, 28, 30, 34, 36–7, 42, 141, 170, 181, 203
  Trieste library of, 44, 47, 113, 135
  turn toward Scripture, 11, 42–4, 46–7, 63–4, 88, 181, 185, 198
  unorthodox portrayal of Christ, 117n25
  view of mind-soul-body relationship, 149
  wealth of learning of, 192
Joyce, John Stanislaus, 38, 45, 54
Joyce, Stanislaus, 26, 31, 44–5, 47, 53, 56–7, 59, 65, 94, 112, 121n88
  negative view of Christ, 94

Kain, Richard, 94
kairotic time, 109
Kane, Jean, 3–4, 194n23
Kaufmann, Michael W., 4
Kavanagh, Patrick, 17n21
Kawin, Bruce F., 152n3
Kearney, Richard, 8–9, 14, 59, 61n39, 148–50, 189, 193–4
  diacritical hermeneutic of the Other, 9
Kelleher, Corny, 71–2, 75, 87, 99, 102, 115n1
Kelly, Bridie, 97
Kelly, H. P., 128
Kenner, Hugh, 2, 55, 75, 81, 97–8, 117n34, 122, 126, 128, 132, 134–5, 142

Kermode, Frank, 76, 92, 191
Kernan, Mr, 12, 19, 68–70, 72–5
Kernan, Mrs, 68
Kershner, Brandon, 16n16, 80
Kiberd, Declan, viii–ix, 11, 42, 51–2, 63, 89, 91, 123, 137, 139, 148, 154n31, 180–1
Kiernan, Barney's pub, 167–9
Killeen, Terence, 54–5
King James Bible, 44–5, 47, 67
Klossowski, Pierre, 35
Knight, Mark, 4, 203–4
Kristeva, Julia, 120n82

Lamy, Thomas Joseph, 60n8
"Lass of Aughrim, The" 28–30, 36
Last Supper, The, 30
Latham, Sean, 86n54, 139, 157n71
Lawrence, D. H., 42
Lawrence, Karen, 3, 20, 23, 33, 93, 99, 146, 158n96
Lawton, David, 49, 208
Lenehan, 92, 143
Lernout, Geert, 16n16, 43–5, 47–8, 60n8, 116n11, 121n88
Levinas, Emmanuel, 17n24, 41n38, 103, 206
Levite, 101–2, 111, 114, 124
Lewis, Pericles, 5, 83n3
Lily (as character in "The Dead"), 25–6
literary criticism/literary theory, viii, 4, 6, 190, 196n41, 205–7, 210n5
  a new moment in, 205
Litz, Walton, 146
Logos, 165
love, 6, 9, 13–14, 16n10, 17n21, 23, 27, 29–30, 32–3, 35–7, 40n25, 43, 45, 48, 50–3, 63, 82, 89, 91, 95, 103–4, 109–10, 114, 118n35, 123, 128–9, 140, 143, 146, 149–51, 156n68, 173, 177, 181, 184–6, 189–90, 194n2, 202, 209; *see also* charity
Lowe-Evans, Mary, 5
Lucifer, 78–9, 85n41, 85n43, 110

Luke, Gospel of, 12, 42, 66, 73, 75–9, 82, 84n34, 92, 94, 101–2, 105, 110–11, 114, 123, 127, 152n14, 183–5, 187, 194n2, 202
   depiction of Christ, 94
   literary qualities of, 75–7, 84n34
   narrative of, 12, 77, 96, 102–3, 107, 114, 142, 183, 187, 189, 203;
   see also Good Samaritan parable
Luther, Martin, 52

McBride, Margaret, 141–2, 147, 160, 176
McClure, John, 5
McCole, Camille, 195n23
McCourt, John, 40n25, 58
M'Coy, Mr, 68
McDonald, Ian, 111, 157n73
MacDuff, Sangam, 49–50
Macé, Marielle, 3
McGinn, Bernard, 50
McHugh, Roger, 45
Maddox, Brenda, 31
Maddox, James H., 119n69, 120n69, 147, 165
Magalaner, Marvin, 84n24
Mahaffey, Vicki, 19, 188–9, 192
Maher, Father, 143
Malins, Freddy, 24
Malone, Reverend Charles, 168
Malory, Sir Thomas, 96
Marais, Mike, 17n24
Martello Tower, 54, 57, 98, 202
Mary and Martha, 111
Mary Ellen, 21
Mason, Emma, 4, 95
Mason/Masonic, 12, 69–70, 105–6, 110
May, Herbert G., 94
Maynooth Catechism, 181
Melchiori, Giorgio, 62n62
Menton, John Henry, 73
Miller, J. Hillis, 7
Mills-Knutsen, Joshua, 141
Milton, John, 52
modernity, 4, 10, 47, 109, 200
   "modernity as secularization," 4, 96

Mooney, Mrs., 20–1
Mooney, Polly, 21, 166
Moore, Thomas, 28, 31–2
Morkan, the Misses, 21–7, 31, 36–7, 41n41
Moseley, Virginia, 45, 50, 86n54, 131–2, 181
Mulligan, Buck, 2, 12, 47, 57, 81–2, 88, 97–8, 122–3, 125, 135, 143, 145, 147, 165–6, 169, 202
Munkácsy, Mihály, 95–6, 117n25
Murphy, 143–4, 147
   as false father figure to Stephen, 143–4
Mutter, Matthew, 5
My Brother's Keeper, 65
mystery, 135, 144

Nadel, Ira B., 113
Nannie (in "The Sisters,"), 75
narratives/narrative frame, vii, 2–4, 6–8, 12–15, 20–1, 25, 32–6, 38, 42–7, 49, 51–2, 55–6, 60n8, 63–8, 74–7, 80, 82, 85n49, 86n54, 88–9, 92, 95–7, 102–3, 106–9, 115, 127, 132, 136–7, 141–4, 147, 157n74, 163, 167, 170–2, 174, 176, 180–3, 185–9, 191–3, 203, 206–7, 209
   Good Samaritan narrative *see* Good Samaritan parable
   Homer's narrative delay, 143
   mythic narratives, 108
   narrative voice, 137
   of modernity as secularization, 47
   scriptural narratives *see* Scripture
narrator/narration, vi, 13, 29, 35, 50, 69–70, 73–4, 76–7, 80, 82, 87–9, 97–100, 106, 109, 113, 122, 126, 128, 131–2, 134, 137–8, 140–5, 147–8, 152n12, 153n15, 154n26, 162–3, 166–9, 172–3, 182, 189–90, 194, 196n37, 204
   Circean narrator, 99–100, 134, 144, 190
   Ithacan narrator, 167
   of "Eumaeus," 132, 137, 143

narrator/narration (*Cont.*)
nationalism, 10, 26, 138, 156n68, 168–70
National Library, 135, 145
neighbor/good neighbor/neighborliness, 1, 2, 6, 14, 48, 51–3, 59, 63, 67, 92, 94–5, 103, 109–11, 113–14, 118n50, 120n73, 123, 130, 160, 181, 183–4, 186, 190, 194n2, 200, 207–9
Neuman, Justin, 5, 64
New Criticism, 16n16
new Jerusalem, 110
Newman, John Cardinal, 45
New Testament 11, 46, 48–51, 63, 65, 77, 104, 123, 154n31, 184, 187, 204, 206–7; *see also* Scripture
New Year's feast, 19
Nighttown district, 72, 74, 77, 98, 101–2, 111
Nolan, Emer, 5
Norris, Margot, 13, 29, 69, 102, 115n6, 120n78, 131–4, 142, 166, 171–2, 178n26, 182–3
"Nostos," vi, 11, 13, 78, 125, 140, 142, 152n6, 180, 191
Nouss, Alexis, 209n2

O'Brien, Darcy, 10
O'Connor, Frank, 19
Odysseus (Ulysses), 35, 79–82, 85n47, 92, 102, 108, 135, 142–3, 146, 155n54, 161, 182, 207
Odyssey, The, 7, 11, 47, 81, 85n47, 85n49, 135, 142, 146, 155n54, 165, 184, 187
  and hospitality, 7, 81
  Odyssean narrative, 142
O'Gorman, Farrell, 5
Old Testament, the, 11, 42, 46–7, 51, 60n8, 77, 118n54, 121n95, 123; *see also* Scripture
O'Molloy, J. J., 88
O'Neill, Christine, 126, 129, 136–7, 142, 153n21
O Ríordán, Seán, 17n21

orthodox/orthodoxy, 6, 12, 60n26, 64, 72, 79, 93, 107, 113–14, 116n17, 117n25, 119n61, 122–5, 128–9, 131–2, 141, 152n12, 152n14, 153n15, 165, 181
Osteen, Mark, 199
Other, the/otherness, 3, 5, 8–9, 11, 14–15, 19, 36–7, 45–6, 50–1, 59, 90, 97, 103–4, 111, 120n82, 134, 137–8, 141, 143–5, 147–9, 151, 163–4, 170, 181, 183–4, 186, 189–91, 193, 197n52, 202–3, 206, 208–9, 209n2, 210n14
Otis, Harrison, 66, 179n40
Owens, Cóilín, 17n21

parable(s)/parabolic, vi–viii, 1–3, 6, 8, 11–15, 16n10, 17n21, 19–20, 22, 24, 33, 36, 38, 42–3, 45–6, 48, 50–3, 56, 59, 61n39, 63–8, 70, 73–82, 83n8, 84n24, 84n26, 84n34, 86n54, 87, 89–92, 94, 96, 98–102, 106–15, 118n50, 119n59, 120n79, 121n95, 122–4, 128–34, 139–40, 147, 150, 152n3, 152n14, 153n14, 155n42, 157n73, 157n74, 157n77, 159n116, 160–3, 170–2, 175–6, 177n5, 179n40, 180–90, 192, 194n2, 195n36, 201–4, 206–9
  and their literary context, 194n2
  demanding embodied response, 208
  ethics revealed by, 121n95, 181–2, 185–6, 201, 208
  interpreting the reader, 121n95, 182
  literary and theological dimensions of, 83n8, 109
  Parable of the Good Samaritan *see* Good Samaritan Parable
  parabolic reading of Bloom's and Molly's relationship, 176–7, 179n40
  parabolic reading of Bloom's and Stephen's relationship, 74–86, 87–121, 122–59, 160–75, 177–9, 180–97, 201–2
Parnell, Charles Stewart, 41n41, 49, 56, 61n35, 65, 145

Passover, 169
Paul, Saint, 146–7, 158n103, 175
Peake, C. H., 84n24, 129, 136, 144–5, 167, 171
Pecora, Vincent P., 22–3, 39n10, 40n26
Penelope, 35, 80–1
Pentateuch *see* Scripture
philosophy, 4
Pierce, David, 88, 180
Pilate, Pontius, 41n41
Pinkerton, Steve, 5, 48, 60n26, 179n41
Polyphemus, 182
postcritical, 4, 15, 198, 200, 203–7, 211n21
postsecular/postsecularism, 4, 15, 198, 200, 206–7
Power, Colum, 5, 48
Power, Mary, 22, 39n7
Power, Mr, 68, 71–2
Prezioso, Robert, 40n25
priest, 20, 45, 100–2, 111, 114, 124, 162, 168, 195n28
Prodigal Son parable, 76, 80, 82, 84n34, 86n54
Protestant/Protestantism, 14, 17n21, 22, 47–8, 52, 70, 73, 81, 87–8, 106–7, 115n1, 124, 130, 168, 184, 187, 190, 203, 208
Proust, Marcel, 194
Purefoy, Mina, 93, 96, 116n16

Quinlan, Kieran, 5

Rabaté, Jean-Michel, 16n10, 195–6n36
Rahoon Cemetery, 31
Raleigh, John Henry, 126–7, 135, 142
reader/readers, viii, 2–4, 9, 11, 14–15, 26, 41n26, 48, 50, 64, 66–7, 77, 80–2, 83n11, 87, 89, 108, 110, 115, 116n6, 121n95, 125–6, 131, 135–6, 140, 143–5, 151n3, 154n26, 159n116, 167, 171–2, 177, 179n40, 180–92, 194, 194n2, 195n23, 195n28, 195n36, 200–4, 206–9, 209n1, 210n5
  affective response of, 190, 204
  as developing a habitus of *caritas,* 202, 204
  as generous, 200
  as Good Samaritan, 184, 187, 189
  as loving interpreter of Joyce's novel, 188
  as mediating consciousness between characters and myths, 108
  as Samaritan rescued by Bloom, 186
  as rescuing/caring for characters, 82, 143, 182, 186, 188, 190, 201, 207
  as witnesses, 189
  caring for characters, 191
  in relationship with characters, 192, 201, 203
  in relationship with Joyce, 187–8
  in relationship with the text, 201
  responsibility of/role of, 180–4, 188, 191–2, 195n28, 195–6n36, 201, 206, 208
reader-response theory, 67
reading, viii, ix, 1–4, 7–8, 10–15, 30, 33, 35, 38, 39n10, 41n26, 41n41, 43, 45–6, 48, 50–2, 61n33, 61n43, 62n62, 64, 66–9, 79, 81–2, 83n8, 85n49, 86n54, 87, 92–6, 99–100, 105, 107, 109, 112, 115, 116n17, 117n34, 118n50, 120n82, 121n88, 124, 127–9, 132–5, 137, 140–2, 145–8, 150, 153n21, 154n25, 154n30, 154n31, 156n60, 156n68, 157n77, 162–4, 166–7, 171–2, 176, 178n21, 178n28, 179n41, 180–3, 186–94, 194n23, 195n28, 195n36, 198, 200–7, 209, 209n3, 210n5, 210n8, 211n2
  as active love, 189, 209
  attentively and immersively, 202
  charitably/hospitably/generously, 15, 187–8, 198, 200
  creatively, 3
  disinterestedly, 200, 210n8
  hermeneutics of, 190, 198, 200
  humbly, 207
  parabolically, 14, 74–175, 177–97, 201–2

reading (*Cont.*)
  postcritical, 200, 203–7, 211n21
  postsecular, 200, 206–7
  through religious viewpoints, 206
  through the Good Samaritan parable, 132, 167, 171, 176
realism, 76
Reece, Steve, 7
Reformation, the, 1, 48, 187, 208
Reilly, Terry, 61n33
relationship of Bloom and Stephen, 3, 74–175, 177–97, 201–2, 203
  as banal, 144–5
  as empathetic, 156n64
  as genesis of *Ulysses,* 142
  as pedestrian, 145
  its highpoint, 172
  read parabolically, 74–175, 177–97, 201–2
religion/religious, 3–6, 8, 10, 12, 16n16, 17n21, 43–5, 47, 49, 52, 60n8, 60n26, 64–5, 68–70, 73, 82, 89, 95–6, 100, 103–4, 112, 114, 116n11, 128, 168, 189–90, 194, 198, 203–8
  as "a candidate for the truth," 16n18
religious turn in literary criticism, 4, 5, 205
Renan, Ernest, 112–13, 117n25, 121n, 128, 141
rescue/rescue narratives, vii, 1, 12–14, 19–20, 37–8, 42, 53–9, 63, 68–70, 72, 74–5, 77, 79–82, 89, 91, 96–7, 100–4, 107–8, 111–12, 114, 115n1, 119n62, 120n78, 122–3, 127, 130, 132, 138, 140–4, 146–7, 154n28, 163, 171, 175–6, 178n28, 179n36, 181, 184, 188, 192–3, 202, 207, 209, 210n3
Richards, Grant, 66–8
Ricoeur, Paul, viii, 8, 14–15, 51, 66–8, 93, 111–12, 118n50, 138, 147, 149, 151, 159n116, 163, 182, 186, 190, 192–3, 197n52, 200, 203, 206
Riquelme, John Paul, 145, 187
Roberte Ce Soir, 35
Romanus, Lentulus, 165

Rome, 1, 21–2, 38, 42, 53, 56–9, 62n62, 63, 207
Rudy *see* Bloom
Russell, Harry K., 114, 121n94
Ryken, Leland, 44

Sacher, Harry, 113
sacrifice/sacrificial, 20, 24–5, 27, 30, 32, 34, 37–8, 41n41, 48, 93, 104, 110, 132, 150–1, 154n31, 157n74, 169, 177, 202
  of Christ *see* Christ
  of Michael Furey, 38
Saint-Amour, Paul K., 24, 34, 35
St. Stephen's Green, 54
Samaria, 113
Samaritan/Samaritans, 113–15, 116n17, 119n61, 122, 124–5, 128–32, 141, 153n14, 160–1, 163, 171, 176, 181–6, 188, 190, 208–9; *see also* Good Samaritan
Sambrooke, Jerilyn, 82
Scarry, Elaine, 13, 173–4
Schlossman, Beryl, 110
Scholes, Robert, 94
Scripture, 1–2, 8, 11, 14–15, 17n21, 18n46, 42–52, 60n, 63–6, 68, 73–7, 90, 94, 104, 107, 147–8, 154n31, 175, 182, 184, 187, 189, 199, 202, 204, 206–7
  authority of, 43, 206–7
  Gospels, 42, 51, 66, 75–9, 82, 84n34, 94, 102, 123, 127, 147, 182, 184, 187, 202
  prophetic narrative, 51
  scriptural narratives, 42–4, 46, 64, 76, 107, 182
Second Coming of Christ *see* Christ
secular/secularization, 4, 6, 10, 12, 14–15, 43–4, 47–8, 51–2, 63–4, 81, 82n3, 92, 95–6, 107, 109, 112–14, 116n11, 120n82, 123, 125, 141, 151, 164, 166, 170, 175, 184–5, 189, 198, 200, 206, 208
Sedgwick, Eve Kosofsky, 204, 210n5
Seeley, John R., 95, 117n25, 140–1

Seidel, Kevin, 198, 207
Seidman, Robert J., 124
Senn, Fritz, 138, 152n14
shade *see* the dead
Shakespeare, William, 45, 135, 145, 202
Shashaty, Jill, 66, 181
Shepherd, Andrew, 41n38
similitude, 197n52
simony/simoniac, 20, 65, 74, 83n12
Sir Gawain and the Green Knight, 35
Skeffington, 61n39
Slote, Sam, 105, 123–4, 153n21, 178n28
specter *see* the dead
spiritual/spiritual aspect/spiritual register, 10, 27, 32–3, 68, 72–4, 84n24, 115, 130, 143, 149–51, 161, 164–5, 171, 190–1, 206, 208
spiritual awakening *see* conversion
Steiner, George, 2
Stephen Hero, 38, 53
Stockstad, Ray, 178n21
stranger/the Stranger, 2, 6–9, 11–14, 21, 28, 33–6, 45–6, 48, 51, 59, 62n47, 70–1, 74–5, 77, 81, 87–9, 92, 98–101, 103, 107–9, 114, 115n5, 130, 138, 141–2, 146–7, 150, 155n54, 160–1, 163, 169–71, 174–7, 179n40, 181–2, 185, 188–9, 193, 202, 207–9
Strauss, David Friedrich, 154n30
street sweeper, the, 143
style, 13, 15, 23, 64, 76, 79, 96, 98, 117n34, 125–30, 136–7, 142–5, 152n12, 153n14, 153n15, 153n21, 154n25, 157n74, 161, 172, 177n5, 183, 187, 199, 207
Sultan, Stanley, 126–8, 155n42
Suter, Paul, 92
sympathy, 16n15, 35–8, 96–7, 116, 139, 157n77
Synge, J. M., 17n21

Talbot, Florry, 50
Tate, Allen, 33
Taxil, Léo, 154n30

Taylor, Charles, 35, 104, 109, 112, 186, 208
"Telemachiad," 78
Telemachus, 81–2, 135, 143, 146, 155n54
TeSelle, Sallie McFague, 207–8
Tess of the D'Urbervilles, 35
theology *see* religion; *see also* Christian
Thornton, Weldon, 14, 99, 108, 116n16, 117n29, 117n34, 118n35, 140, 152n3, 153n18, 157n74, 177n5, 187, 190, 195n28, 195n36, 201
Thrailkill, Jane, 196n41
Thurston, Luke, 29, 39n15
Toíbín, Colm, 22, 38
Torah *see* Scripture
Torchiana, Donald, 21, 178n15
transcendence, 109, 195n23, 208
transformation, 12, 35, 38, 80, 95, 142, 144, 173, 176, 203, 209; *see also* conversion
traveler, 7, 12, 20, 69–70, 78, 81, 84n24, 84n26, 87, 91, 96, 101, 107, 111, 114, 128, 140, 182–3
Trench, Samuel Chenevix, 57
Trieste, 57–8, 62n62, 95, 113
Trinity, the, 165
truth, 13, 16n18, 21, 31, 44, 49, 147, 184
Turner, Mark, 65

"Ulysses," 55–6, 79
Ulysses, 14–15, 20, 22, 24, 30, 36–8, 40n25, 42–4, 46–59, 60n8, 61n39, 63–4, 66–7, 69, 75–7, 79, 81–2, 90–1, 95, 104–5, 108–9, 115n6, 116n6, 118n36, 119n69, 122–3, 126, 130, 133–4, 137, 140–2, 144, 164, 173, 180–1, 183, 185, 187–92, 194, 198–201, 203–9, 209n2
  additions to "Cyclops" and "Circe," 118n36
  apotheosis of, 131
  as bridge between postcritical and postsecular, 206
  as call to reader to help the Other, 193, 203

Ulysses (Cont.)
  as Christian hospitality text, 81
  as hospitality text, 23, 58, 186–7, 207
  as less accessible text, 192
  as placing ethical demands on reader, 193, 207
  as prophetic, apocalyptic "sacred" book, 109, 189
  as wisdom literature, 181
  biblical allusions in, 152n3
  early drafts of, 152n6
  Homeric parallels of, 124, 142, 184
  Joyce's inspirations for, 12, 53, 59, 142
  metafictional reading of, 142
  parabolic structuring of, 87, 192, 201, 209
  parallels between mythic and modern times in, 120n69
  self-transcending power of, 192
  to be read apocalyptically, 189
  to be read parabolically, 74–175, 177–97, 201–2, 206
  "Aeolus," 76, 80, 82
  "Calypso," 93, 136, 160, 162
  "Circe," vi, 20, 49–50, 55, 58, 63, 69, 70–2, 74–5, 77, 82, 87–9, 92–3, 96–8, 100–6, 109, 114, 117n34, 118n35, 120n78, 122–3, 130, 137, 139, 142, 146–9, 152n3, 162–4, 166, 185, 189–90, 207
  "Cyclops," 71, 87–92, 95, 105, 130, 138–9, 156n68, 168, 171
  "Eumaeus," vi, 13, 71–2, 77–82, 87, 89, 98, 100, 104, 107, 109, 111, 113–15, 116n17, 118n50, 120n69, 122–59, 161, 163–6, 170, 173, 175–6, 181–3, 185, 187, 189, 193, 207; Bloom as narrator of, 125–6, 128, 132, 136–7, 153n18; insufficient critical attention to, 151n1; style of, 125–8, 136–7, 157n74, 183
  "Hades," 69–70, 72–3, 75, 95, 104, 130
  "Ithaca," vii, 13, 71, 77, 82, 89, 104, 114, 118n50, 122, 130, 138–42, 146–7, 152n6, 156n60, 160–76, 177, 178–89, 181–2, 185, 189, 193, 207; catechistic style of, 161, 177n5; objective style of, 177n5
  "Lestrygonians," 75, 93, 105, 116n16, 148
  "Lotus Eaters," 75, 105, 110, 117n, 152n3
  "Nausicaa," 130, 170
  "Nestor," 88, 130
  "Oxen of the Sun," 77, 87, 93, 96–7, 101, 110, 123, 126–7, 135, 152n3, 202
  "Penelope," 13, 123, 152n6, 160, 176–7, 179n40, 179n41, 185, 186, 189, 207
  "Proteus," 78, 106, 145–6, 154n30
  "Scylla and Charybdis," 80, 135–6, 145, 187, 202
  "Telemachus," 82, 88, 106, 136, 145, 147, 165
  "Wandering Rocks," 64, 131, 133, 141
unheimlich, 35
University College, Dublin, 43, 45

van Mierlo, Chrissie, 5
Via, Dan Otto, Jr, 83n8
Virgin Mary, the, 99, 165, 178n15
Vulgate, 44–5, 67, 199

Walzl, Florence, 35
Ward, Graham, 149
Weinstein, Arnold, 162
Weir, David, 81
Westland Row, 96–8, 101
Wimsatt, W. K., 190, 196n40
Winant, Johanna, 156n64
Wirzba, Norman, 149
Woolf, Virginia, 68

words as permanent living sites of dynamic memory, 187
Wordsworth, William, 135
Wyse, John, 91

xenos/xenia see hospitality

Yates, Christopher, 6
Yazell, Bryan, 156n68
Yeats, William Butler, 17n21, 38, 88, 100, 102, 106, 115n5, 189
Young, Brad H., 102

EU representative:
Easy Access System Europe
Mustamäe tee 50, 10621 Tallinn, Estonia
Gpsr.requests@easproject.com

www.ingramcontent.com/pod-product-compliance
Lightning Source LLC
Chambersburg PA
CBHW070340240426
43671CB00013BA/2379